Crime, State and Citizen

A FIELD FULL OF FOLK

David Faulkner is a Senior Research Associate at the University of Oxford Centre for Criminological Research, where he writes about and teaches criminal justice, penology and government and public administration. He also works with charities concerned with penal reform, community safety and opportunities for young people, and is a former Chair of the Howard League. He was a Fellow of St. John's College, Oxford, from 1992 to 1999. In *Crime, State and Citizen* he also draws on a 30-year career working at the heart of government – including eight years as Deputy Secretary in charge of the Criminal, Research and Statistical Departments of the Home Office. He was Private Secretary to one Home Secretary (James Callaghan) and senior adviser to six others.

For 20 years he held direct responsibility for key aspects of the workings of criminal justice in the UK. His career included secondment to the then Prison Commission in 1963 (working on the reform of aftercare and associated changes in the then Probation Service), and appointment as special adviser to the Lord Privy Seal (Lord Shackleton) to work on Labour's 1960s attempt to reform the House of Lords. He returned to the Prison Service as head of P4 Division in 1970 (working on modernisation of the borstal system; the first schemes for bail hostels and bail information systems; and the redevelopment of Holloway Prison). Later he was concerned with matters of police pay and organization. In 1978, at the Cabinet Office, he co-ordinated the Government's policies on home affairs, its legislative programme, and reform of the select committees of the House of Commons.

In 1980, back at the Home Office, he implemented the organizational changes which followed Lord Justice May's inquiry into the Prison Service including the creation of HM Inspectorate of Prisons and later, as Director of Operational Policy, began a debate on justice in prisons which anticipated Lord Woolf's recommendations ten years later. As Deputy Secretary (1982 to 1990) he worked to promote support for victims, racial equality, crime prevention and the co-ordination of criminal justice (all then new as a focus of government policy); to improve communications with the judiciary at all levels; and to develop a more systematic relationship between the formation of policy and the commissioning and application of academic research. He guided the process of consultation which led to the Criminal Justice Act 1991. From 1990 to 1992 he had charge of Home Office staffing and organization.

David Faulkner was a member of the UN Committee on Crime Prevention and Control and of the Advisory Board of the Helsinki Institute for Crime Prevention and Control. and led the UK delegation to the UN Congresses on Crime and He was appointed CB in 1985.

D1381886

3 1111 01319 3212

Crime State and Citizen
A Field Full of Folk
David Faulkner

SECOND EDITION

Published 2006 by
WATERSIDE PRESS
Domum Road
Winchester SO23 9NN
United Kingdom

Telephone 01962 855567/UK Local-rate call 0845 2300 733
E-mail enquiries@watersidepress.co.uk
Online catalogue and bookstore www.watersidepress.co.uk

Copyright © 2006 David Faulkner. All rights reserved. No part of this book may be reproduced, stored in any retrieval system or transmitted in any form or by any means, including over the Internet, without prior permission.

ISBN 1 904380 23 9

First edition (2001) **ISBN** 1 872 870 98 8

Catalogue-in-Publication Data A catalogue record for this book can be obtained from the British Library

Printing and binding CPI Antony Rowe Ltd, Chippenham and Eastbourne

Cover design Waterside Press

Sole North American distributors International Specialised Book Services (ISBS), 920 NE 58th Ave, Suite 300, Portland, Oregon, 97213-3786, USA
Telephone 1 800 944 6190; Fax 1 503 280 8832; website: www.isbs.com; email: orders@isbs.com

Crime, State and Citizen

A FIELD FULL OF FOLK

David Faulkner

SECOND EDITION

WATERSIDE PRESS

WINCHESTER

This book is dedicated to my grandchildren, Louise, David, Jonathan, Heather and James, in the hope that the values it tries to express will still be respected in the world in which they enter upon their adult lives, and that those values will inform their careers as they have, however imperfectly, informed my own.

Crime, State and Citizen

CONTENTS

Continued overleaf

Foreword

For many years David Faulkner occupied senior, highly influential positions in the Home Office, at the heart of policy-making. He developed a legendary, possibly unique approach to the job, consulting widely with practitioners, academic researchers and specialist policy analysts outside Whitehall. He built a wide social network and earned great respect. After leaving the Home Office in 1992 he became a Fellow of St John's College Oxford and an associate at the University of Oxford Centre for Criminological Research, a base from which he has maintained his network within and without Whitehall. He has also had time to absorb, sift and analyse the welter of criminal justice policy developments, and subject them to critical scrutiny born of experience shaped at the highest level. The result is an unusually broad and penetrating analysis of criminal justice policy yoked to a deep, personal commitment to an ethical view of the proper role of the state and the rights of citizens.

Crime, State and Citizen remains as relevant today as it was when it first appeared five years ago. The second edition contains an additional chapter reviewing events since 2001 – a huge raft of further legislation, the embedding of the Government's managerial framework for criminal justice, the Carter review of sentencing trends and offender management, New Labour's victory in the 2005 General Election, the London bombings of July 2005, a record high prison population, the plan that probation services be extensively marketised, and so on. What readers will find interesting is how so wise an observer as David Faulkner would now go about achieving the Government's objectives on subjects such as contestability, sentencing and civil renewal, and that he has found it necessary to express increasing, critical concern about our direction of travel. His approach and his concerns merit close attention.

Rod Morgan
Chair, Youth Justice Board January 2006

Preface to the 2006 Edition

Almost five years have passed since the first edition was published in the spring of 2001. A lot has happened since then, but the issues I discussed at that time have lost none of their importance, and most of the arguments are equally valid today.

In this second edition, I have left the original text as it stood, but I have added a new chapter to bring the narrative up .to date and to refocus the arguments where necessary. I have included a more or less factual account of the main developments since 2001, but I have not tried to examine all the issues in the same degree of detail. I have concentrated on those subjects on which I am reasonably well informed and on which I believe I have most to contribute. I have not, for example, attempted any extensive treatment of policing, youth justice, victims or community safety, not because I think those subjects are unimportant – far from it – but because I feel I have less to say about them that is not already being said by others. Policing in particular deserves a separate study on another occasion.

I have tried to make the new chapter relatively optimistic. That optimism does however depend on a number of conditions. One is the quality of the criminal justice services themselves – their skills and expertise, but also their morale and commitment, their integrity, their professional values and leadership. Those things must never be taken for granted, especially at a time of constant change and upheaval. Another is the extent to which communities and individual citizens are prepared to make their own contribution to the prevention of crime and the re-settlement of offenders, and – very important - the spirit in which they do so. A third is the context of public opinion and debate, the influences of the media and of the political parties, and the sources from which the nation is able to draw its maturity and wisdom.

How those conditions can be achieved and sustained is a difficult question. But answers are more likely to be found through relationships and education in the widest sense, than they are in legislation, bureaucratic re-organization or threats of punishment.

I owe an immense debt of gratitude to the friends, colleagues and students with whom I have worked over the last 45 years. Most of the ideas in this book have come from them. I very much appreciate the support of Lord Hurd and Lord Windlesham at the launch of the first edition in 2001, and special thanks are due to Rasha Albazaz, Ros Burnett, John Croft, John Graham, Sue Raikes, Graham Towl, Patsy Townsend and Aidan Wilcox for their advice in preparing this second edition. Many other people have contributed indirectly, in conversation, conferences, seminars and through their own writings. I would not have attempted a second edition without the encouragement of Bryan Gibson, and as before I have relied on his wisdom and patience and on the support of Jane Green his house editor at Waterside Press.

David Faulkner January 2006

Preface to the First Edition

I was in a wilderness, I could not tell where, and looking Eastwards I saw a tower high up against the sun, and splendidly built on top of a hill; and far beneath it was a great gulf, with a dungeon in it, surrounded by deep, dark pits, dreadful to see. But between the tower and the gulf I saw a smooth plain, a Field Full of Folk, thronged with all kinds of people, high and low together, moving busily about their worldly affairs.

> William Langland, *The Vision of Piers Ploughman* (c. 1380)
> Adapted from the translation into modern English by J. F. Goodrich[1]

This book is an attempt to identify some of the questions of governance, citizenship and public service which Great Britain has to face at the start of a new century, especially in relation to crime and criminal justice; and to suggest how they might be approached through legislation, policy and professional practice. I have drawn on, and tried to share, the experience, impressions and ideas which I have gathered during a working life spent mostly in the Home Office, but for the last nine years in Oxford and with several voluntary organizations where I have been able to share ideas both with colleagues from other professional backgrounds, and with students from other generations.

At a time when governments have to use words like 'new', 'modern', 'effective' and 'reform' to give an appearance of novelty to any statement or publication, it is worthwhile to acknowledge that an understanding of the past may still serve as a guide to the future. That understanding can help to avoid mistakes, to see connections and recognise implications, and provide a sense of continuity and confidence which far from inhibiting change can help sustain and accelerate progress. I have therefore included some historical references and some accounts of events which will be outside the memory of many of today's public servants, and which are being rapidly lost from the collective memory of their services or departments. But their purpose is always to illuminate the present, and to try to anticipate the future.

Public servants and academics always have to judge how far they can or should separate their public duty, or the study of their discipline, from the ethical values in which they believe. They must not compromise their professional integrity in order to pursue some personal agenda or indulge their personal prejudices. But nor should they compromise their personal integrity for the sake of some supposed career or institutional advantage. No public policy or academic discipline is 'value free', and to present or evaluate a policy as if it were, for example because it 'works', is to impose an implicit set of values without the discipline of explaining or justifying them. There is nothing new about that situation, but the pressures to conform have become

---

[1] London: Penguin Books, revised edition, 1966.

more acute, and the temptation to compromise has become stronger, during the past 20 years.

Governments introduce new legislation and issue guidance and reports, academics publish books and articles, and voluntary organizations arrange conferences and seminars, at a rate which would have seemed incredible ten years ago. Some of today's issues will soon be old news. But in the midst of all this activity, there are some questions which remain unaltered and which are not often discussed. I hope some of the suggestions I have made will be adopted as a matter of policy or practice. But I also hope that the book will encourage some more thoughtful reflection - about the character of British society and citizenship, the relationship between the state and the citizen, the role of government, public services and civil society, the nature and foundation of their authority, and the means of sustaining their accountability and legitimacy. I hope it will prompt questions about our understanding of justice and freedom; of qualities such as integrity and compassion, and the value we attach to them; the purpose and limits of punishment as it is applied on behalf of the state; the relationship between politics, professional practice and morality; and the norms according to which we balance rights and responsibilities, safety and risk, equality and diversity, and the interests of the public or of the state and those of the individual. Those are the judgements which define our character as a nation, and as individuals in our own lives. I hope this book will provide some points of reference for those who have to make those judgements in their own working lives, and for students who are preparing for their own careers.

Most of the questions I have discussed are immediately relevant to issues which Parliament, the Government, public services and scholars are now considering as matters of policy, professional practice and research. Their attention is often directed more towards immediate political and practical benefits, or 'quick wins', than towards longer-term strategic and normative questions. But those questions are now receiving more attention: from Parliament in the reports which the House of Commons Select Committee on Public Administration published in the Spring of 2001; from practitioners who are beginning to ask more questions about the ethics of their professional cultures and working practices; and from academics. All these developments are considered in later chapters of the book.

The focus of this book is almost entirely on England and Wales. But there is a great deal that we can learn from and share with Scotland, and for better or worse with the United States. We have much to learn from Canada, Australia, New Zealand and Ireland, and from less developed countries where we should not suppose that the traffic in ideas should only be in one direction. We should be ready to ask whether our traditional values of justice and freedom may not be as well or better protected in continental Europe or Scandinavia than they are at home. But these are questions for another time and another project.

David Faulkner March 2001

PART I The Modern Scene

CHAPTER 1

Introduction

The last years of the twentieth century will almost certainly be remembered as a period of rapid and confusing change, and sometimes difficult adjustment. Historians may have difficulty in giving a coherent account of what they find. They will see advances in medicine and surgery, and increases in life expectancy, overshadowed by administrative turmoil and constant criticism in and about the National Health Service. An education system which is seen from one perspective as educating more children to higher standards than ever before is criticised from another as devaluing those standards, and as failing the nation in its ability to teach the basic elements of literacy and numeracy. A diverse society in which some members of its cultural or ethnic minorities are increasingly accepted and successful is still perceived as institutionally racist in many of its organizational structures and social and working relationships. More opportunities and choices are available than ever before, but for many people their social and economic circumstances put them out of reach. Advances in science and technology have not been matched by similar progress in social wisdom.

The country has difficulty in recognising, and still more in coming to terms with and resolving, its problems of drugs, mental health, the environment and transport. It is sometime unsure of its own identity - whether it is as the United Kingdom or Great Britain, or as England, Scotland and Wales – and of what its special character might be. The country is uncertain of its place in Europe or of its relationship with the rest of the world. Writers like Anthony Giddens in *The Third Way*[1] give a generally optimistic impression of inevitability and progress; others like Will Hutton in *The State We're In*, Richard Sennett in *The Corruption of Character,* and Frank Furedi in *The Culture of Fear*[2] give more sombre accounts.

A government committed to the values of fairness, opportunity and social inclusion is seen as pursuing policies which risk intensifying the exclusion of a minority whom its programmes may not be able to reach or who are unable to conform to the government's expectations. Its confidence in taking to itself decisions which were once regarded as matters of professional or managerial, even judicial, judgement is accompanied by surprising hesitation in grasping some of the more complex, longer-term, strategic issues such as those already mentioned, and confusing ambiguity in its approach to such matters as human rights and constitutional reform. The conflicts inherent in any p government and in any public service seem to be increasingly harder to resolve – between rights and responsibilities, bet individual and society or the state, between equality and diversity, between centralisation and delegation or devolution. The Government relies on, and claims to value, public servants and the support and services they provide, but seems to be constantly frustrated by their supposed inefficiency and conservatism. It is trying to form a vision of a new kind of society, and of a new relationship between the citizen and the state based on concepts of rights and responsibilities, but the outline is still obscure, and shapes emerge only to be lost in the shadows of slogans and 'sound-bites', and in the smoke of adversarial politics.

The combination of progress and confusion is to be found in the areas of crime and criminal justice, as it is elsewhere. Measures to reduce or prevent crime through various forms of social intervention, and to support and reform those who commit it, are matched by a constant expansion in the scope of the criminal law through the creation of new criminal offences; and by increasingly severe punishment, for example through mandatory sentences of imprisonment and proposals for the extended or indefinite detention of those who continue to offend or who may be perceived to be a danger to the public. Measures which are set to transform the structure and process of youth justice contrast with apparent complacency over the state of the prisons. Policing which is targeted on previous or suspected offenders, and measures to increase the number of arrests and convictions may have been successful in reducing the number of burglaries, but they can come to be applied oppressively against vulnerable individuals or disadvantaged groups. A commitment to evidence-based policy and 'what works' stops short of questioning the deterrent effect of sentencing or the social costs of imprisonment. The Human Rights Act 1998 has implications which cannot as yet be more than dimly perceived.

This is the complex and changing situation in which all public services - including the criminal justice services, the judiciary, the practising legal profession, and the voluntary and community organizations which work alongside them - now have to operate. It is also one in which they are subject to increasing direction from central government, through statutory requirements, public service agreements, departmental instructions, performance indicators and the processes of inspection and audit. Few people would deny the need for improvements in efficiency or for greater coherence in the formation and execution of government policy, and the early years of the Labour Government elected in 1997 were generally seen as a time of optimism and of a sense of opportunity. But progress does not depend only on the volume and quality of legislation and the policy initiatives which are set by Parliament and government. It also depends on the skills, commitment and leadership of public servants themselves, and the mood and temper of the country as a whole.

The following chapters offer an analysis of the changes which have been taking place, and of the political, professional and managerial responses to those changes. It sets them in a social and historical context. *Part I* examines the vision of a new kind of society, a new concept of citizenship and public service, and a new relationship between the citizen and the state, which the government and the country seem to have before them; and considers the implications for government and governance, and for the leadership, management and organization of public services. Later chapters apply the ideas of public service and citizenship, and some of the lessons which can be learned from history, to the more specific questions which arise in relation to crime and criminal justice. *Part II* is concerned with the theories and politics of crime and criminal justice, including some recent developments and current issues; and *Part III* with the role of the criminal law and the principles of punishment and sentencing. *Part IV* deals with some special cases – children, victims and questions of racial justice, and with the special responsibilities of the state and of civil society in relation to vulnerable groups. *Part V* is concerned with the various criminal justice services and their structure, culture and leadership; with the functions and organization of the criminal courts; and with the machinery of central government.

Some of the arguments are that governments and public services cannot operate as if they were in a value-free environment; that they need more than scientific, technological or managerial skills and judgement; and that the values they adopt, or assume, come from but also influence the country, the communities and the citizens whom they serve. In a civilised society, they need to include humanity, social inclusion, reciprocal responsibility, respect for dignity and diversity, and a sense that all people are of equal value. Crime threatens those values, and the criminal justice process puts them severely to the test. Crime can cause great suffering and serious damage. But it cannot be dealt with by the criminal justice process alone. The criminal justice process has important limitations which need to be recognised and understood. It is easy for a country, or a government, which feels threatened by crime to look for solutions which increase the criminalisation and punishment of those thought to be immediately responsible. But those measures may not be effective in reducing crime, and may have damaging consequences of their own. The services and institutions which are concerned with criminal justice have an influence on society, and on the character of the country, which extends far beyond their success in catching and punishing criminals. Their organization, culture and accountability must be structured in ways which enable that influence to be both constructive, beneficent and also accountable and legitimate. How that is done raises practical but also constitutional questions about the character and role of the state, the rights and responsibilities of citizenship, the relationship between them and with the government of the day, and the nature and purpose of democracy.

In criminal justice, as in other aspects of public and political life, the country is facing a democratic dilemma. Political power is concentrated in the hands of the government of the day, and especially Prime Minister. Every five, or more often every fo government submits itself to the electorate for a vote on the political parties' programmes for the next Parliament. the government's record and the parties' programme as increasingly on the personalities of its leading figures - are they competent, can they be trusted? The electorate has no opportunity to express a view on individual elements within the programme; the government, and the opposition parties, make judgements on how those elements, and their own handling of particular initiatives and events, are likely to 'run with' the electorate on the basis of opinion polls, focus groups, news reports and editorial comments in the media, and contacts with their constituents. All this works quite well up to a point, and the Labour Government has tried to extend the democratic legitimacy of its programme by developing new ways both of listening to public opinion and of consulting those with relevant experience and expertise. But the demonstrations over the price of fuel in September 2000 showed that the dynamics of public protest, and the means by which public feeling can be expressed, are changing in ways which are unfamiliar and often unexpected.

At the same time a range of commercial organizations, interest groups and well-connected individuals are using their own methods for influencing government policy and public opinion, employing consultants, promoting articles in newspapers and sometimes conducting their own opinion polls. Most of this activity is legitimate and conducted in accordance with ethical principles. But there have been abuses, for example when Members of Parliament have been paid to ask Parliamentary Questions; and attempts to mobilise the expression of particular, usually reactionary, opinions and present them as if they were those of the country as a whole.[3] Even the Government's own attempts to canvass public opinion, for example on the National Health Service, have been subject to criticism.

Despite the Government's efforts, and perhaps partly because of attempts to manipulate or even subvert the democratic process, there is a sense of a 'democratic deficit'.[4] The public generally feels cut off from the decision-making processes which affect them, and many of them are disillusioned with or have no interest in politics. This situation was dramatically demonstrated by the protests already mentioned. As citizens, they may - though many do not - vote in elections, but they have little sense of ownership or responsibility for the programmes which governments develop on their behalf, or for the public services for which they pay, mostly through taxation. Those who are asked to advise on the basis of their experience and expertise too often feel the government prefers to lecture than listen, and that they have been called in more to give an appearance of legitimacy to what the government has already decided than to make a contribution of their own. Governments become increasingly 'executive' or 'management' minded, and more and more directly involved in the running of public services, whose 'efficiency' then becomes part of their appeal to the electorate. Paradoxically, as responsibility for services is withdrawn further away from the communities which they serve, their management becomes increasingly politicised and a potential focus for political and populist opportunism. Services' accountability to central government begins to occlude their

responsibility to citizens and the public. Efficiency is r
democratic, and democracy is not usually efficient.

This new form of politicisation is to some extent a rea
influence of the so-called elites which were thought,
justification, to have dominated the country's professional and public life
until the 1980s, and whose remaining influence the Labour Government
associated with 'conservatism' and resistance to change. The situation
and influence of elites - and of their opposite, those members of society
who are in various ways deprived and socially excluded - is a good deal
more complicated than most political debate is prepared to
acknowledge.[5] Attempts to discredit one so-called 'elite' – for example by
labelling it as 'liberal' - may serve, and may be intended, only to promote
the interests of another. The immediate point is that no group in society
should be able to promote its sectional interests without regard to the
interests of society as a whole, and no group should be so deprived of
influence that it feels alienated or excluded (as farmers and road hauliers
seem to have felt during the summer of 2000). How this obvious, but still
difficult, balance is to be achieved in a complex modern society is what
might be called 'the democratic challenge'. Experience over the last few
years of the twentieth century suggests that it cannot be achieved by
central government acting on its own, and that public services and civil
society have also to play a part.

Possible methods of achieving the balance include more frequent
and intensive consultation, for example through reference or focus
groups or referendums, and greater devolution to local areas and
communities. The Labour Government has shown cautious interest in
both. Neither will by itself reduce the influence of self-interested elites,
although the elites may come to be composed or to behave in different
ways. Nor will they improve the situation of those who are
disadvantaged or excluded, unless or until they become a larger and
more organized section of society. But a good deal could be achieved by
the development of more locally-based, responsive, accountable and
legitimate forms of organization in which citizens and public servants
feel a shared sense of responsibility for the social situations in which they
live and work, and for the public services which they use or on which
they rely. *Chapter 18* gives some examples.

Arguments against this kind of devolution are the assumption that it
leads to inconsistency and inequality, and that it tolerates or even
encourages inefficiency. Arguments of a different kind are that without
central control, locally-based services will behave in ways which are
politically unacceptable - either because they are too 'liberal' or because
they might be too repressive in their desire to please local opinion and
appease local prejudice. All these arguments are in different ways
condescending and 'elitist', based on a belief that 'we know best', and
that 'other people' are somehow not to be trusted. Examples and
anecdotes can always be found to support whatever claims might be
made; but if people are ignored or diminished, whether as citizens or as
public servants, the dangers are just as great as if they are given some
autonomy and independence.

Power, responsibility and the resources to use them are distributed very unequally at present. Later chapters will suggest how more equitable distribution might be achieved for the institutions, professions and services concerned with criminal justice, and how the country as a whole might come to adopt a more comprehensive, coherent and socially responsible approach to the problems of crime and criminality.

ENDNOTES for *Chapter 1*

---

[1] Anthony Giddens, *The Third Way: The Renewal of Social Democracy*, Cambridge, Polity Press, 1998.

[2] Richard Sennet, *The Corrosion of Character. The Personal Consequences of Work in the New Capitalism*, New York, W. W. Norton and Co, 1998. Will Hutton, *The State We're in*, London, Vintage Press, 1996. Frank Furedi, *The Culture of Fear: Risk Taking and the Morality of Low Expectation*, London, Cassell, 1998.

[3] For example the *Sun* newspaper's poll of its readers on the period of detention to be served by the children convicted of the murder of Jamie Bulger, and Brian Souter's private poll in Scotland on the legislation relating to teaching about homosexuality in schools. See also Magnus Linklater's claim that anyone with enough money can pick their subject and bypass the democratic process, 'Beware the Dangers of Too Much Democracy', *The Times*, 3 May 2000. And more recently the *News of the World*'s poll on the treatment of paedophiles, on which see Alan Travis, 'Figure It Out', *Guardian*, 23 August 2000. He claims that the results of the poll, conducted by Mori, were distorted by that newspaper's report.

[4] The 'democratic deficit' in the health service is the subject of a report *New Life for Health* by the Commission on the National Health Service set up by the Association of Community Health Councils for England and Wales and chaired by Will Hutton. Its report argues that a 'democratic voice and accountability must be deployed as buttresses against inequality and inefficiency of provision'. It calls for a 'new constitution' for the National Health Service, and a new relationship with ministers, which would provide some protection from government interference and would entrench and extend 'the concept of social citizenship and a wider view of the public interest in the health service'. London, Vintage, 2000.

[5] Mick Ryan discussed the role of the 'elites' which he sees as having dominated the process of policy making from 1945 onwards in his article 'Penal Policy Making Towards the Millennium: Elites and Populists; New Labour and the New Criminology', *International Journal of the Sociology of Law*, 1999 27, pp. 1-22. He argues that these elites came to be displaced under the political pressure first of the 1970s and then of the 1980s; that the Conservative Government attempted a direct appeal to popular opinion, and the newspapers which influenced it, during the 1990s; and that the Labour Government appeared to have set itself the task of bringing power and perhaps responsibility, to the people after its election victory in 1997, although its rhetoric in this respect was likely to be contradicted by its practice. For a further account, see Simon Hallsworth, 'Rethinking the Punitive Turn', *Punishment and Society* 2 (2), pp. 145-160, 2000.

George Walden considers the motivation and influence of the 'new elites' which became established under the Labour Government in *The New Elites: Making a Career in the Masses*, London, Penguin Press, 2000. A cynic might argue that whereas the 'old' elitists acted in what they saw, however misguidedly, as the public interest, the 'new' elites have been more concerned with gaining and manipulating power for its own sake.

Thomas Frank links the attacks on elites with the rise of market capitalism: a situation in which markets come to be represented not only as a medium of exchange but as a medium of consent, with its own legitimacy independent of any democratic process or other source of authority. It is depicted as representing 'ordinary people' against the forces of obstruction and privilege, with entrepreneurs and professional service people – accountants, lawyers, consultants, public relations experts – as their champions. His points of reference are in the United States but the pattern can be discerned in political and public life in Britain. *One Market under God: Extreme Capitalism, Market Populism and the End of Economic Democracy,* New York, Secker and Warburg, 2001. See also 'The Big Con', *Guardian,* 6 January 2001.

CHAPTER 2

Coming to Terms with Change: Developments in Society, Politics and Governance

... the dilemmas of an ancient island democracy trying to catch up with a continual scale of organization and power, and to develop its own safeguards and counterweights, against centralised authority ...

From the cover of Anthony Sampson *The Essential Anatomy of Britain*, Hodder and Stoughton, 1992.

Society in most countries in the world is changing and becoming increasingly complex. Examples of social and economic change in Great Britain include

- the transition to more plural and multi-cultural society - in matters of class, tradition and outlook, as well as race and ethnicity;
- change in the patterns, opportunities and expectations of employment;
- for some people, especially for men, the loss of confidence and status which comes from security in employment; for young men, the loss of the support they received from fellow workers in the older industries as they made the transition to adult life;
- changes in patterns of personal relationships, and in the formation and break up of families;
- change in the position and expectations of women;
- the fragmentation of traditional communities, and perhaps a weakening of the sense of individual, family and national identity;
- the development of new technology, and its uncertain social, economic and political consequences.

The economic background has included chronic economic weakness; anxiety over inflation, exchange rates, and the cycle of boom and recession; and in more recent years the globalisation of markets, concern for national competitiveness, and the prospects for the single European currency. There are fewer opportunities for unskilled employment, and much of the employment that is available demands skills which seem to be beyond the reach of a substantial part of the population (especially those who are or have been in prison). There is an increasing gap between those in prosperous if sometimes precarious circumstances, and those in relative and sometimes absolute poverty. Developments in technology may widen the gap if a technologically disenfranchised section of society is excluded from the skills to apply them and the benefits they can provide. The combination of social and economic changes has been accompanied by, and has contributed to, an increase in crime, in the fear of crime, and in public anger when crime is committed.

The changes described so far are factually quite straightforward. They are reflected in national statistics such as the *Social Survey* and in reports of research, and they are vividly described in the Social Exclusion Unit's *National Strategy for Neighbourhood Renewal: Report by Policy Action Team 12: Young People.*[1] They can be observed in most people's own experience. But other, more subtle, changes are taking place in outlook and attitude, in social groupings and relationships, and in the distribution of power and influence. The 1980s were a period during which personal security, health, education and housing became commodities to be purchased, not services which the state, communities and individuals had a shared responsibility to provide, and still less rights or goods to be protected by the state and enjoyed by the citizen.

Citizens came to be defined as consumers of services, not as people who shared a sense of common interest or identity or who were joined by any sense of mutual obligation or trust. Public service was judged by the achievement of internal targets and performance indicators rather than by social or economic outcomes. The values of public service become those of managerial efficiency, to be achieved for its own sake and not in pursuit of any wider purpose or obligation. The state, or rather the political administration of the day, became increasingly powerful, centralised and remote, while seeming to divest itself of its responsibilities towards its citizens and placing those responsibilities in the hands of private or intermediate organizations with their own, often commercial or quasi-commercial, interests and objectives.

These changes were usually presented as common sense, as necessary and even inevitable in a world of global markets and resource constraints, and as uncontroversial and politically and ethically neutral. In fact they have had a profound effect not only on the character of public services, but also on the nature of modern society, the relationships within it, and the quality of justice. Some of the changes continued when the Labour Government came into office in May 1997; others were interrupted or brought to an end but their effects often remained.

INSECURITY AND FEAR

A sense of personal insecurity, and especially a fear of crime, has led to a widespread pre-occupation, sometimes even obsession, with safety, security, and the avoidance of risk.[2] Often because of increased publicity, people are more conscious of the dangers from crime, accidents on the road or when using public transport, and from environmental pollution including contaminated food. They are increasingly ready to demand that the government should protect them from those dangers, although they may not be so ready to accept protection if it involves restrictions on the use of motor cars or of tobacco and alcohol. They take increasing precautions on their own account to protect or insure themselves against crime, accidents and mechanical failures.

Such precautions are hard to criticise and sometimes amount to no more than ordinary responsible behaviour. But they can have unfortunate consequences, for example when large numbers of parents take children to school by car for the protection which a car is thought to provide; when people are afraid to leave their homes or travel by public transport, so that places which should be the centre of a community's social life are left deserted; or when residential or commercial areas become fortresses defended by electronic and other forms of physical security. Such fears may not be irrational, but there are some activities in which people are happy to engage (smoking, some sports) although the actual risk is much greater than those involved in activities which they avoid (such as letting children walk to school). It is notorious that people are much more frightened of violence from strangers in public places than they are of violence from people known to them in their own homes, although the actual risk of the former is much less than the risk of the latter.

Social attitudes are hardening in some respects, and softening in others. There is an emphasis on the values of individual initiative, self-reliance and personal responsibility. There is less regard for those of equity, team spirit and public duty. There is greater concern and sympathy for victims, of accidents or natural disasters (or even stress at work) as well as of crime; and a willingness to accept counselling or other forms of help is no longer - or less often - seen as a sign of weakness. There is arguably more tolerance of what are sometimes described as 'alternative life-styles', at least in personal and social relationships if not at a public or political level. But there is rightly less tolerance of certain forms of behaviour, especially violence, including domestic violence, and sexual abuse. Intolerance may however extend beyond criminal offences which might previously have been concealed or overlooked to other less damaging forms of behaviour which are perceived as dangerous or threatening, or just inconsiderate.

The dividing line between proper precautions against a repeated offence by a known sex offender professionally judged to be dangerous, and oppressive behaviour by self-appointed vigilantes against a suspected offender, or a person of unusual appearance or behaviour, is not always easy to draw in practice. Intolerance may extend beyond particular identifiable actions, or forms of unacceptable behaviour, to people who are known or supposed from their appearance or background to be dangerous, threatening or just a nuisance; and beyond them to groups of people who incur disapproval not for what they do but for the kind of people they are or are thought to be. They become the 'other', from whom 'ordinary people' wish to distance themselves, with whom they want to avoid contact, from whom they expect to be protected.[3] Examples include those with criminal records, single parents, the unemployed, travellers, refugees (typically characterised as 'illegal' or 'bogus'), and members of ethnic or cultural minorities. Hostility towards minorities may take the form of open, sometimes violent, racism; or it may appear in a less overt form as indirect or institutional discrimination. Young people seem to be especially exposed to public hostility. Children causing trouble have been demonised as 'vermin' or 'animals' needing to be 'tamed'; groups of teenagers are likely to be called 'yobs' or 'layabouts' even when they are doing no harm.[4] The country as a whole often seems to have little time for its children and young people; they are commonly seen simply as a nuisance, they are unwelcome as neighbours or in public places, and they are to be avoided in restaurants, shops, and on public transport. (See also *Chapter 14.*)

Drugs are widely used as a form of supposedly harmless recreation, but their use can damage or destroy people's lives and their supply has created a criminal industry with a powerful, widespread and corrupting influence. Measures to deal with it must clearly include education (in the broadest sense), treatment and the criminal law and its enforcement: but the balance between them, the energy and resources to be devoted to them, and the means of co-ordinating the various programmes and activities, are a continuous source of argument and frustration.

A form of intolerance which has some affinity with violent racism is the violence associated with football. Its manifestations are different from most of those forms of intolerance described in the previous paragraph, and football hooligans are themselves a group for whom there is - rightly - little public sympathy. They can be distinguished from the other groups mentioned by the fact their behaviour is itself an expression of intolerance and supposed superiority over the supporters of other teams, and at international matches over the citizens of other nations. For that behaviour to be effectively prevented requires the condemnation, not only of particular acts of violence - for which those concerned may try to evade responsibility by blaming provocation from opposing fans or the tactics adopted by the police - but also of the underlying social attitudes which are more widely shared in modern British society. In December 2000 the Government published proposals for a comprehensive programme to deal with the violent and racist elements among football supporters of both domestic and international matches.[5] By tackling the structure and dynamics of support for the game, they offer a more promising way forward than the creation of new criminal offences and their rigorous enforcement.

SOCIAL DIVISIONS AND VALUES

The country is divided along several different dimensions, all with important social implications. They include affluence or poverty; being in work or unemployed; living with or without children; membership of what is seen as the majority or host community, or of an ethnic or cultural minority; a reputation for being hard working and reliable, or troublesome and potentially or actually criminal. These are in addition to the longstanding divisions of social class or socio-economic groups, and between adults and young people. There are 'insiders' wh[...] more resources and have greater access to social, economic power or influence than the 'outsiders' who are, or feel them[...] excluded and alienated. Those with access to new technol[...] skills to use it, may gain a range of social and economic increase their influence and standing in their communities; those without it might become a disadvantaged and excluded underclass.[6]

From another point of view the change can be seen as a transition from 'modern' to 'late modern' or what are sometimes called 'post-modern' values and attitudes. 'Modern' values are seen typically as respect for authority, including the professions, the state and the institutions; belief in technical and scientific progress, and confidence in 'scientific' solutions; support for representative bodies such as Parliament, political parties and trade unions; and 'male' values, such as authority, objectivity, hierarchy and rationality. 'Late-modern' values include an emphasis on quality of life, rather than wealth for its own sake; belief in individual self-expression and creativity; respect for social and cultural diversity; sensitivity to risk; a preference for individual participation and single-issue campaigns, rather than mass democracy; and 'female' values of relationships: exchange, intuition and subjectivity.[7]

Both 'modern' and 'late-modern' values co-exist and compete in today's society. The Labour Government's programme to modernise the processes of government and the public services is mostly based on 'modern' values (although the academic debate about 'modernity' and the political and mangerial debate about 'modernisation' otherwise have little in common). Evidence of the transition to 'late-modern' values can be seen in the decline in membership of political parties and in voting at elections; the rising number and importance of voluntary and community organizations; and increasing concern for such issues as the protection of the environment and the treatment of victims of all kinds. Another feature which academics would associate with 'late-modernity', prompted partly by the Labour Government's proposals for devolution and the reform of the House of Lords, has been the intellectual debate about the possible break-up of the United Kingdom and the history and identity of the 'English'.[8]

Some of these changes are generally welcome, others will be matters of regret. Some may be inevitable and irreversible, others may be challenged and suppressed. Different people will see them in different ways. However they may be perceived, the country has to acknowledge them and work with them. Whether as government, public servants, professional practitioners, parents or simply as concerned citizens, people have variously to reinforce, compensate for or challenge the influences which are at work.

SOCIAL INCLUSION AND EXCLUSION

There is nothing new or unique about a situation in which substantial sections of the population, or substantial numbers of individuals, feel themselves to be 'outsiders' excluded from the mainstream of the country's political, economic and social life. That situation has at various times and for various reasons arisen in many parts of the world. Different populations and different individuals have found different ways of dealing with it - in extreme cases by resorting to terrorism or 'ethnic ·leansing'; by seeking refuge in other countries; or by forming groups such as trade unions or new political parties. Whether the situation is opposed or defended violently or peacefully, it is fundamentally unjust, and inherently precarious. Divisions based on class and culture have been familiar in Great Britain for a long time, and even more so in Ireland, but some of the forms in which those divisions now exist are quite recent and largely unfamiliar. They are constantly evolving and extremely complex, with political, economic and social aspects, including elements of race, class and culture. How they are dealt with, whether by reducing or simply by 'managing' them, will have a profound effect on the country's social and economic stability.

Government, political parties, and other institutions of the British state have naturally responded, and sometimes contributed, to the developments described earlier in this chapter. During the 1980s and early 1990s there emerged what might be described as a 'politics' of social exclusion, and social control, which depicted British society as divided between a deserving majority who are self-reliant, responsible and law-abiding, and entitled to the protection of the state so that they may benefit themselves and those around them without interference from others; and an undeserving, feckless, welfare-dependent, potentially criminal minority - or under-class - from whom they need to be defended. It assumed the existence of a 'host' or 'majority' community, to whose customs and standards 'minorities' should be required to assimilate themselves. The benefits of citizenship, or membership of a community, should be confined to those who conform to accepted standards or who can afford to pay for them. Human behaviour was thought to be motivated mainly by a desire for material gain or by fear of punishment or disgrace. There was not much interest in, or respect for, notions of equality or social justice, or of public duty or service. The 'exclusionary' view of society and its relationships has been put forward on several occasions by the American writer Charles Murray, especially in his reference to the 'under-class';[9] the dangers when it is taken to an extreme form have been described by Andrew Rutherford.[10] Dorothy Rowe has argued that countries and individuals like to have more enemies because they give a collective sense of political and social cohesion, and a personal sense of excitement and self-esteem.[11]

'Exclusionary' social policies will promote self-reliance and personal independence rather than support for those who are vulnerable or disadvantaged. They will favour the placement for adoption of the children of unsatisfactory parents. In schools, the interests of disruptive children may be sacrificed to those of the more able and to the school's overall academic performance, typically its performance in league tables. Policies on housing will focus more on the removal of disorderly tenants than on other means of creating harmonious relationships and of maintaining high standards of behaviour and maintenance. The administration of social security will concentrate more on identifying and punishing abuse than on making sure that claimants receive the full amounts to which they are entitled. Minorities will be expected to conform to the attitudes, behaviour and customs of the 'majority' culture.

Criminal justice policies reflecting an 'exclusionary' view of society include an emphasis on law enforcement and punishment rather than prevention and resettlement, and on imprisonment rather than community-based penalties.[12] They give more prominence to the protection of the public than to the interests of suspects or offenders. They favour access to criminal records; public identification of 'dangerous' people, especially sex offenders; the reporting of suspicious persons or events; the use of technology for surveillance and social control; and requirements to carry and produce identity cards. Policies on immigration and asylum are restrictive and vigorously, perhaps oppressively, enforced, especially against refugees and others who might add to the 'under-class' or become a burden on the state. An extreme version of an 'exclusionary' policy would be one which gave powers of coercion to the police on a basis of suspicion and subjective judgement of the suspect's possible future behaviour, as in the Football Disorder Act 2000.

Exclusion, in one form or another, has been practised by most societies in most periods of history. When people or governments feel threatened, unsure of themselves or uncertain of the future, they look instinctively for an 'enemy', for the 'other' on whom their fears can be projected in the hope that they can be protected if the 'other' can be controlled or overcome. The 'other' can easily be found in wartime, as it could during the cold war; it is harder to find in peacetime and then has to be discovered among threatening, dangerous or alien groups within the country itself. A civilised society has to overcome these fears, and to prevent exclusion and the hatred which can be associated with it, by promoting inclusive policies and values. Policies must be designed and administered with a sense of respect for human dignity and personal identity. Disadvantaged groups need to be protected. Damaged and vulnerable individuals need to be given opportunities to change, with guidance, encouragement and material support. The individual's responsibility to conform to society's standards of civilised and considerate behaviour needs to be matched by society's responsibility to respect and care for its disadvantaged members. History shows that a society in which exclusive attitudes and policies are dominant is likely to become unjust and oppressive. Its decision-making processes will be cautious, closed and secretive. It is likely to be vulnerable to corruption in public life.

The contrasting 'inclusive' view has been less commonly expressed. It recognises the capacity and will of individuals to change - to improve if they are given guidance, help and encouragement; to be damaged if they are abused or humiliated. It emphasises respect for human dignity and personal identity, and a sense of public duty and social responsibility. It looks more towards putting things right for the future than to allocating blame and awarding punishment, although the latter may sometimes be part of the former. Citizenship and membership of the community are seen as permanent and unconditional, and the duty to conform to society's or the community's standards is matched by the community's own obligation to support its vulnerable and disadvantaged members.

The 'inclusive' view is likely to be characteristic of a society which is open and compassionate, which accommodates and respects plurality, and which has some confidence in the future. In criminal justice, it is reflected in the ideas of restorative justice, respect for diversity and the promotion of racial equality and the promotion of community safety, which are discussed in *Chapters 10, 15* and *18.*

The policies of most governments are likely to include both 'exclusive' and 'inclusive' elements. The argument in this book is that 'inclusive' policies are generally to be preferred to 'exclusive' policies and attitudes; some 'exclusive' elements - for example some use of imprisonment or compulsory detention for people who are dangerous - will be inevitable; but they should always be subject to safeguards and due process. Writing from an American background, Robert Sullivan has argued that some 'schizophrenia' in criminal justice is necessary for success in politics and for stable government in a modern, neo-liberal and social democratic state.[13]

The contrasting approaches are not characteristic of particular political parties.[14] The ideas of inclusion and exclusion do however provide a framework of reference within which legislation, policy and administrative and professional practice can be examined and tested, and some insight obtained into the motivation, likely appeal, and possible consequences of proposals which may be put forward and of options which may present themselves.

An interesting illustration relates to the notion of 'community'. An emphasis on communities can readily be seen as an expression of the 'inclusive' approach, with its implications for mutual co-operation and a sense of mutual obligation. But communities can be defined in several different ways. Those which are most easily recognised - such as those based on culture, religion, occupation of common interests - implicitly exclude those people who do not have the characteristics which qualify them for membership or conform to its requirements. A community based on geographical location is more likely to be 'inclusive' but will only have a recognisable identity if certain social conditions are satisfied, and even then - as in gated housing developments - it may be more concerned to exclude outsiders than to promote inclusive relationships of mutual respect and support. Or the language of communities may be used to imply approval not only of local self-reliance, initiative and independence, but also disapproval of interference by the state and perhaps also of the support, protection and safeguards which the state exists to provide. In much ordinary language the word is almost meaningless: in expressions like community sentences, care in the community and community health the expression only means that the sentence is not served in prisons or the service is not provided in hospitals or other establishments. There is no resonance with the energy, skills, services and obligations which can be found within communities which are more positively identified or defined, or to the means of mobilising those communities in a spirit of common citizenship and enterprise.

LIVERPOOL JOHN MOORES UNIVERSITY
LEARNING SERVICES

The language of 'communities' needs to be used with caution, and scrutinised with care. But it is difficult to avoid. It will be used in later chapters in the sense of people living and working in a geographical area and connected by a common interest in its environment, in the quality of its services, in its safety and in its social relationships - the things that are critical for making it a good place in which to live and work (or not). Ideally those people will be connected by a sense of mutual respect and responsibility; of citizenship; and of contributing to and receiving support from civil society.[15] Mike Nellis[16] has provided a valuable account of the development of 'communitarianism' in British thinking, especially its relevance to the ideas of 'community punishment', 'community safety' and 'community justice' which are discussed in later chapters.

NATIONAL IDENTITY AND CULTURAL DIVERSITY

One of the tests of a civilised country is its approach to crime and criminal justice, which is the subject of later chapters. Another is its attitude to racial and cultural diversity. That is itself a reflection of its sense of national identity - how its people think of themselves as citizens, of their relationships with the communities and the state, and whom they acknowledge as sharing that identity and that common sense of 'belonging' and whom they do not.

Mention has already been made of the different ways in which Britishness, or Englishness, is conceived and interpreted. It means different things, and has different associations, for different people. Simon Schama has described the process through which the English nation, and the British people, came to be formed and the different 'stories' or historical interpretations through which it can be described.[17] Neither of the stories he mentions - the imperial triumphalism of the 'island race' or the 'socialist' struggle against oppression and inequality - is an adequate basis for a sense of national identity; although both, and more especially the first, still have a powerful influence on many people's imagination. In particular, they do not easily allow for an inclusive identity which extends beyond England to Scotland and Wales, which accommodates both London and the English regions, or which embraces those from what are sometimes called 'minority' cultures and backgrounds. 'Britishness' has been a unifying force in periods of national expansion or in times or war. But in times of political change and social transformation, the notion of the British as a superior island race can be deeply offensive to many people who would still like to consider themselves as British; and the 'socialist' view is mostly dismissed as hopelessly out of date. 'Britishness' in those terms can then seem divisive or obstructive, while attempts to redefine Britishness by reference to different stories or symbols can be criticised as disloyal or unpatriotic. And yet some unifying sense of national identity and purpose, based on an understanding of the past and some optimism for the future, is still needed. As Robert Hazell has put it:

The government needs to understand and articulate clearly a sense of the wider loyalties which bind us together ... it will require an acceptance of multiple identities and indeed a celebration of them .... and a clear statement of the common core of rights and responsibilities.[18]

Simon Schama has seen national identity as having a more fluid quality, in which allegiance might over time move from place to place or institution to institution, which embraced 'historical impurity as our great strength', which valued 'generous heterogeneity' and complexity rather than simplicity. In slightly less abstract terms, the Commission on the Future of Multi-Ethnic Britain saw the future in terms of a 'community of communities' and a 'community of citizens'.[19] In other words, a truly inclusive society would think in terms of a single nation comprising different cultures, rather than a dominant culture to which others should be assimilated or by which they should be tolerated on suitable terms. Many of the progressive and well-intended reforms from the 1960s onwards have reflected the attitude and used the language of separate communities and identities, with an implied sense of ownership and superiority on the part of the host culture or community. The notion of a single, inclusive British nation will not by itself resolve the conflicts which arise when customs accepted by one community are repugnant to another; or reconcile, in ways which are intellectually consistent, the competing claims of equality and diversity when they occur in day-to-day practical situations. But some common framework of understanding and good will, and of shared interests and obligations, is needed if the actual and potential conflicts are to be resolved on a basis of mutual respect and legitimate authority. *Chapter* 4 suggests how such a framework might be constructed. The press and political reactions, both to the report of the Commission on the Future of Multi-Ethnic Britain (see also *Chapter 16)* and to the earlier report of the Stephen Lawrence Inquiry (see *Chapter 17)*, show the difficulty which the country still finds in debating these questions on a basis of rational argument and objective judgement.

POLITICS AND POLITICAL PARTIES

The social and economic changes described so far in this chapter have been accompanied by, and have influenced, other changes in politics, public service and criminal justice.

In politics, the Liberal Party lost its traditional basis of support when the Party split during the period between the two world wars.[20] It has remained on the margins of national politics ever since. During the last 20 years of the century, both the Conservative Party and the Labour Party have found that their traditional bases of support have become weaker, both in numbers and in political influence; that the values which they represented have lost some of their authority and respect; and that they have to appeal to an electorate which has become less accepting and more diverse, restless and cynical - a situation which could be observed in the local elections, the election of the Mayor of London, and the

Parliamentary by-election in Romsey on 4 May 2000. In a country whose values are presented as mainly material, practical and commercial, a government's vision, ideals, and aspirations have less appeal than a reputation for, or a promise of, competent government. Competent government then comes to mean successful management of the economy - and hence increasing prosperity for at least the majority of those who can be expected to vote in elections; and the efficient and economical management of the business of government, and of the public services which government provides, pays for, or regulates. It is not surprising that people begin to lose interest, except for those for whom politics is a full-time career. And for them it becomes a career like any other, to be pursued ambitiously and single-mindedly for the personal advancement it can provide.

NEW PUBLIC MANAGEMENT

One of the reactions to economic weakness has been the emergence of the 'new public management'.[21] This was originally an attempt to reduce public expenditure by improving the efficiency of public services, and to do so by applying the methods, and where possible the structures, of the commercial sector and a competitive 'market' with opportunity to choose between different services and providers. The driving force came partly from public frustration at the real or perceived inefficiency of public services, and the industrial action which had been taken in some of them during the 1970s; and from a natural political wish to exploit that frustration. But an equally powerful influence, affecting all the major political parties, was the sense that in a world of global markets the country could not afford to sustain public services and a public bureaucracy, paid for from taxation, on the scale that it had in the past. Characteristics of the new public management included the emphasis on economy, efficiency and effectiveness and on value for money; on the assessment of performance through the measurement of inputs and outputs and the use of quantified indicators; on competition and fixed-term contracts of employment; on performance-related pay; on the privatisation and contracting-out of services; and on the creation of executive agencies of government functioning at 'arm's length' from the responsible ministers.

The new public management was associated politically with the idea of a new commercial or 'market' relationship between the state as purchaser, public services as providers, and the citizen as consumer. The relationship found practical expression both in the creation of executive or 'Next Steps' agencies, within the civil service but distanced from the government itself; in the *Citizen's Charter*; and in the programme of privatisation and contracting-out. The Government saw itself as the board of directors of a company trading and competing as Great Britain PLC, concerned primarily with its trading performance and therefore with its need for a modern image and symbols of its up-to-date, commercially successful, character. It thought that the social changes described earlier in the chapter could be handled by the operation of market forces and neo-liberal economies; by the re-structuring of public services in accordance with the new public management and what was thought to be commercial practice; and by tough - critics would say oppressive - policies on crime and criminal justice.

With the White Paper *Competing for Quality*,[22] the Conservative Government launched a programme for privatising or contracting-out various government services and functions. In his Autumn Statement in 1992 the Chancellor of the Exchequer announced the Private Finance Initiative to enable capital projects in the public sector, for example new hospitals or prisons, to be funded by finance from the private sector. The Government, and committees of both Houses of Parliament, published numerous other reports as these programmes gathered momentum. Legislation was sparse, most of the changes being carried out by executive action under the Royal Prerogative, but included the Civil Service (Management Functions) Act 1992, the Deregulation and Contracting-Out Act 1994, the provisions on compulsory competitive tendering in the Local Government Act 1988 and the provisions on contracting-out prison services in the Criminal Justice Acts 1991 and 1993. The Labour Government continued the policy with no less enthusiasm.

The 'central' civil service had never been far from controversy and criticism since the Fulton Commission's criticisms of its elitism, exclusiveness and amateurism in the 1960s.[23] It had continuously been compared unfavourably with the business sector, to the surprise of some observers from other countries who were more ready to acknowledge the quality of the United Kingdom's system of public administration than they were to admire the achievements of its industry and commerce. However that may be, the 'central' civil service has felt itself to be on the defensive for most of the last 30 years; and it has been engaged in, and sometimes subjected to, a process of more or less rapid change throughout that time.

Measures to correct the shortcomings criticised by the Fulton Committee, and later to apply the new public management, concentrated largely on skills in management, drawn mainly from the disciplines of economics and accountancy, while the social sciences and other academic disciplines were largely neglected (and sociology was treated with contempt). Civil servants had little encouragement to become experts in their own fields, as distinct from public managers in general. They were often positively discouraged, partly by the increasing pressures to which they have had to respond, and partly by the fear that they would be regarded as too specialised to make impartial judgements or to be qualified for more senior posts.

Most civil servants agreed that changes were needed, and were able to identify themselves with the process - although some aspects of the 'bureaucracy of efficiency', and of the new public management as it came to be adopted, attracted a certain amount of scepticism and occasional ridicule.

The new public management undoubtedly brought important benefits - an increase in efficiency, a discipline of quantitive and cost-conscious analysis, a focus on achieving results rather than administering a process, sometimes improvements in safety or in openness and accountability. It broke down some of the secrecy, and some of the professional mystique, in which some professions, for example the law, medicine and the police, had been able to operate. It was a period in which local services came to be withdrawn from local democratic control, but it put a different - though arguably less legitimate - form of accountability in its place. None of these benefits should be underestimated. But it also, sometimes, brought a loss of trust, a culture of blame, and a loss of respect for equity, loyalty and even integrity. Public administration came to be portrayed as if it were a technical matter, indistinguishable from other forms of management, in which values or principles had no place.[24] A reaction is now beginning to take place.[25]

GOVERNMENT, STATE AND CIVIL SERVICE: THE TRADITIONAL RELATIONSHIP

One consequence has been a confusion between the role and authority of the government of the day - political, temporary and subject to renewal by the electorate; and of the state, or perhaps in the British tradition the Crown - non-political, permanent, and the source of a different form of authority. The role and authority of the state has come increasingly to be assumed by the government of the day, and in effect by the political administration which controls it. It is to the government, rather than the state, that civil servants are considered in practice to owe their loyalty; it is the government which, to a large extent, controls Parliament; and because it controls Parliament it has become - in normal language - the government which claims to give the courts and the rest of the apparatus of the state their powers. It is to the government, rather than to local communities or stakeholders, that public services are now held to be primarily responsible.[26] All are required not so much to serve the national, local or public interest as they may perceive it, but to work in accordance with the centrally and politically determined policies of the government, communicated to them through an increasingly elaborate structure of legislation, instructions, objectives, targets, performance indicators, league tables, contracts and service-level agreements. It is ironic that a movement which had as its declared objective a reduction in the role and bureaucracy of the state has resulted in an increase in the power and influence of central government and in the bureaucracy needed to support it.

Stephen Sedley has written '... the fact that the government of the day now controls both Parliament and the executive has profound implications both for the constitutional separation of powers and, less often recognized, for the political distinction between party and state'.[27] Parties which think of themselves, and behave, as commercial rivals in the market place cannot expect the loyalty and commitment which previous generations of their supporters gave them 30 or 40 years ago.

Nor can Parliament be thought of and respected as the forum in which the great issues of the day are debated and decided. Political parties, whether in government or in opposition, must find other ways of engaging the public's imagination and capturing their support. One consequence is the much greater attention which they have to pay to public opinion, to the ways it is expressed or influenced through the media, and to other ways of gaining access to it such as surveys and focus groups. A second is the political importance which successive governments have attached to public services and to public service reforms, often accompanied by criticism of the services themselves. A third is the greater political salience of crime and criminal justice.

During the later years of the Conservative Government, the question began to be asked whether the new public management, in the form in which it was being applied in Great Britain, involved not only a change in the way in which public business was organized and conducted, but also in the constitutional relationship between ministers and civil servants. That relationship had always been based largely on shared understandings and unwritten assumptions, communicated orally and informally between colleagues when people were appointed as ministers, to positions in places like the Cabinet Office or ministers' private offices, or to the civil service itself. There was no statutory or definitive code to which it was possible to refer when those understandings were questioned or departures were made from them. The nearest there was were the 'Haldane' doctrine of a 'partnership' or 'fusion' between ministers and officials, in the sense that they understood one another and officials always acted as if in the person of the minister; and the *Carltona* judgment in which the courts upheld that doctrine in a dispute about the legitimacy of civil servants taking decisions on behalf of their ministers.[28]

The comfortable relationship established by Haldane and confirmed in *Carltona* continued, with some interruptions, until the 1960s. It came under strain with the change of government in 1964 and the Labour Government's impatience with what it saw as the elitist, conservative and complacent attitudes, especially of the higher civil service and its administrative class. That impatience is described in the diaries of Richard Crossman and Tony Benn, and led to the Fulton Report already mentioned. Similar strains appeared with the election of the Conservative Government in 1979. Attempts to improve ministers' confidence in the civil service included not only the structural and procedural reforms associated with the new public management, but the 'Note by the Head of the Home Civil Service on the Duties and Responsibilities of Civil Servants in Relation to Ministers', known as the Armstrong Memorandum, with its crucial assertion that 'civil servants are the Servants of the Crown. For all practical purposes the Crown in this context is represented by the government of the day'.[29]

All civil servants would acknowledge that it was implicit in the tradition of Haldane and *Carltona* that their first loyalty was to their ministers and their task was to do what ministers expected. Loyalties might be strained when ministers were divided among themselves, but public disloyalty to the government would have been unthinkable and probably unforgiveable. But many civil servants also felt that their duty to the Crown included duties of integrity, impartiality, care, thoughtfulness, thorough preparation and attention to detail which should not be compromised for the sake of good relations with ministers or benefits to one's career. Nor should they be sacrificed for the sake of quick political returns. Although for practical purposes the Crown was represented by the minister, and the minister had a similar duty to the Crown to place the public or national interest above that of his or her party or his or her career in politics. If disagreements took place, both ministers and civil servants should recognise that shared duty to the Crown and differences should be respected, with the understanding that the minister had the final decision, having taken any differences into account. It is natural for ministers to value civil servants who provide 'can do' advice, and right for civil servants to put forward solutions rather than difficulties, but essential if those solutions are to be soundly based and properly considered.

It is not for civil servants to be arbiters of the national interest, but nor is that a matter only for ministers. It is also a matter for Parliament and the courts. All three, together with the civil service, have to operate in a constitutional framework in which all the institutions of state can be seen as accountable and legitimate. The fact that these concepts are difficult to handle as matters of day-to-day politics and public administration does not make them any less important. It is an abdication of responsibility for a civil servant, or any professional public servant, to comply unthinkingly with what he or she thinks is expected - perhaps with the excuse that 'it's my job' without regard for its legitimacy and propriety.[30]

CHANGING ASSUMPTIONS AND RELATIONSHIPS

The Haldane and *Carltona* tradition was coming under strain in other respects by the end of the Conservative administration. Ministers were beginning to make a distinction between their own 'accountability' and their 'responsibility'. Under the Haldane tradition, the two expressions were more or less equivalent and ministers were accountable and responsible, both for their own actions and for the work of their departments. In theory, they could in the last resort be required to resign not only for indiscretions or errors of judgement in which they were directly and personally involved, but also for mistakes in their departments of which they might know nothing.[31] In practice, the only error of judgement for which there is no alternative to resignation is knowingly to mislead Parliament; serious financial indiscretions come close but personal indiscretions depend on the circumstances of the case. Failures of policy have occasionally led to resignations (Lord Carrington over the Falkland Islands), but not departmental failure or mistakes of which the minister might not be aware. Even so, ministers have sought to reduce the notion of 'accountability' to an obligation to explain the facts and take remedial action if necessary, but not to accept personal blame or criticism. 'Responsibility' is stronger and contains a personal element but is confined to matters of which the minister has personal knowledge and actions which he or she has deliberately taken.[32]

Ministers were also beginning to distance themselves from their civil servants by making a distinction between 'policy' (for themselves) and 'operations' or 'implementation' (for civil servants). The distinction was fundamental to the concept of executive agencies, as put forward in the Ibbs Report. Mark Freedland has pointed out that if agency status was intended to imply a real separation of powers, duties and responsibilities between ministers and their chief executives, there would have been serious questions of accountability and legitimacy which would eventually have to be resolved by legislation and the creation of a new statutory relationship with mechanisms to support it.[33]

Other aspects of the Haldane tradition which Rosamund Thomas described in her book were its emphasis on the ethics of government and public administration, and on thought and investigation. None of those featured significantly in the new public management, or in the politics of the mid-1990s.

In the event the separation of executive agencies from their parent or 'core' departments was rarely seen in Westminster or Whitehall as a serious political or constitutional issue. Agency status has had some administrative and presentational benefits, for example by helping to create a sharper managerial focus, a stronger sense of accountability, and a greater feeling of corporate identity. But it has rarely been significant at times when an agency has been under strain and the government has come under criticism, and such occasions have so far been resolved in the usual way as matters of political confidence and expediency.

A distinction between policy and operations is in any event difficult to sustain as a basis for the relationship between ministers and civil servants. When things go well it is unlikely to be an issue; when things go wrong the minister will, rightly, be called to account for a failure which is serious, whether it is seen as a failure of policy or operations. The outcome will depend on whether he or she still has the confidence of colleagues and Parliament. For civil servants the failure can sometimes be attributed to specific lapses by clearly identified individuals, or to inadequate management for which managers should be held responsible. But more often the situation will have built up over a period of time and it may be difficult to hold anyone individually to blame. The important task is then to put the situation right and prevent its recurrence, and for that purpose a distinction between policy and operations is unlikely to be relevant, if it can be made at all.

The Labour Government's relationship with the civil service, and its attitude to the tradition of Haldane and *Carltona*, is one of the subjects considered in the next chapter.

ENDNOTES for *Chapter 2*

[1] See for example Office for National Statistics, *Social Trends*, London, Stationery Office, 2000; also *Job Insecurity and Work Intensification: Flexibility and the Changing Boundaries of Work*, York, Joseph Rowntree Foundation, 1999. *The National Strategy for Neighbourhood Renewal: Report of Policy Action Team 12* is published by the Cabinet Office and available on the Cabinet Office Website http://www.cabinet-office.gov.uk/seu/2000/pat12, 2000.

[2] Frank Furedi *The Culture of Fear: Risk Taking and The Morality of Low Expectation*, London, Cassell, 1998. For an account of the effects, both on individual behaviour and on the politics of crime and criminal justice in Great Britain and the United States, see David Garland, 'The Culture of High Crime Societies: Some Preconditions of Recent Law and Order Politics', *British Journal of Criminology* 2000 40 347-375.

[3] For an account of this 'criminology of the other', see David Garland 'The Limits of the Sovereign State: Strategies of Crime Control in Contemporary Society', *British Journal of Criminology* 36/4: 445-471, 1966); also Simon Hallsworth 'Economies of Excess and the Criminology of the Other' *Punishment and Society* 2(2): 145-160, (2000).

[4] Elizabeth Burney examines the problem of children who are 'out of control' in *Crime and Banishment: Nuisance and Exclusion in Social Housing*, Winchester, Waterside Press, 1999. Emma Brokes described the life of one of the notorious 'child offenders' of the early 1990s (the 'balaclava boy'), and his eventual death from an overdose of drugs, in the *Guardian*, 15 May 2000.

[5] Home Office, *Review of Football Related Legislation*, London, Home Office, 2000.

[6] Foresight Crime Prevention Panel, *Just Around the Corner: a Consultation Document*, London, Department of Trade and Industry, 2000. Also, *Turning the Corner*, the final report, *ibid.*, 2000.

[7] The notions of 'modernity'; 'late modernity' and 'post modernism' are all the subject of intriguing but not always illuminating academic dispute. 'Modernity' generally relates to the institutions, conditions and relationships which were associated with and grew out of the Industrial Revolution; 'late modernism' to their adaptation or replacement during the post-industrial period; and 'post modernism' to the fragmentation which some writers view as taking place at the beginning of the twenty-first century. Opinions differ on whether that period should be seen as 'late modern' or 'post modern'. The most recent and perhaps the most complete account of 'late modernity' and its consequences for criminal justice and criminology is in David Garland, *The Culture of Control: Crime and Social Order in Contemporary Society*, Oxford, Oxford University Press, 2001. Other writers who have addressed the subject include Anthony Giddens, *The Consequences of Modernity*, Cambridge, Polity Press, 1990: see also his later work *The Third Way*, Cambridge, Polity Press, 1998; Jock Young 'Writing on the Cusp of Change: A New Criminology for an Age of Modernity' in Paul Walton and Jock Young (eds.), *The New Criminology Revisited*, Basingstoke, Macmillan, 1998; and Anthony Bottoms and Paul Wiles, 'Environmental Criminology' in Rod Morgan and Robert Reiner, (eds.), *The Oxford Handbook of Criminology*, Oxford, University Press, 1997; and 'Understanding Crime Prevention in Late Modern Societies' in Trevor Bennett, (ed.), *Preventing Crime and Disorder*, Cambridge, University Institute of Criminology, 1998.

[8] Norman Davies, *The Isles*, Basingstoke, Macmillan, 1999; Jeremy Paxman, *The English*; Peter Hitchens, *The Abolition of Britain: the British Cultural Revolution from Lady Chatterly to Tony Blair*, London, Quartet, 1999. Simon Heffer, *Nor shall my Sword: the Reinvention of England*, London, Weidenfield and Nicholson, 1999 and Andrew Marr, *The Day Britain Died*, London, Profile Books, 2000 are some examples written from different points of view and comprising different opinions and beliefs.

[9] Richard Hernstein and Charles Murray, *The Bell Curve*, New York, The Free Press, 1996. See also the articles by Charles Murray, 'The Underclass: The Crisis Deepens', and 'The Emerging British Underclass', (both published by the Institute of Economic Affairs, in 1990 and 1994 respectively).

[10] Andrew Rutherford, 'Criminal Policy and the Eliminative Ideal', *Social Policy and Administration* 1997, London, Michael Joseph, 1998, 31/5, pp. 116-135.

[11] Dorothy Rowe, *Friends and Enemies*, London, Harper Collins, 2000.

[12] For an account of the relationship between social exclusion and criminal justice, see Lorraine Gelsthorpe, *Understanding Social Exclusion, Crime and Justice*, Buckingham, Open University Press, 2000.

[13] Robert Sullivan, 'The Schizophrenic State: Neo-liberal Criminal Justice', in Kevin Stenson and Robert Sullivan, (eds), *Crime, Risk and Justice: the Politics of Crime Control in Liberal Democracies*, Cullompton, Devon, Willan Publishing, 2001.

[14] The Labour Government elected in 1997 claimed, probably rightly, to be more 'inclusive' than its immediate predecessor, in the sense that it appealed to, and sought to represent, the interests of this country as a whole, in the same way as the 'One Nation' Conservative Party had once tried to do. However the 'old' Conservative and Labour Parties were probably both more inclusive, in the sense that more people could more readily identify themselves with political parties, their personalities, and what each stood for and believed in, than any of the political parties today.

[15] Amitai Etzioni, *The Spirit of Community: Rights, Responsibilities and the Communitarian Agenda*, London, Fontana, 1995; *The New Golden Rule: Community and Morality in Democratic Society*, London, Profile Books, 1997; and *The Third Way to a Good Society*, London, Demos, 2000. See also 'You have Fixed the Economy, Mr Blair - Now You Must Mend Society', *The Times*, 5 July 2000. And Giddens *op. cit.*, n. 7.

[16] Mike Nellis , 'Creating Community Justice' in Scott Ballintyre, Ken Pease and Vic McLaren, (eds.), *Secure Foundations: Key issues in Crime Prevention, Crime Reduction and Community Safety*, London, Institute for Public Policy Research, 2000.

[17] Simon Schama, *A History of Britain, 3000 BC–AD 1603*, London, BBC Worldwide Ltd, 2000, p. 15.

[18] Robert Hazell, (ed.), *Constitutional Futures*, Oxford University Press, 1999, pp. 45-6.

[19] Commission on the Future of Multi-Ethnic Britain, *The Future of Multi-Ethnic Britain*, London, Profile Books, 2000. See also Mike Nellis *op. cit.* n.14 and Yasmin Alibhai-Brown, *Who Do We Think We Are: Imagining the New Britain*, London, Penguin Press, 2000.

[20] A situation which may have had its origins in the politics of the period between the Liberal Party's election victory in 1906 and the start of World War I, and especially between 1910 and 1914. George Dangerfield identified as reasons: the Party's ambiguous commitment to progress; its failure to confront capital; and its handling of such issues as Ireland, the emancipation of women, the recognition of organized labour, and the reform of the House of Lords. See *The Strange Death of Liberal England*, New York, Capricorn Press, 1935, reprinted 1961. Similar features which can perhaps be discerned in the politics of the beginning of the twenty-first century, in relation to issues such as modernisation, globalisation, social exclusion, racial inequality and constitutional reform, (not to mention Ireland).

[21] The new public management is the subject of an extensive literature, by writers who have approached it from different perspectives, in different countries. The American writers Osborne and Gaebler famously promoted the ideas of small or 'hollowed out' government and 'steering not rowing' in their book *Reinventing Government*, Reading Mass., Addison-Wesley, 1992. In Britain, Derek Rayner introduced the Financial Management Initiative in the early years of the Conservative Government, and Robin Ibbs and Kate Jenkins wrote their report *Improving Management in Government: The Next Steps*, London, HMSO, 1988 proposing that large areas of the civil service should be re-established as executive agencies – a report which became the basis of a major programme of reform during the second half of the Conservative Government. The Conservative Government also produced the *Citizen's Charter*, Cmnd. 1599, London, HMSO, 1991, and the various charters associated with it, telling citizens as consumers what they could expect from the services provided for them. Numerous academic commentaries include Christopher Foster and Francis Plowden, *The State Under Stress*, Buckingham, Open University Press, 1996; Mark Freedland 'Government by Contract

and Public Law' in *Public Law,* pp. 86-104, Spring 1994; and 'Law, Public Services and Citizenship – New Domains, New Regimes' in Mark Freedland and Silvana Sciarra, (eds.), *Public Services and Citizenship in European Law: Public and Labour Law Perspectives,* Oxford, Clarendon Press, 1998; Christopher Hood *The Art of the State: Culture, Rhetoric and Public Management,* Oxford, Clarendon Press, 1998; and Michael Power, *The Audit Society, Rituals of Verification,* Oxford, University Press, 1997. Michael Pusey has provided a sobering account of similar developments in Canberra. *Economic Rationalism in Canberra.,* Sydney, Cambridge University Press, 1991.

[22] Cmnd. 1730, London, HMSO, 1991.

[23] Lord Fulton, *The Civil Service: Report of the Committee,* (The Fulton Report), London, HMSO, 1968.

[24] A series of seminars held in St John's College, Oxford, explored these and other questions of public administration, public law and citizenship during the period between 1992-1999. Participants came from the civil service, other public services, universities, the practising legal profession and voluntary organizations. Records of the seminars are available from St John's College or the University of Oxford Centre for Criminological Research.

[25] See, for example, Peter Neyroud and Alan Buckley, *Policing, Ethics and Human Rights,* Cullompton, Devon, Willan Publishing, 2001, who conclude that 'good policing requires more than "good performance". It needs . . . a new commitment to ethics at the core of poliicing.'

[26] Cabinet Office, *The Ministerial Code,* 1997 and Cabinet Office, *The Civil Service Code,* 1999 available on the Cabinet Office website. For discussion, see Simon Jenkins, *Accountable to None: the Tory Nationalisation of Britain,* London, Hamish Hamilton, 1995 and Christopher Vicenzi; *Crown Powers, Subjects and Citizens,* London, Pinter, 1998 especially *Chapters 7, 10* and *11.* Also *The Ministerial Code: Improving the Rule Book,* Third Report from the House of Commons Select Committee on Public Administration, Session 2000-2001 (HC 235). The report is concerned principally with relations between ministers, the Prime Minister and Parliament. It recommends that 'a free-standing code of ethical principles is devised', with 'greater coherence and clarity to its structure . . . Its status should be properly recognised. Its Prime Ministerial ownership should be clearly acknowledged and tied to responsibility. The lines of accountability should be strengthened. There should be proper investigation of alleged breaches. Its key elements should be clearly identified and endorsed by Parliament. Its publication should be put on a formal footing.'

[27] Stephen Sedley 'The Sound of Silence', *Law Quarterly Review* 110, 1994, pp. 270-282.

[28] See Lord Haldane's *Report of the Machinery of Government Committee,* Ministry of Reconstruction, Cd. 9230, HMSO, 1918, and Green MR's judgement in *Carltona v. Commissioners of Works,* 1943, discussed in T. Daintith and A. Page, *The Executive in the Constitution,* Oxford, University Press, 1999. For a fuller account see Rosamund Thomas, *The British Philosophy of Administration,* London, Longman, 1978.

[29] *The Civil Service Code, op. cit.,* n. 26. Anthony Sampson considers the change in perception which took place during the 1980s, and the different ways in which the civil service's duties were described by different heads of the civil service - Ian Bancroft and Robert Armstrong at different times during the Conservative administration. *The Essential Anatomy of Britain: Democracy in Crisis,* London, Hodder and Stoughton, 1992 p. 34. The Treasury and Civil Service Committee of the House of Commons had declared that 'the civil service as such has no constitutional personality or responsibility separate from the duly elected government of the day', *Report of the Treasury and Civil Service Committee Vol. III,* 1985-86, HC 92-II.

[30] In a paper 'Continuity and Change in the Home Office' written in August 1991, the author considered some of those features as they appeared in the Home Office at that time. Its purpose was to give staff some understanding of the Department's history and of its values and traditions as they affected, for example, the balance between public protection and the rights and freedoms of the individual; and to set in that context the

changes both in organization and management and in criminal justice policy, which were then taking place. It included the following:

> It is our job to support [Ministers] in responding to ... [the] pressures [which are increasingly being placed upon them], whilst stopping short of involving ourselves in party political activity; we must not engage in any public activity in which we know they would disapprove; and if we think they might but ought not to disapprove, we should obtain their clearance in advance. But the official's relationship with Ministers is emphatically not one of passive obedience. It is not the official's job to give Ministers the advice they want to hear, but to make sure that the financial, practical and other consequences of a course of action have been properly worked out, and are firmly in the Ministers' minds, before a decision is taken. It is a serious professional failure on our part if we are unprepared or so anxious to please that we fail to provide properly thought out judgement or advice. The other side of the relationship is that Ministers should respect and expect that advice, even if they decide not to accept it. If that happens it is the duty of officials to give effect to the decision unless they can be moved to other work or in an extreme case they are prepared to resign.

Copies of the paper are available from Waterside Press or the University of Oxford Centre for Criminological Research.

[31] Sir Thomas Dugdale's resignation over Crichel Down is the example most often quoted, although it is now generally accepted that he resigned not so much to uphold the principle of ministerial accountability as because he had lost the confidence of his party in the House of Commons.

[32] Sir Robin Butler (now Lord Butler) expressed this view in evidence to Sir Richard Scott's inquiry into the sale of arms to Iraq. Sir Richard Scott, *Report of the Inquiry into the Export of Defence Equipment etc.*, Cmnd. 115, Vol. IV, pna K8.15, 1994. See also Vernon Bogdanor 'Ministers, Civil Servants and the Constitution: a Revolution in Whitehall', *Institute of Advanced Legal Studies Bulletin*, October 1993. Diana Woodhouse gave an interesting analysis of the notions of 'accountability' and 'responsibility' in her professorial lecture *Lock, Stock and Two Smoking Barrels*, delivered at Oxford Brookes University on 30 May 2000. See also Christopher Vincenzi, *op. cit.*, n. 26. It is interesting that in the debate over the escape from Parkhurst Prison in 1995 and the Home Secretary's decision to dismiss the Director General of the Prison Service, the Opposition chose to concentrate on a narrow and rather continued argument that the Home Secretary, Michael Howard, had misled the House of Commons. They did not criticise him for the state of affairs in the Prison Service for which they presumably accepted that he was 'accountable' but not 'responsible', and therefore not personally vulnerable – a situation which would of course be helpful to a Labour Home Secretary if he came into office. Derek Lewis has written his own account of the events and exchanges leading up to his dismissal as Director General of the Prison Service, *Hidden Agendas: Politics, Law and Disorder*, London, Hamish Hamilton, 1997.

[33] See his article 'Government by Contract and Public Law', (n. 21 above) and his paper *Constitutional and Administrative Law in Public Service, the State and Citizenship* in the report of the series of seminars held in St John's College, Oxford in 1998, (n. 24 above). He expressed similar concerns about the Private Finance Initiative in his article 'Public Law and Private Finance – Placing the Private Finance Initiative in a Public Law Framework', *Public Law*, 1998, pp. 288-307.

ıısing Government

THE LABOUR GOVERNMENT FROM MAY 1997

At the heart of all our work, however, is one central theme: national renewal. Britain rebuilt as one nation, in which each citizen is valued and has a stake; in which no one is excluded from opportunity and the chance to develop their potential; in which we make it, once more, our national purpose to tackle social division and inequality. My political philosophy is simple. Individuals prosper in a strong and active community of citizens.

Tony Blair

The goal is to create a more open, diverse and professional Civil Service in which people put the public's interests first; innovate, create and learn; take personal responsibility; work in partnership with others; and use new technology to deliver results of high quality and good value.

Sir Richard Wilson, *Civil Service Reform*, December 1999

The Labour Government elected in May 1997 brought a change of direction in some respects, and continued the Conservative Government's approach in others. The changes include its much greater concern to reduce poverty; to recognise cultural diversity; to support people who are in difficulty; to promote opportunities, especially for work; and to reduce social exclusion. It was strongly committed to what it called modernisation, and to achieving a transformation both in social conditions and relationships, and in the quality of public services. It came into office with an ambitious programme of constitutional reform – on human rights, devolution to Scotland and Wales (but with some anbiguity in its attitude to the regions in England), reform of the House of Lords and freedom of information. The continuity was in the Labour Government's emphasis on individual enterprise, in its commercially oriented approach to public management, and in its generally punitive penal policies.

The Government's aims and values
The Treasury's White Paper *Public Services for the Future: Modernisation, Reform, Accountability* stated that the Government's overall objectives were to

- increase sustainable growth and employment;
- promote fairness and opportunity; and
- deliver efficient and modern public services.

Other publications, for example the Government's Annual Report for 1998, and the Prime Minister's Fabian Society Pamphlet on *The Third Way*, referred to principles, aims or values such as equal worth, responsibility, community, social inclusion, democracy, tolerance and decency.[1] The Home Office logo displays the words 'building a safe, just and tolerant society'. The five principles of good regulation set out by the Better Regulation Task Force were 'transparency, accountability, targeting, consistency and proportionality'.[2]

The means of achieving the three overall objectives included a series of Public Service Agreements (PSAs), both for individual departments and for 'cross-cutting areas' such as criminal justice. Each of those Agreements contained the following 'key elements':

- an introduction, setting out the minister or ministers accountable for delivering the commitments, together with the coverage of the agreement
- the aims and objectives of the department or cross-cutting areas
- the resources which had been allocated to it in the Comprehensive Spending Review.
- key performance targets for the delivery of its services, together with, in some cases, a list of key policy initiatives to be delivered
- a statement about how the department will increase the productivity of its operations.

The emphasis was to be on social and economic outcomes, as well as on processes and outputs. The Objectives and Performance Measures and Indicators for the criminal justice departments, and the criminal justice system as a whole, are discussed in more detail in *Chapter 9*.

The Government developed its thinking in its subsequent White Paper *Modernising Government*.[3] That document dealt with the responsiveness of public services to their users and to citizens, with the use of information technology for that and other purposes; with policy making that is 'joined-up and strategic'; and with internal reforms in the civil service to increase the numbers of women and of members of ethnic minorities and disabled people, especially in senior positions. Government was to be 'inclusive and integrated', and to be 'more forward - and outward - looking'. Boundaries between the public and the private sector were to be broken down still further. Services were to 'reflect real lives', with programmes that were 'citizen-focused', 'group-focused' and ' area-based'. The public service was to be the agent of the changes to which the Government was committed, but there was to be more movement within the public service and between the public service and other sectors, and greater diversity. Public servants were to be 'valued, not denigrated'.

Human rights and citizenship
The Government has generally presented its programme on consitutional reform as distinct from its programmes in areas of social and economic policy, criminal justice and the modernisation of public

services. But if the Government is serious about its constitutional programmes, their practical application will be intimately connected. Each aspect of the constitutional reform has the capacity to give an extra edge of legitimacy, and of public ownership and commitment, to the country's governance and public administration. *The State and the Nations*, edited by Robert Hazell, describes how the work of Parliament at Westminster has already changed, and perhaps become more effective, since devolution.[4] The Freedom of Information Act has not so far been tested; properly used in a spirit of confidence and goodwill it should help to increase the quality and standing of public services, although it must be a matter of disappointment that central government itself remains largely exempt. The House of Lords is in a state of transition, and its long term future remains undecided. For immediate purposes, potentially the most powerful of the Government's constitutional reforms is probably the incorporation of the European Convention on Human Rights through the Human Rights Act 1998.

There has always been a strand of opinion in Great Britain which has seen the European Convention on Human Rights as something rather alien, unnecessary and potentially troublesome; and the enactment of the Human Rights Act as a measure justified only, if at all, by the saving in embarrassment and expense through not having to argue cases in Strasbourg. This was not the view of the Labour Government when it arrived in office. Like the European Court of Human Rights itself, the Government saw the Convention as a 'living instrument', capable of promoting a culture of human rights which would come to inform and perhaps to transform the quality and character of British public administration. While the Convention itself was a statement of minimum rights, its application through the Human Rights Act would ensure that even higher standards were achieved. The state, through Parliament and the courts, had a 'positive obligation' to promote and develop the rights stated in the Convention, and to adopt a 'purposive approach' in which it would if necessary look beyond the precise words of the Convention to the purpose it was seeking to achieve.[5] Some of those who supported the Act hoped that the Government would go further and provide for the appointment of a Human Rights Commission which would act positively to promote and protect human rights.[6]

Two significant texts are the Constitution Unit Annual Lecture, which the Home Secretary, Jack Straw, delivered on 27 October 1999[7], and his address 'Building a Human Rights Culture' to a Civil Service College seminar on 9 December 1999.[8] In his lecture, he spoke of a new relationship between the citizen and the state, to be created by the Government's programme of constitutional reform. That relationship was to be founded upon a formalisation of rights, through the Human Rights Act 1998, and of responsibilities, through measures such as the Crime and Disorder Act 1998. He emphasised the need for policies to give practical expression to pluralist, democratic and inclusive values. People were to be thought of as citizens rather than subjects, and as citizens they should be actively involved in their communities, especially by voting in elections. He referred to the devolution of power and authority from central government to local authorities and to local services such as the police, and invited suggestions on how citizenship could be given more practical content.

In his address at the Civil Service College, the Home Secretary spoke of building a 'culture of rights and responsibilities', which he seemed to see as primarily a matter for government and especially for public servants: 'it' s about what counts as a winning argument, what really matters, what makes things tick'. He referred to the United Kingdom's honourable history in matters of human rights during the seventeenth and eighteenth centuries, and approvingly to the Lord Chancellor' s statement in 1762 that 'As soon as a man sets foot on English ground he is free'. He went on to examine the significance of the Human Rights Act, emphasising that Parliament ultimately retains supremacy over any interpretations by the courts, and the need for courts to interpret the Act in accordance with what Parliament intended. He saw the Act as a 'living instrument', constantly adapting to changing social conditions and standards, and as providing 'a common set of values to help unite a diverse society ... to underpin the rights and responsibilities culture we want to build - unity in diversity, and inclusiveness'; a guarantee of fairness in public administration; and a support for public confidence in the institutions of state. He went on to argue that rights are conditional in the sense that they can legitimately be interfered with in order to protect other rights, and that they have to be balanced with responsibilities towards others, the wider community, and the state. Rights depend on the performance of duties, and that performance is 'a moral obligation based as much on self-interest as on concern for the common good'.

The Chancellor of the Exchequer, Gordon Brown, has also spoken about the Government's vision of citizenship, with a particular emphasis on the role of voluntary organizations.[9] He referred to '... what defines us as a nation - the most precious things, our tolerance, strong sense of fair play, our sense of civil responsibility ...' and to the case for 'a new and stronger relationship between individual, community and government - for the renewal of British civil society - a great society which not only defines anew the importance of voluntary organizations, but engenders a civil patriotism.' He saw a strong and effective civil society occupying the middle ground between markets and the state, rooted in a 'positive and optimistic view of human nature'; and a country in which individuals 'felt at home in society by virtue of being a member not only of a family but of a neighbourhood, a community, and a society network'. He went on to announce new arrangements to encourage financial support for the voluntary sector, and indicated that the Government would be prepared, not only to engage voluntary organizations in delivering programmes such as Sure Start (for children under four) and the New Deal (for young people who have difficulty in finding employment), but also to pass over the responsibility for those delivering services to partnerships between the voluntary organizations themselves.

A new form of governance?

A new form of governance, and with it a new approach to public administration and citizenship, now seems to be emerging. Compared with the situation at the end of the 1970s, it is more centralised, more politically directed and more business oriented. It places more emphasis on efficiency and accountability through published reports and the processes of inspection and audit, but it is consequently more bureaucratic. It is more sensitive to what is perceived to be public opinon, as expressed through certain newspapers or by certain individuals or interest groups, but it is arguably less democratic and more remote from the population as a whole. In criminal justice it includes a process of creeping criminalisation. The Government no longer sees public service as the administration of a process but as a means of achieving 'real' outcomes and results. Civil servants are encouraged to think of themselves as 'social entrepreneurs'.

Some of the words on the signposts – 'modernisation' or 'effectiveness' - are clearly displayed, but it is not always clear where the signposts are pointing. In some respects they point to a major change of direction, for example the Labour Government's programme of constitutional reform - the Human Rights Act, devolution, perhaps, to some extent, freedom of information and the reform of the House of Lords. In others they suggest that the previous Government's approaches will be continued - the use of performance indicators and league tables, contracting out and the Private Finance Initiative. This ambivalence is not a matter of criticism, but there may be problems of ambiguity and an unclear sense of longer-term direction.

The governance of a modern state, or nation, is a complex matter. It includes managing not only change, but also diversity, conflict, and ambivalence of the kind just mentioned. It often includes managing uncertainty, risk and irrationality. It involves relationships not only between the government and the citizen, but also between a host of other interests, 'stakeholders', professions and communities. Some of these interests may be seen as obstructive or even subversive, but most of them have a legitimate part to play and some of them are essential for a healthy (in the widest sense of the word), prosperous, fair and stable society. Few problems can be dealt with 'at a stroke'; most call for multiple forms of action, involving several agencies and a variety of interests; and any course of action is likely to have effects which extend much more widely than the problem at which it is immediately directed. Decisions to tackle a problem, and very often decisions about how to treat an individual, are also likely to involve conflicting considerations and arguments. The conflict may be a matter of empirical judgement and verifiable fact, but in the public sphere, more often than in the commercial sphere, it may also involve judgements on matters of principle, values or attitude. It will often have to be resolved by local managers, or by individual public servants, on the ground. How the arguments are both put forward and reconciled is one of the tests - perhaps the most important test - of a modern legitimate state and liberal democracy.

How it looks and feels

Critics have made much of the fact that many people, including some public servants, have found difficulty in understanding what the Government believes or where it is going. They have been conscious, and sometimes suspicious, of its preoccupation with matters of presentation and handling. They have recognised, and many of them have supported, the Government' s commitment to modernisation and reform, but they have not been sure what difference it will make in practice. They have been conscious that most public services have room for improvement, and some services may be portrayed as failing the nation in more serious ways. Many people will not use public services much themselves - they may not have children at school, or have much need of the National Health Service - and arguments about consitutional reform often seem remote and academic. But they do want public services to be available and to work when they need them. They do want to live their lives without too many restrictions or frustrations, and without having to worry too much about becoming a victim of crime. And most of them would like to feel that society as a whole has some principles and values, and a sense of direction, with which they can identify themselves and which they think the Government also shares. Whether that sense is one of 'decency', or of 'Britishness', or 'Englishness', 'Scottishness' and 'Welshness'; how much diversity it is able to accommodate; and whether it is something which governments can legitimately impose, or only respond to it as it develops in society as a whole, have so far been unfamiliar questions to which they have rarely given much thought. When they do, they find that it is an uncomfortable subject.

People do however see a Government which in some areas of public life seems prepared, with varying degrees of commitment or enthusiasm, to surrender power or influence to other bodies - the assemblies in Scotland, Wales and Northern Ireland; the Bank of England on interest rates; the courts under the Human Rights Act; the commercial sector through privatisation, contracting out and the Private Finance Initiative. It is keen to improve local communities through the processes of consultation and participation which local authorities are required to undertake in order to comply with the Local Government Act 2000. At the same time the Government is seeking to increase its control over public services, through public service agreements, the continuing development of standards and performance indicators, the issue of league tables ('naming and shaming') and the extension of performance-related pay. Ministers seem constantly to be putting themselves in charge of reforms to ' failing' services, whether in health, education, transport or criminal justice, with implied criticism of the public servants involved. Measures originally designed to promote freedom of choice, such as league tables and the *Citizen's Charter*, have come to be treated as instruments of audit and control. Those procedures can themselves produce a creeping politicisation of public services, no less than political interference with public appointments. They can destroy trust. They produce a situation of responsibility without control, which is a recognised cause of stress and poor performance (see Richard Sennett's important book on *The Corrosion of Character* and the Rowntree Foundation's report *Job Insecurity and Work Intensification: Flexible and Changing Boundaries at Work,* already mentioned in *Chapter 2*[10], and also *Chapter 5*).

The drive to promote social inclusion by various forms of social support is often directed towards those who 'deserve it' and are able to co-operate. It may be matched by punishment and exclusion for those who are 'difficult' and unwilling to conform. Desmond King has described how 'illiberal' social policies having this effect have over the years have been pursued by supposedly 'liberal' governments in 'liberal' countries, both the United Kingdom and the United States. Kevin Stenson has described how the word 'liberal' has come to be given new meanings and to be used as a term of abuse, especially in criminal justice.[11] Attempts to improve the opportunities available to members of minority groups and the respect shown to them, including the Government's own commitment to implementing the recommendations of Sir William Macpherson's report on the investigation into the death of Stephen Lawrence[12], are for many people undermined by increasingly restrictive policies on immigration and asylum.

Attempts to promote joined-up government are still frustrated at national level by pressure of work and competing demands within government; and joined-up implementation at local level presents serious difficulty where services have conflicting priorities and loyalties and have to respond to, and if possible take advantage of, an ever-increasing range of separate government demands and initiatives. Apparent willingness to consult is accompanied by an almost self-righteous hostility to criticism. Protestations by ministers that action is in hand, and defensive claims by public service managers that services as measured by performance indicators are improving, often seem out of touch with the public's experience of the services themselves. Three, very different, examples are the performance of the privatised railways, the situation in some prisons, and - dramatically and tragically - the inquiry into the death of Stephen Lawrence. The loss of an effective Parliamentary opposition has left the press and broadcasting as the only sources of criticism which the government thinks it needs to take seriously, and certain sections of the press have gained enormous influence as a result.

Recognising the limitations of elective Parliamentary democracy, ministers have been keen to exploit supplementary forms of democracy such as opinion surveys, the People's Panel, focus groups and citizens' juries. They rightly attach importance to the views which are put to them by constituents. All these are valuable ways of keeping ministers in touch with public opinion. But they cannot take account of the full complexity or ramifications of many of the choices which have to be made. They are not a substitute for ministers' own judgement, or for advice from colleagues, officials, the relevant services or representative bodies, all of which can pay attention to a wider range of arguments and opinions. They may give ministers a sense that they are better informed; they do not give the public a sense that they are actually involved.

The Government seems to feel that it must always give the impression that it is in charge of everything, has a solution for everything, and has everything under control. It is so important to give an impression of movement that the direction does not seem to matter, even if it is backwards (as sometimes in criminal justice). Anything that goes wrong must be made to seem someone else's fault: incompetent managers, self-seeking professionals, dishonest manipulators. The Government is deeply committed, and rightly so, to evidence-based policy, to making things work, and to developing and exploiting new technology. But its commitment carries the risk of believing, or giving the impression, that science and technology can provide all the answers, and that problems can be reduced to questions either of management or of technical knowledge. An exclusive emphasis of this kind, if not balanced by a broader vision, understanding and judgement, will generate a form of pseudo-science, with its own language and patterns of thought, which will come to gain an air of spurious authenticity. Danger signals should be raised whenever strings of nouns are used as adjectives, when arguments are presented in 'bullet points' or 'sound bites' rather than complete sentences, or when dead metaphors (words like 'streamline' or 'spearhead') are used to conceal gaps in thought.

THE PROCESS OF POLICY-MAKING

The Labour Government deserves full credit for its commitment to evidence-based policies and practice, to promoting and respecting knowledge and to improving professional and public understanding. That commitment is essential for any civilised modern society. Without it, the country is vulnerable to a politics of conviction, populism and prejudice, of the kind which is described in *Chapter 8* as it has affected crime and criminal justice. But the commitment must be wholehearted; and evidence, knowledge and understanding must be sought and applied with diligence and integrity. It is all too easy, in government or any public service, to assemble or pay attention only to the evidence which suits a person's prejudices or help their career, or to accept convenient conclusions which are superficial and hurriedly prepared.

Policy-making needs expertise, judgement and time. Decisions need to be preceded by research and analysis, and by consultation; and followed by implementation, often including legislation, and then by evaluation and review. All too often, policies have been formulated without adequate research or analysis, perhaps because the material was not available, or it was of poor quality; because it would take too long to assemble; or because political imperatives made it irrelevant or unimportant. Preparatory research or analytical studies are always conducted under pressure of time and the product sometimes suffers as a result. Consultation may be perfunctory; legislation may be badly prepared; and implementation, even if it includes pilot schemes, may not take full account of local relationships and circumstances. Evaluation is more often applied to the programmes, schemes and projects which are developed in accordance with a policy than to the policy itself. Arrangements for evaluation may not take adequate account of the wider social and economic context, including the impact of other government programmes or the working conditions of those who have to put them into effect. Serious attempts to review policies are difficult for governments if they are likely to be embarrassed by the result. Failure of programmes can be blamed on the officials in charge even within the changing conventions described in *Chapter* 2; failure of policy is more likely to be seen as a direct responsibility of the minister. When policies are reviewed in retrospect, their success or otherwise is usually judged by the way in which they have come to be portrayed by the media or by ministers (sometimes of a different administration) who later became responsible for them. Today's success can easily become tomorrow's failure, or less often vice-versa. Some examples are given in later chapters.

The Government has recognised the difficulty and importance of the policy-making process in its creation of special, often multi-disciplinary, units and task forces to achieve 'joined-up policy' and tackle 'cross-cutting issues'; in its proposals to give a more strategic direction to the management of the criminal justice system[13]; and in the two excellent reports from the Cabinet Office's Performance and Innovation Unit: *Adding it Up: Improving Analysis and Modelling in Central Government;* and *Wiring it Up: Whitehall's Management of Cross Cutting Issues and Services.*[14]

Ministers themselves would probably agree that more must be done to achieve successful implementation on the ground. *Chapter 18* makes some suggestions.

Conditions for success
Success in the formulation and implementation of policy is likely to involve a number of conditions.

(i)   A reasonably long-term and clearly stated vision and sense of direction, recognised and accepted by the professionals and practitioners whose task is to put the policy and legislation into effect and by those who are affected by it.

(ii) Open consultation at the stage when the policy is being formulated and legislation is being drafted, with effective contributions from producers and providers, from other relevant groups and representative bodies, including academics and those representing users and minority interests, and with a sense of shared ownership of the outcome. The Hansard Society's Commission on the Legislative Process attached considerable importance to this point in its report published in 1993.[15]

(iii) Genuine understanding and careful attention to the dynamics as well as the cost of the policy's implementation, both to avoid any unforeseen damaging consequences, and to take account of any wider consequences for other areas of policy and other aspects of the public or national interest.

(iv) Continuous and open consultation with those affected by the policy as it is prepared and as it is put into operation, in a spirit which is creative and inclusive, based on mutual confidence, respect and trust.

(v) A sense of local and professional 'ownership' of the policy as it is implemented, and a commitment to its success.

(vi) The ability to work effectively across organizational, and institutional and cultural boundaries, without appearing defensive, secretive or bureaucratic.

(vii) A 'problem solving' rather than an 'institutional' approach which looks first to the outcomes to be achieved, rather than to organizational change in the services concerned, and which regards organizational change not as an objective in itself but as a necessary means of achieving the outcome.

(viii) Well planned programmes of research, including both short-term and long-term projects, with stable funding and commissioning authorities which are able to look beyond the immediate political concerns of the government of the day.

(ix) A holistic approach, with joined-up policies and programmes at the local as well as the national level. Citizens and civil society must be fully engaged, with shared ownership of the programme and a shared commitment to the outcome.

Programmes should be based on practical experience and evidence of 'what works', but it is important to recognise the limitations of much of the existing data and existing methods of monitoring and evaluation. Social outcomes should be assessed as well as quantified inputs, outputs and internal processes. Disappointing outcomes may be the results of lack of commitment or support, or failure to carry the programme through in the way that was intended; such results do not indicate that the original ideas were misconceived.

Reliable information is an essential ingredient of success, but it is often difficult to collect in a form which is of practical use. Different organizations collect information for their own purposes, and especially to satisfy their own performance indicators which can have a distorting effect on any programme which involves partnership with others. Organizations working in partnerships, as they must increasingly be prepared to do, must have a sense of responsibility and accountability which extends beyond their own internal structure.

Partnerships should be based on mutual respect and equal status. No single organization should consider itself entitled to impose decisions on others, or to ignore their legitimate views or requirements. Arrangements for funding should be stable and creative, avoiding situations where prospective partners have to compete with one another or accept terms which prevent them from looking or planning ahead, or where restrictive conditions are imposed which frustrate imagination or initiative. Steve Hamer has written 'sadly, recent experience with the

Prison Service is of contracts that seek to load the demand on providers and limit the responsibilities of the purchaser: they seem to have been less about partnership and closer to marriage Hollywood style, with contract-terms that anticipate divorce and ensure that the division of the family-spoils is one-sided'.[16]

There is a long distance between those who make decisions in Whitehall or Westminster, those who have to put them into effect, and those who are intended to benefit (or perhaps in criminal justice to suffer) from them or who may be affected by them. At each stage there are likely to be 'insiders' who are involved in the processes of consultation and implementation and who can have some influence, and 'outsiders' who are likely to be excluded. Consultation should not be adversarial. It should where possible start from the bottom and work upwards: people should not be put in the position of having to say 'yes' or 'no' to a proposal to which those in positions of power are in effect already committed. They should feel they have an opportunity to join in setting the agenda, not just to confirm it or make it seem legitimate. The process should acknowledge and respect differences of culture and class, it should where necessary make use of intermediate representative groups, and focus groups should where possible have some identity separate from the particular occasion for which they have been assembled. Those who are consulted should if possible be given the chance to 'own' the programme and feel part of the solution to whatever problem is being addressed. Authority should be responsible without being populist.

The Cabinet Office published a report *Professional Policy-Making for the Twenty-First Century* in September 1999.[17] The report refers back to the White Paper *Modernising Government* and provides a 'model' of professional policy-making which resembles in many ways the arguments in this chapter. The model contains

- nine features: clearly defined outcomes and a long-term view; account of the national, European and international situation; a holistic view of the Government's strategic objectives; flexibility and innovation; best available evidence from a wide variety of sources; constant review; fairness to everyone concerned; involvement of stakeholders; learning from experience
- three themes: vision, effectiveness and continuous improvement
- core competencies: forward and outward looking, innovative and creative, use of evidence, inclusive, joined up, evaluation and review, learning lessons.

The 'big ideas' emerging from the report are the use of peer review to change culture and share experience; joint training for Ministers and civil servants; a policy knowledge pool, again to share information and experience and provide a more accessible source of evidence; and a system of benchmarking.

The ' big ideas' would be unfamiliar to civil servants who learned their trade before the Fulton report,[18] or even during the 1970s. But in some respects the 'model' corresponds quite closely to what they would have recognised as good practice during an earlier period. Their sources of information would have been more limited and they might have experienced less pressure to be innovative and creative. Those who were innovative or creative were not necessarily respected, still less rewarded, for it. They might be surprised to see what they had taken for granted discussed in such an earnest and self-conscious way, but they would probably support and welcome the general sense of the report. Their experience would have taught them to be sceptical of the extent to which the good intentions of the report would be carried into practice among the pressures and distractions of civil service life - probably a good deal more intense than it would have been during most of their own working lives. But they would recognise that it still belongs in the tradition of Haldane and *Carltona* (see *Chapter 2*).

CIVIL SERVANTS IN MODERN GOVERNMENT

Perhaps the most significant comment comes almost at the end of the Cabinet Office report, where it states that civil servants will need new skills to meet the demands of 'modernised' policy-making. These should include:

- understanding the context - organizational, political and wider - in which they are working. This should include some first-hand experience of the way the policy area in which they are working affects the wider world;
- managing complex relationships with a range of key players, relinquishing the residual command and control culture that still exists in some policy-making areas;
- well developed presentational skills, not just the usual written and oral communication skills, but the ability to work with others to explain and to gain ownership of their ideas by different groups;
- a broader understanding of information technology and how it can be used to facilitate and support policy-making;
- a grounding in economics, statistics and relevant scientific disciplines in order to act as 'intelligent customers' for complex policy evidence;
- understanding of and familiarity with using project management disciplines to keep work on track;
- willingness to experiment, managing risks as they arise; and
- willingness to continue to learn new skills and acquire new knowledge throughout a career in policy-making and elsewhere.

Features of the situation in which the civil service has to operate include the following:

- changes in the working environment resulting from advances in technology, globalisation and the developing relationship with European countries and institutions;

- the Government's policies and legislation on human rights, devolution, the reform of the House of Lords and Freedom of Information, and their service-wide implications;
- increasing pressure from the Government to 'perform' in carrying out its policies and showing results from them; and
- the greater complexity of much government business, its increasing politicisation, the confrontational style in which it is often handled and reported, and ministers' political need for 'quick wins'.

The Service has also had to cope with the consequences of various developments which had taken place during the period of the previous governments.

- The emphasis on the efficient management of internal processes as distinct from understanding and expertise in subjects such as education, health or criminal justice themselves. Associated with that emphasis, a sense that management is a 'value free' activity, to which principles and values had no relevance (talk of principles or values was thought rather precious and self indulgent in the early 1990s).
- Loss of continuity, and of a sense of departmental identity and history, as staff moved rapidly from one position to another in what often appears to be a constant process of reorganization. Experienced staff and the support they can provide have been lost through 'delayering'; and newly recruited staff (as in many other occupations) no longer expect or wish the organization they have joined to provide a long-term career.
- A professional culture in which the civil servant's relationship with ministers was perceived as waiting to see what ministers wanted to do, finding ways of doing it, and carrying out their instructions, rather than exercising an independent judgement and working jointly with ministers to identify options, consider their merits and devise the best means of putting the preferred option into effect. Advice to ministers would tell them what they wanted to know, not what they needed to hear. This is the culture which prevented successive administrations from giving an adequate response to the threat from BSE, and which led to a structure for the privatized railway which failed to give proper attention to safety or to the national interest.
- A decline in some of the traditional skills of consultation, preparation and presentation of advice, use of research, drafting of Green Papers and White Papers, even the preparation of legislation, which ministers had not generally sought or valued.

For these and other reasons related to their experiences in opposition, and despite the generally enthusiastic welcome they received from their civil servants on coming into office, ministers seem to have felt some disappointment with the service they found when they came into office, and some frustration at the pace at which their ideas could be turned into policies and their policies into action. The expertise which had been run down under the previous administration needed to be restored, and new working relationships between ministers and civil servants - including, it could be argued, a revival of the Haldane tradition - needed to be established.

This was the situation which Sir Richard Wilson, Head of the Home Civil Service, addressed in his report to the Prime Minister, *Civil Service Reform*, published in December 1999.[19] The report identified six themes to which the civil service is committed - stronger leadership, better business planning, sharper management of performance, a dramatic improvement in diversity, a service more open to people and ideas and a better deal for staff. The goal, as stated at the beginning of this chapter, was to create a civil service which would be more open, diverse and professional. There was a civil service-wide statement of vision and values:

> Our Aim is to help make the UK a better place for everyone to live in, and support its success in the world. We want to be the best at everything we do.
> In support of successive administrations, we will

- act with integrity, propriety and political impartiality, and select on merit
- put the public's interests first
- achieve results of high quality and good value
- show leadership and take personal responsibility
- value the people we work with and their diversity
- innovate and learn
- work in partnership
- be professional in all we do
- be open and communicate well.

The report responded to most of the points raised earlier in this chapter, and included some significant features which have not received much public attention. They include '360 degree' feedback, designed to improve self-awareness but with the potential, if successful, to improve the fairness of the procedures for assessment and selection; diversity awareness to support the targets for recruiting and promoting members of ethnic minorities, and women, with a more thorough understanding of different communities and cultures; and a better deal for staff. The last should respond to concerns such as those described by Richard Sennett and the Rowntree Foundation's report and mentioned earlier in this chapter (provided that it is treated more seriously than the Civil Service Department's Wider Issues Review was treated in the 1970s).

The Government produces an annual report on the Civil Service Reform Programme and the report for 2000 recorded progress on the programme's various aspects. It gave particular prominence to leadership and a new 'competence framework' for the Senior Civil Service; and to a new 'deal' for staff, starting with a 'vision statement': 'To make a difference to the success of the country to serve with integrity, drive and creativity'. That 'deal ' goes on to set out the 'values and behaviour we seek and the expectations civil servants can have in return'.[20] There are some important subjects which the report did not address. Understandably, it did not deal with relations between civil servants and ministers and ministers' political advisers. Mutual confidence, respect and trust, will be crucial, and civil servants' creativity will depend as much on their relationship with ministers and political advisers as it will on any skills of their own. Ministers' relationships with their departments - and with the services related to their departments - should be one of partnership and should not always be 'top down'.

The report referred to an urgent review of the key competences for the senior civil service. But it did not deal with the skills and expertise which civil servants need in their changing and increasingly demanding relationships with statutory services and voluntary organizations, in the commissioning and interpretation of research, in monitoring and evaluation, in consultation, and in the use of surveys, focus groups and other means of judging opinion. Civil servants also need, to an increasing extent, an understanding of the work of other organizations, and to earn their respect, if their departments' instruction and guidance to those organizations are to have any credibility. They must not use the processes of monitoring or consultation as a means of confirming their own opinions or prejudices, but nor must they allow those processes to set the agenda or determine the options without exercising an independent judgement of their own.

Nor are those only matters of skills and expertise. Civil servants also need time, space and energy to gain and apply those skills - not only by attending courses but also by visiting, talking and reading. Pressure of work has not in the past left room for this kind of activity and the 'performance culture' has not attached any value to it.

Sir Richard Wilson's Report, *Civil Service Reform* (i.e. the 1999 report, see n. 20), provides a good foundation for the continuing reform of the home civil service, especially if the programme is expanded to include subjects such as those just described. But the spirit in which it is carried forward is just as important as the programme itself. It needs in particular a combination of energy, imagination, commitment and trust.

FIVE LAWS OF PUBLIC ADMINISTRATION

There are five 'laws of public administration' that governments and public servants do well to remember.

The first is Parkinson's well-known law that work expands to fill the capacity available, usually quoted as a warning to resist the natural temptation continuously to expand an organization, especially its bureaucracy. The warning has been well heeded in recent years, but the converse is worth heeding as well. That is to say that capacity cannot be reduced without some effect on the work being done. The effect may be salutory, but beyond a certain point it may lead to a coarsening of working relationships, a decline in quality or a corrupting effect on the character of the workforce of the kind which Richard Sennett described in *The Corrosion of Character*. This is not to deny that the discipline of cost effectiveness should always be rigorously applied, but it is to say that the consequences of reducing capacity (or increasing the work without expanding capacity) should be fully thought out. It is not possible indefinitely to do more with less.

The second is that once a policy or a programme starts to go wrong, it is likely to keep on going wrong. Lord Windlesham gives us an example in the attempts to reform the arrangements for compensation for criminal injuries preceding the Criminal Injuries Compensation Act 1995.[21] This law is sometimes stated as 'if you're in a hole, stop digging', 'get out while you can' or 'don't reinforce failure'. It is usually sound advice, but this too has a converse - mistakes on matters of detail, especially in the early stages of a policy or programme, can have a disproportionately damaging effect. Early attention to the detail is always worthwhile.

The third is that there is a limit to the number of priorities to which any organization can pay attention at any one time - at a strategic level, probably not more than two or three. The demands which the Government is imposing on the health and education services, and on local government, make it unlikely that they will have much capacity or energy to spare for community safety or the prevention of crime (see *Chapter 18*). The number of priorities to which the Prison Service has inevitably to pay attention, and the potential conflicts between them, make it an exceptionally difficult service to manage.

The fourth is that simplistic error drives out complex truth. This is a warning of the dangers of 'conviction politics' and of relying on 'common sense', and a reminder of the importance of 'evidence-based policy'. But it is also a warning that the evidence may be complex, ambiguous and difficult to interpret; and that even in an evidence-based environment, there is a temptation to rely on uncertain evidence because it is politically convenient, or to neglect other evidence because it is not. Examples are to be found in youth justice, crime prevention and programmes to tackle offending behaviour: see *Chapters 14* and *18*.

The fifth is that dynamics count for more than structure. Dynamics, not structure, are what bring about social and economic outcomes and have an effect in the 'real world'. Changes in structure may sometimes be necessary to bring about a change in dynamics, as later chapters in this volume recognise and argue, but a new structure is only as good as the dynamics it creates. The process of structural change will also distract attention from the dynamics, and therefore from the activity or service itself, for the period during which the change is planned and put into effect. But that process should not take place without thorough consideration of the dynamics which will flow from it. They will be influenced not only by the structure, but also by the character of the relationships, and the trust, confidence and motivation of those who work within it.

ENDNOTES for *Chapter 3*

[1] HM Treasury, *Public Services for the Future: Modernisation, Reform, Accountability*, London, Stationery Office, Cm. 4181, 1998. See also Tony Blair, *The Third Way*, London, the Fabian Society, 1998 and the Government's *Annual Report 1998-99*.

[2] Better Regulation Task Force, *Principles of Good Regulation*, adopted by the Prime Minister, 5 March 1998, London, Cabinet Office, 1998.

[3] Cabinet Office, *Modernising Government*, Stationery Office, Cm. 4310, 1999.

[4] Robert Hazell (ed.), *The State and the Nations: the First Year of Devolution in the United Kingdom*, London, Imprint Academic, 2000.

[5] Bryan Gibson (ed.), *Human Rights and the Courts: Bringing Rights Home*, Winchester, Waterside Press, 1999.

[6] Sarah Spencer and Ian Bynoe, *A Human Rights Commission: the Options for Great Britain and Northern Ireland*, London, Institute for Public Policy Research, 1998.

[7] Jack Straw, *Constitution Unit Annual Lecture*, London, Constitution Unit, 1999.

[8] Jack Straw, *Building a Human Rights Culture*, Address to a Civil Service College Seminar: London, Home Office, 1999.

[9] Speech by Gordon Brown to the Annual Conference of the National Council of Voluntary Organizations, 9 February 2000.

[10] Richard Sennett, *The Corrosion of Character: The Personal Consequences of Work in the New Capitalism*, New York, W. W. Norton, 1998; and the Joseph Rowntree Foundation, *Job Insecurity and Work Intensification: Flexible and Changing Boundaries at Work*, York, Joseph Rowntree Foundation, 1999.

[11] Desmond King, *In the Name of Liberalism: Illiberal Social Policies in the United States and Britain*, Oxford, University Press, 1999. Kevin Stenson, 'The New Politics of Crime Control' in Kevin Stenson and Robert Sulllivan (eds.), *Crime, Risk and Justice: the Politics of Crime Control in Liberal Democracies*, Cullompton, Devon, Willan Publishing, 2001.

[12] Sir William Macpherson of Cluny, *The Stephen Lawrence Inquiry*, Cm. 4262, London, Stationery Office, 1999.

[13] *The Government's Strategic Plan and Business Plan for the Criminal Justice System 2000-2001*, May 2000.

[14] Cabinet Office, 'Adding it up: Improving Analysis and Modelling' in *Central Government. Performance and Innovation Unit Report*, London, Cabinet Office, 2000. Cabinet Office, 'Wiring It Up: Whitehall's Management of Cross-Cutting Policies and Services' in *Performance and Innovation Unit Report*, London, Cabinet Office, 2000.

[15] The Hansard Society, *Making the Law: The Report of the Hansard Society Commission on the Legislative Process*, London, The Hansard Society, 1992.

[16] Steve Hamer, 'I'll Keep the House and the Kids, You Get the Dog', in *Criminal Justice Matters*, 40, Summer 2000, p. 9.

[17] Cabinet Office, *Professional Policy-Making for the Twenty-First Century: A Report by the Strategic Policy Making Team*, London, Cabinet Office, 1999.

[18] Lord Fulton, *The Civil Service: Report of the Committee* (The Fulton Report), London, HMSO, 1968.

[19] Sir Richard Wilson, *Civil Service Reform*, Report to the Prime Minister from Sir Richard Wilson, Head of the Home Civil Service, London, Cabinet Office, 1999. See also the supporting reports on *Vision and Values; Performance Management; Bringing In and Bringing On Talent*, and *Diverse Civil Service*.

[20] Cabinet Office, *The Civil Service Reform Programme: Annual Report 2000*, London, Cabinet Office, 2001.

[21] Lord Windlesham, *Responses to Crime*, Volume 1: *Legislating with the Tide*, Oxford, University Press, 1996, pp. 433-478.

CHAPTER 4

A New Framework of Principles ar Values: Citizenship, Civil Society and Human Rights

> He who is unable to live in society, or who has no need because he is sufficient for himself, must be either a beast or a god.
>
> Aristotle, Politics, Book 1, 1256b

> Instead of being so mesmerised by debates over British identity, it would be far more productive to concentrate on renovating British citizenship, and on convincing all of the inhabitants of these islands that they are equal and valued *citizens* irrespective of whatever identity they may individually select to prioritise.
>
> Linda Colley, from her Millenium Lecture on
'Britishness in the Twenty-first Century', 3 December 1999

The Labour Government recognised that its generally pragmatic approach, free from political dogma or any attachment to the past, and concentrating on efficiency, effectiveness, modernisation and new technology, needed to have some larger vision and some other source of inspiration if it was to retain its credibility and public support. Liberal, or legitimate, states cannot afford to be ethically neutral about the character or culture of the societies they serve. Nor can public services. The Government saw the need to bring some principle and coherence to what might otherwise appear as a series of unconnected initiatives based on short-term opportunism. It acknowledged that more was needed than statements of aims or values in terms of abstract nouns such as fairness, opportunity, inclusion and decency. In opposition the Labour Party did so by exploring the notion of a 'stakeholding' society, drawing for example on the writing of John Kay in *The Business of Economics:* and on notions of 'community' such as those put forward by the American writer Amitai Etzioni, already mentioned in *Chapter 2*. In government, it became attracted to the idea of a 'Third Way' in politics and in social and economic relationships, articulated principally in Anthony Giddens' book *The Third Way: The Renewal of Social Democracy*, and it has contributed its own political interpretation, for example in Tony Blair's Fabian pamphlet and in various political speeches.[1]

THE 'THIRD WAY'

The 'third way' asserted that the views of socialism or 'old Labour' have become obsolete, and those of the 'new right' had been proved inadequate. The time had come for a new way forward, drawing eclectically on ideas from both left and right, and adding new ones which

e account of modern phenomena such as globalisation and the
anging character of Europe. There would be a new, international
consensus of the centre left, with a new policy framework to match the
new global order and, in developed countries, a new diversity and
pluralism in cultural backgrounds and in personal, social and working
relationships. The new consensus would respond, and bring some order
to, the changes and conflicts described in *Chapter 2*.

Features which Anthony Giddens identified for a 'third way'
programme include

- greater democratisation - more diverse mechanisms by which the public can influence decisions which the government or public services take on their behalf (focus groups, citizens' juries, the People's Panel, and electronic referendums);
- greater efficiency and more transparency in the business of government;
- partnerships between government and civil society or the 'third' (voluntary and community) sector; community-based crime prevention (see *Chapter 18*);
- strong relationships within families (but not necessarily based on the traditional institution of marriage);
- positive management of risk, and investment in human capital; and
- global interventions to reduce world inequality and environmental damage.

Some of these features could be easily recognised in the Government's
policies, others less so. The Government had itself identified as examples
of the third way some features of its policies which do not appear in
Anthony Giddens' list, for example the Private Finance Initiative and its
application, especially and most topically, to hospitals, prisons and the
London Underground.

The third way has not so far proved a source of public or political
inspiration, partly because it is easier to define negatively - *not* socialism,
not the 'new right' - than it is to describe positively by reference to any
distinctive characteristics or underlying values. Critics can associate its
practical application more easily with ambiguity, compromise and
opportunism than with any new vision or fresh insights. By the summer
of 2000 it was beginning to recede from day-to-day political debate, but
the need for the Government, and the Conservative Opposition, to find
and articulate on a new sense of direction and purpose remained as
strong as ever.[2]

CITIZENSHIP: THE GOVERNMENT'S VIEW

After three years in office there were signs that the Labour Government
might be looking to the notion of citizenship to provide the vision, the

sense of national unity and direction, and perhaps the political support, which it needed for a successful second term in office.

The previous Government had seen the citizen as a consumer of public services, entitled (in theory but not always able in practice) to make choices about which to use or whether or not to use them; to expect certain standards of service (but with little or no opportunity to say what those standards should be); and to complain if they are not met. At least part of the *Citizen's Charter's* original purpose was to bring pressure to bear on public services to 'drive up standards' and give better value for money, and in this sense it was as much a matter of supply-side economics as it was of citizens' rights. The Charter, and the Charters for particular services associated with it, were concerned only with the expectations of the individual (the position of the apostrophe was significant): they were not about the interests of groups or communities or the public interest in any larger sense.[3] The speeches described in the previous chapter show that the present Government's vision of citizenship is founded on a combination of rights and responsibilities and on its interpretation of the Human Rights Act. It is different from, and larger and more generous than, the view which was taken by the previous Government. For the Home Secretary, the citizen holds those civil and political rights which are specified by the European Convention on Human Rights, but they are also subject to his or her obligation to respect the rights of others. The state and its institutions, and especially its public servants, have a responsibility under the Human Rights Act to observe, protect and promote those rights (see *Chapter 3*). Home Office 'Aim 5' is

> . . . helping to build, under a modernised constitution, a fair and prosperous society, in which everyone has a stake, and responsibilities of individuals, families and communities are properly balanced.

The Home Office Annual Report for 1999-2000 lists a range of supporting objectives, performance measures, targets and milestones by which they are to be achieved. The objectives include 'promote an inclusive society with equal rights, responsibilities and opportunities for all' and promote a fairer and more open society in which the rights of individuals are balanced within a clear legal framework'.

THE STATE AND THE CITIZEN

Beyond that point, the nature of the 'balance', and of the 'contract' (if that is how it is seen) between the state and the citizen becomes less clear. In exchange for their rights as result of the Act (although not a part of the Act itself or the European Convention) citizens are seen as having a responsibility to carry out various duties. These obviously include a duty to obey the law; probably an obligation to bring up their children, if they have them, in a responsible manner; a duty to behave with due consideration towards other people; and a responsibility to respect other people's individuality, dignity and feelings, especially if they come from a different cultural background. Further obligations may be to attend school, reach a reasonable standard of education, to support oneself and one's family economically, and to look after one's health. The state for its part has a responsibility to provide services efficiently, cost effectively, and with due regard to the user's, or customer's, wishes and expectations. More controversially, the state may have a right, and even a responsibility, to intervene in the lives of its citizens to make sure that they not only obey the law, but also carry out their wider responsibilities as those responsibilities come to be defined.[4]

The Government is also keen to encourage 'active' citizenship in the form of volunteering and other forms of unpaid charitable work. But there has been no suggestion so far that citizens have any further responsibility or obligation, for example to act in support of fellow citizens who may be disadvantaged, threatened, vulnerable or in danger, either individually or in any public or professional functions they may perform. Nor is there any indication that the rights and duties of citizenship have any application to the commercial sector, except in narrowly defined areas such as health and safety, or the avoidance of discrimination in employment or in the supply of goods or services.

'Conditional' citizenship

The Government's view of citizenship, and especially its extension of the notion of rights and responsibilities - but mostly responsibilities - into the area of social and economic affairs; the connection it makes between those rights and responsibilities and the rights stated in the European Convention On Human Rights and enacted through the Human Rights Act; and their practical application in legislation, policy and administrative practice, all raise questions of huge public importance. Its view of the citizen's rights, even the rights enacted through the Act, is plainly conditional, but the citizen's responsibilities seem to be unconditional in the sense that failure to discharge them renders the citizen liable, if not actually to the loss of rights under the Act, then certainly to coercive intervention by the state – intervention which may override the rights in the Convention. The Crime and Disorder Act 1998, and the anti-social behaviour order and other orders which that Act creates (see *Chapter 9*), provide what is so far the most obvious example of this approach. Another is the withdrawal of social security benefits from people who do not attend training courses or accept jobs which are offered to them, who are in arrears with payment of child support maintenance, or who fail to comply with the conditions of community sentences (on which see *Chapter 9*). In contrast, the responsibility of the state to provide efficient services does not carry a corresponding right on the part of the citizen to have access to them, and both are in practice subject to qualifications such as delay or the availability of resources. Where a citizen is in trouble for not carrying out his or her responsibilities, there is no suggestion that they could counter or mitigate by saying that the state had failed to provide them with the means or opportunity to discharge such responsibility. Nor could the citizen claim that the state had failed to protect them from influences or circumstances which might have contributed to their situation. Nevertheless, the state's right to make demands on the citizen, although limited to some extent as a result of the Human Rights Act and the public law doctrines of reasonableness and legitimate expectations, is otherwise restricted only by the Government's, and Parliament's, judgement of what is politically acceptable.

There is almost infinite scope for extending the Government's view of rights and responsibilities to other areas of social and economic life. Withholding of medical treatment from people who have not taken proper care of their health is an obvious example, but the manipulation of social security benefits shows that the penalty need not even be related to the act of irresponsibility which is in issue. The state has a wide range of possible sanctions which it can use against those of whom it disapproves, of which the issue of passports or driving licences are only two examples. The fact that the commercial sector already operates its own forms of exclusion - from insurance, credit facilities, access to certain shops, shopping precincts, football matches or public houses, sometimes with serious consequences for the freedom of the individual concerned - is another indication of the scale on which people thought to be dangerous, suspicious, irresponsible, or just idiosyncratic, could be excluded from opportunities, services and facilities which most people would take for granted. Advances in technology will add to the possibilities, especially if they are combined with a requirement to carry identity cards on which a person's history and background can be encoded. (The connection between the Government's view of citizenship and its view of punishment is discussed in *Chapter 10.*)

A NEW CONCEPT OF CITIZENSHIP

The rest of this chapter suggests a less confused, less conditional and more generous view of citizenship. Such a view might come to provide the basis for a more principled vision of the country's future, and a more coherent sense of direction for the future development of policy and public service.

Citizenship is not a word which has until recently been much used in political debate or ordinary discussion. The dictionary definition of a citizen is a native or inhabitant of a state or city, often in the sense of possessing its 'freedom' or franchise. Aristotle developed the idea that it involves both 'ruling' and 'being ruled', and citizenship thus came to imply a combination of rights and obligations of the kind on which the Government rightly insists - a right to protection, and perhaps to consideration and respect; a right or qualification to participate in the running of the state; and an obligation to comply with the law of the land, to pay taxes, and historically for men to perform military service if required.[5]

In the period following the Second World War, citizenship came to be associated especially with the ideas of rights - for example the rights expressed in the United Nations' Universal Declaration of Human Rights, the United Nations Covenant on Civil and Political Rights, and the European Convention On Human Rights. The work of T. H. Marshall[6] extended the notion of rights from those civil and political rights to the economic and social rights associated with the welfare state. In ordinary language, citizenship may also imply for example a willingness to contribute to charity, to help neighbours, or to undertake voluntary public services (for example as a lay magistrate or a special constable).

Christopher Vincenzi describes the current debate on citizenship, the background and the growing body of literature associated with it, in his chapter 'From Subjecthood to Citizenship'.[7] A collection of papers *Tomorrow's Citizens: Critical Debates in Citizenship and Education*, published by the Institute for Public Policy Research (2000) describes the notions of citizenship and its relevance from a variety of practical, theoretical and religious perspectives, especially its inclusion in the core curriculum for schools.[8] In his essay in that volume, 'Citizenship: What Does it Mean and Why is it Important', David Miller points out that the concept has a more problematic status in Great Britain than in many other democratic countries. He describes three models - one in which rights and responsibilities are balanced to give all citizens equal status; a 'consumerist' model; and one which involves active civil engagement.

Elements of citizenship
For the purpose of this chapter, citizenship will be taken as comprising three elements - rights, responsibilities, and a voice in the country's and the local community's decision-making processes. None of them should be pursued without regard for the other two. As the Commission on the Future of Multi-Ethnic Britain has argued in its report[9], they must be brought together in a new sense of national identity which reconciles cohesion with difference, and equity with diversity. That sense of identity, based on an understanding of history and an acknowledgement of and respect for, the different traditions, cultures and experiences which go to make up that history, may help to generate a new sense of 'Britishness' which includes but is much more than the memory of an empire and two world wars. *Chapter 2* has however described the difficulty of establishing a genuinely inclusive sense of Britishness, and a national story to go with it. A more immediately useful project, as Linda Colley has argued, is to renovate a vision of citizenship which is inclusive, accepting and tolerant; and one which believes in itself, has a realistic understanding of its place in the world, and is confident of its future.[10] The task is then to give that vision some reality in politics, public life and public service.

Rights of citizenship
Rights can be thought of as those which are protected by the European Convention On Human Rights and enacted in the Human Rights Act, or as the 'legitimate expectations' which can be enforced in public law by judicial review. Other rights are established in international law by instruments such as the United Nations Convention on the Rights of the Child. Others again can be regarded as rights in ordinary language,

where services such as education, health care, social services, access to justice, or compensation for criminal injuries are provided on a universal basis. Some of those rights can be reduced to matters of eligibility if conditions are attached such as age limits or means tests, but they can still be regarded as rights for those who qualify. Rights of a different kind include the right to hold a passport or a driving licence, which is conditional upon certain procedural requirements and may be withdrawn in certain specified and sometimes controversial circumstances (for example the withdrawal of passports from those thought likely to cause trouble at football matches, or of driving licences as a penalty for a non-driving offence). Yet another set of rights is concerned with freedom from injury or loss caused by crime, or to go about one's business without the fear of crime. The right to liberty and security of the person is protected under the Convention, but it has usually been interpreted in terms of freedom from unlawful detention, by the agencies of the state - not as a guarantee of protection against criminal activity.

The rights described here are different from one another in their character, in the means by which they can be protected or enforced, in the extent to which they are conditional upon rules of eligibility, procedural requirements, the behaviour of the individual, the availability of resources, or practicability. They are not by any means a comprehensive statement of the rights of citizenship. Even those in the European Convention are rarely absolute (an exception is the right to freedom from torture), and they have to be balanced against one another - for example the rights to free speech and to freedom from racial hatred. But it is possible to specify some rules or principles. It is convenient to express them in terms of public services, because it is through public services that rights can be articulated and made effective. For example,

- all public services must be available without discrimination on grounds of status or of factors such as race, ethnicity, culture, gender, disability or religion;
- any restrictions on eligibility must be objectively related to the nature of the service and to the needs and situations of the persons concerned, and should not operate to deprive individuals of services on grounds of 'lesser eligibility' (see *Chapter 10*) or because the person does not 'deserve' them, for example because of a criminal conviction;
- all procedures should treat everyone with equal dignity and respect, or in David Miller's terms all citizens have equal status;
- an individual's disqualification from access to a particular public service should be related strictly to that individual's abuse of the service or facility, not to any judgement of the person's previous behaviour or character, and must be open to appeal and review;
- public services must operate within a structure which not only ensures that they are efficient and reliable, but which also guarantees openness, accessibility, accountability and legitimacy;

- public services should in a real sense be 'owned' by the citizens whom they serve, not just by the state or the government - citizens have a responsibility to support and certainly not to abuse them, and central and local government have a responsibility to acknowledge in their policies the social and economic conditions which affect their work.

Public services as such are discussed more fully in the next chapter.

Responsibilities

Responsibilities clearly include personal and individual responsibilities to obey the law, to treat other people with consideration and respect, to contribute (or at least avoid doing harm) to one's neighbourhood or community, to avoid putting unnecessary burdens on the state and its services, to perform some public service in a voluntary capacity if it is needed and if possible, and to bring up one's children to become responsible citizens themselves. When these responsibilities are discussed, it usually assumes that 'we', or 'people like us', carry them out without difficulty, and that the problem is with 'other people's' failure to conform to 'our' standards and comply with 'our' requirements, especially those requirements whose purpose is to protect our own safety and comfort. There has been less emphasis on the equally important responsibilities of all citizens to promote and protect the interests of the nation's children, or more generally to support or care for those who are vulnerable, disadvantaged or at risk of being socially excluded. Citizens may do so by their direct efforts as volunteers, by supporting charities, or through the payment of taxes Or they may do so in the broader sense of being prepared to subordinate their immediate personal interests to a larger sense of public duty or purpose.

Nor has there been much emphasis on the responsibilities of the commercial sector to adopt practices which promote the public interest, whether through the goods and services they provide; in matters such as their practices relating to employment and their effect on the environment, or their own support for voluntary and community activities. It can be argued for example that the insurance industry has a responsibility to make sure that affordable insurance is available in deprived neighbourhoods or to disadvantaged individuals; or that banks have a responsibility to provide locally accessible facilities (a matter which became controversial when Barclays Bank closed a number of branches in April 2000). It can also be argued that employers have an obligation to train and employ people who are vulnerable or disadvantaged, as well as those who may be disabled; or that their working conditions including their working culture - should not be unnecessarily stressful, involve excessively long hours, or prevent staff from giving proper attention to their families (see the references to Richard Sennett and the Joseph Rowntree Foundation in *Chapter 2*). And it can be argued that one of the tests of a good company is the financial or material support it is prepared to give to voluntary activities and organizations, including time for members of staff who wish to take part.

All these should be seen as citizenship. They are not matters to be required or enforced by law, but they could become normal expectations, reinforced by teaching when citizenship becomes part of the national curriculum in English schools.

The citizen's voice
The citizen's voice in the running of the country, and confidence that it will be heard, are what give governments and the state their legitimacy and authority. The right to vote is one of the most fundamental rights of citizenship, even if it does not always seem to be the one that is most prized. The vote in general and local elections has historically been the principal means by which ordinary citizens have been able to make their voices heard, but those in positions of influence have always been able to do so in other, sometimes subtle, usually indirect, but usually effective ways. Changes in the social structure of society and the political orientation of parties, combined with the rise of lobbying organizations, interest groups and large, sometimes global, businesses have changed the dynamics of politics and the distribution of power among those who try to influence them. *Chapter 1* has already referred to the changing character of so-called 'elites'. Parliament seems to have become less effective as an institution for challenging the government. Interest in politics as such has given way to support for single issues, for example the abolition of nuclear weapons (during the period of the cold war), and more recently those associated with protecting the environment or the welfare of animals. Many people feel that the day-to-day decisions of government, and those of the public services, are beyond their influence. They have opportunity every four or five years to bring about a change of government, but even then they have little opportunity to affect particular policies or the handling of individual issues except by narrowly focused public campaigns. The frustration caused by that situation found a new and previously unprecedented form of repression in the demonstration against the price of fuel during September 2000.

Chapter 3 has pointed out that the Labour Government has tried to respond to these concerns by developing other procedures for consulting public opinion - focus groups, the People's Panel, citizens' juries, opinion surveys. But those procedures are likely to be inaccessible to more than a small minority, and the questions put to them cannot easily match the complexity of the decisions which have to be made in real political, public service and administrative life. Members of Parliament still pay attention to complaints and arguments which are put to them in their constituencies, and those put to the Labour Party during its period in opposition and the campaign for the 1997 general election clearly had a powerful influence on the Labour Government. But people who call on or write to Members of Parliament, or attend constituency meetings, do not necessarily express views which are representative of the constituency, still less of the country, as a whole. When accountability is discussed in government, it is not usually democratic accountability that is at issue, but internal accountability brought about by the processes of inspection, audit and performance management. Successive

Governments, in their ordinary handling of events, have often given an impression that they are more concerned to suppress any opposition or criticism than to show any sense of responsibility to Parliament or to the country. (See *Chapter 2* for a discussion of the difference between 'accountability' and 'responsibility' in this context.)

The situation raises issues and has ramifications which go well beyond the scope of this book. It cannot be dealt with adequately by marginal adjustments to Parliamentary procedure or the application of modern technology. The issues range from the representative role, if any, which is to be taken by the reformed House of Lords, through devolution to Scotland and Wales and to any future regional assemblies in England, to the functions and character of local government. They include the concept of European citizenship, the rights which are derived from the developing case law of both the European Court of Human Rights and the European Court of Justice, and the frustrations which arise from European institutions' lack of accountability. They extend to the public duties of commercial companies and transnational corporations, and certainly include the means by which public services can make themselves accountable, and responsible, not only to central government but also to their own communities. Christopher Vincenzi considers some of the issues in his chapter already mentioned. Later chapters in this book will return to public services' accountability and responsibility to the citizens and communities whom they serve. Whatever structures or procedures may emerge in the future, citizens will need to make their voices heard collectively as well as individually. To do this they will need the resources of civil society.

CIVIL SOCIETY

Civil society is closely associated with citizenship.[11] It is part of the framework within which citizenship is put into practice. It consists of those associations, networks and relationships which are neither part of the mechanisms of the state nor run for commercial profit. It includes the voluntary and community sector, but also the less formal meetings, groups and associations, and the individual acts of generosity or kindness, which provide opportunities for personal development, service to others, and support in times of difficulty. These are part of the responsibilities of citizenship. Civil society is also the source of the energy, the resilience and the will which provide a country's, a nation's, or a community's, social capital. Social capital is what enables them to deal with social turbulence; with disturbance, including crime; and when necessary with war. Lord Hurd has argued that it was Great Britain's greater social capital that enabled the country to sustain the first World War for longer than Germany, and so ultimately to prevail - although at appalling cost.[12] Building or re-building civil society is seen as an important task in many former communist countries in central and eastern Europe. The Home Office *Annual Report for 1999-2000* includes 'helping to strengthen civil society' as one of its objectives under 'Aim 5', already mentioned. One of the most significant consequences of the Labour Government's programmes to support young people and their parents is that many more people are becoming involved, in many different capacities, not as full-time salaried employees but as citizens contributing to civil society.

Trust is an important element in social capital - trust between citizens and public servants, between public servants themselves, and between both citizens and public servants and the government of the day. In some environments, trust can be a source of exclusiveness or complacency. It is important to make sure that when measures such as those characteristic of new public management are introduced to challenge a culture of exclusiveness or complacency, the result is not a collapse of trust or a culture of blame.

THE VOLUNTARY AND COMMUNITY SECTOR

The voluntary and community sector has a valuable and perhaps essential role in listening to and articulating the voices of citizens; and in making them heard in government, in the statutory public services and in the country as a whole. Voluntary and community organizations, many of them charities, represent groups such as children, the elderly, the disabled, or victims of crime; or interests such as the environment, conservation or penal reform. Some of them provide services for those whom they represent or whom they aim to support, often with funding from central government. The Conservative Government viewed most of them with some suspicion, regarding them as self-seeking and politically motivated; the Labour Government has embraced them enthusiastically, joining with them in publishing the *Compact on Relations between the Government and the Voluntary and Community Sector in England*[13], inviting them to join advisory groups and encouraging partnerships with statutory bodies to provide certain public services. 'Helping to achieve a healthy voluntary sector and community sector and an effective partnership between it and government' is another objective of the Home Office under Aim 5.

Voluntary and community organizations have much to offer the Government in both of the ways indicated in the previous paragraph. But the Government should not expect them, and they should not allow themselves, to compromise their independence, or to become conscripted into the service of the state, whether it is represented by the Government itself or by the statutory public sector. A contract or partnership between a government department or a statutory service and a voluntary or community organization (such as the arrangement between HM Prison Service and the voluntary sector currently being promoted[14]) is not an equal relationship. The organization should not feel - and should not be allowed to feel - that it is compelled by that relationship to act against its own better judgement or what it considers to be the wider public interest. Nor is it easy for a voluntary organization, dependent as it must be on its sources of funding and the interests of its trustees, to represent or promote the public interest or the interests of citizens in the widest sense. The point has particular relevance to minorities: there is an opportunity, and a need, for a strong and diverse voluntary and community sector to provide services which match the diversity of minority groups and represent their interests; but charities which are not specifically focused on those interests have found it difficult to do so.

The Centre for Civil Society at the London School of Economics and Political Science is studying the developing role of the voluntary and community sector, its relationships with central government and statutory public services, and any possible changes in its statutory framework. Questions needing to be explored include the balance between a voluntary or community organization's independence and its accountability; and the means by which those organizations should be regulated or held to account, given the wide range of the objectives for which they are established and of the functions which they perform, and the differences in character among the organizations themselves. Some are for public and some for private benefit. Some are vehicles for unpaid voluntary effort; some employ paid staff and professional managers. Partnerships with the public sector are also of different kinds. Their purpose may be to commission or to deliver services, to facilitate or promote initiatives or ideas, to provide a different balance of power or interest, or to give a greater sense of 'inclusiveness' and perhaps legitimacy than a statutory service could achieve on its own. No single framework or mechanism of accountability is likely to match the variety of situations and relationships which are involved.

Other questions concern the nature of the Government's involvement with the voluntary and community sector, and especially the Government's aversion to risk, its prescriptive approach, its continuing faith in 'markets' and measurements as providing adequate mechanisms of accountability, and the burdensome nature of the bureaucracy which it has felt obliged to impose. Voluntary and community organizations must not become pre-occupied with their relationship with central government, and with the structures and mechanisms through which they might hope to influence government and in particular increase their access to funding, to a degree which distracts their energy or compromises their independence. Neither government nor the voluntary and community sectors should lose sight of the longer-term and more strategic questions, such as the means by which citizens might gain a voice in the running of their public services and the role of voluntary and representative organizations in helping them to do so. Lord Dahrendorf's advice, at a policy symposium at the London School of Economics on 7 June 1999, should always be borne in mind.[15]

EXCLUSION AND INCLUSION

Citizenship, like community, can be defined exclusively or inclusively. Just as 'community' can be defined by reference to a geographical area, a social or religious group, the members of a profession or the employees of a firm, with the implication that all those outside the group are excluded, so 'citizenship' can be defined by reference to narrow legal criteria of birth, descent or residence. It can thus exclude foreigners, aliens, visitors, guest workers, refugees or members of identifiable ethnic minorities whom a government wishes to exclude from the benefits available to the 'host' or majority population. As already discussed in *Chapter 2*, it can also exclude those whose behaviour or life-style does not conform to the expectations of the majority, the state, or the government of the day. Desmond King's final chapter has a discussion of 'who should be admitted to membership in a liberal democracy' with sections on the obligations of membership, coercive obligations, and paternalistic policies which focus on targeted individuals with the aim of enforcing conformity regardless of their own wishes or inclinations, or sometimes their own abilities.[16] It is a salutary warning.

That is not the version of citizenship that is intended in this chapter. While the restricted or exclusive interpretation may in many circumstances be linguistically and technically correct, the sense intended here is one of social inclusion, acceptance and respect, on a universal basis which extends to all those present in the country or in particular neighbourhoods or institutions, without discrimination or exception and regardless of differences of race, ethnicity, culture, class, nationality, descent, situation or circumstances. It is a recognition of their common humanity.

To say this is not to deny that some control will be necessary over access to some services, or that the rights (and with them the responsibilities), of citizenship may sometimes have to be curtailed, for example as a result of a sentence for a criminal offence. But they should not then be controlled or curtailed to any greater extent than is required by the aim which has to be achieved, and by the national interest or the sentence of the court. The principle of proportionality, increasingly recognised in the jurisprudence of the European Court of Human Rights, should always apply. The spirit in which the control is exercised, or rights and responsibilities are curtailed should still be one of universal humanity, dignity and respect.

The direct and immediate effects of the European Convention and the Human Rights Act may prove to be quite limited, in terms of the outcome of cases which turn on their interpretation, or of successful challenges to the legislation or articles. But the Convention provides what the Home Secretary has called a 'living instrument' whose interpretation can evolve as attitudes and circumstances change, and which can itself influence those changes as they take place. In this way, the Act and Convention may lead in the longer-term to a culture of human rights which reinforces and gives some substance to a spirit of universal humanity and the values associated with it. Such a spirit will be of particular importance in relation to minority groups, whose concerns have generally been addressed as an issue about minorities themselves, not in a spirit of citizenship and human rights or as a matter which affects society as a whole.

POLICIES BASED ON CITIZENSHIP AND HUMAN RIGHTS

Policies to give practical expression to this view of citizenship would reflect the 'inclusive' rather than the 'exclusive' view described above and in *Chapter 2*. Much of the Government's language, in its references to social inclusion, fairness, democracy, tolerance and decency, is in accordance with a notion of citizenship based on a spirit of universal humanity and its associated values. So are many of its policies, for example those designed to reduce poverty, support parents who are in difficulty, improve standards in education and reduce exclusions and truancy from school, create new opportunities for young people and help them to make the transition from adolescence to adult life and employment, revive run-down neighbourhoods and communities, prevent crime and reduce juvenile delinquency. The test will be the scale on which those policies achieve success; the extent to which problems of social exclusion continue, whether because the policies themselves are inadequate, because the problems are too deep-seated to be within their reach, or because some people choose not to take advantage of them; and how the country then treats the people who remain vulnerable, disadvantaged, marginalised and neglected.

In her Millenium Lecture on Britishness in the twenty-first century, quoted at the beginning of this chapter, Linda Colley made five suggestions:

- A better, more inspiring and far more accessible definition of citizenship, including a new Millenium Charter or Contract of Citizen Rights.
- To acknowledge the essential equality of the people of these islands far more than at present.
- On the one hand a constantly reforming centre, and on the other hand a diffusion of power away from the centre.
- A revivified Citizen Nation committed to equality must take positive steps to improve the position of ethnic minorities and women, and deal with these groupings in tandem.
- A healthier, more comprehensive, less apologetic view of our past.[17]

ENDNOTES for *Chapter 4*

[1] John Kay, *The Business of Economics*, Oxford, Oxford University Press, 1996; Amitai Etzioni, *The Spirit of the Community: Rights, Responsibilities and the Communitarian Agenda*, London, Fontana, 1995; *The New Golden Rule: Community and Morality in Democratic Society*, London, Profile Books, 1997; Anthony Giddens, *The Third Way: The Pursuit of Social Democracy*, Cambridge, Polity Press, 1998. See also Tony Blair, *The Third Way*, London, the Fabian Society, 1998.
[2] Perhaps the last word on the third way will prove to have been a short debate in the House of Lords on 31 December 2000, *Hansard*, Vol. 618, No. 158, cols. 860-875. Lord

Dahrendorf described the third way as a narrative intended not as a programme in itself, but as a 'big story' which pulled together and gave some inspiration for the diverse strands of government policy. As such he considered it to be inadequate, partly because the story was superficial in what it had to say about the economy and social solidarity, and partly because it made no reference to liberty.

[3] Ian Bynoe, *Beyond the Citizen's Charter. New Directions of Social Rights,* London, Institute of Public Policy Research, 1996.

[4] The Crime and Disorder Act 1998 is a clear expression of the Labour Government's wish for the state to demand standards of responsible behaviour in matters which are not themselves within the scope of the criminal law, but where failure to observe those standards can render the person liable to a civil order which is then subject to a criminal penalty. See *Chapters 9* and *11.* In his speech at Kent Police Headquarters on 31 August 2000, the Prime Minister said 'I believe this [the money which the Government had made available to help poorer parents and the unemployed] entitles us to speak very plainly about the responsibility we expect in return … law abiding conduct … decent, civil behaviour …'.

[5] Desmond King has an interesting section on the histories and significance of military service in his book, *In the Name of Liberalism: Illiberal Social Policies in the United States and Britain,* Oxford, University Press, 1999.

[6] T. H. Marshall, *Clan, Citizenship and Social Development,* London, University of Chicago Press, 1977.

[7] Christopher Vicenzi: *Crown Powers, Subjects and Citizens,* London, Pinter, 1998.

[8] Institute for Public Policy Research, *Tomorrow's Citizens; Critical Debates in Citizenship and Education,* Institute for Public Policy Research, 2000. Also see Bernard Crick, *Education for Citizenship and the Teaching of Democracy in Schools,* Final Report of the Advisory Group on Citizenship, London, Qualifications and Curriculum Authority, 1998.

[9] See the report of the Commission on the Future of Multi-Ethnic Britain, *The Future of Multi Ethnic Britain,* London, Profile Books, 2000.

[10] Linda Colley, *Britishness in the Twenty-first Century,* Millenium Lecture, 3 December 1999.

[11] The Centre for Civil Society at the London School of Economics and Political Science has considered a number of interpretations of the expression 'Civil Society'. It has adopted the following: 'Civil Society refers to the set of institutions, organizations and behaviours situated between the State, the business world and the family. Specifically, this would include voluntary and non-profit organizations of many different kinds, philanthropic institutions, social and political movements, forms of social participation and engagement, the public sphere, and the values and cultural patterns associated with them'. Helmut Anheier, 'Can Culture, Market and State Relate', London, *LSE Magazine,* Summer 2000.

[12] Lord Hurd of Westwell, *The Search for Peace: a Century of Peace Diplomacy,* London, Little Brown and Co., 1997 and the related programmes for television.

[13] Home Office and National Council of Voluntary Organizations, *Compact on Relations between Government and the Voluntary and Community Sector in England,* London, Home Office, 1998.

[14] Shane Bryans and Roma Walker, *The Prison Service and the Voluntary Sector: Delivering Services in Partnership,* Winchester, Waterside Press (forthcoming).

[15] Many of these questions are discussed in Helmut Anheier (ed.), *The Third Way, Third Sector,* Proceedings of a Policy Symposium organized by the LSE Centre for Civil Society on 7 June 1999, London, LSE, 2000. The report quotes Lord Dahrendorf as follows:

I look with a degree of scepticism and interest at a growing overlap between governmental and voluntary agencies and institutions because I suspect they are really quangos - quasi non-governmental institutions – in the strict sense of the word. Quangos are structures of the voluntary sector used to pursue governmental purposes. While it may sound nice, as far as government is concerned, it reduces accountability and control. I suspect that a compact is ultimately justifiable only for this area of overlap. It is justifiable only in the area in which one is no longer talking about truly voluntary initiatives in civil society, but where government had abandoned its own concerns to organizations, which are not strictly part of governmental structures. In this case it is useful to have some degree of accountability in this otherwise non-democratic area of activity.

In conclusion, a civilised government should open up space for the work of voluntary and charitable organizations and institutions. It should open up legal space. The instrument of a Charity Commission is better than detailed legislation, which tries to put into primary legislation a definition of who belongs. A civilised government will also open up funding opportunities and make certain concessions, although one can argue that that is not the function of government. On the whole, however, I argue that a civilised government should offer certain opportunities and concessions which encourage activity which is in no sense governmental, I very much hope that, whatever happens in the present Government – inspired discussion of third sector, the creative chaos will not be turned into a controlled para-governmental area of activity.

[16] Desmond King, *op. cit.*, n. 4.
[17] *Loc. cit.*, n. 10.

CHAPTER 5

Public Service: Status, Structure and Accountability

There is a public service ethos and by harnessing it, there is considerable potential for enhancing the impact that senior managers in public services have on public value. By ignoring it or by imposing systems that attempt to override it, there is danger of undermining the value that public services can produce.

Jane Steele, *Wasted Values: Harnessing the Commitment of Public Managers,*
Public Management Foundation, 1997

PUBLIC SERVICE AND PUBLIC DUTY

The terms 'public servant' and 'public service' are often used but they are not clearly defined. Public servants certainly include civil servants, employees of local government and those who work in statutory services such as the police, education or the health service. They can be defined fairly precisely as those working for services which are paid for from taxation, or whose pay and conditions of service are determined nationally by the government, and less precisely as those whose work is closely aligned to the policies of the government of the day. Alongside them are the staff or volunteers working in the voluntary and community sector who may be providing services to the public, either on their own account or in partnership with statutory agencies or the government itself. 'Public service' may be used to describe the service being provided, or the organization which provides it. Public services include those already mentioned. They include the remaining nationalised industries and, probably still, those which have been privatised. The boundary becomes less clear when it reaches banks, insurance, and financial services. The retail trade, newspapers and broadcasting companies provide services to the public but (with the exception of the BBC) would probably not be thought of as public services.

Many groups or individuals, or organizations, could also claim to be public servants or public services in the sense that they not only supply goods or services to the public, but also have a sense of public duty and the public interest which influences the service they provide and how they provide it. Members of professions, privatised industries and utilities, providers of services on the internet, banks, insurance companies, major retailers and large international companies are some examples. The nature of that public duty, and of the public interest which it has to serve, may involve considerations of public law if an organization's or an individual's actions or judgement are liable to be challenged by way of judicial review or under the Human Rights Act.

For the purpose of this chapter, public servants comprise principally civil servants, those employed by local government or statutory services, and those working alongside those services in the voluntary and community sector.

Successful public services depend not only on the framework of legislation, policy and public finance which is properly set by Parliament and government, but also on how government expects or requires its policies to be implemented on the ground, and on the leadership, commitment and expertise of public servants themselves. Success depends on the way in which not only change, but also complexity and conflict, are managed in day-to-day situations; and on the principles and values according to which conflicting considerations are resolved - the balance between public safety and individual freedom, between public service and commercial profit (or financial viability), between uniformity and diversity, between central direction and local discretion, between certainty and ambiguity or risk, between efficiency and equity, between effectiveness and due process. It depends on how those principles and values come to be defined, by whom and with what authority, and how they should be communicated and interpreted. It raises questions about the location and distribution of power and authority; about accountability and legitimacy; and about the expertise, leadership and culture which are needed in a modern public service. Peter Neyroud and Alan Beckley explore those questions in their important analysis of policing and ethics *Policing, Ethics and Human Rights.*[1] The same questions gained a high profile at the end of 2000 in connection with the privatised railway.

Relationship with the state and with government

Power and authority are not the exclusive prerogative of the state, of gvernment, or of elected assemblies. Public services and professions draw their authority and legitimacy not only from the state, but also from civil society and from citizens' need, and respect, for their skills and expertise. So do voluntary and community organizations, especially those which are charities. Although they operate within a framework which is set by Parliament and government, and for charities by the Charity Commission, public servants should not be seen simply as agents of the government. Doctors, nurses, teachers, police officers and many civil servants - perhaps especially those in specialised agencies like the Prison Service - join their services to serve the public, not to serve the political administration of the day. So do the trustees and employees of charities. The Labour Government's commitment to improve the standard of public services is thoroughly welcome, but it does not follow that public services should be conscripted into a relationship of subordination to the political administration of the day, as appears to be implied, for example, in public service agreements or in the Government's intentions for the Probation Service (see *Chapter 20*). The point arises in a particularly acute form where services are provided by charities such as Barnado's, the National Society for the Prevention of Cruelty to Children or Crime Concern.

Questions of power and authority are closely linked with questions of accountability, legitimacy and democracy. Public services in a modern society must be accountable in several directions, through mechanisms which take different forms.[2] They have some accountability to central government, but also to their employing authorities, to their users, to other services with whom they work and on whom they may depend (sometimes known as their 'stakeholders'), to their own staff, and to the citizens whom they serve including those who may not be direct users of the service. The fact that they are publicly funded, with money paid to the government through taxation and then distributed on behalf of the taxpayer, does not give the government exclusive rights of ownership. Those wider accountabilities, and the mechanisms for making them effective, should be as much part of democracy as elections to Parliament. They will be especially important for the future of policing in the developing areas of community safety and youth justice; in the reform of the Probation Service; and in the partnerships which are a prominent feature of many of the Government's new policies. They have always been recognised for the police and the Probation Service and must remain so, and they should also be recognised for prisons. Peter Neyroud and Alan Beckley make an important connection between forms of accountability and professional ethics.[3] It must be a matter of regret that the present Government, like its predecessor, should have so little confidence in local government, and that it should be thought unacceptable for more services to be democratically accountable at local level.

Professionalism and the role of public servants
Governments rarely use the word 'professional'. Other people use it quite often, for example to distinguish a person's 'professional' or working life from their personal life, or to express vague approval for something they have done well. But the word has no consistent meaning. Strictly speaking, it involves a vocation or calling, especially one which involves an organized body of learning or science, often with qualifications for membership, standards of conduct and a system of discipline. The word may also be used to distinguish specialist, qualified or expert staff from others who are not so qualified; and sometimes to imply that their decisions or judgements have a special authority which cannot be challenged except by another member of the same discipline. It usually assumes a commitment to placing the interests of the client, or the interests of the public, above those of the practitioner concerned; to impartiality; and to a refusal to become sentimentally or emotionally involved. More loosely, the word may be used to imply skills or competence of a more general kind, or a disciplined or productive working relationship between colleagues engaged in a similar occupation or enterprise.

There is now decreasing respect for professional judgement or professional status in the original, more narrow, sense. Successive governments have seen some professions, for example the medical and teaching professions, as obstructing progress and protecting their own 'provider' interests against what the government itself regards as a necessary programme of modernisation and reform. They have seen the Probation Service and social workers as holding attitudes and assumptions associated with their 'profession' which have no place in the modern world as they see it. They are suspicious of all forms of expertise which appeal to experience of the past or to abstract principles or values, or which cannot demonstrate their benefits in quantative and preferably 'value for money' terms. Business people, accountants and consultants are regarded as having more authority on how services should be organized and delivered than members of the services themselves. Judgements which public servants have made, or could reasonably be expected to make, on a basis of their own authority, experience and expertise are increasingly becoming matters of ministerial direction, statutory duty, or departmental guidance. Not only is professional status devalued, but professional ethics can become compromised.

Public servants are subject to most of the strains which affect the working lives of many people in modern societies and economies, especially the loss of security and a sense of trust; long and sometimes unpredictable hours of work; the pressure to do 'more for less'. These pressures may 'drive up' the organization's performance and sometimes standards of service to the public, but the organization's gain is often the public servant's loss - and whether it is the public's gain may be more open to question than it is made to appear. Use of technology may improve efficiency but it can reduce the need and opportunities for human contact.[4] It can de-personalise working relationships (whether e-mail has this or the opposite effect is an interesting subject for debate). Public servants may not be as vulnerable as some of those in the commercial sector, but nor do they enjoy the same rewards. Richard Sennett has described some of the consequences in his book *The Corrosion of Character*[5]; and the Joseph Rowntree Foundation has done so in *Job Insecurity and Work Intensification*[6], both of which have been mentioned in earlier chapters. Richard Sennett sees a way forward in the development of a sense of community, which values diversity and acknowledges incomprehension, and which he distinguishes from communitarianism and protectionism. His idea of community resembles that of citizenship as it is discussed in *Chapter 4*. The Joseph Rowntree Foundation's report shows that 'work intensification and job insecurity are both associated with increased tension within the household ... and damage the social environment'. It states that 'one of the most striking aspects of our organization's employment practices was the extent to which they had attempted to collectivise effort and decollectivise risk .... largely unconditional demands are being made on workers by their employers, whilst .... promises by employers to their employees are conditional'. A similar contrast can be seen in the Government's view of the relationship between the citizen, whose rights it treats as conditional and their responsibilities as unconditional; and the state or the government, whose rights it treats as unconditional and its responsibilities as conditional, as discussed in *Chapters 4* and *10*.

An interesting contrast is to be found in the concluding section of the Government's Business Plan for the criminal justice system for 1999-2000, where the Government, having taken credit for the plan, seems to distance itself from responsibility for its successful implementation.[7]

> Achieving the aims and objectives set by Ministers will depend crucially on the response by Departments at national level and by local services and agencies. The importance of successfully delivering CJS services at the local level cannot be over emphasised.

> The challenge is now for the criminal justice system to respond by improving its performance through better joined-up working at a national and a local level.

Other references to public servants and public services have characterised them as inefficient and obstructive, with threats of restructuring or replacement for organizations which do not perform and of loss of pay or redundancy for individuals. Talk of rapid promotion and higher pay for high achievers (often people brought in from elsewhere) implies that there are others - perhaps the majority - who will be excluded from those benefits. Methods by which the high achievers will be identified are not usually made clear, but there is an underlying suspicion that those methods will operate as much through patronage, and rely as much on individuals' skills in self-projection (and perhaps ability to overshadow or even discredit their colleagues) as on an objective, all round assessment. Stephen Covey has described how in America the 'personality ethic' focused on images, skills, techniques in human and public relations and 'positive mental attitudes' has displaced the 'character ethic' focused on such qualities as integrity, courage, patience and industry as a criterion for success.[8]

NORMS, ETHOS AND VALUES

An important report is Jane Steele's *Wasted Values: Harnessing the Commitment of Public Managers,* based on interviews with a large number of managers in the public, private and voluntary sectors.[9] She concluded that

> There is a public service ethos and by harnessing it, there is considerable potential for enhancing the impact that senior managers in public services have on public value. By ignoring it or by imposing systems that attempt to override it, there is danger of undermining the value that public services can produce.

By public service ethos, the author explains that the principal motivation of public sector employees is not their own self-interest (a belief that it was seemed to underlie a lot of the 'new public management'), but a sense of 'public spiritedness on which policy-makers can draw to ensure proper implementation of their policies'. It follows that success depends on knowledge, information and skills, not on material rewards, fear of blame, threats of redundancy or dismissal, competition or heavy monitoring of performance.

Jane Steele's research showed strong evidence that managers feel confused and overwhelmed by the demands made upon them. It argued that local leaders need a clear vision of local priorities and the strategies for achieving them. There is plenty of common ground on which to build a stronger common culture of motivation and values, both within and between public sector organizations. The government has to set the framework for delivery: senior managers are looking for clarity of purpose, but experience the current agenda for modernisation as chaotic and confusing. Managers should work with communities and users of services to define goals, establish a vision and strategy; accept a sense of responsibility for outcomes wider than those attributable to their own departments or functions; and take control of the system of evaluation to ensure that they do not allow themselves to be driven by short-term measures of performance. Government should lead with a clear and consistent vision of intended outcomes, building on the motivation and values of people working in the sector, rather than on an ideal of organizational excellence; it should show more trust in public service managers and allow innovation and variation in local approaches. The report acknowledges that many of these ideas are implicit in the Government's White Paper *Modernising Government*,[10] and its author hopes that the report will help to inform the Government's programme for putting them into effect. Peter Neyroud and Alan Beckley are more critical. They argue that the techniques of managerialism can compromise public service (in particular police) ethics, that they are inconsistent with a 'learning' culture, that they discourage innovative, problem-solving strategies and that they lead to ritualised forms of control. They argue instead for value-based controls and a 'morally informed professionalism' within a framework of ethical standards.[11]

FUNCTIONS AND FORMS OF PUBLIC SERVICE

Public services perform a wide range of different functions, take different forms and operate under different conditions. They provide a framework for maintaining social order and protecting the public (the police, the courts and other criminal and civil justice services); they provide essential services which are universally available (public utilities and transport); they provide necessary services for those who need them (health and social services or social security, but also - for those who can afford them - banking, insurance and financial services); or they provide desirable amenities (shopping or recreation). The services may be provided publicly, by central or local government, or by statutory agencies; privately, by charities or other voluntary organizations; or by the private sector (commercially or under contract).

Public services can be placed in different positions on various scales, such as whether they

- are large or small;
- are publicly funded, or raise their funds from fees or charges;
- involve a complex organization and relationships, or are relatively simple;
- provide services direct to the public, or to other organizations;
- provide services which are politically sensitive or relatively uncontroversial;
- involve a substantial degree of professional discretion or judgement, or consist mainly in applying standard rules or procedures;
- provide services which are important to the national interest or marginal to it;
- provide services whose use is compulsory or a matter of individual choice.

The nearer a service is to the 'top' of each of these scales, the more complex its relationships - with government, with stakeholders, with users and with citizens or the public more generally - are likely to be. Its mechanisms and procedures for accountability should correspondingly be more highly developed and effective.

English and European law distinguish between public and private functions and relationships, but that distinction is not clear cut, and the boundary is becoming less straightforward. The European Union has begun to develop, in Article 26 of the Treaty of Amsterdam, a concept of 'services of general interest' which would exclude those directly provided by the state but which would include some of those provided by commercial companies.[12] As society becomes more complex, an increasing number of functions and relationships are likely to take on a public aspect. By the same token, most providers of private or commercial services would be regarded as having public duties or obligations. Those duties would certainly extend, for example, to health and safety and the avoidance of racial discrimination, and sometimes also to hours of opening or to practices in employment. Such matters are often the subject of regulatory legislation. The public obligations of private organizations, especially those providing services which have been contracted out from the public sector, are likely to involve applying some of the same procedures for public accountability as those which are or should be followed by public organizations.

STRUCTURE AND ACCOUNTABILITY

The structure and accountability of most public services has been the subject of intense debate, and in some instances of radical or frequent change, throughout the last 20 years. In some instances, such as the police and the Prison Service, the debate has gone on for a good deal longer than that. Earlier arguments were based on constitutional integrity and propriety (the Royal Commission on the Police and the Police Act 1964, the formation of the Crown Prosecution Service in 1986), or on administrative convenience (the dissolution of the Prison Commission and its integration with the Home Office in 1963). In more recent years, pressure for change has usually been driven by a demand for greater economy or for greater effectiveness; sometimes by a call for greater consistency; occasionally (but perhaps ambiguously) by a desire to improve a service's responsiveness to its customers (as in the *Citizen's Charter*, where economic arguments were sometimes just as powerful as those based on the interests of citizens themselves). Accountability, when it was considered, was usually seen more as accountability to ministers and central government than as accountability to users, other organizations or stakeholders, or citizens. And it was seen more as a matter of finding someone to blame than of maintaining or improving standards.

Criminal justice services, like other public services, have been the subject of government programmes to improve efficiency and effectiveness, to create closer and more co-operative working relationships, and to adopt common boundaries. Attempts to achieve closer co-operation and interdependence preceded by 15 years the election of the Labour Government in 1997, but their benefits were dissipated by the style adopted during the last years of the previous administration (see *Chapters 7* and *8*). There has also been radical change in the structures to be adopted in particular services and the requirements imposed upon them - the changes for the police and the magistrates' courts brought about by the Police and Magistrates' Courts' Act 1994; the creation of the Crown Prosecution Service and the successive changes which were then made to its internal organization; the restructuring of the prison and court services as executive agencies of government;[13] a series of other changes in the status and internal structure of the Prison Service; the contracting out of prison escorts and of various prisons and functions within prisons; and most recently the creation of a unified Probation Service directly accountable to the government.

Central government has also come to exercise a progressively stronger influence, and often control, over the services' practice and management through the setting of objectives, standards, targets and performance indicators and the processes of inspection and audit. The methods and techniques have been similar in each service, but their application has not been co-ordinated across the services and the standards or measures for one service have sometimes been in conflict with those for another. Procedural requirements for the police, the Crown Prosecution Service and the Probation Service in preparing cases for court may for example conflict with requirements for courts to reduce delays before trial.

What has been missing from the debate has been a coherent discussion of the proper balance between national direction or control on the one hand and local discretion or independence on the other; or between national and local forms of accountability. Arguments can be and have been deployed for and against a national police service, and for and against a national Prison Service. But it is not clear why those for a national police service have (so far) always failed and those for a national Prison Service have always prevailed; or why a national Probation Service should now find favour, at a time when more local autonomy is being introduced into the Crown Prosecution Service. It is difficult to argue that any one form of structure or status is always to be preferred to others, but certain tests can always be applied and certain conditions satisfied. These tests and conditions relate especially to the service's accountability.

Accountability is one of a family of expressions which includes for example responsibility, legitimacy, answerability and responsiveness. The ideas which they represent will often overlap, and accountability may sometimes be used in a broad sense which embraces all of them. It is so used in this chapter. Accountability can also take different forms - political, financial, managerial, operational, legal, professional. It can be to different authorities, institutions or individuals - Parliament, ministers, managers, the courts, auditors, professional bodies, inspectors and regulators. It may be to users or customers, including patients in the health service, children and young people in education, claimants for social security benefits, victims of crime, and no less important suspects under investigation by the police and offenders under supervision or in prison. Ultimately it is to citizens or to the general public. It may operate only in one direction, or it may involve reciprocal obligations. Organizations are not normally regarded as 'accountable' to their own staff, but they certainly have obligations towards them. Employment practices and labour law are an important element in the relationship between public service and citizenship. (Ministers' accountability, or responsibility, to Parliament was discussed in *Chapter 2*, and will not be considered again here.)

Accountability can operate through direct supervision or contact, through formal arrangements for reporting or consultation (in public or in private), through inspection and audit, through procedures (such as complaints) which can be activated when required, and in various other ways. It can be based on a constitutional or employment relationship, on statute, on contract, or on various types of unwritten or informal recognition or understanding. It is very often - perhaps too often - seen as a process identifying the person who should be vulnerable if something goes wrong and of seeing that the person is corrected or removed. It is also, less prominently, about enabling people to complain and giving some satisfaction to those who justifiably do so (as in the *Citizen's Charter*); and about identifying and rewarding success. It is about making the service known, understood and respected, both for the quality of the service at the point of contact with the customer, where that is relevant; and also for the integrity of its operations and the longer term benefits which result from them. The last is arguably - for Parliament and the country as a whole - the most important and most neglected aspect.

The structure of a public service's accountability should include some or all of the following features

- appointments made openly and on merit;
- accessible and well understood procedures for public consultation;
- clearly stated objectives, standards and expectations;
- monitoring of performance to establish how far those objectives are being met;
- independent inspection and audit;
- reasons for decisions explained to those affected by them;
- opportunities and a recognised structure for representation and complaints;
- effective means for correcting mistakes, abuses or errors of judgement, and for preventing them from being repeated - but not an obsession with blaming and punishing individuals;
- informative, accessible and well-presented reports;
- recognition of, and sensitivity to, issues of race, gender and culture;
- independent evaluation and research;
- a statutory framework within which these requirements can ultimately, but exceptionally, be enforced through the courts.

The more complex, sensitive or inter-dependent the service to be provided, the more features are likely to be needed. Ann James describes the multiple forms of accountability that are needed in a modern public service, their potential for supporting creative new developments, and the political conflicts between financial, administrative, political and professional modes of accountability, in her book *Managing to Care*.[14] Peter Neyroud and Alan Beckley consider the same theme.[15]

More recently, the Government's Public Services Productivity Panel issued a report, *Public Services Productivity: Meeting the Challenge*.[16] It reflected the Government's impatience with the perceived inefficiency and lack of production of many public services and began with the statement that by 'increasing productivity by three per cent, the public sector can free up over £6 billion per annum to reinvest in services, making a significant contribution to Britain's economic performance'. It identified the need for strengthened leadership, better arrangements for tackling variations in performance, more focused and rationalised measures of performance, a sharper focus on customers, and improved rewards and reinforcements for public servants. It went on to make a number of sensible, but mostly rather vague and conventional, recommendations for more specific actions.

There were also hints that the panel had perceived some of the underlying tensions and complexity which made simplistic solutions difficult to apply and often ineffective. They acknowledged that as well as a need for improvement in the public sector there is also excellence and a tremendous amount of enthusiasm; and they recognised that 'systems alone cannot deliver high performance. They need to be embedded in the culture and values of the organization ...'. They recognised that programmes have to be judged by their outcomes, or social impact, as well as by their outputs, but did not acknowledge that outcomes are difficult to measure except in the long-term and may then be a matter of political rather than empirical judgement. They saw the need for 'organizational ownership' and for top managers to be 'personally committed', but ownership and commitment cannot be imposed by political direction, and the panel made the important statement that 'a more fundamental debate is required about the respective roles of politicians and managers.' Cynicism or lack of interest among senior members can rapidly bring disillusion and loss of motivation to more junior staff, but so too can the appearance of too close a political attachment to the government of the day. In a personal contribution to the Report, Lord Simon wrote 'The improvements will only be captured by intense commitment to change both in the civil service leadership and through the system and in the Government's political management process.' Perhaps the most significant passage in this report is John Mackinson's personal comment, 'underlying all these problems is a real dilemma about accountability. Are individuals ... accountable first and foremost to the Government that sets the agenda, to the management that is responsible for their careers, to the customers who create the need for this service, or to the taxpayer who foots the bill?'

The Government has given legislative expression to its ideas for the accountability of public services, as applied to local government, in the Local Government Act 2000. Their main features are requirements for political decision-making in local government to be efficient, transparent and accountable; for the efficiency and quality of services to be continuously improved, with an emphasis on outcomes rather than process (although the Act is very prescriptive on the processes to be followed); and for local communities to be actively involved in local decisions. Local authorities have a new duty to draw up community strategies for promoting the well-being of their areas, and new powers to do anything which they consider likely to promote it. Local partnerships are to be established, with a shared commitment to implementing the strategy and local action plans. The Government has issued detailed guidance to local authorities on how this Act is to be implemented.[17]

The Act and the ideas discussed in this chapter have a great deal in common. The outcome, as the Government recognises, is to be an improvement in the well-being of areas and communities. But the outcome will also depend on the culture and style of the services concerned, on how 'communities' are identified and engaged, on the character of the various relationships which are involved, and on the legitimacy of the processes through which the outcome is achieved.[18] Perhaps the greatest danger is that pressure to conform to the detailed prescriptions in the Act will result in what is in the end a lifeless bureaucracy. (See *Chapter 18* for a discussion of how the approaches might be applied to community safety.)

Culture, style and relationships

The structure of a service's accountability, and the dynamics through which it operates, will have a direct effect on its culture, management style and internal and external relationships. They will affect the extent to which it is open and accessible, and the interests and influences to which it is most likely to respond. They will affect the service's attitude to risk (whether it is one of careful assessment and readiness to take risks when they are justified, or one of risk avoidance). They will influence the extent to which staff feel supported, valued, confident and secure. The influence may be progressive in the sense of creating a will to adopt new ideas and approaches and an ability to do so in a spirit of optimism and confidence; or regressive in the sense of generating a culture of blame and a climate of rigidity, suspicion, secrecy and fear.

Mechanisms for accountability, and the information they provide, are of little value unless they are properly and effectively used. Information must be relevant and accessible to the various parties and interests, including citizens in general; it must be understood by them; questions put to them must be intelligible and capable of intelligent answers; it must be possible for views to be volunteered as well as sought; and views once given must be respected, taken into account and responded to by those in positions of relevant responsibility. Procedures for complaint should be open and accessible; complaints when they are made should wherever possible be treated as helpful feedback and an opportunity for improvement, and not defensively as an attack on a person's competence or integrity from which they need to be defended (see also *Chapters 16* and *17*). Accountability must not be perfunctory, or appear as if its purpose is only to gain support or to create a favourable impression.

The privatisation of British Rail has had the effect of replacing an operating culture with a culture of financial performance, of substituting skills in financial management and accountancy for skills in running the railway and railway engineering. Operating staff have, over many years and not only since privatisation, been de-skilled and devalued. Authority, discretion and respect have been withdrawn from them, and the industry has progressively acquired a higher and more precarious centre of gravity.[19] The catastrophic consequences have become all too visible. There is no directly comparable situation in other public services, but there are warnings to be heeded - about the effect of a performance culture which is too internally or financially driven, of a structure of accountability which operates only in one direction or on too narrow criteria, and of the loss or corruption of a spirit of public service.

A larger subject is preparation for leadership and professional practice in public services and professions, and the role of universities in that respect. It is too large a subject for this book, and similar questions arise in every area of national life. But Mike Nellis has drawn attention to the need for higher education to provide not only 'underpinning' knowledge - the practical or vocational knowledge required to be a competent and qualified practitioner - but also 'overarching' knowledge. The latter is academic rather than vocational, not in any way superior on that account, but different. Quoting Barnett, and addressing in particular the form of training which is needed for the reformed Probation Service, he writes 'overarching knowledge ... is what enables the university to play its civic role ... both in expanding the frames of understanding of the wider world, and assisting in their assimilation'. He sees it as fostering 'a certain depth and breadth of thought' which will help to give the public servant the vision and confidence, both to question, adapt and innovate, and also to sustain his or her professional and moral integrity in situations where it might be challenged. He is concerned that 'overarching' knowledge might be neglected under the pressure for economy and effectiveness although he writes primarily in the context of the Probation Service, his arguments apply to public services as a whole.[20]

LEGITIMACY

Public services, especially those which exercise powers over people's lives, must be not only accountable but also legitimate.[21] They must function with the consent and support of society as a whole. The authority of those who exercise them has to be respected in its own right and not simply imposed on those made subject to them. The police, for example, cannot function without the consent of the public; or a prison, in the last resort, without the consent of the inmates.

Legitimacy is an elusive but important concept. It has elements of accountability, of fairness, and of natural and procedural justice. For an authority, or service, a decision or an instruction to be legitimate, all of these have to be present. Legitimacy is not only what helps to persuade a person that a decision by a public authority or an instruction by a public official is fair, but also what persuades them to accept the decision or instruction even though they may not like it or it may be painful to them. For that to happen, the necessary conditions include both a satisfactory formal structure which gives at least a reasonable degree of accountability and expectation of fairness and natural and procedural justice; and a relationship of mutual confidence, trust and respect between those taking or conveying the decision and those to whom it is directed. The former may themselves be acting under instructions or in accordance with rules by which they are bound, but they still represent the state, the authority or the system which they serve. The quality of that relationship may be as necessary a part of the authority's legitimacy as the *vires* or validity of the decision itself. Once an authority loses legitimacy, or if it fails to achieve legitimacy, a great deal is lost with it - as with the Royal Ulster Constabulary and the nationalist community in

Northern Ireland, and as has been at risk between the Metropolitan Police and some minority groups in London. See also *Chapters 17* and *18*.

ACCOUNTABILITY IN ACTION

Ministers, Members of Parliament and departmental officials must use the mechanisms of accountability to make themselves aware of the state and effectiveness of the service concerned, and of public attitudes towards it (not necessarily the same as those which appear from reports in the media). They must use that information to inform legislation, policy, the allocation of resources and their own relationships with the service itself; and at the same time to increase effectiveness, raise standards and promote public confidence. There are arguments for saying that Parliament should be much more effective in this respect, and the effectiveness of Parliament is of course a subject in itself, with its own extensive literature.

Managers of services, including those at a very local level, and individual officers and practitioners, must use information to shape local practice, priorities and relationships. They will be concerned to resolve local problems which may not be so easily visible at national level. The extent to which services or local managers should have local discretion to resolve them on their own and in accordance with local opinion, and the extent to which justice requires the uniform, consistent application of national requirements and standards, will always be a source of tension. The aim should not however be to impose absolute uniformity, which would deny or make harder the possibility of progress or change, but to ensure that differences can be explained and understood. There is evidence that people may be quite well satisfied with what they think of as their own local services, while criticising the same service's peformance at national level - see for example *Hitting Local Targets*, published by the Public Management Foundation. [22] Their satisfaction may result in complacency or carelessness, which must then be corrected through inspection and the enforcement of national standards; or it may reinforce a sense of professional pride and local ownership of the service concerned.

The structures and mechanisms for a service's accountability must be suited to the types of function it exists to perform. The functions of some services are relatively straightforward. They may involve complex procedures, sophisticated technology or large organizations, but their purpose is reasonably clear and performance can ultimately be judged by objective and usually quantifiable standards of accuracy, consistency, timeliness and cost. Services performing these functions must satisfy their users or customers, but they do not have to engage in sensitive relationships with, or account to, other organizations or local communities. They can often be best provided by an organization whose accountability is of a 'vertical' kind, under a chief executive who in the public sector is in turn accountable to ministers. The issue of passports, or of vehicle and driving licences, or the payment of social security benefits, are broadly of this kind, and were natural sites for the creation of the executive agencies under the 'Next Steps' programme. They typically require the unswerving pursuit of a single-minded, top-down management agenda and their accountability is relatively uncomplicated.

Other public services and institutions, especially those involved in criminal justice, are considerably more complex. Their purpose is less easy to define, and although reasonably robust statements of purpose have been devised those statements can be interpreted in various ways. National standards and quantified indicators of performance have brought a valuable discipline to many services, but they do not provide a complete account of how well a service is performing. High and improving scores on the indicators would still be combined with an overall performance which would be perceived as harsh, oppressive or unjust. A prison or a police service may perform well on its key performance indicators, but still be the subject of public criticism or an adverse inspection report. The statutory principal aim of the youth justice system to 'prevent offending' has been generally welcomed as helping to bring some much needed coherence to the system, but it must not override principles such as equity, equality and proportionality.

Criminal justice services and institutions also have to manage some very complicated relationships - with each other; with other public services; with witnesses, suspects and offenders; with their families; with victims; with organizations, communities and individual citizens who expect their help and protection. Those communities and groups include cultural minorities, their members and those who speak for them. Few policies, programmes or initiatives, whether from government or the services themselves, can succeed without their consent and co-operation - or often without their commitment and enthusiasm. Nor is the relationship with the government straightforward. The constitutional independence of the judiciary, the operational independence of chief officers of police (and until the Criminal Justice and Court Services Act of chief officers of probation), and the legal independence of Crown prosecutors are all regarded as important safeguards. The extent to which ministers can properly give directions regarding the detention or treatment of individual prisoners is a matter of continuing debate, and a similar debate will arise for the Probation Service when it is reformed on the lines set out in the Criminal Justice and Court Services Act (see *Chapter 20*).

PUBLIC SERVICES AND CITIZENSHIP

All public services, but especially those concerned with crime and criminal justice, are intimately connected with the rights and responsibilities of citizenship. Lines of accountability must run vertically, connecting the services' managers and practitioners with government departments, ministers and Parliament; and horizontally connecting them with other organizations, interests and the citizens whom they serve. Ministers may understandably find that a service which is locally employed and managed, and supervised by a locally-appointed board or committee, will not be sufficiently accountable or responsive to themselves or the national responsibilities which the service has to undertake. On the other hand, a service which only looks to central government, to Whitehall and Westminster, for its direction and guidance may not be able to generate the local understanding, support and commitment which are needed if Parliament's legislation and the government's own policies are to be successfully put into effect.

Services should always be provided as locally as possible. De Tocqueville wrote of the United States

> the strength of free peoples resides in the local community. Local institutions.... put [liberty] within the people's reach.... and accustom them to make use of it. Without local institutions a nation may give itself free government, but it has not got the spirit of liberty.... Municipal Institutions constitute the strength of free nations.[23]

The tension between central direction and local discretion is one of those which is now at the heart of British society and the British state, and affects the governance of the country in fundamental ways.

Public services must themselves contribute, not just to the formation of policy and the development of professional practice, but also to the character of the society and the communities they serve. They must not be treated simply as the agents of central government. They must have what Brian Cooke, in his important analysis of American public administration and policies, has described as a 'constitutive' as well as an 'instrumental' role.[24]

It was probably a salutary experience for 'professional' public servants to lose some of the political influence they once enjoyed as members of 'elites'; and similarly some of the unquestioned authority they once enjoyed both with professional colleagues in other disciplines and with their own patients, pupils and clients. Changes in the character and circumstances of public service are taking that development a stage further. Colleagues in other services and disciplines can no longer be over-ruled or ignored: they have to be listened to, understood and relied upon. Work with patients and clients must similarly be founded on a more equal relationship of communication, trust and agreement. And where there is an element of inequality in power or authority – as in schools, and in a different sense in the criminal justice services – the use of that power or authority has to be legitimate and founded on principles of mutual respect and proportionality.

Drawing the threads together, some principles of modern public service might be

- equity and fairness between individuals, including the equal value of people regardless of race, gender, social class, religion or cultural background;
- respect for people as citizens and for human dignity;
- proportionality of response whenever public servants have to intervene in citizens' lives;

- subsidiarity, with decisions being taken and services provided as locally as practicable;
- openness, transparency and accessibility;
- accountability, taking multiple forms and operating in multiple directions, both nationally and locally.

Later chapters will consider how these principles might be applied to crime and criminal justice.

ENDNOTES for *Chapter 5*

[1] Peter Neyroud and Alan Beckley, *Policing, Ethics and Human Rights*, Cullompton, Devon, Willan Publishing, 2001.

[2] *Chapter 2* considered the distinction which governments now make between 'accountability', understood in the narrow sense of being prepared to give an explanation, and 'responsibility' in the broad and more dynamic sense of an obligation to make improvements, to put right what may have gone wrong, and if necessary to accept blame. Historically, and usually in ordinary language, 'accountability' has itself been used in this broader sense, and it is so used in this and later chapters.

[3] Peter Neyroud and Alan Beckley, *op. cit.* n. 1, pp. 145-165.

[4] Michael Schluter and David Lee, *The R Factor*, London, Hodder and Stoughton, 1993.

[5] Richard Sennett, *The Corrosion of Character: The Personal Consequences of Work in the New Capitalism*, New York, W. W. Norton and Co, 1998 .

[6] The Joseph Rowntree Foundation, *Job Insecurity and Work Intensification: Flexible and Changing Boundaries at Work*, York, Joseph Rowntree Foundation, 1999.

[7] *The Government's Strategic Plan and Business Plan for the Criminal Justice System 2000-2001*, May 2000 .

[8] Stephen Covey, *The Seven Habits of Highly Effective People*, London, Simon and Schuster, 1989, quoted by Peter Neyroud and Alan Beckley, *op. cit.* p. 171.

[9] Jane Steele, *Wasted Values: Harnessing the Commitment of Public Managers*, London, Public Management Foundation 1999. The crisis in the public sector was the subject of a series of articles and interviews under the general title, 'The Common Good' in the *Guardian*, 20 and 21 March 2001. The series gave support to many of the arguments in this chapter.

[10] Cabinet Office, *Modernising Government*, Cm. 4310, London, Stationery Office, 1999.

[11] Peter Neyroud and Alan Beckley, *op. cit.* n. 1.

[12] Mark Freedland, 'Law, Public Services and Citizenship – New Domains, New Regimes?', in Mark Freedland and Silvana Sciarra (eds.), *Public Services and Citizenship in European Law*, Oxford, Clarendon Press, 1998.

[13] Except for the magistrates courts, which remain under the control of the local magistrates' courts committees insofar as their management (but not judicial) functions are concerned. However even these courts are subject to the pressures of budgets, key performance indicators and other influences which stem from the centre.

[14] Ann James and John Raine, *The New Politics of Criminal Justice*, London, Longman 1994.

[15] Peter Neyroud and Alan Beckley, *op. cit.* n. 1.

[16] Public Services Productivity Panel, *Public Services' Productivity: Meeting the Challenge*, London, HM Treasury, 2000.

[17] Department of the Environment, Transport and the Regions, *Preparing Community Strategies: Government Guidance to Local Authorities*, London, Department of the Environment, Transport and the Regions, 2001.

[18] A conference at Oxford Brookes University in December 2000 identified the following as being among the questions which have to be considered:
- What should be the points of focus? Geographical areas or groups of people - young people, the elderly, minority groups? Or communities, and if so what kinds of

community - those based on occupations, racial or ethnic backgrounds, different faiths?

- Whose responsibility is it to take the initiative and the lead? Services, prominent citizens, voluntary organizations? Who should be seen as being 'in charge'? How should they be held to account?
- Should it be a collective or bilateral process? If it is to be based on consultative groups, should they be assembled for particular or more general purposes? How often should they be stood down or replaced? How is membership to be decided?
- What mechanisms should be employed? Public meetings, focus groups, meetings with representatives, written communication? What about groups who are hard to reach - travellers, minorities, those who are for various reasons alienated or disaffected?
- What information is needed - about services, people or situations and conditions? From what sources should it be obtained, and how should it be assembled and communicated?
- What skills are needed - in analysis, presentation and communication? Are they already available, should they be developed through training or in other ways, should they be brought in from consultants or other specialists? The process must be reciprocal and multi-directional, and all parties to the process will need the skills to make it effective.
- How will the process, and the relationships it involves, affect relations with existing structures and institutions, including central government, elected members of local authorities and the audit and inspection authorities? How will they relate to existing mechanisms for accountability?

[19] For an example, see 'Railtalk' and Roger Ford, 'The Forgotten Driver', both in *Modern Railways*, vol. 58, no. 628, January 2001, pp. 4 and 45-52.

[20] Mike Nellis, 'The New Probation Training in England and Wales: Realising the Potential', *Social Work Education*, (forthcoming). He quotes R. Barnett, *Realising the University in an Age of Super-Complexity*, Buckingham, Open University Press, 2000.

[21] For arguments about the importance of legitimacy in public services and public institutions, see Tom Tyler, *Why People Obey the Law*, New Haven, Yale University Press, 1990; David Beetham, *The Legitimation of Power*, London, Macmillan, 1991; Anthony Bottoms and Will Hay, *Prisons and the Problem of Order*, Oxford, Clarendon Press, 1996; and Anthony Bottoms, *Compliance and Community Penalties* (A paper prepared for the twenty-fourth Cropwood Conference, University of Cambridge Institute of Criminology, forthcoming).

[22] Office For Public Management, *Hitting Local Targets: Public Value of Public Services*, London, Public Management Foundation, 1997.

[23] Quoted in Brian Cooke, *Bureaucracy and Self Government: Reconsidering the Role of Public Administration in American Politics*, Baltimore, John Hopkins University Press, 1996.

[24] Brian Cooke, *op cit*, n. 23.

PART II Politics and Crime

CHAPTER 6

Approaches to Crime and Penal Policy

The mood and temper of the public in regard to the treatment of crime and criminals is one of the most unfailing tests of the civilisation of any country.

Winston Churchill, 20 July 1910[1]

Crime and criminal justice, and with them the protection and liberty of the citizen, are now intensely political issues. They have become more so during the last 20 years, partly because of the increase in crime and public fears about it, but also because governments committed so wholeheartedly to efficient management lose credibility if they seem unable to control it. But the politics of crime has some rather odd features. The Conservative Party was for many years able to give an impression that it was more 'tough' on crime than its opponents, and the Labour Party was portrayed as more 'soft' or 'liberal'. But an analysis of the policies which successive Governments have pursued during the past 50 years does not support that comparison, and it is easier to see contrasts between individual Home Secretaries than it is to generalise about the attitudes of the parties of which they were members. Crime and criminal justice have rarely produced specific issues on which the parties have been seriously divided (legislation on Irish terrorism was perhaps until recently the main example), and it was not until 1979 that any party made policies on crime part of its appeal to the electorate. Even in the period since then, the opposition's criticisms of the government of the day (whichever party was in office) have focused more on its handling of particular situations (such as crime figures or release or escapes from prisons) than on its policies or proposals for legislation.[2]

DIFFERENCES OF ATTITUDE AND APPROACH

There are fundamental divisions between some of the approaches to crime and criminal justice, especially between those who see crime as a social phenomenon to be dealt with by social measures, including the rehabilitation of offenders; and those who see it as an expression of individual wickedness to be dealt with by punishment and especially imprisonment (or even by capital punishment). The latter view is prevalent, but by no means universal, in the United States of America. No political party in Great Britain has in recent times adopted one approach to the exclusion of the other, and no issue has been the subject of a debate where the political parties have been divided along precisely those parameters. But a government committed to managerial efficiency and effectiveness will find it easier to attribute continuing or rising crime to the wickedness of criminals or to the failure of public servants than to any lack of success in its own policies. (For examples see *Chapters 8* and *9*.)

Scholars have identified several different traditions in the approaches which different countries have taken to crime and criminal justice at various times in their history. Those traditions have gained or lost ground as a result of different social and political influences, and - perhaps rightly - none has ever completely dominated a country's legislation or practice.[3] Governments are always keen to emphasise the novelty of any measures they may propose; judges the fairness and sometimes the difficulty of their sentencing decisions; and police, prison and probation services the success of their current practice. They may relate any or all of these to their own set of aims or principles, but for ministers or practitioners to attach them too closely to an academic theory or an historical tradition is likely to invite a sceptical and probably scornful response from colleagues and the media.

Even so, most of the supposedly new approaches to crime and criminal justice can be located within the pattern set by the different historical traditions. An appreciation of those traditions may help towards an understanding of the ideas which influence existing and proposed legislation and practice, and of the possible consequences when they are applied to today's problems and circumstances.[4]

The classical view of crime and criminal justice, sometimes called the retributivist view, asserts that people who commit crime do so of their own free will as individual moral agents; and that they deserve to be, and should be, punished for it. They should not however be punished more, or less, severely than their crime deserves. Similar crimes should attract similar punishments: there should be proportionality and consistency in sentencing. Retributive justice is often thought to be harsh justice, but the classical view's insistence on proportionality imposes a restraint on the degree of punishment to be imposed on a particular individual. This was, essentially, the view which informed the original proposals for the legislation which became the Criminal Justice Act 1991 - see *Chapter 7*. The theory does not however help to decide the scale or tariff or punishments which are proportionate to different types of offence and its failure to do so is one of the criticisms which academics such as Nicola Lacey have made of the Act.[5]

The contrasting 'utilitarian' view claims that punishment, and the suffering associated with it, is justified not so much because it is deserved but because of wider benefits, either to society or to the individual, and including the possible deterrent effect which would follow from it. The limiting factor here was the extent of those benefits: the suffering was to be proportionate not to the offence but to the benefits it would bring. This view is associated with writers such as Jeremy Bentham and to some extent John Stuart Mill. Again, it is a poor guide to the amount of punishment to be imposed in any particular case.

Leon Radzinowicz and Roger Hood wrote at the beginning of Volume 5 of *A History of the English Criminal Law*[6]

> It is an almost instinctive response on the part of those who are not criminals to look upon those who are as being different. From there it is a short and easy path to the assumption that this difference originates in characteristics peculiar to the transgressor's individuality alone.

They describe how this interpretation came to the forefront of criminal thinking in the 1880s under the influence of the Positivist School of criminology and its founder Cesare Lombroso. Its followers rejected the concepts of criminal responsibility and proportionality to the seriousness of the offence; and argued for sanctions based on the dangerousness of the offender, including indefinite detention for curative or incapacitative purposes. It reflected to some extent the practice in Victorian England of detaining children for long periods in industrial schools and reformatories, but which had become discredited by the end of the nineteenth century. The reasons were partly a reaction against the oppressive nature of industrial schools and reformatories and the long periods which children spent in them, and partly a sense that they made little or no contribution to the country's social and economic progress.

Radzinowicz and Hood contrast this approach both with the classical view already described, and with what might be called a 'socialist' view associated with the earlier ideas of reformers such as Robert Owen and later William Morris. Socialists saw crime as the product of social conditions, poverty, inequality, the pursuit of wealth and the ownership of private property. The criminal law existed to protect the capitalist state, and criminals were its victims. They came to recognise that a socialist state might still have a problem of crime, but were not clear about how to deal with it. Similar views were expressed by Engels and Marx, and by criminologists in the Soviet Union and in Eastern Europe during the period of communist rule.

A more recent version of the 'socialist' approach is the 'new criminology' developed by writers such as Ian Taylor, Paul Walton and Jock Young - the authors of *The New Criminology*, published in 1973 - together with Stan Cohen and Colin Sumner.[7] This approach saw crime as a feature of the modern world, widespread in society as a whole, but with criminality - the identification, labelling and treatment of individuals as criminals - confined largely to the working class. While most utilitarian and all positivist approaches sought to deal with crime by persuading, conditioning or coercing criminals to conform with society's expectations, they saw criminality as the creation of a flawed and unjust society. The solution was not to change individuals but to change society. A more recent account of the new criminology, updated to take account of earlier criticisms that it did not pay enough attention to subjects such as the interests of victims or the position of women or cultural minorities, is in *The New Criminology Revisited*, a collection of essays edited by Paul Walton and Jock Young.[8]

APPLICATION TO POLICY AND LEGISLATION

None of the four approaches discussed so far has on its own provided a foundation which a government has found satisfactory for its own criminal justice policy, or for the practice of a country's criminal justice services. Radzinowicz and Hood have shown how ideas from all four traditions were promoted, modified or abandoned during the later part of the nineteenth century, and how they informed legislation and professional and operational practice. In a chapter which is interesting for its topicality in view of the Government's present ideas on sentencing, they describe 'four basic approaches' to 'incapacitating the habitual criminal'.[9] The first, which they term 'Sequestration and Surveillance', involved indefinite periods of imprisonment until the offender could be shown to have been reformed, with life imprisonment for those who were incorrigible. The second, 'the Cumulative System', involved progressively heavier punishments which follow with certainty upon each reconviction, and was aimed at incapacitating the whole 'criminal class' rather than particular individuals. The third was a 'Dual Track scheme', with life imprisonment for a second or third felony conviction, to be served in stages of which the first would be severely deterrent and later stages would be more relaxed. The fourth focused on the persistent petty offender with progressively longer, automatic sentences for each conviction, all to be served in severely penal conditions. The chapter goes on to describe the arguments put forward for and against these approaches and the legislative provisions which followed from them: the Penal Servitude Act of 1864, the Habitual Criminals Act 1869, the Prevention of Crimes Act 1871. None of these measures was a success and by 1891 the sentencing structure had been brought back to where it was 30 years earlier. The arguments closely resemble those which were heard 130 years later.[10]

The Gladstone Committee of 1894
The legislation from that period was generally found to be unjust and ineffective in practice, and criticism came to a head in 1894 when the Prime Minister, Herbert Asquith, announced the appointment of a Departmental Committee under the chairmanship of Herbert Gladstone. The Committee brought the classical and utilitarian approaches together (more or less) in its report which was published less than a year later. It established six principles of penal policy, which can be summarised as follows[11]

- reformation should be a purpose of punishment alongside deterrence;
- prison treatment should be matched to the needs and circumstances of individual prisoners;
- prisoners should be divided into different categories according to their record and background;

- prisoners should be allowed useful employment and association and useless and humiliating activities should be stopped (the treadmill, the shot and the crank);
- there should be a stronger local influence on local prisons through the visiting committees of local justices; and
- the system as a whole should be unified and integrated, with wider processes of consultation and sources of advice.

Legislation and policy in the twentieth century

The Gladstone report was given statutory effect in the Probation of Offenders Act 1907 and in the Prevention of Crime Act and the Children Act, both of 1908. The Probation of Offenders Act established the Probation Service and the probation order, not just as an alternative to punishment or imprisonment but also as a means of reducing crime by advising, assisting, befriending, supervising and reforming offenders. (Probation officers had in effect been appointed as 'court missionaries' since 1878). The Prevention of Crime Act established the sentence of borstal detention (later borstal training) and the system and institutions to administer it. That Act also established the system of preventive detention for adults, essentially a survival from the 1860s, which came more quickly into disrepute. The Children Act established the separate system of juvenile courts, abolished imprisonment and penal servitude for any child under 14, and placed severe restrictions on the imprisonment of those aged between 14 and 16. Children and young persons accused of offences were always to be given bail, except in certain limited circumstances, and if remanded in custody they were to be sent to special places of detention separate from prisons.

These measures laid the foundation for a, broadly speaking, liberal set of criminal justice and penal policies, most of which were not seriously challenged for another 60 years.

All four traditions can be traced in the subsequent legislation and practice of the twentieth century. The utilitarian view persisted in the use of indeterminate sentences for borstal training and preventive detention, and in the 'welfare' and 'medical' models of penal treatment which were prominent until disillusion set in during the 1970s (see *Chapter 7*). The classical approach was then revived, sometimes described as the 'justice model', and found legislative expression in the abolition of the indeterminate sentence of borstal training (a sentence much resented by classically-minded judges after the alternative power to impose medium term sentences of imprisonment on young offenders had been removed under the Criminal Justice Act 1967). It had a powerful influence on the green and White Papers which preceded the Criminal Justice Act 1991, and to a large extent on the 1991 Act itself.

More recently, the utilitarian approach has been revived in the Labour Government's strategy for reducing crime and disorder (see *Chapters 9* and *18*). The positivist approach can be seen in the notions of eugenics, which became intellectually, and to some extent politically, fashionable in the 1920s,[12] but morally repugnant in the version which was put into practice in national socialist Germany. It is strongly reflected in the writing of Charles Murray in the United States,[13] and to some extent in policies both in the United States and under the Conservative Government in Great Britain in the 1990s (see *Chapter 8*). The socialist approach formed part of the influences on the early Labour Party, and on the development of social work and sociology, and it has influenced a number of academic criminologists. It has not had much influence on Labour Governments when in office, but has perhaps been the reason why the Labour Party's political opponents have been able to claim that Labour Governments are likely to be 'soft on crime', and why measures which could be described as 'liberal' have more often come from Conservative rather than Labour Home Secretaries.

The landmarks during the 1930s were the Children and Young Persons Act 1933, and the Criminal Justice Bill which was introduced in 1938 but abandoned on the outbreak of the Second World War. The 1933 Act established the welfare of the child as the primary consideration to be taken into account in matters affecting children, including proceedings for a criminal offence. The Criminal Justice Bill would have abolished judicial corporal punishment and the sentence of penal servitude; and would have restricted and eventually abolished imprisonment for young people aged under 21, leaving borstal training, remand homes, detention centres (at that stage to be known as 'Howard Houses') and attendance centres as alternatives. For persistent offenders, it would have introduced a new sentence of corrective training and a new version of preventive detention. The Labour Government revived the Bill after the war, and it was passed as the Criminal Justice Act 1948. It was still too soon to attempt the abolition of capital punishment, which took another 20 years.[14]

After the Second World War: the 'medical' and 'justice' models

Various ideas and ways of expressing them have entered and receded from the debate during the years since the passage of the Criminal Justice Act 1948. The 'medical' or 'treatment' model, based on the utilitarian tradition, had some prominence during the 1960s: the criminal justice process was compared with the medical process of diagnosis, treatment and cure; with a similar progress from assessment, through suitably designed programmes in institutions or in the community, to a period of after-care - of 'recuperation' after release. Risley and other remand centres were built, and Holloway Prison was rebuilt, with this model in mind[15]. The arrangements for social inquiry reports (now pre-sentence reports prepared on a different basis), and various therapeutic programmes for offenders in prison or on probation, had similar origins.

The 'medical' model fell from favour during the 1970s and was followed by the 'justice' model. This was much closer to the classical tradition and emphasised fairness, due process, accountability, the need to explain and give reasons for decisions, mechanisms for dealing with complaints and grievances, and inspection and audit. In some ways it anticipated the new public management of the 1980s (see *Chapter 2*) and was in effect overtaken by it. In their book *The Prison Governor: Theory and Practice*, David Wilson and Shane Bryans[16] describe its application to prisons, in Great Britain and Minnesota, and it was the subject of a discussion at the Prison Governors' Conference in 1982.[17] Perhaps the most consistent expressions of the classical or retributivist tradition in recent government policy are the Green Paper *Punishment, Custody and the Community*, published in 1988; the White Paper *Crime, Justice and Protecting the Public*, published in 1990;[18] and the Criminal Justice Act 1991 which followed, although some 'utilitarian' provisions on sentences to protect the public from serious violent or sexual offences had by then been added.

NEW PUBLIC MANAGEMENT AND THE NEW PENOLOGY

New public management brought with it the paradigm shift which Malcolm Feely and Jonathan Simon first identified in the United States and termed the 'new penology' in their article 'The New Penology: Notes on the Emerging Strategy of Corrections and its Implications', written in 1992.[19] This approach concentrated attention on efficient custody and control, without embracing the traditional ideas of retribution or rehabilitation. It had some resemblance to the rather bleak ideas of 'humane containment' which Roy King and Rod Morgan put forward in their book *The Future of the Prison System;*[20] and of 'positive custody' which Mr. (now Lord) Justice May had offered as a rationale for imprisonment in his report on the prison officers' industrial action in 1979.[21] In a later article 'Actuarial Justice: the Emerging New Criminal Law',[22] Malcolm Feely and Jonathan Simon broaden the argument and link the 'new penology' with the development they had described as 'actuarial justice'. Its features include a belief in the incapacitating effect of prison sentences as a means of reducing crime, and the use of pre-trial detention for the same purpose. Both depend on a process of selection and assessment, based not on study of the character of the offender or the nature of the offence, still less on any consideration of rights or due process, but on profiles of risk and dangerousness and on actuarial predictions of future behaviour, and danger to the public. Because actuarial justice is 'forward-looking', rather than looking 'backwards' to the offender's history and to the offence, it can be presented as more 'progressive' or 'hopeful' than more traditional approaches. And because it operates according to formal systems of internal rules it can be compared with - or even reduced to - a computer programme which can be presented as 'modern' and as applying the latest technology. In their article 'Expanding Realms of the New Penology: the Advent of Actuarial Justice for Juveniles', Kimberly Kemf-Leonard and Elicka Peterson describe how actuarial justice has infected the juvenile justice system in the United States, extended not only to children identified as offenders or as being at risk, but also to their families[23].

Actuarial justice fits well with the Labour Government's approach to public management, based on efficiency and effectiveness, performance targets and indicators, league tables and the use of modern technology, although the Government also emphasises the 'reformative' aspects of imprisonment which it promotes through a range of tested and accredited courses to reduce offending behaviour.

Arguments in favour of actuarial justice and formalised procedures for risk assessment are usually based on the greater protection they can give to the public in comparison with procedures based on individual 'clinical' assessment. In this repect the application of the procedure is typically to sentencing, any form of discretionary release from custody, or to any restrictive condition which might be imposed as a condition of release or of a community sentence. There are however practical and ethical questions which need to be resolved. No method of assessment has so far avoided a proportion of 'false positives' (offenders assessed as likely to commit offences who do not in fact do so) or 'false negatives' (those assessed as unlikely but do). Judgements still have to be made about what level of risk is acceptable to any particular purpose or in any particular situation. Debate continues on which factors should or should not be taken into account, the weight which should be given to them, and the balance between 'static' risk factors in a person's history and background which they can do nothing to change, and 'dynamic' factors which can be affected by the programmes and opportunities provided for them and the choices they make for themselves. There is as yet no evidence on whether the choice of risk factor is likely to have a discriminatory effect in relation to particular racial or ethnic groups.

Ethical considerations present few problems when the assessment is made in order to judge whether a person is suitable or likely to benefit from a particular course or programme. They present more difficulty if a person is likely to lose their freedom or to have serious restrictions placed upon it, especially if the assessment is based on 'static' risk factors which the person cannot and never has been able to alter. On the other hand, actuarial forms of assessment may potentially benefit offenders to the extent that risks calculated by those methods may prove to be lower than those which sentencers and other decision-makers calculate by using more subjective methods.

Richard Jones offers a more speculative vision of the future with what he terms 'digital rule' in his article 'Digital Rule: Punishment Control and Technology'.[24] Drawing on the work of Foucault, Garland and others, he sees sentencing and punishment as part of a wider spectrum of penalty and social control, in which electronic technology is increasingly used as a means of maintaining social order. It does so by monitoring and restraining those belonging to groups or having characteristics which identify them as presenting a potential risk. Social order which is imposed by technology in the end has little need for institutions, human relationships or individual judgement. The state can maintain control by electronic means, not only to impose a curfew during the hours when a person is required to be at home, but also to send a warning when a person approaches a place which is forbidden to them, or by the use of a 'smart card' which can be programmed to allow or deny access to any of the places, persons or facilities where control is thought to be needed. Decision-making can be made similarly automatic and impersonal, for example decisions about breaches of the conditions of court orders for those under supervision. Discretion can be removed, and enforcement - at least in the sense of denying access to some or all of the offender's means of livelihood - can be made automatic.

Michael Cavadino, Iain Crow and James Dignan have put forward a modern classification of the different strategies which successive governments have adopted in their approaches to criminal justice in their book *Criminal Justice 2000: Strategies for a New Century*.[25] Following Andrew Rutherford[26] they identify

- Strategy A - the punitive 'law and order' approach which relies on law enforcement, detention and punishment;
- Strategy B - 'managerialism' which aim to organize and run the criminal justice system and its services and institutions as efficiently and effectively as possible; and
- Strategy C - 'human rights' which seeks to minimise punishment and ensure fairness and due process - for victims as well as offenders - throughout the system.

Recent governments of both parties have pursued a mixture of all three, although different strategies have been more or less prominent at different times.

Drawing on an analysis of 'post modern' developments in social conditions and politics which is similar to the account in *Chapter 2*, David Garland[27] distinguishes between those approaches which focus primarily on the offender or criminal as a person, with that person's punishment or rehabilitation as their objective; and those which focus on criminal actions or events where the objective is to prevent or reduce them. He argues that the former were predominant in Great Britain and the United States during the nineteenth century and until the 1970s, and that social, economic and political changes in both countries have brought the latter into prominence since then. He claims that the resulting strategies and criminological ideas often have more relevance to the politics of the moment than to the problems of crime itself.

THREE RECURRING PROBLEMS

Three problems have continually troubled governments, judges and the criminal justice services throughout the last 150 years. They are:

- how to recognise and deal with persistent or dangerous offenders;
- how to treat those who are thought to need a sharp and in some sense painful lesson; and
- how to identify and deal with the causes of crime, or in today's language 'what works' to prevent re-offending.

Persistent offenders

Victorian attempts to deal with persistent offenders have already been described. Those of the twentieth century have included preventive detention in the first half of the century; corrective training and a new form of preventive detention in the third quarter of the century; and various arrangements or proposals for extended, mandatory and possibly 'seamless' and reviewable sentences as the century came to an end. None of those which have been tried in the past has been found satisfactory for very long. Attempts to identify persistent or dangerous criminals otherwise than by their previous records have not proved successful, and attempts based on previous records have so far produced too many false positives and false negatives to be used with great confidence. It remains to be seen whether modern techniques of risk assessment will prove sufficiently accurate, or sufficiently fair in their application, to be used credibly and legitimately in future. The lesson of history is that severe and rigid statutes invite evasion, and are difficult to apply without inconsistency and injustice.[28]

Sharp lessons

Attempts to administer sharp lessons have included corporal punishment in the nineteenth and early twentieth centuries; the 'short sharp shock' in detention centres in the 1950s and again, briefly, the early 1980s; and more recently, 'boot camps' and training at a military correction centre (later abandoned in the UK on grounds of cost). Other attempts were made in the Victorian reformatories and industrial schools and later in approved schools. Experience has shown that such attempts do not produce any better results in terms of the offender's re-offending or other behaviour; and usually end either in cruelty or abuse by staff or, sooner or later, in a transformation to a more constructive programme. Only staff who are bullies seem able to sustain a deliberately punitive regime over an extended period of time.

The causes of crime - preventing re-offending

Governments, judges, clerics and reformers have always been interested in the causes of crime, and the related question of what to do to prevent people from offending. The conclusions have usually been based more on moral or political conviction or subjective impressions than on empirical evidence, but an attempt to provide better answers led to the Government's support for academic criminology from the late 1950s onwards (with an interruption during the mid 1990s). In the event, academic research such as that carried out by Donald West and then by David Farrington in the 1980s and 1990s was able to identify a number of social and personal factors - poverty, poor housing, criminal parents, brothers or sisters, poor performance at school, harsh or erratic discipline at home - which are correlated with offending.[29] A Home Office research study *Reducing Offending*,[30] drawing on this and other research, suggested a range of possible initiatives which might help to reduce offending, and this study provided the basis for the present Government's crime reduction programme - see *Chapter 18*. Research has not, however, been able so far to find any 'causes' of crime in the sense that if they were removed, certain crimes would no longer be committed or crime generally would be reduced; or that if they are present, crime will invariably follow.

More recent research has sought to find out 'what works' in programmes to reduce re-offending by those who have already been convicted and sentenced. Much effort is going into the monitoring, evaluation and accreditation of programmes which will have that effect, and some factors have been identified, especially in programmes based on 'cognitive behaviour', which seem to be correlated with success in that respect. The hope must obviously be that a sufficiently direct causal relationship will be established for the application of such programmes to have a direct, quantifiable, effect on individual behaviour and so on future rates of crime. But the range of factors which may affect a person's future offending is so wide and various, and many of them are so difficult to control, that the search for what works may be as uncertain as the search for the causes of crime. Some correlations can be established, which will help to inform the design of programmes for those in prison or under supervision in the community, but predicting and preventing offending is unlikely ever to become an exact science.

It is now commonplace to say that there are no simple causes of crime (although there are plenty of correlations), and hard to assert that there are any simple solutions. And yet it is hard for governments, or political parties, to resist the argument that the solution is to be 'tough on criminals', and perhaps the suggestion that nothing else much matters. The lesson from history, and from more recent research,[31] is that in the long term there is little to be gained from detailed adjustments to the legislation or practice on sentencing, whether in terms of a reduction in crime or of a supposed increase in public confidence. The more important question for sentencing is whether the process and the outcomes are fair and just - for the offender, for the victim and for the community more generally. There is also an important connection between sentencing and the means of putting the sentence into effect. If the means are inadequate, whether because of conditions in prisons or because of unrealised expectations of enforcement, treatment or rehabilitation, sentencing and the whole criminal justice process is brought into disrepute.

Perhaps the most promising focus for any study of the 'causes' of crime, and the means of preventing individuals from committing it, is the range of 'risk' and 'resilience' factors which can be found in the social, cultural and moral environment in which young people grow up and spend their adult lives. The most comprehensive account is *Anti-Social Behaviour by Young People* by Michael Rutter, Henri Giller and Ann Hagell.[32] Governments and statutory services find it hard to engage with those factors as a matter of policy or professional practice, rightly so because they involve a serious degree of intrusion into personal lives, and judgements about cultural norms which can quickly be seen as illegitimate and unacceptable. But they cannot be ignored, and later chapters refer to some of the programmes - for example for various forms of early intervention with children and their parents - which are now being pursued.

THE POLITICS OF PUNISHMENT

The 'new penology' and what has been described as actuarial or digital justice have much in common with the positivist tradition described earlier in this chapter and with the new public management described in *Chapter 2*. Like the new public management, they operate as if they were in a controlled and value-free environment. The immediate aim, and what is recognised and rewarded, is the efficient, economical and trouble-free management of institutions and operations. The more procedures can be mechanised and made impersonal and automatic the better: costs will be reduced and the uncertainties of human contact, human judgement and individual discretion will be removed. Failures to comply with the system can be instantly recognised and the blame can be laid immediately on the individual suspect, offender, or member of staff concerned, with no room for argument or excuses. If a potentially troublesome situation seems likely to develop, especially if the public might be put at risk, the supposed trouble-maker can be quickly identified and challenged or removed. If measures to identify potentially persistent or dangerous offenders, or to reduce crime or prevent re-offending, are not successful, the fault will not be in the measures themselves but in the staff's failure to apply them properly or the offender's failure to respond. Staff or offenders can then be punished accordingly.

On this view, all that matters is what can be counted or measured; questions about how people think or feel, the character of their relationships, the extent to which there is a spirit of confidence, respect for human dignity and decency or a sense of compassion or mutual trust and understanding are reduced to tick-boxes concerning the completion of processes or procedures, compliance with requirements or indications of failure - for example complaints, adjudications, absences by staff, or escapes by prisoners.

It is now possible to detect a 'new punitiveness' or 'authoritarian populism' which seems to be seeping, perhaps even surging, through the English-speaking countries of the developed world. It departs both from the classical principles of retributive justice, especially their emphasis on due process and proportionality, and from those of utilitarian or instrumental justice, with their emphasis on results and empirical evidence of 'what works'. Typical features which can be perceived to different degrees in all those countries, including Great Britain, include mandatory sentences of imprisonment; 'naming and shaming' of offenders, either in the form of public humiliation (ranging from chain gangs to distinctive clothing worn in public), or of public notification of offenders' addresses ('Megan's Law' in the United States and the campaign conducted after the murder of Sarah Payne in Great Britain); automated procedures for surveillance and control, including electronic monitoring; curfews; restrictions on the use of judicial, operational or administrative discretion (and public criticism of its supposed misuse); and attention to popular opinion rather than professional advice or judgement. Criminal justice becomes less a matter of punishing, deterring or reforming individuals than of collectively controlling a dangerous criminal underclass. The mood, and the movement, are probably driven by the increase in the volume of crime; the extent to which people have experience of it as victims or as friends or relatives of victims; perhaps by the scale on which crime, especially sensational but isolated crimes, are reported in the media; and the anger which people feel as a result. The natural demand is for 'something to be done' - partly for punishment and partly for protection.

Measures such as those described would have been thought 20 years ago as objectionable in principle. How far they can be located within traditional approaches to crime and justice and treated as ordinary reactions to new situations and opportunities (such as new technology); and how far they represent a departure from those traditions and a return to the ideas of an earlier period, perhaps 200 years ago, is the subject of John Pratt's article in the British Journal of Criminology.[33] He writes

> clinical diagnosis begins to give way to actuarial prediction. But this new means of classifying offenders at the same time lends itself to a way of ordering and assessing criminality that goes beyond the boundaries of penal modernity; a shift away from making judgments on individual cases, and into a new realm where the kind of group which one is judged to belong to becomes the determinant of the penalty that is to be imposed. At the same time risk rather than crime comes to play a crucial role in this judgment; it is not so much the gravity of the particular offence that will determine the penalty to be imposed, but the risk that one is thought to pose to the security of the community.

and continues

> What we have lost is the sense of certainty about where the boundaries of punishment now lie, and the sense that we are following, long-term at least, an irreversible path of reform, amelioration and progress. In its place, a penal relativism opens up the possibilities for much more localised practices, that go off from one another at diverse tangents - while at the same time indicating the privileging of public sentiment rather than bureaucratic rationalism as an important driving force of punishment.

John Pratt has especially in mind the situation in the United States, where the developments he describes are especially prominent[34], and in Australia and New Zealand, as well as in Great Britain. Whether policy, law and practice in Great Britain are overtaken by the 'post modernism' and the retreat into the past which he fears, will depend very much on the Government's actions. Continuing insistence on evidence-based practice, and the presence and application of the Human Rights Act 1998, and a liberal understanding of citizenship and an increasingly strong civil society, should provide effective protection against the influences which John Pratt fears. But recent events, especially the attitude which the Government displayed towards offensive behaviour and football hooliganism during the summer of 2000, and the language in which it announced its review of sentencing (see *Chapter 12*), give grounds for serious concern.

THE 'LIBERAL' TRADITION

The term 'liberal' has an honourable history in political debate about crime and criminal justice. It is now used, often with the adjective 'woolly', to form a pejorative slogan. The implication is that liberals are careless of the financial and economic costs of crime, indifferent to the actual or potential damage to victims, and too much 'on the side' of the offender. For all those reasons they are irresponsible and present a threat not only to the government but also to their fellow citizens and to society.

It is perhaps worth recalling Leon Radzinowicz's account of what he thought liberalism means in the context of criminal justice:[35]

> free will; criminal responsibility; proportionality between the gravity of the crime and the nature and degree of punishment; retribution and deterrence as the major, if not exclusive, functions of punishment; avoidance of indeterminate sentences and as much restriction as possible on administrative interferences in the enforcement of criminal law; discretionary power of the judges admitted to a certain degree but carefully regulated; only acts or omissions strictly defined as offences and declared to be such in laws duly enacted can be made subject to a penal response; no retroactivity and no filling the omissions or gaps in the law by ad-hoc elastic interpretations; judicial independence; openness of an accountability for decisions; a criminal procedure and evidence operating at each stage of the process in strict accordance with the rule of law and with respect for the presumption of innocence.

He continued:

> the liberal ingredient in criminal justice in a country like Britain [has been] much less susceptible than the social ingredient to radical change or insidious manipulations, for the simple reason that it is grounded in the constitutional fabric of the country. But, even so, its historical stability should not be taken for granted.

The liberal ideas which Radzinowicz described in those paragraphs were for him, as they are still for many traditional thinkers, a baseline which future reforms should take as their starting point, or a set of parameters against which they should be tested. And yet there is among politicians (including ministers), many commentators and some practitioners a sense that the liberal agenda for criminal justice has 'failed', in the sense that it has not succeeded in controlling or reducing crime, that it places too much emphasis on individual rights, at the expense of individual and collective responsibilities. For both the Conservative and Labour Governments, that agenda has had the expansion and enforcement of the criminal law, severity of punishment, and increasing use of imprisonment among its prominent features. Both assume the existence of a dangerous, criminal underclass from whom society has to be protected.

A difference between the two governments has been the Labour Government's evangelical determination to rescue, or save, potential offenders and those at an early stage of offending from becoming part of the underclass. The Government is supported in this mission by its faith in new technology, in the mechanisms of risk assessment, and in the various schemes and programmes for confronting offending behaviour. The mission itself is honourable and laudable. Where there are legitimate doubts, they relate to the simplistic view which the Government seems to take of the diverse social and personal situations in which crime comes to be committed; of the complex nature of the institutions, procedures and relationships which make up the criminal justice system and the criminal justice process; and of the inevitably uncertain and often unpredictable outcomes which it expects its policies to produce. The agenda is uncompromisingly utilitarian, and in relation to those who are perceived as belonging to the dangerous underclass, deliberately exclusionary and potentially oppressive. It has very little to say about collective or social responsibilities, or about social justice. Its 'effectiveness' in reducing crime is as yet unproven.

Writers and practitioners who approach crime and criminal justice from a restorative perspective, often founded in the Christian (and especially the Quaker) tradition, share the view that the 'liberal' agenda has been inadequate – not so much because they reject any of its principles, but because it does not in their view pay enough attention to 'communitarian' ideas of public duty and of individual and collective responsibility.[36] Their vision is, however, 'inclusive' in the sense that all people deserve equal respect and there is 'good in everyone', and they reject any idea of a dangerous or undeserving underclass. The 'restorative' agenda, which complements rather than replaces the 'liberal' agenda, is discussed more fully in *Chapter 10*.

Neither retributive nor liberal ideas contain the whole truth about a country's or a society's proper response to crime. Utilitarian and restorative ideas have their place as well. There may, in particular, be a role for restorative or community justice although its scope and character are still, in many ways, uncertain. To acknowledge this is not, however, to say that liberal principles are of any less account, still less to accept that those who support them speak from self-interest or represent some dark and sinister force which is opposed to progress.[37] Leon Radzinowicz argued that

no meaningful advance in penal matters can be achieved in contemporary democratic societies so long as it remains a topic of party political controversy instead of a matter of national concern, cutting across the conventional political alignments.

He was perhaps unrealistic if he supposed that crime or criminal justice can or should be removed from politics; they are matters for political debate, no less than health, education, the environment or levels of taxation. But progress is not helped if the debate is conducted in a spirit of competition, where any proposal from one side has to be criticised from the other, or where the currency is one of slogans, soundbites and half-truths.

ENDNOTES for *Chapter 6*

[1] The complete quotation is

> We must not forget that when every material improvement has been effected in prisons, when the temperature has been rightly adjusted, when the proper food to maintain health has been given, when the doctors, chaplains and prison visitors have come and gone, the convict stands deprived of everything that a free man calls life. We must not forget that all these improvements, which are sometimes salves to our consciences do not change that position. The mood and temper of the public in regard to the treatment of crime and criminals is one of the most unfailing tests of the civilisation of any country. A calm and dispassionate recognition of the rights of the accused against the state, and even of convicted criminals against the state, a constant heart-searching by all charged with the duty of punishment, a desire and eagerness to rehabilitate in the world of industry all those who have paid their dues in the hard coinage of punishment, tireless efforts towards the discovery of curative and regenerating processes, and an unfaltering faith that there is treasure, if only you can find it, in the heart of every man - these are the symbols which in the treatment of crime and criminals mark and measure the stored-up strength of a nation, and are the sign and proof of the living virtue in it.

Winston Churchill, speaking in the House of Commons on 20 July 1910.

[2] The Debate in the House of Commons on the second reading of the Criminal Justice and Court Services Bill on 28 March 2000 was one example.

[3] Barbara Hudson, 'Public Safety and Human Rights' Bill McWilliams memorial lecture 2000, (forthcoming).

[4] Useful sources are Leon Radzinowicz and Roger Hood, *A History of the Criminal Law and its Administration from 1750*, Volume V: *The Emergence of Penal Policy*, London, Stevens and Co, 1986. Also see Leon Radzinowicz's more recent *Adventures in Criminology*, London, Routledge, 1999. From a different perspective, David Garland's *Punishment and Welfare*, Aldershot, Gower, 1985, and *Punishment and Modern Society: A Study in Social Theory*, Oxford, Clarendon Press, 1991.

[5] Nicola Lacey, 'Government as Manager, Citizen as Consumer: The Case of the Criminal Justice Act 1991' in *Modern Law Review*, 54, pp. 534-54, 1994.

[6] *Op. cit.*, n. 4. See also Andrew Ashworth, *Sentencing and Criminal Justice*, third edition, London, Butterworths, 2000, pp. 160-9.

[7] Ian Taylor, Paul Walton and Jock Young, *The New Criminology*, London, Routledge Kegan Paul, 1973.

[8] Paul Walton and Jock Young, *The New Criminology Revisited*, Basingstoke, Macmillan, 1998.

[9] *Op. cit*, n. 4, 231-87.

[10] Jack Straw, *Honesty, Consistency and Progression in Sentencing*, London, Labour Party, 1996. See also *Chapter 12*.

[11] Report from the Departmental Committee on Prisons (The Gladstone Committee), C. 7702, Parliamentary Papers, 1895.

[12] See Desmond King, *In the Name of Liberalism: Liberal Social Policies in the United States and Britain*, Oxford University Press, 1999.

[13] See *Chapter 2*, n. 7.

[14] Capital punishment in the United Kingdom was suspended by the Murder (Abolition of Death Penalty) Act 1965, and effectively made permanent by a vote of both Houses of Parliament on 16 December 1969 'That the Act should not expire'. For an account of the Parliamentary debates and of subsequent attempts to restore capital punishment see Lord Windlesham, *Responses to Crime*, Volume 1 pp. 144-73 and Volume 2 pp. 86-90, Oxford, Clarendon Press, 1987 and 1996; also, for a general historical account based upon Parliamentary proceedings and newspaper reports, see *Hanging in the Balance: A History of the Abolition of Capital Punishment in Britain*, Brian P. Block and John Hostettler, Winchester, Waterside Press, 1998.

[15] D. E. R. Faulkner, 'The Redevelopment of Holloway Prison', *Howard Journal of Penology and Crime Prevention*, 1971 pp. 122-32.

[16] David Wilson and Shane Bryans, 'The Prison Governor: Theory and Practice', *Prison Service Journal*, 1998.

[17] *Prison Service Journal*, September 1982.

[18] Green Paper, *Punishment, Custody and the Community*, Cmnd. 424, London HMSO, 1988. White Paper, *Crime, Justice and Protecting the Public*, Cmnd. 965, London, HMSO, 1990.

[19] Malcolm Feely and Jonathan Simon, 'The New Penology: Notes on the Emerging Strategy of Corrections and its Implications', *Criminology*, 1992, 30 4 pp. 449-74.

[20] Roy King and Rod Morgan, *The Future of the Prison System*, Farnborough, Gower, 1980.

[21] Home Office, *Report of the Committee of the Inquiry into the United Kingdom Prison Services* (The May Report), London, HMSO, 1979.

[22] Malcolm Feely and Jonathan Simon, 'Actuarial Justice the Emerging New Criminal Law', *Punishment and Society*, 2000, 2 1, pp. 23-65.

[23] Kimberly Kempf-Leonard and Elicka S. L. Peterson, 'Expanding the Realms of the New Penology: The Advent of Actuarial Justice for Juveniles', *Punishment and Society*, 2000, 2 1 pp. 66-97.

[24] Richard Jones, 'Digital Rule: Punishment, Control and Technology', *Punishment and Society*, 2000, 2 1, pp. 5-22.

[25] Michael Cavadino, Iain Crow and James Dignan, *Criminal Justice 2000: Strategies for a New Century*, Winchester, Waterside Press, 2000.

[26] Andrew Rutherford, *Criminal Justice and the Pursuit of Decency*, Oxford, Oxford University Press, 1993; reprinted Winchester, Waterside Press, 1996.

[27] David Garland, *The Culture of Control: Crime and Social Order in Contemporary Society*, Oxford, Oxford University Press, 2001.

[28] For a discussion of this problem of 'false positives' see Thomas Mathieson, *Prison on Trial*, second English edition, Winchester, Waterside Press, 2000, pp. 93-101. Michael Tonry has described how punitive and rigid sentencing statutes in the United States are being 'undermined from within' by 'new individualised approaches' originating for example from the burgeoning drug court movement. The movement creates opportunities for diversion which are being extended to more serious offences and offenders so that more offenders who face mandatory sentences if convicted are diverted from prosecution altogether. Michael Tonry 'The Fragmentation of Sentencing and Corrections in America', in *Sentencing and Corrections: Issues in the 21st Century*, No 1, Washington National Institute of Justice, 1999.

[29] David Farrington, 'Human Development and Criminal Careers' in Michael Maguire, Rod Morgan and Robert Reiner (eds.), *The Oxford Handbook of Criminology*, Oxford University Press, 1997 and other sources quoted in that chapter.

[30] Home Office, *Reducing Offending*, Home Office Research Study No. 187, 1997.

[31] Andrew von Hirsch, Anthony Bottoms, Elizabeth Burnet and Per-Olof Wikstrom, *Criminal Deterrence and Sentence Security*, Oxford, Hart Publishing, 1999. For an account of a German study with similar conclusions, see Mathieson, *op. cit.*, n. 28.

[32] Michael Rutter, Henri Giller and Ann Hagell, *Anti-Social Behaviour by Young People*, Cambridge, Cambridge University Press, 1998.

[33] John Pratt, 'The Return of the Wheelbarrowmen: On the arrival of Post Modern Penality' *British Journal of Criminology*, 2000, 40, pp. 127-43.

[34] Lord Windlesham, *Politics, Punishment and Populism*, Oxford, University Press, 1998.

[35] Leon Radzinowicz, *Adventures in Criminology*, London, Routledge, 1999, p. 116.

[36] For example Mike Nellis 'Creating Community Justice' in Scott Ballintyre, Ken Pease and Vic McLaren (eds.), *Secure Foundations: Key Issues in Crime Prevention, Crime Reduction and Community Safety*, London, Institute for Public Policy Research, 2000; Tim Newell, *Forgiving Justice*, Quaker Home Service 2000; Martin Wright, *Restoring Respect for Justice*, Winchester, Waterside Press, 1999.

[37] Kevin Stenson and Robert Sullivan have edited a collection of papers *Crime, Risk and Justice: the Politics of Crime Control in Liberal Democracies*, Cullompton, Devon, Willan Publishing, 2001 which reviews the changing politics of crime and criminal justice in English-speaking 'liberal democracies'- principally Great Britain and the United States but also Canada and Australia and with some references to France and Germany. The authors analyse the shifts in ideas such as liberalism and justice itself; the emergence of risk as a dominant theme in criminal justice and politics more generally; the significance of the new public managerialism, especially as it affects the police; the tensions between central direction and local empowerment; and the influence of the media. They relate their analysis to the 'third way' politics of Tony Blair in Great Britain and Bill Clinton in the United States, and to changes in government policy and in professional and operational practice in areas such as sentencing, crime control, policing and the treatment of suspects 'and criminals'. Reference has already been made to their volume in *Chapters* 2 and 3.

David Garland has described the transition, in Great Britain and the United States, from what he calls 'penal welfarism' (the dominant approach in the 1950s and 1960s), through the process of social change associated with 'late modernity' and the associated predicaments of penal policy, to what he sees as 'a new culture of crime control'. *The Culture of Control: Crime and Social Order in Contemporary Society*, Oxford, Oxford University Press, 2001.

CHAPTER 7

The Politics of Criminal Justice 1979-1992

There is not one single law connected with my name which has not had as its object some mitigation of the severity of the criminal law; some prevention of abuse in the exercise of it; or some security for its impartial administration.

Robert Peel, 1827

POST-WAR CONSENSUS AND CONFIDENCE

Like health and education, criminal justice was part of the post war liberal consensus of the 1950s and 1960s. A progressive measure - the Criminal Justice Act 1948 - was followed by a period of reasonable confidence in which it seemed that the system was working reasonably well and crime could be effectively controlled or even significantly reduced. There was a strong belief in science and its ability to produce more rapid responses and increased detection rates for the police; more accurate assessment of offenders for purposes of sentencing or allocation to prisons or types of regime; and better-designed programmes of training and supervision to reduce rates of re-conviction. Crime would be solved by the resulting combination of deterrence and rehabilitation. Criminology was beginning to emerge as an academic discipline. There was a new interest in research, reflected in the formation of the Home Office Research Unit and the Cambridge Institute of Criminology. It was the age of C. P. Snow and his vision of 'two cultures' and a scientific revolution; a more general belief in the capacity of science to bring about a social transformation, and the need for it to do so; and the 'white heat of scientific revolution' (a slogan of the Labour Government in the mid-1960s).[1] The approach was expressed in the White Papers *Penal Practice in a Changing* Society (1959) and *The War on Crime in England and Wales* (1964). Interesting comparisons can be made with today's emphasis on new technology, risk assessment and 'what works'.

Government was ready to listen to expert opinion, expressed through Royal Commissions, for example on capital punishment and the police; and advisory bodies, such as the Advisory Council on the Treatment of Offenders (later the Advisory Council on the Penal System). The Howard League and the Institute for the Study and Treatment of Delinquency (now the Centre for Crime and Justice Studies) were influential as voluntary organizations. Tensions were beginning to develop between the Prison Service - then the Prison Commission - and the Home Office and ministers, but generally speaking it was still the professionals who, like the doctors and the teachers, had the power and ran the system.

Successive governments saw themselves as responsible for matters of law, structure and finance, but as providing a framework within which the courts and the operational services could carry out their functions to suitable standards and subject to suitable safeguards. Measures to prevent crime were seen mainly in terms of the criminal justice process and not of wider social policies; but the services' functions were not always clearly defined, and their operational tasks were for the most part determined by the services themselves, and often by individuals within them. Governments could not afford to appear 'soft on crime'; the executions of Derek Bentley and Ruth Ellis were to some extent political demonstrations of Maxwell Fyffe's determination to be 'tough'; and Conservative party conferences were always a painful experience for his more liberal successors. But ministers did not think of themselves as managing a system, and certainly not as setting specific objectives which services were expected to achieve on behalf of the government. The political parties did not make their ability to reduce or punish crime a test of their credibility or part of their appeal to the electorate.

There are several features in what has been described which may appeal to a liberal audience at the start of the twenty-first century, and several points of comparison with the situation as it is today. But the 1950s and 1960s were not a golden age to which liberals or technocrats should try to return. The system was often complacent, elitist and exclusive, with little regard for victims or for the rights of offenders, children or minorities. The international instruments on human rights, developed by the United Nations and the Council of Europe with United Kingdom support, were for other nations, not for the British. Little regard was paid to first-line staff. Accountability, if it was thought about at all, was seen in narrow, legalistic terms of statutory powers and duties, or in Parliamentary terms of Members' Questions and letters. Today's notions of openness, responsiveness and accessibility, or of cost-effectiveness and value for money, would scarcely have been understood. The 'establishment' and its social and political influence had come to be recognised, but the significance of culture in the institutions of state was not a focus of serious attention.[2]

The beginnings of doubt
The situation began to change in the 1960s. The confidence of the 1950s and the optimism of *Penal Practice in a Changing Society* gave way to doubt and then to disillusion. Towards the end of its life, the Conservative Government set up a Royal Commission on the Penal System, but it was abandoned after the Labour Government came into office in 1964. (The reasons were complicated: for one account see Leon Radzinowicz's *Adventures in Criminology*.[3]) Investigative journalists were showing that all was not as well as might be supposed with the Prison Service and the police. The Mountbatten Report, following the escape of George Blake from Wormwood Scrubs in 1966, called for and produced a fundamental change in the culture of the Prison Service, with a high status for jobs involved with security and little regard for work with prisoners as people.[4] Police and probation services were amalgamated and the Prison Service acquired a regional organization, seen for a time as a source of power for governors and the service in the field against

what was perceived as the Home Office bureaucracy at headquarters. The academic claim that 'nothing works', overstated and misunderstood though it may have been, led to disillusion in the prison and probation services and with the sentencing practice of the courts. The effectiveness of beat policing came under challenge.[5] Awkward discoveries were made about the significance of race and gender; about situations of discrimination and prejudice; and about the difficulty which all professional and service cultures found in dealing with them. Traditional practices like the censorship of prisoners' letters were successfully challenged in the domestic courts and the European Court of Human Rights. The end of the 1970s saw disturbances in the prisons and large-scale industrial action by prison offices. A pay dispute in the police led first to a breakdown of the negotiating machinery and then to the Edmund Davies review[6], followed by a decade of privileged status (at least in terms of pay) under the Conservative administration. The familiar landmarks of law, structure and culture were being progressively obscured or removed.

The utilitarian approach, and the 'medical' or 'treatment' models associated with it, began to lose favour. The change to a belief that 'nothing works' has sometimes been attributed to the work of R. M. Martinson.[7] But in England the work of Herman Mannheim and Leslie Wilkins[8], and subsequently Vernon Holloway's study of borstal typology[9], had already shown that an offender's subsequent progress could be more or less accurately predicted by reference to the person's history and personality at the time of sentence, regardless of the type of institution or regime to which they might subsequently be allocated. The 'IMPACT' study in the Probation Service, and the Sundsvall experiment in Sweden, similarly suggested that different types of community-based programme made little or no difference.

The 1970s were also a period of administrative upheaval and professional disillusion in the Prison Service, as the prison building programme was abandoned in the face of the country's financial crisis and resources within the service were diverted from young offenders' and training institutions to the high security prisons required by the Mountbatten Report. The Probation Service was similarly under pressure and was making what were at that time professionally painful adjustments to accommodate the new community service order. The imaginative and progressive, but in the circumstances of the time unrealistic, proposals from the Advisory Council on the Penal System, in the report of its Young Offender Review published in 1974[10], made no progress at the time. Some of them - for example the amalgamation of the detention centre order and the borstal training order into a single determinate sentence - were however implemented piecemeal during the 1980s; and the plan for 'clusters' of establishments providing different facilities and regimes and serving defined geographical areas, was revived (for the prison system as a whole) in the Woolf Report in 1991 (see *Chapter 8*).

Managing criminal justice

The 1980s saw an attempt to introduce a greater sense of order to the criminal justice system. While disturbances and industrial action continued to take place in prisons, and the police were facing accusations of malpractice in the Confait Inquiry and disorder on the streets in Brixton, Toxteth and other places, both the Government and the courts and services themselves were trying to develop a stronger sense of coherence and principle. The immediate stimulus was the emphasis on efficiency, economy and effectiveness, which was characteristic of the Conservative administration as a whole. By the Government's own tests of value for money and efficiency, economy and effectiveness, an indefinite expansion in the numbers of police officers or prison places did not score very highly, and stability in prisons - for which some control over the size of the prison population was seen as a necessary condition - was an important political objective. But the search for order and principle, and for a coherent strategy, was proceeding throughout the system, professionally and managerially as well as politically. The underlying principles, which gradually came to be articulated during the decade, were those of proportionality in sentencing, of due process and accountability in administration, and of equity and respect for individuals.[11]

It is easy to think of the change of government in 1979 as a turning point. So it was in many ways, but many of the subsequent changes were built on ideas which had been developed some time previously. The Criminal Justice Acts of 1982 and 1988, for example, built on proposals for the custodial sentencing and treatment of young adults which the Advisory Council on the Penal System had put forward in 1974; and attempts to 'manage' criminal justice as a coherent 'system' can be found in the crime policy planning documents which the Home Office had published in the mid 1970s.

In a 'working paper' published in May 1984[12], the Home Secretary, Leon Britain, announced that the Government had established

a strategy which would enable us to establish and pursue our priorities and objectives in a deliberate and coherent way

and in which

the criminal justice system [was to be] treated in all that we do as a system.

The objective was

to sustain the rule of law:
(a) by preventing crime wherever possible;
(b) when crimes are committed, by detecting the culprit;
(c) by dealing adequately and appropriately with those who are guilty and by giving proper effect to the sentences or orders which are imposed.

A more substantial version of the working paper appeared in November 1986, by which time Douglas Hurd had become Home

Secretary[13]. The strategy had become more complete, and considerably more sophisticated. A chapter on *Principles and Management* included the following.

> Crime is a widespread, intractable and complex phenomenon for which no simple 'causes' can be proved. Its incidence is commonly associated with the presence of wider social problems such as a weakening of the family and a decline in standards of conduct and respect for authority. It follows that there are no simple 'solutions' to the problem of crime as such and that crime cannot be overcome and the needs of the victim cannot adequately be met through the operation of the criminal justice system alone. That system can only react after the crime has taken place. Wider social policies, for example for education, housing, employment and support for the family, must also play a part. Special attention must be given to providing help for victims . . .

> The Government's strategy for dealing with crime has five main elements:

> (i) Promoting action to prevent crime.
> (ii) Providing the criminal justice services, such as police, prisons and probation, with the extra resources they need to meet the increasing demands made on them.
> (iii) Strengthening the powers of the police and the courts while maintaining the necessary safeguards for the individual.
> (iv) Improving the efficiency and effectiveness of all parts of the criminal justice system.
> (v) Providing more effective support and increased reassurance for the victims of crime.

> The Home Office and the various services are working on the design of measures of performance or output. Statistics on criminal justice were in the past produced mainly for the information of Parliament and the public, but they are now being increasingly developed as the basis of a management information system. Research is similarly used to measure performance and the results of new initiatives and changes in practice; and longer term research provides an essential part of the background against which new ideas and fresh options can be considered in the future. An important function of both the Home Office Statistical Department and the Research and Planning Unit is to assemble and analyse the relevant information, from this country and abroad, on the basis of which options can be identified and new approaches can be considered.

Results were becoming available from the *British Crime Survey*[14] which showed that considerably more crime was being committed than the numbers recorded by the police and included in the Criminal Statistics, and that some areas and some groups of people were at much greater risk than others. The elderly, although regarded as especially vulnerable, were least likely to be victims of crime. Victims' views about punishment were broadly in line with police and court practice. Other research showed that about a third of young men had a conviction for a 'standard list' (roughly speaking 'indictable') offence by the age of 30; that of the crime uncovered by the *British Crime Survey* only about two per cent ultimately resulted in a conviction in court. About five per cent of known offenders committed about 70 per cent of detected crime. No clear picture had so far emerged of the extent to which drug misusers were engaged in other forms of crime.

Legislation and policy
Legislation introduced during the 1980s included the Criminal Justice Acts 1982 and 1988, with provisions to give courts more flexibility in sentencing young offenders, but within a more coherent and structured framework; the Police and Criminal Evidence Act 1984, and the Codes of Practice issued under the Act, designed to increase is the openness and accountability of the police; the Prosecution of Offences Act 1985, which established the Crown Prosecution Service as a service independent of the police; and the Public Order Act 1986 which codified a number of common law offences, strengthened police powers in various respects and reinforced the law on incitement to racial hatred.

Policy initiatives included the development of both physical and 'situational' measures for crime prevention (locks, cameras, lighting, the design of buildings and estates) and social measures (focused on potential offenders' motivation and opportunities). The Safer Cities programme sought to encourage comprehensive and 'holistic' approaches to community safety, which combined measures of both kinds and linked them to other programmes in areas such as education, housing, employment and transport (see *Chapter 18*). The Government introduced a major programme of funding for victim support schemes (see *Chapter 15*); supported the development of community policing; and continued its attempts to improve community relations, mainly through training and efforts to recruit or appoint members of ethnic minorities to relevant services and positions (see *Chapter 16*). The emphasis in the Probation Service continued to be on efficiency and effectiveness and on the confidence of the courts, and in the Prison Service on managing overcrowding, the building programme and industrial relations, including new arrangements for pay and working hours ('Fresh Start') designed to eliminate the culture of overtime working. The Home Office sought and cultivated close working relations with voluntary organizations, especially at that time the National Association for the Care and Resettlement of Offenders (NACRO) the National Association of Victim Support Schemes (now Victim Support) and later Crime Concern; and with the academic community.

Sentencing
Sentencing, and the relationship between sentencing and the prison population and prison overcrowding - and less prominently between the use and the design and management of community-based programmes run by the Probation Service - had always been a difficult issue for government. A government which has to provide, run and account for the country's prison system cannot for long remain indifferent to the courts' use of the system through their sentencing practice. Chronic overcrowding, combined with precarious industrial relations, periodical

unrest among prisoners, persistent anxiety over prison security, and continual complaints about prison conditions, were a source of constant concern throughout the 1980s.

Sentencing practice was itself under criticism for being haphazard and inconsistent, too lenient in some cases and too harsh in others. The courts themselves were alive to this criticism. The Lord Chief Justice, Lord Lane, had developed the Court of Appeal's practice of issuing 'guideline judgments' for particular types of offence at the beginning of the 1980s, with his judgments in the cases of *Upton* and *Bibi* (which referred explicitly to the need for courts to be sparing in their use of imprisonment), and the Magistrates' Association subsequently issued its own *Sentencing Handbook*. The Judicial Studies Board became increasingly active in issuing sentencing guidance - cautiously presented as information about recent cases - through seminars and publications. The Government, for its part, had to appear 'tough' on sentencing when the occasion required, for example by promoting legislation to increase the powers available to the police when dealing with public disorder (in the Public Order Act 1986), and also to enable the Attorney General to refer sentences which appeared over-lenient to the Court of Appeal with a view to having them increased.

Direct communication between the judiciary, especially the higher judiciary, and the Home Office was however difficult, particularly if the Home Office appeared to be asking for more leniency in sentencing in order to relieve prison overcrowding; to complain about apparent inconsistency; or to propose, or draw attention to, research on sentencing which might challenge assumptions on matters such as the deterrent effect of a severe sentence.[15] Reasons for the difficulty were partly the risk of appearing to challenge the judiciary's constitutional independence, and partly the political risk to the Government of seeming to be 'soft' on crime. For the most part, prison overcrowding was managed internally within the Prison Service, or by occasional ventures into executive action such as, in 1984, the reduction of the minimum qualifying period for parole, and in 1986 the increase in the period of remission for good conduct. The aim in both cases was to enable more prisoners to become eligible for early release and so reduce prison overcrowding.

Even so the Home Secretary, Douglas Hurd, in a speech to the Magistrates' Association in 1986, said

I would . . . emphasise the importance of doing justice for the offence; of making the punishment fit the crime . . . But doing justice does not just now mean that serious crime needs to be dealt with severely. It also means that the punishment should not be any more severe than the crime warrants. An offender with a long record, for example, deserves the full punishment his offence merits, with no mitigation. He does not deserve to be punished more severely than is justified by the current crime because of offences for which he has already been dealt with. Nor does he deserve to be sent to prison, if the current offence does not call for it, simply because he has previously been given non-custodial sentences . . .

More generally, the search for a broad consistency of approach among magistrates is very important for continued public confidence in the courts. In saying that, I am not suggesting you should strive for a slavish uniformity of outcome. Each case must be judged on its merits. And there must always be a place for a local response to local concerns in what is rightly a local based service. But discussion of sentencing policy and principles has a vital part to play.

Despite the courts' resistance to any suggestion of executive interference in sentencing, the evidence from the figures for the prison population and receptions during the 1980s shows that the courts did generally respond when ministers drew special attention to the problem of overcrowding. It may however have been an unspoken condition of their response to such appeals that the Government should at the same time be pursuing a major programme of prison building which was expected to resolve the problem in the longer term.

Re-appraisal and consolidation

The summer of 1987 brought a re-appraisal and consolidation. The most important strategic question was whether to leave sentencing to the courts, to give political support to severe sentencing as an expression of moral authority or political leadership (there was not much confidence in its deterrent or rehabilitative effect), and to build whatever new prisons were needed to cope with the resulting population. This would have been the easy option. The alternative was to continue and intensify the efforts to control the prison population, and therefore to try and place some limitations on sentencing; and simultaneously to pursue other policies to reduce crime and to deal more effectively with those who committed it. At a meeting at Leeds Castle in September, ministers decided that the prospective increase in the prison population - perhaps reaching 70,000 by the year 2000 - and the associated costs, were more than the country could reasonably afford. They accordingly settled for the second option.[16] The Labour Government faced the same question when it came into office ten years later.

The Home Office, together with the Lord Chancellor's Department and the Crown Prosecution Service, then started to prepare the legislation which became the Criminal Justice Act 1991. A Green Paper *Punishment, Custody and the Community* appeared in 1988, followed in 1990 by two White Papers - *Crime, Justice and Protecting the Public* (on the proposed structure for sentencing); and *Supervision and Punishment in the Community* (on the organization and practice of the Probation Service).[17] The latter included a suggestion that the Probation Service might be reconstructed as an executive agency of the Home Office, but this was not pursued until the Labour Government came into office in 1997. The two papers were the subject of intensive consultation with the criminal justice services, voluntary organizations, academic criminologists and, tentatively but with increasing confidence, the judiciary. The White Papers followed a major, and still probably unique, conference which brought together all the most senior figures of the criminal justice system in England and Wales, with representatives from Scotland and Northern Ireland, at Ditchley Park in the autumn of 1989.

The Act was passed two years later. It laid out a sentencing framework in which a custodial sentence could be imposed only if the offence was so serious that no other sentence could be justified; and a community sentence - probation and community service orders and a new 'combination order' combining both probation and community service - could be imposed only if the offence was serious enough to justify the restriction of liberty involved. Courts were to give reasons for certain decisions, but 'seriousness' was not defined and its interpretation was left to the courts themselves. Other sections of the Act introduced a system of means-related 'unit fines', reduced the maximum penalties for theft and non-domestic burglary, provided for curfew orders backed by electronic monitoring, and created a youth court to exercise the criminal jurisdiction of the former juvenile court (aspects of family jurisdiction having been separated from it under the Children Act 1989). There was also provision for the contracting-out of escorts and other functions of the Prison Service, and various measures to improve the efficiency of criminal justice services generally. Detailed and subsequentially controversial sections dealt with the treatment of multiple offences and previous convictions.[18] The sentencing provisions of the Criminal Justice Act 1991, and of other criminal justice legislation, were subsequently consolidated in the Powers of Criminal Courts (Sentences) Act 2000. References in this book are to the original statutes.

Reform of parole

While consultations were proceeding on the Green and White Papers, a committee had been sitting under the chairmanship of Lord Carlisle to examine the future of the parole system, and in particular to resolve the anomaly which had arisen from the reduction in the minimum period of imprisonment to be served. This anomaly had resulted in the custodial part of many prison sentences - those between 12 months up to and including two years - becoming much the same (about eight months). The judges had found this situation deeply objectionable, and in their concern to have it corrected they may have acquiesced more readily than they might otherwise have done in the sentencing proposals as they had been set out in the Green and White Papers.

The new structure which the Carlisle Committee recommended was largely implemented by the 1991 Act, with the following effect.[19]

- All prisoners sentenced to less than four years would be released on licence after half their sentence (except for any days added for offences committed in prison).
- Prisoners serving four years or more would have to serve half their sentence (instead of one third previously) before becoming eligible for parole. Those granted parole would then be released on licence, others would be released on licence after serving two thirds of the sentence.

- All prisoners serving 12 months or more would be 'at risk' of having the unexpired portion of their sentence added to any new sentence which a court might impose if they were convicted of another offence.

The intention and the effect was to make the whole of the sentence, as imposed by the court, 'count' in the sense that the prisoner would be subject to restrictions for the full term of the sentence including that portion which might be served in the community. The Carlisle Committee's aims, consistently with those which now informed the Government's criminal justice policy as a whole, were among others to provide for a greater degree of consistency, and to introduce a greater degree of openness, fairness and procedural justice into the decision-making process.

Wider criminal justice and social policies
In parallel with the Criminal Justice Act 1991, and complementary to it, the Government promoted a wide range of policies to prevent crime, reduce offending, and improve the fairness and efficiency of the criminal justice system. They included the following.

- A vigorous programme of crime prevention, including the Safer Cities programme already mentioned, and the formation and support for the new voluntary organization Crime Concern, and work with established voluntary organizations such as NACRO.
- A nationwide service to victims of crime, especially through Victim Support but also through statutory services such as the police and probation services, formalised by the first *Victim's Charter*, issued in 1990.
- Measures to reduce discrimination against ethnic minorities and women, including the recruitment and training of staff, ethnic monitoring and a provision in the Criminal Justice Act itself (Section 95) which required the Secretary of State to publish information which would help those working in the criminal justice system to perform 'their duty to avoid discriminating against any person on the ground of race or sex or any other improper ground'.
- The development of 'community policing', with an emphasis on prevention and responsiveness as well as on arrests and law enforcement, together with a programme to improve the quality of the police service to the public.

Regular trilateral meetings were held between the Home Office, the Lord Chancellor's Department and the Crown Prosecution Service to share information and agree objectives, but attempts to extend this form of 'joined-up government' to other departments were less successful. Ministers did not proceed with a suggestion for a broadly based, inter-departmental programme of 'action for youth', which would to some extent have anticipated the Labour Government's later initiatives on the

New Deal for training and employment, youth justice, truancy and exclusion from school, and social exclusion.

The Woolf Report

A series of disturbances, which began at Strangeways Prison in Manchester and subsequently spread to a number of other large prisons, led to an inquiry by Lord Justice Woolf and Judge Stephen Tumim, Her Majesty's Chief Inspector of Prisons (as they then were), whose report was the most comprehensive and penetrating one on prisons and imprisonment since the Gladstone Committee report 100 years before.[20] The disturbances extended over a period of two or three weeks, and probably brought the prison system nearer to the point of breakdown - in the sense of being unable to accept prisoners from courts - than it had been before or has been since. The only comparable situation, in that respect, had been brought about by prison officers' industrial action some ten years before. The Inquiry was remarkable for the degree of openness with which it was conducted and the range of organizations and individuals who contributed to it. It comprised an 'Overview', with 12 major and potentially far reaching recommendations; and an analysis, with more detailed recommendations, of the disturbances themselves.

The recommendations in the 'Overview' were entirely consistent with the Government's approach to criminal justice as it has been described in this chapter, but it is ironic that politically it would have been virtually impossible for the Government - or any recent government - to put them forward on its own account. They are worth quoting in full.

We recommend

1. Closer co-operation between the different parts of the Criminal Justice System. For that purpose a national forum and local committees should be established;
2. More visible leadership of the Prison Service by a Director General who is and is seen to be the operational head and in day-to-day charge of the Service. To achieve this there should be a published 'compact' or 'contract' given by Ministers to the Director General of the Prison Service, who should be responsible for the performance of that 'contract' and publicly answerable for the day-to-day operations of the Prison Service;
3. Increased delegation of responsibility to Governors of establishments;
4. An enhanced role for prison officers;
5. A 'compact' or 'contract' for each prisoner setting out the prisoner's expectations and responsibilities in the prison in which he or she is held;
6. A national system of Accredited Standards, with which, in time, each prison establishment would be required to comply;
7. A new Prison Rule that no establishment should hold more prisoners than is provided for in its certified normal level of accommodation, with provisions for Parliament to be informed if exceptionally there is to be a material departure from that rule;
8. A public commitment from Ministers setting a timetable to provide access to sanitation for all inmates at the earliest practicable date not later than February 1996;

9. Better prospects for prisoners to maintain their links with families and the community through more visits and home leaves and through being located in community prisons as near to their homes as possible;
10. A division of prison establishments into small and more manageable and secure units;
11. A separate statement of purpose, separate conditions and generally a lower security categorisation for remand prisoners;
12. Improved standards of justice within prisons involving the giving of reasons to a prisoner for any decision which materially and adversely affects him; a grievance procedure and disciplinary proceedings which ensure that the Governor deals with most matters under his present powers, relieving Boards of Visitors of their adjudicatory role; and providing for final access to an independent Complaints Adjudicator.

Of these the first and last were probably the most significant. The Government accepted the 'direction' set by the key recommendations and announced its conclusions, including the formation of the National Criminal Justice Consultative Council, the intention to establish area committees, the appointment of a Prisons ombudsman, and the longer-term development of community prisons in the White Paper *Custody Care and Justice*.[21]

Principles and objectives
There had thus begun to emerge a reasonably coherent set of principles and objectives, and the beginnings of a strategic vision of the direction which future developments might take. The principles underlying these objectives included proportionality in sentencing; structured decision-making; due process and accountability in administration, including the giving of reasons; recognised and accessible channels for complaint; equity in the provision of services; and respect for individuals, including members of ethnic or cultural minorities.

The objectives were to

- prevent and reduce crime;
- establish a more coherent and principled basis for sentencing and parole;
- avoid the unnecessary use of imprisonment and stabilise the prison population;
- develop schemes of supervision in the community which would effectively reduce re-offending;
- give greater consideration to victims; and
- make the system more efficient, effective and accountable.

New statements of purpose were issued for the police, prison and probation services. For the police it was

The purpose of the police service is to uphold the law fairly and firmly; to prevent crime; to pursue and bring to justice those who break the law; to keep the Queen's peace; to protect, help and reassure the community; and to be seen to do this with integrity, common-sense and sound judgement.

For the Prison Service it was

> Her Majesty's Prison Service serves the public by keeping in custody those committed by the courts.
>
> Our duty is to look after them with humanity, and to help them to lead law-abiding and useful lives, in custody and after release.

And for the Probation Service:

> The Probation Service serves the courts and the public by:
>
> * supervising offenders in the community;
> * helping offenders to lead law-abiding lives;
> * safeguarding the welfare of children and family proceedings.

For a brief period at the end of 1992 and during 1993, the prison population was below the nominal capacity of the system, as measured by the certified normal accommodation (the population was only 40,600 in December 1992).

Ambiguity and weakness

A paper presented to a conference of European judges and prosecutors, convened by the Dutch Ministry of Justice and by NACRO in Breda in The Netherlands in October 1990, tried to give an impression of that emerging strategic vision.[22] The situation was however precarious, as the paper recognised. It was difficult for Ministers to express those objectives, and still more the principles, in a straightforward, unambiguous way when it was at the same time politically necessary to give an over-riding impression of being 'tough on crime'. One consequence was the 'twin track' or 'bifurcatory' approach to sentencing which came to be embodied in the Criminal Justice Act 1991. This approach promoted community sentences for minor offenders and longer prison sentences for serious, and especially violent and sexual offenders, but the public emphasis was always on the latter. Different messages were given to different audiences, and were interpreted accordingly. Another consequence was the rhetoric of 'punishment in the community', with its emphasis on the demanding nature of the requirements imposed by probation orders and community service orders to the exclusion of their rehabilitative or preventive effect (admittedly difficult to demonstrate from any evidence which has been available then or subsequently). A third consequence, although consistent with the traditions of English legislative drafting, was the absence from legislation of any statutory sentencing principles, as distinct from procedural requirements, to reinforce the provisions on sentencing in Criminal Justice Acts of 1982 and 1987 and especially the Act of 1991.[23]

A more fundamental problem may have been that the Government's commitment to efficiency and effectiveness carried an implication that it should be possible to deal with the problem of crime simply by improvements in management and the deployment of resources. Not only that, but the view was beginning to gain ground that criminal justice is a process which exists not so much to achieve justice (admittedly a rather nebulous concept), but to control crime by catching, convicting and punishing offenders. Its outputs are convictions and sentences, and its outcome is public safety. Against this view, the information emerging from the *British Crime Survey* and other sources was particularly damaging. Examples were the small proportion of offences which are traced to an offender who is then convicted in court; the fact that a large proportion of crime is attributable to a relatively small number of young men in their late teens; and the realisation that community sentences seem to be no more 'effective' in terms of reconvictions than imprisonment. The situation was particularly difficult for a Government whose political convictions prevented it from pursuing social policies which might have had a greater effect on the level of crime, for example in relation to employment, housing and social security, or by giving a greater role to local government. The result was a sense that the criminal justice system was somehow failing the nation, a sense which was compounded by the discovery of the notorious miscarriages of justice in cases involving Irish terrorism and other conspicuous offences. Critics made it appear that the system was doing very little to prevent crime, that it was allowing many criminals to go free, and that when people were convicted, the conviction turned out too often to be unsafe.

The consequences of the Government's ambiguity, and of the increasing weakness in its political position, are described in the next chapter.

ENDNOTES for *Chapter 7*

[1] *Penal Practice in a Changing Society: Aspects of Future Development*, Cmnd. 645, London, HMSO, 1959 and *The War on Crime in England and Wales*, London, HMSO, 1964.

[2] Mick Ryan, 'Penal Policy Making Towards the Millennium: Elites and Populists; New Labour and the New Criminology', *International Journal of the Sociology of Law*, 1999, 27, pp. 1-22.

[3] Leon Radzinowicz, *Adventures in Criminology*, London, Routledge, 1999.

[4] Home Office, *Report of the Inquiry into Prison Escapes and Security* (The Mountbatten Report) , Cmnd. 3175, London, HMSO, 1966.

[5] Ronald Clarke and Michael Hough (eds.), *The Effectiveness of Policing*, Aldershot, Gower, 1990; Ronald Clarke and Michael Hough, *Crime and Police Effectiveness*, London, Home Office Research Unit, 1984; Michael Hough, 'The Police Patrol Function: What Research Can Tell Us', in W. Saulsbury, J. Mott and T. Newburn (eds.), *Themes in Contemporary Policing*, London, Police Foundation/Policy Studies Institute, 1996.

[6] Committee of the Inquiry on the Police (Chairman, Lord Edmund Davis), *Report on Negotiating Machinery and Pay*, Cmnd. 7283, London, HMSO, 1978.

[7] R. M. Martinson, 'What Works? – Questions and Answers about Penal Reform', *Public Interest*, Spring 1974, 35, pp. 22-54.

[8] Herman Mannheim, *Prediction Methods in Relation to Borstal Training*, London, HMSO, 1955. The work of Leslie Wilkins includes: *Social Policy, Action and Research: Studies in*

Social Deviance, London, Tavistock, 1967 and *Evaluation of Penal Measures*, New York, Random House, 1969.

[9] Vernon Holloway, Sheila Speirs and David Grayson, *Neighbourhood Borstals: Interim Papers on their Evaluation*, London, Home Office, Directorate of Psychological Services, 1977.

[10] Advisory Council on the Penal System, *Young Offender Review - Report*, London, HMSO, 1974.

[11] More detailed accounts of the way in which legislation, policy and practice developed during the 1980s can be found in Lord Windlesham's *Responses to Crime: Penal Policy in the Making*, Volume 2, Oxford, Oxford University Press, 1996; Ian Dunbar and Anthony Langdon, *Tough Justice Sentencing and Penal Policies in the 1990s*, London, Blackstone Press, 1998; and in Michael Cavadino, Iain Crow and James Dignan, *Criminal Justice 2000*, Winchester, Waterside Press, 2000.

[12] Home Office, *Criminal Justice: a Working Paper*, London, Home Office, 1984.

[13] Home Office, *Criminal Justice: a Working Paper*, Revised Edition, London, Home Office, 1986.

[14] In 1982 the Home Office initiated the *British Crime Survey* to complement the annually published *Criminal Statistics*. The survey consisted of over 10,000 interviews with members of the general population who had been victims of crime. It has been repeated regularly since then.

[15] Doubts about the deterrent effect of sentencing began to be expressed in an article by Robert Baxter and Christopher Nuttall, 'Severe Sentences: No Deterrent to Crime', *New Society*, 2 January 1975. A more substantial study followed later that year: Stephen Brody *The Effectiveness of Sentencing*, Home Office Research Study No. 35, London, Home Office, 1995.

[16] Lord Windlesham describes the meeting in Volume 2 of *Responses to Crime*, , Oxford, Oxford University Press, 1993, p. 215.

[17] Home Office, *Punishment, Custody and the Community*, Cmnd. 424, London, HMSO, 1988; *Crime, Justice and Protecting the Public*, Cmnd. 965, London, HMSO, 1990 and *Supervision and Punishment in the Community*, London, HMSO, 1991.

[18] Section 2(2) and Section 29.

[19] *The Parole System in England and Wales, Report of the Review Committee*, Cmnd. 532, London, HMSO, 1988.

[20] Lord Justice Woolf, *Report of an Inquiry into the Prison Disturbances of April 1990*, Cmnd. 1456, London, HMSO, 1991.

[21] Home Office, *Custody, Care and Justice: The Way Ahead for the Prison Service in England and Wales*, Cmnd. 1647, London, HMSO, 1991.

[22] David Faulkner, 'Policy, Legislation and Practice', a paper presented to a conference of European and Canadian judges held in Breda, the Netherlands in October 1990. Copies are available from Waterside Press or from the University of Oxford Centre for Criminological Research.

[23] Nicola Lacey, 'Government as Manager, Citizen as Consumer: the Case of the Criminal Justice Act 1991', *Modern Law Review*, 1994, 57, pp. 534-54.

LIVERPOOL JOHN MOORES UNIVERSITY
LEARNING SERVICES

CHAPTER 8

The Conservative Government 1993-1997

Before long a consistent pattern could be detected of conforming to perceived public opinion, taking particular notice of the coverage of crime and editorial comment in the broadsheet and tabloid press. As an inevitable result, decisions began to be taken piecemeal, often dictated by what was thought most likely to appeal to an insecure and resentful general public.

Lord Windlesham, *Responses to Crime*, Volume 3, p. 41.

A change of political mood took place at the end of 1993, accompanied by a dramatic change in the Government's own political style and direction. The change at this time was probably more fundamental than any which could be associated with a change of government, for example in 1979 or 1997. It was partly a response to the figures for recorded crime, which were rising again after slight falls at the end of the 1980s. It was also a reaction to the situation described in the previous chapter, and to the ambiguity which had been inherent in the Government's previous approach. But it can also be traced to the difficulties within the Conservative Party and its leadership after the United Kingdom's withdrawal from the European Exchange Rate Mechanism, and later its accession to the Maastricht Treaty, in the autumn of 1992. Those events created an urgent need for the Government to re-unite the Party around a suitable populist issue, and crime and law and order were a natural choice. However that may be, the change was for the most part supported by other political parties. No party can easily oppose a populist law and order campaign once it gathers momentum.

JUVENILE CRIME

During the two years 1992-1993, the police conducted a sophisticated and mostly successful campaign for more punitive action to be taken against persistent juvenile offenders. This campaign gained a special and tragic momentum from the murder of two-year old Jamie Bulger by two ten-year-old boys, and the public impression that the whole country was at risk from dangerous children who were somehow out of control. A parallel campaign argued for a more restrictive use of bail, with a claim that 'bail bandits' were committing large numbers of offences while on bail in the belief that they could do so with impunity. The police also argued for changes in the law to prevent the 'abuse' of the criminal justice process by defendants who exercised their rights to silence under police questioning and to decline to give evidence in court, and also their right of access to evidence which the police might have collected but which was not to form part of the prosecution case.

The campaign on juvenile crime came as a surprise to many practitioners, and seemed hard to explain in any rational terms. The policy of diverting juvenile offenders from custody and substituting programmes of 'intermediate treatment' in the community had been regarded as quite a success in the 1980s. The number of juveniles sent into custody had fallen, but so had the number of offences which were attributed to juvenile offenders. The peak age of known offending had risen from 15 to about 18. The police claim, and the public and political perception, that juvenile crime was rising, and that juvenile offenders were becoming both more persistent and nastier, was difficult to reconcile with the statistics or to substantiate with more than anecdotal or impressionistic evidence. With hindsight, the fact is that the police themselves were probably ignoring quite a lot of juvenile crime, perhaps in the belief that 'nothing would happen' if they made an arrest or began a prosecution. Programmes of intermediate treatment were also of variable quality, and were not always consistently applied. Reviewing the situation in 1996, the Audit Commission thought that actual juvenile crime had probably not fallen, but nor was there any evidence of a substantial increase.[1] There was however seen to be a need for a much tighter, more systematic and more closely co-ordinated set of arrangements for youth justice and this became a prominent part of the Labour Government's programme on its return to office in 1997.

ABUSE OF THE SYSTEM

The supposed abuse of the criminal justice process by unscrupulous defendants and their lawyers was a theme which had persisted throughout the 1990s. So had abuse of the social security system (although not the evasion of income tax). Complaints of manipulation or abuse surfaced again under the Labour Government with proposals to restrict legal aid; to provide incentives (such as 'discounted' prison sentences) for early admissions of guilt; to limit access to trial by jury in the Crown Court. The Conservative Government introduced legislation to create new offences which were 'absolute' and easy to prove in order to deal with various forms of protest, nuisance, and public disorder (for example in the Criminal Justice and Public Order Act 1994, and the Prevention of Harassment Act 1997). The Labour Government took the process further in the Crime and Disorder Act 1998. The extent of any such abuse is always difficult to judge; and it is equally difficult to judge whether for every unscrupulous defendant or unscrupulous lawyer there may be ten confused or vulnerable defendants, or conscientious but frustrated lawyers, who need the protection or support of the safeguards which are being criticised. There is no reason to be complacent about the system's ability to produce outcomes which are invariably fair and just, especially at a time when governments are inclined to see the proper outcome of the process as public safety rather than justice for its own sake.

THE ROYAL COMMISSION ON CRIMINAL JUSTICE

The dramatic miscarriages of justice in cases such as the Guildford Four and the Birmingham Six alerted the country to the problem and the Royal Commission on Criminal Justice was set up to address it. But it is significant that the Royal Commission was required by its terms of reference

> to examine the effectiveness of the criminal justice system in England and Wales in securing the conviction of those guilty of criminal offences and the acquittal of those who are innocent, having regard to the efficient use of resources . . .

These words place the Royal Commission firmly within the managerial and instrumental culture of the time, and the Commission responded accordingly. Its report[2] gave as much attention to securing more convictions as it did to protecting those who might be innocent or vulnerable, and most of it reads more as a management consultant's review of the criminal justice process than a study of the means of balancing collective and individual human rights.[3] Neither the Commission nor the Government would have had much time for Blackstone's dictum that *it is better that ten guilty persons escape than one innocent suffers.*[4] The Commission did however recommend the long overdue creation of an independent commission to consider allegations of possible miscarriages of justice with a view to their reference to the Court of Appeal, so removing this function from the Home Office where it had for many years been a source of external complaint and internal discomfort. Its recommendation became the basis for the Criminal Appeal Act 1995. It also commissioned some valuable research, including some inconclusive comparisons with inquisitorial systems of justice in other European jurisdictions, and it made some useful practical recommendations, which have generally been adopted, on the treatment of victims and members of minority groups.

No action was, however, taken on its recommendation that the Contempt of Court Act 1981 should be amended to enable research to be undertaken into juries' reasons for their verdicts. Nor was action taken until after the report of the Stephen Lawrence Inquiry on its recommendations for more systematic ethnic monitoring, and for further research into the extent to which minority communities suffer discrimination. And no action taken on the recommendation for a system of prosecution fines, which *Chapter 21* suggests should now be revived. The majority of the Commission was against changes in the defendant's 'right of silence' which later formed part of the Criminal Justice and Public Order Act 1994; but the Commission recommended in favour of restrictions on a defendant's right to insist on a trial before a jury, similar to those eventually proposed in the Labour Government's abortive Criminal Justice (Mode of Trial) Bills in 2000.

The programme for improving the efficiency of the courts, and of the criminal justice process, continued with the Review of Delay in the Criminal Justice System, whose report (the Narey Report) was published early in 1997.[5]

THE FATE OF THE CRIMINAL JUSTICE ACT 1991

In relation to sentencing, it quickly became evident that Home Secretaries Kenneth Clarke, and still more Michael Howard, did not share their predecessors' confidence in the Criminal Justice Act 1991. Open criticism came from the judiciary, especially and in surprisingly fierce language, from the newly appointed Lord Chief Justice Lord Taylor (who had not been present at the earlier discussions at Ditchley Park mentioned in *Chapter 7*). In a speech in Scotland on 23 March 1993 he described the Act's sentencing provisions as 'forcing the judge into an ill-fitting straightjacket'. Other criticism focused on the lack of flexibility in unit fines, and for a time the Act and those associated with its preparation were the subject of ridicule by the media. A series of judgments by the Court of Appeal, delivered together early in 1993, especially those in *Cunningham* and *Cox* had the effect of reinterpreting (some critics[6] have said undermining) the intentions of the Act, for example by reintroducing the notions of deterrence and prevalence to the test of seriousness and of weakening the requirement for courts to give reasons.

In a series of hastily prepared amendments, the Government extended the scope of a relatively routine Criminal Justice Bill then before Parliament to abolish the system of unit fines and to amend the 1991 Act's most controversial provisions on related sentences and previous criminal records. The introduction of unit fines had not been well managed, mainly because the 'gearing' between unit and monetary values, carefully tested in pilot schemes, had been thrown into disorder by a simultaneous increase in maximum penalties. But it should not have been necessary to abandon the whole scheme, as Alun Michael argued for the Labour Opposition at the time.

The other two amendments were probably necessary, and they enabled the Lord Chief Justice to say later in the year

> I believe the philosophy of the Criminal Justice Act 1991 as it was envisaged still holds good. I believe, though, that the amendments have improved it and made it more realistic. The philosophy of the Act is very simple as far as custody is concerned. It is just this - that the courts should not send anybody to a period of custody unless the seriousness of the offending behaviour makes a custodial penalty the only viable option or where, in the case of serious violent or sexual offences, the public needs to be protected from a dangerous offender.[7]

Even so, the Government and the judiciary had demonstrated that the Act's intention of limiting the use of imprisonment was no longer to be taken seriously. The prison population began to rise as courts responded to the new political climate.

The Government took its punitive and populist approach a stage further in the following year. Following the Home Secretary's speech at the Conservative Party Conference in October 1993, the Government introduced the Bill which became the Criminal Justice and Public Order Act 1994. Its provisions included

- a new secure training order for persistent juvenile offenders, to be served in secure training centres built and run by commercial companies;
- a range of new 'absolute' offences aimed at squatters, travellers, demonstrators and other troublesome groups with the intention that convictions should be easier to obtain;
- changes in the law of evidence designed to strengthen the prosecution's position against the defence, for example the abolition of the so-called 'right of silence' - in effect a provision which allowed the court to draw adverse influences from a defendant's silence when questioned.
- increased penalties for various offences and increased maximum periods of custody for children and young offenders;
- restrictions on the grant of bail.

Two years later, the Government introduced the Bill which became the Crime (Sentences) Act 1997. The Act broke new ground in modern times by providing mandatory sentences of life imprisonment for second convictions of certain serious violent or sexual offences, and mandatory minimum sentences of seven years for second convictions for offences involving the manufacturing or supply of class A drugs. It also provided for mandatory minimum sentences of three years for third convictions for burglary, although the implementation of this provision was delayed because of its expected effect on the prison population. The Labour Government brought it into effect early in 1999. Their purpose was partly deterrent, in defiance of the evidence that severe prison sentences do not have a significant deterrent effect but also, and more importantly, to remove the judges' discretion to impose what the Government considered to be unacceptably lenient sentences, even if they thought a less severe sentence was justified by the circumstances of the case. The Act further provided for 'truth in sentencing' in the sense of requiring the term to be served in prison to correspond much more closely with the term of the sentence expressed in court (in effect setting aside the conclusions of the Carlisle Committee as enacted in the Criminal Justice Act 1991), but this part of the Act was never brought into effect.

The Government had now effectively abandoned its earlier attempts to establish a principled and coherent approach to sentencing, to restrain the growth in the prison population and reduce prison overcrowding, and to promote community sentences as the normal disposal for all but the most serious offences. 'Prison works' became a political slogan, and the language of warfare - the 'war on crime', police 'in the front line', an 'armoury of weapons' to 'defeat criminals' - came back into common use. Because of its implications of an 'enemy', and its suggestion that any methods could be justified if they succeeded, the Government had avoided language of warfare since the Scarman report ten years before.[8]

OTHER CRIMINAL JUSTICE POLICIES

Crime prevention receded from the active political agenda, and no action was taken on the principal recommendation of the Home Office Standing Conference on Crime Prevention - namely that crime prevention should become a clearly defined, statutory duty of local authorities in its important and widely welcomed report on *Safer Communities* (the Morgan Report).[9] Issues relating to victims became dominated by controversy over the Government's proposals for reforming the Criminal Injuries Compensation Scheme in order to control its costs, and the eventual passage of the Criminal Injuries Compensation Act 1995. The Government ignored the carefully considered proposals put forward by an independent working group set up by Victim Support; and its own proposals, designed principally to control expenditure on compensation with little regard for wider considerations, were successfully challenged by an application for judicial review when the Government thought it could bring them into effect without legislation.[10]

The practical managerialism of the early 1980s was giving way to a more assertive and more dogmatic form of central direction, across the whole of government, based on notions of contracts and markets. Power was increasingly concentrated at the centre; and responsibility, and blame when things went wrong, was devolved to local managers. A new commercial model was being superimposed upon the professional, bureaucratic and (in the police and prison services) command structures which had competed with one another in the past.

The managerial or instrumental view of justice was also reflected in a White Paper on Police Reform[11], with its emphasis on law enforcement and the detection and arrest of criminals as the principal functions of the police; and its neglect of those public service functions which had featured in the statement of purpose three years earlier - for example to prevent crime and to protect, help and reassure the community. The White Paper, and the Police and Magistrates' Courts Act 1994 which followed, were accompanied by political and media campaigns to reinforce the culture of aggressive law enforcement and to discredit the ideas of public accountability, responsiveness and community policing which the police themselves had successfully developed following the Scarman report on the urban disorders at the beginning of the 1980s and the Police and Criminal Evidence Act 1984. Opposition in the House of Lords forced the Government to make a number of concessions during the passage of the Bill.[12]

A further White Paper *Protecting the Public* published in 1996[13] once again recognised the importance of the preventive role of the police and of public trust and local consultation, as well as emphasising the importance of efficiency and effectiveness in controlling crime. In relation to the courts, the White Paper restated the Government's (or more accurately it should have said Parliament's) traditional role in providing a statutory framework for sentencing. It proposed a range of measures - community service and attendance centre orders or disqualification from driving - for those who were unable or who refused to pay fines, together with the range of mandatory sentences which have already been described. The proposals in the White Paper were subsequently enacted in the Crime (Sentences) Act 1997.

STANDARDS AND INDICATORS

Standards for the treatment of prisoners had originally been conceived, for example by the United Nations and the Council of Europe, and as an instrument of penal reform. The Prison Service had seen them as a means of limiting prison overcrowding when it had proposed the preparation of a code of standards in 1982 - a proposal which the Government had for a short time accepted. Standards, or 'key performance indicators', came to be applied - in prisons and elsewhere - as an instrument of standardisation, audit, risk avoidance and government control. Combined with the emphasis on punishment, intended in the 1980s to give credibility to community sentences, the new form of political managerialism began to substitute a culture of mechanical enforcement and compliance for the ideas of personal progress and development which had traditionally informed probation programmes and prison regimes. The Government's development of Probation Service standards, its proposals effectively to remove the professional content from probation training, and its consultation paper on *Strengthening Punishment in the Community*[14] were obvious examples. The service itself was submitted to unremitting criticism and frequent humiliation for its supposed lack of effectiveness.

THE PRISON SERVICE AS AN EXECUTIVE AGENCY

Under the Government's 'Next Steps' programme[15] of public service reform, the Prison Service became an executive agency of the Home Office with effect from 1 April 1993. The change was designed to give the Prison Service a greater degree of managerial and operational autonomy, within a framework of 'tough and demanding' targets and standards. It was also intended to give the service a degree of independence from day-to-day ministerial control, symbolised by the fact that the Director General, rather than the prisons Minister, would reply to enquiries and Questions from Members of Parliament. The change followed soon after the Woolf Report and the Government's White Paper on *Crime, Justice and Protecting the Public*. The Prison Service itself, and many penal reformers, welcomed it as providing a platform from which the service would be able to adopt a higher public profile and assert its interests, and those of prisoners themselves, more effectively than had been possible under the normal civil service rules of conduct. With the population apparently stable at around 44,000 and a Government still apparently committed to a programme of penal reform on the lines of the Woolf Report, the service's future looked more promising than at any time during its members' previous careers. The Director General, Joe Pilling, expressed this spirit of optimism in a remarkable address at the end of 1992.[16]

Disillusion set in as the prison population began to rise, and the prospects for prison reform began to recede under the renewed pressure of overcrowding and a different political agenda. The expected freedom from political intervention gave way to day-to-day ministerial involvement in the running of prisons and the treatment of prisoners, usually in pursuit of harsher, or 'more austere', conditions and more restrictive treatment of individuals. The situation was exacerbated by the notorious escapes from Whitemoor and Parkhurst prisons, the inquiries and damaging reports which followed, and the measures which were taken as a result (including the dismissal of Derek Lewis (Joe Pilling's successor as Director General: see *Chapter 2* for a discussion of its wider constitutional significance). Even so, the service was able to make progress during this period by virtually abolishing the practices of slopping out and of accommodating prisoners three in a cell, in increasing the time which most prisoners spent out of their cells and engaged in constructive activity, and in improving its professional skills, especially in matters of security and control. A provision in the Criminal Justice and Public Order Act 1994 finally removed by statute the right of prison officers to take industrial action. (Their status as constables had probably denied them that right many years before, but neither ministers nor Prison Service managers had been willing to test the issue in the courts.)

It is possible to argue that the failure to realise the hopes generated by the Woolf Report and by agency status was a consequence of the political situation at the time, to which the service's status and structure as an executive agency had no relevance. So it was to some extent, and no organizational structure can, or should, remove a public service entirely from ministerial, political or democratic influence. But agency status for the Prison Service was unique in the sense that the service had argued, successfully, that in the prison setting 'policy' could not be separated from 'operations' in the way which had been fundamental in the setting up of other agencies elsewhere in government (see *Chapter 2*). Whereas for other agencies the 'policy', or 'purchasing' or 'commissioning', function had remained in the central department concerned, with the 'operational' or 'providing' function going to the agency, the Prison Service retained both functions within itself.

The Service was right to argue that policy for prisons cannot be entirely separated from operations. But the service was not able to sustain the argument (and probably did not try) once it became politically convenient, perhaps indeed necessary, to make the separation in order to secure a minister's political survival after the escape from

Parkhurst. What the events of the mid-1990s show is the need to re-examine the status and structure of the Prison Service in order to define more clearly the respective functions of the Secretary of State and the managers of the Service, and the relationship between them. The Woolf report had recognised the need for a new and clearer definition, which would ultimately have to be enacted by statute, and it had recommended that there should be a new Prison Act. The Government had accepted this recommendation in *Crime, Justice and Protecting the Public*, but without giving it any priority. The status and structure of the Prison and Probation Service are considered in more detail in *Chapters 19* and *20*.

CONCLUSIONS

Lord Windlesham summed up the period from 1993 to 1997 in the words quoted at the beginning of this chapter.

Many of those who write from a ' liberal' point of view are inclined to portray the mid-1990s as a 'dark age' in British, or certainly English, criminal justice, marked by oppressive legislation, exclusive or exclusionary policies, and punitive attitudes. But another and potentially more telling criticism, at any rate in the short term, is that it was a period in which - for all the managerial and political skills which were supposedly brought to bear - the management and politics of criminal justice were badly handled, with too little strategic direction and too little regard for professional judgement or advice. The blatant attempts to achieve political popularity did not seem to bring the Government much credit, and in criminal justice as in other matters the country hoped for better things from a change of government. What exactly it was hoping for is harder to judge, but it certainly seemed ready to welcome a government which would be tough not only on crime but also on the causes of crime. How the incoming Labour Government put its election slogan 'Tough on crime, tough on the causes of crime' into legislative and administrative effect is the subject of the next chapter.

ENDNOTES for *Chapter 8*

1 Audit Commission, *Misspent Youth, Young People and Crime*, London, Audit Commission, 1996.
2 Report of The Royal Commission on Criminal Justice, London, HMSO, 1996.
3 Nicola Lacey, 'Missing the Wood... Pragmatism and Theory in the Royal Commission' in Michael McConville and Lee Bridges (eds.), *Criminal Justice in Crisis*, Aldershot, Edward Elgar, 1994.
4 Blackstone's *Commentaries on the Laws of England*, 1765.
5 Martin Narey, *Review of Delay in the Criminal Justice System: Report*, London, Home Office, 1997.
6 *R v. Cunningham* [1993] 2 ALL ER 15. In this judgment, the Court of Appeal held that the primary purposes of a custodial sentence were to punish and deter. The Court interpreted the phrase 'Commensurate with the seriousness of the offence' in section 2(2) of the 1991 Act to mean 'commensurate with the punishment and *deterrence* which the seriousness of the offence requires.' (Emphasis added). Lord Windlesham states in

Responses to Crime (op. cit. above, p. 20) that contemporary Home Office records demonstrate that such an interpretation departed from the intention of the original framers of the Act. The reinstatement of deterrence could have been an attempt by the judiciary to undermine the unpopular regulation of their sentencing power that the 1991 Act had brought about. *R v. Cox* [1993] 2 ALL ER 15 caused further problems when the Court of Appeal adopted an earlier dictum on the relevance of public opinion when passing sentence on juveniles. See *Responses to Crime* p. 21.

[7] Lord Taylor, speaking at the annual general meeting of NACRO, November 1993.

[8] Lord Windlesham tells the story of this legislation – the policies and attitudes which produced it, and the surrounding debates in Parliament, the media and the political parties – in Volume 3 of *Responses to Crime (op. cit)* from which the quotation at the beginning of this chapter is taken. He shows how many of its features could be traced to American examples and influence, and in his later book, *Politics, Punishment and Populism*, (Oxford, Oxford University Press, 1998) he describes the contemporary situation in the United States. The comparison is not reassuring. He also makes an interesting link between the Government's refusal to consult and the techniques of the new managerialism, or new public management, as described in *Chapter 2* of this work. Other accounts of the influence of managerialism on criminal justice can be found in Ann James and John Raine, *The New Politics of Criminal Justice*, London, Longman, 1998 and in Michael Cavadino, Ian Crow and James Dignan, *Criminal Justice 2000*, Winchester, Waterside Press, 2000. Ann James and John Raine emphasise in particular the loss of respect for professional judgement and the decline in professional influence, together with the higher status accorded to generalist (and often ambitious and competitive) managers. Michael Cavadino, Ian Crow and James Dignan see managerialism as one of the three strategies for criminal justice which had its origins in the 1980s, but which became more fully developed during the 1990s and was combined with the first, punitive or 'law and order' strategy with damaging results.

Ian Dunbar and Anthony Langdon provide another account in their book, *Tough Justice: Sentencing and Penal Policies in the 1990s*, London, Blackstone Press, 1998, including a description of the interplay between the Government and the higher judiciary. Their account indicates a state of affairs which cannot have done much good to either, and which can only have been damaging to the country as a whole. They also reveal their concern, not to say contempt, for the way in which the Government exploited the Prison Service for the sake of what it thought to be its own political advantage.

[9] James Morgan, *Safer Communities: The Local Delivery of Crime and Disorder Prevention through the Partnership Approach*, (The Morgan Report), London Home Office, 1991.

[10] See Lord Windlesham's account, in *Chapter 11* of *Responses to Crime*, Volume 3, *Legislating with the Tide*, Oxford, Oxford University Press, 1996.

[11] Home Office, *Police Reform: a Police Service for the Twenty-first Century*, Cmnd. 2281, London, HMSO, 1993.

[12] Lord Windlesham, *op. cit.*, note 9.

[13] Home Office, *Protecting the Public*, Cmnd. 3190, London, HMSO, 1996.

[14] Home Office Consultation Paper, *Strengthening Punishment in the Community*, Cmnd. 2780, London, HMSO, 1995.

[15] For a discussion on the significance of executive or 'next-steps' agencies see *Chapter 2*.

[16] Joe Pilling, 'Back to Basics: Relationships in the Prison Service' in *Perspectives on Prison: A Collection of Views on Prison Life and Running Prisons* (supplement to the *Annual Report of the Prison Service 1991-1992*, Cmnd. 2087).

CHAPTER 9

The Labour Government from 1997

To build a safe, just and tolerant society, in which the rights and responsibilities of individuals, families and communities are properly balanced, and the protection and security of the public are maintained.

To reduce crime and the fear of crime and their social and economic costs; and to dispense justice fairly and efficiently and to promote confidence in the rule of law.

The Government's aims for the Home Office and the criminal justice system respectively, published with the *New Public Spending Plans 2001-2004*, London, HM Treasury, 2000.

The Labour Government which came into office in May 1997 faced what it saw as serious loss of public confidence in the criminal justice system and a serious loss of operational effectiveness in the criminal justice services. Its policies were summed up by the slogan, used effectively during the election campaign and often repeated since then, *tough on crime and tough on the causes of crime.*

RESTORING CONFIDENCE, PROMOTING EFFICIENCY AND EFFECTIVENESS

As described in the previous two chapters, public confidence and the services' efficiency and effectiveness had been issues for some years. During the Labour Party's period in opposition, its members and Parliamentary candidates had heard complaints of children running out of control and terrorising their neighbourhoods; of parents who were ineffectual or not interested; of people committing anti-social acts to the distress of neighbours or others; and of potentially dangerous people at large and liable to commit sexual or violent offences against the vulnerable and innocent. All were apparently beyond the reach of the law. Further complaints concerned the general level of crime, especially burglary and car crime; the low level of successful prosecutions, including the number of cases discontinued by the Crown Prosecution Service for lack of evidence or on 'public interest' grounds; and the impression that community sentences were neither sufficiently punitive nor properly enforced.

Concerns relating to efficiency and effectiveness were focused mainly on the youth justice system, the Crown Prosecution Service and the Probation Service, all of which seemed to be 'failing' in various ways; and on the continuing lack of co-ordination and strategic direction in the criminal justice system as a whole. Those focused on the youth justice system reflected the criticisms expressed by the Audit Commission and are discussed more fully in *Chapter 14*. Most important for the new Government were the delays in bringing young people accused of offences to trial in the youth court; the failure of the process to 'face young offenders with the consequences of their actions', and the opportunities it gave to deny or evade their responsibility for those actions; and the disproportionate cost of processing cases through the system, compared with the resources devoted to prevention or the reform of offenders. The Crown Prosecution Service was seen as badly managed, too ready to allow offenders to 'get off' because of technical faults in the evidence or the process; and not sufficiently co-ordinated with the police. The Probation Service was seen as ineffective, out of date, 'on the side of the offender' and careless of any duty to protect the public.

NEW FEATURES AND PROGRAMMES

Most of the policies which the Labour Government adopted, and most of the measures which it introduced, can be seen as responding to those criticisms and concerns. Many of them form the subject of later chapters. They included the following:

- A strong Ministerial commitment to strategic planning and management, across the whole of the criminal justice system and the relevant government departments (see below).
- The transformation of the system of youth justice brought about by the Crime and Disorder Act 1998 and the Youth Justice and Criminal Evidence Act 1999 (see *Chapter 14*).
- A comprehensive strategy for preventing crime and reducing criminality, based on statutory partnerships between the police and local authorities and informed by empirical research.[1] The Home Secretary announced the strategy in the summer of 1998; it included an investment of £250 million to fund innovative new schemes (see *Chapter 18*).
- A range of new court orders designed to support the police and local authorities in reducing crime and public disorder (see below and *Chapter 18*).
- An unprecedented emphasis on evidence-based policy and practice; on monitoring, evaluation and research; on the assessment of risk; and on targets, performance indicators,

benchmarks and comparisons; together with a large scale
programme of funding for pilot projects and innovative schemes.
- Substantial investment in new technology, especially for
information systems, closed circuit television, electric monitoring
and DNA testing of offenders and suspects.
- New measures to prevent racial discrimination and promote racial
equality, especially as a result of Sir William Macpherson' s report
of his inquiry into the death of Stephen Lawrence (see *Chapter 16*).
- The reorganization of the Crown Prosecution Service, and its
closer alignment with the police, following the review by Lord
Justice Glidewell[2].
- The adoption of common boundaries, based on those of the police,
for all criminal justice services.
- The reconstruction of the Probation Service, following the
consultation document *Joining Forces to Protect the Public*[3] together
with the renaming and much more rigorous enforcement of orders
supervised by the Probation Service, under the provisions of the
Criminal Justice and Court Services Act 2000 (see *Chapter 20*).

The Government set up reviews of the criminal courts under Lord Justice
Auld, announced in December 1999 (see *Chapter 21*); and of the
sentencing framework, under John Halliday, announced in May 2000
(see *Chapter 12*). Both were still in progress at the time of writing. It also
published, in February 2001, a White Paper *Criminal Justice: The Way
Ahead*[4] which in effect announced its intention for a comprehensive
overhaul of the criminal justice system if it were returned to office for a
second term. It saw the need not only for changes in process and
method, but also for a 'change in the culture of the whole system' so that
'each of the criminal justice professions are informed by the overriding
social purpose of securing a more peaceful life for our citizens by
delivering justice and reducing crime'. Features included new resources,
changes in law and procedure, measures to deal with drug-related crime,
'effective punishments' to reduce re-offending, 'placing victims more at
the heart of the criminal justice system', modernising the police,
combatting organized crime, and 'joining up the system'.

In other respects the Government continued the policies of its
predecessor. Examples include improving efficiency and reducing delays
in court; contracting out prison services to commercial companies under
the Private Finance Initiative; implementing the provisions for
mandatory sentences of imprisonment in the Crime (Sentences) Act 1997;
and continuing improvements in services for victims, with additional
provision for vulnerable victims in the Youth Justice and Criminal
Evidence Act 1999.

STRATEGIC PLANNING AND MANAGEMENT

One of the Government' s first acts on entering office was to set up comprehensive reviews of all the main areas of government spending. One outcome of the review for criminal justice was a determination to provide a clear strategic direction for the system, and to identify and publish the overarching aims of the system as a whole. A joint statement by the Home Secretary, the Lord Chancellor and the Attorney General in July 1998[5] said that these aims were

- to reduce crime and the fear of crime, and their social and economic costs; and
- to dispense justice fairly and efficiently, and to promote confidence in the rule of law;

and that the Government intended to

- establish joint strategic planning across the system as a whole;
- improve and integrate services' information technology; and
- move to align their boundaries more closely.

The statement went on

> All those in the criminal justice system need to work together to make the system better able to achieve the two overarching aims. In support of the two aims, we propose to set strategic objectives for the criminal justice system as a whole to ensure coherent direction. This must not interfere with the independence of those areas in which it would be improper to exert government control. But if greater coherence is to be achieved, it will be important that individual services' objectives are consistent, mutually-reinforcing and collectively capable of delivering the strategic objectives of the system as a whole. For its part, the Government will adopt a more coherent and co-operative approach to developing policy, consulting practitioners over practical issues.
>
> We will produce and publish for the criminal justice system as a whole:
>
> - a three year strategic plan;
> - an annual forward business plan; and
> - an annual report of performance against objectives.
>
> These will provide a framework for the joint planning and management of the resources needed to run the system, including how new policies and priorities can be funded.

The three ministers published the first of an annual series of Strategic and Business Plans in another joint statement in March 1999. They published their Second Business Plan in May 2000. The two overarching aims were linked with eight objectives and a series of performance measures and targets.[6]

The 'challenge' which the first Business Plan set for all those in the criminal justice system was to work more closely together to deliver the two aims and the improvements in performance sought by the Government. The corresponding words in the Business Plan for 2000-2001 were

> This Plan sets out an ambitious programme of work for the year. The detailed measures and targets for the criminal justice system can only be met if Departments, agencies and services continue to work together to improve performance, especially at the local level.

In practice it is of course the detailed performance measures and targets to which operational services, and the Government, pay attention as a matter of day-today practice and concern. As Barry Loveday has written

> setting objectives and targets for services may be appropriate where that service has almost complete control of the 'product' but may be more problematic where it does not. In the latter case, many other extraneous factors may totally undermine the value of the measurement undertaken when the service measured has little ability to influence those extraneous factors which may impact on the service delivered.[7]

In criminal justice, targets such as reduced levels of reported crime (for the police), or for re-offending (for the prison and probation services) can be valuable in focusing attention and making comparisons, but the process of setting and monitoring them must acknowledge the wide range of social, economic and individual factors which also influence the result, as well as the performance of the service concerned. There are real dangers if people who are responsible for criminal justice services become obsessed with the system itself. Even a target such as reducing delay must acknowledge the need to ensure consideration for victims and witnesses and avoid a wrongful conviction. Loveday refers interestingly to Dilulio's disillusion with performance measures in the United States.

PRISONS AND IMPRISONMENT

Absent from the Government' s policies was any evidence of concern for the size of the prison population, or for the social consequences of the country's use of imprisonment on the present scale. For 30 years before

1993, successive governments had been concerned to limit the use of imprisonment, so far as they could do so without interfering with the judiciary' s independence in the sentencing of individual offenders. Part of the reason was of course concern about the degree of overcrowding, its potential consequences for the stability of the prison system, and the cost of building and maintaining new prisons. But there was a general sense, shared by successive governments and the judiciary, that prisons were an expensive resource, capable of doing harm as well as good, and that they should be used sparingly. (Opinions could and did vary on what 'sparingly' might mean in practice.) As explained in previous chapters, that general sense largely disappeared from 1993 onwards, when the Conservative Government claimed that 'prison works' for its deterrent and incapacitating effect. The Labour Government made no attempt to deny the previous Government's claim, although it also argued that prison 'works' - or should work - because of its potential capacity to reform or rehabilitate those offenders who are sentenced to imprisonment. Much effort and quite a lot of resources were devoted to designing and delivering courses for that purpose, with the monitoring and evaluation that were associated with them. But the Government's belief in deterrence and incapacitation remained, for example in the decision to bring into effect the provision for mandatory sentences of imprisonment for offenders convicted of a third offence of burglary, and in the presumption of imprisonment for a second breach of an order made under a community sentence.

The Government's complacency and apparent insouciance over the size of the prison population came as a surprise to many people as its attitude and its deliberate absence of a policy emerged. It is hard to tell at this stage whether the reason was a political judgement that attempts to limit or talk down the use of imprisonment would be politically unpopular; an empirical but questionable belief that an extensive use of imprisonment prevents crime and protects the public; or a political, or even moral, conviction that a high prison population is an expression, and presumably a necessary consequence, of a responsible society. However that may be, it is surprising that a government so committed to evidence-based policy and practice should take such a relaxed view of a situation which has so little evidence to support it. It is equally surprising that a government so committed to strategic and joined-up planning should exempt from that commitment a programme of expenditure which costs about £2 billion a year, and in effect substitute a policy of 'predict and provide' which has been discredited and abandoned in all other areas of government expenditure (see *Chapter 3*). The outcome of the Comprehensive Spending Review which the Government announced on 19 July 2000 included provision to increase the capacity of prisons by 2,660 places.[8]

POLICY AND RESEARCH

The Labour Government's emphasis on evidence-based policy and joined-up government, and therefore on evaluation and research, is one of the features which distinguishes it most sharply from the previous administration. The relationships between policy and research, between implementation and evaluation, and between policy-makers and academics - or between government departments and universities - are among the most important but also the most neglected in modern governance.

In his paper *Penal Policy and Criminological Challenges in the New Millenium: An Address to the Fourteenth Annual Conference of the Australian and New Zealand Society of Criminology,*[9] Roger Hood commented on the extent to which developments in penal policy had over the last ten years emerged not from the findings of research but from 'ideological and political considerations fuelled by populist concerns and impulses'. He attributed part of the reason to political pressures, and part to governments' limited view of what criminologists have been able to deliver (a view exemplified by Jack Straw's complaint when in opposition that academics had no appreciation of crime as it was experienced by people living in his own constituency).

Criminologists for their part were restricted by the resources at their disposal, and the scientific agenda they were able to pursue. They were also divided on whether their task was one of scientific study and analysis, or whether it extended to a deliberate attempt to promote particular agenda, for example for penal reform. The Home Office Research Unit may have suffered - however unfairly - from a reputation for using its research to promote 'liberal' penal policies. A neutral, scientific approach might have been thought professionally more appropriate, although ministers themselves were understandably more inclined to value research, if at all, for any evidence or ideas it could give them which would help to support their own political position. It was to the credit of the Directorate that it was able during the period of the Conservative Government to produce one report on *Persistent Juvenile Offenders*, and to lay the foundations for another, on *Reducing Offending*, which had a powerful influence on the incoming Labour Government when it took office in 1997.[10]

The Labour Government took a quite different view of research from the view of its predecessor. Paul Wiles, Director of Research, Development and Statistics at the Home Office, has described the change in his paper 'The Contribution of Research to Policy'.[11] The new Government quickly made substantial sums available for research and evaluation, especially in the areas of youth justice and crime reduction, in support of its commitment to evidence-based policy and 'aims-led' management, and made it a requirement of most of the new programmes that they should be rigorously and systematically evaluated. Academics were consulted in the process of formulating policies, and were regularly appointed to advisory groups.

Paul Wiles has however expressed a number of concerns - whether there is an adequate organizational infrastructure to support the programme of research that is now being developed; whether enough skills are available, or skills of the right kind; whether they can be successfully organized into multi-disciplinary teams; whether there is an adequate research base on how to deliver programmes as well as how to formulate them; whether the timescale needed for good quality research and evaluation can be made to fit those which ministerial priorities demand; and how links can more successfully be established between universities and local groups trying to innovate and develop new programmes, perhaps by establishing the equivalent of the 'Cochrane Centres' in medicine. Those concerns are generally shared in universities and other organizations which sponsor or undertake research.

Other concerns relate to gaps in research and therefore in knowledge and understanding. Reasons for those gaps will vary - lack of interest on the part of researchers themselves, lack of funding, opposition from those who feel themselves to be threatened (whatever the reasons may be), fear that the results may be unwelcome because they might encourage prejudice or challenge cherished beliefs. However that may be, there are important questions to which there are at present no satisfactory answers - how much crime is committed by how many people, how reliably can they be identified, and how can efforts to reduce criminality most effectively, but also legitimately, be targeted; how far does criminality run in families or households and how can its transmission most effectively be interrupted; what are the social costs and benefits of imprisonment, or the social costs of a criminal conviction - for the individual or on that person's family or dependants, and for the wider community; what influences affect verdicts and sentences (for example impressions or stereotypes or how evidence is presented), apart from those which are formally acknowledged; how can the quality of the various encounters between criminal justice services and the individual members of the public (including defendants, offenders, victims, witnesses and their families) be assessed and judged and what are the influences upon it; what factors affect the dynamics of the various relationships within and between the criminal justice services and those with whom they work in partnership, especially where different professional cultures or ethnic and social backgrounds are involved, and how can the dynamics be modified by training, management or leadership.

These are serious matters which government, services and the academic community must address. Evidence-based policy, joined-up government and successful implementation all require the formation, development and evaluation of policy to have a broad and firm foundation in principles, experience and ideas. That foundation is essential to a government if it is to resist being driven to populist, exclusionary and probably repressive ideologies and policies. Policies and programmes must not be perceived to fail because their evaluation has been inconclusive or inadequate - for example because they were too narrowly designed, or hastily carried out to meet an arbitrarily imposed timetable or budget. Nor should they be proclaimed as successful on the basis of inadequate evidence or unsound evaluation. Both the reactions are dishonest and damage the integrity of the government or the organization concerned.

Individual projects or activities can rarely be judged in isolation from their context or environment, where changes may be taking place due to quite different factors. Narrowly focused evaluations of specific projects according to closely defined, predetermined criteria, should be related to a larger programme which includes longer term, open ended, strategic programmes designed not only to assess what has been achieved or changed, but also to suggest new approaches, options and possibilities. Research should contribute to assessments of the country's social and economic progress, measured in part by the government departments' success in meeting the aims which have been set for them but look beyond those aims to broader impressions of fairness, justice, inclusiveness, respect for diversity and other social values. The Labour Government's initiatives on youth crime, offending behaviour and support for young people and their parents all have the potential to achieve real progress, but fragmented implementation and evaluation could lead to disillusionment and frustration. The *Edinburgh Study of Youth Transitions and Crime* carried out by the University of Edinburgh is an example of the longer-term, more broadly-based research that is needed to complement individual studies of separate projects.

Paul Wiles has said

> Social policy is not just about efficiency nor is it just about effectiveness. It is also about what kind of vision of civic society we are trying to achieve. In other words it has a moral purpose as well as a technical purpose.

And Roger Hood

> We as criminologists have to establish our scientific credentials. But the authorities themselves have to recognise their contribution to the problem.

The state as the major funder of research (as well as others who may wish to promote it) should create a new institutional structure. Scientific research should not be part of the governmental apparatus - and indeed in most fields it is not. Government funding, as in other areas of research relevant to social policy, should be handled through an independent Criminological Research Council in which considerations of scientific advance and public utility can be weighed in deciding on the allocation of resources to the research community.

That proposal should be seriously considered.

NATURE OF THE GOVERNMENT'S APPROACH

The Government's approach to crime and criminal justice is clearly utilitarian and instrumental, rather than classical or retributive in the sense described in *Chapter 6*. The instrumental view is vividly expressed in the first of the Government's aims for the criminal justice system, and in its insistence on the protection of the public as the first duty of the criminal justice services and those who work in them. It is slightly qualified by the second aim's reference to 'dispensing justice fairly', but the objectives and the performance measures and targets are all expressed in instrumental terms, and there is no suggestion in the Business Plan or other recent government publications that justice or fairness might be an outcome in itself, rather than a means of achieving some other instrumental purpose.

For a broader vision it is necessary to look back to the Government's overall objectives for its programmes as a whole (see *Chapter 3*). The second of these is to 'promote fairness and opportunity'. But it is not clear from the Government's publications on public service agreements, modernisation or strategic planning how criminal justice is intended to contribute to that aim. The Government uses the word 'fairness' alongside other words such as responsibility, social inclusion and decency, but 'justice' seems to be used to refer only to the process of detection, prosecution, trial and punishment - again never to the outcome. It is commonly preceded by the word 'effective'. The adjective 'just' is however used in the Business Plan to refer to the 'processes' and 'outcomes' for which the performance measure is *to monitor a number of measures on just processes and outcomes, and to define effective outcome measures which are consistent with the measures to be agreed for the 2000 Spending Review.*

For a better insight into the Government's beliefs and values, a useful source is the two lectures on human rights and citizenship by the Home Secretary, Jack Straw, already mentioned in *Chapter 3*. Some questions could be asked about the extent of the Government's commitment to the Human Rights Act 1998, for example because of its insistence that Parliament (and therefore in effect the government) should in the last resort be able to insist that its legislation should be applied even if the courts consider it to be in conflict with the Act, and its reluctance so far to agree to the appointment of a human rights commission. But the Government has clearly seen the Act as part of a new relationship which it wants to promote between the state (and again in effect the Government) and the citizen, based on a combination of rights and responsibilities as discussed in *Chapter 4*. In his address to the Civil Service College seminar on 9 December 1999,[12] the Home Secretary described the Human Rights Act as a 'guarantee of fairness'; but went on to dismiss, with contempt, the suggestion that the Act is an instrument to be used on behalf of the individual against the power of the state, and he emphasised the extent to which the different rights established by the Act have to be balanced against one another. He also claimed that the citizen's rights under the Act are conditional upon the performance of duties, 'So you get your rights from your duties'. And he went on to say

> The Human Rights Act is one of the key changes in our programme of constitutional reform. But this constitutional reform is not - or shouldn't be - seen as an end in itself. What we are interested in is what I hope you are interested in - why most of us got involved in public service - to help make a better country for everyone to live in. A modern, successful, society which is enriched by different cultures, different faiths. A society which is plural. But a society where there is also unity. And confidence.

> Where everyone has a guarantee of fairness in the key institutions of the state. A shared understanding about what is fundamentally right and wrong; about the duties we owe to each other and the wider community, and a willingness to fulfill those duties.

The Prime Minister, Tony Blair, spoke in rather similar terms at the Kent Police Headquarters on 31 August 2000 when he said

> I believe the basis of society is respect for others. To each and every citizen we owe opportunity; from each we demand responsibility.

After referring to extra funding for after-school clubs and poorer parents and to the New Deal for the unemployed he went on to say

> I believe this entitles us to speak very plainly... about the responsibility we expect in return. We expect law-abiding conduct; decent civil behaviour towards each other . . .[13]

Human rights and citizenship

The Government's views about human rights, citizenship and its own authority explain some of the themes and some of what might otherwise be thought to be contradictions in its policies. A central theme of the Crime and Disorder Act 1998 is responsibility - not making excuses, not exploiting procedural opportunities, taking responsibility for one's actions. The theme is expressed through the measures to avoid delays in the youth justice process, and through the promotion of alternatives to the traditional adversarial process and of restorative measures in which the victim can be involved. It is expressed in the new orders made available to courts to prevent crime and disorder - the anti-social behaviour order, the parenting order, the drug treatment and testing order, the sex offender order.

All these orders are designed to deal with behaviour which is not in itself criminal, or if criminal is hard to prove, by enabling courts to make orders requiring the person to do or not to do certain things on the basis of the lower, civil standard of proof (the balance of probabilities). Failure to comply with those requirements then, by virtue of novel legislative provision, becomes an easily proven criminal offence, with penalties attached - in the case of the anti-social behaviour order a penalty of up to five years' imprisonment. The fact that the order has been questioned as potentially in conflict with Article 6 of the European Convention On Human Rights (the right to a fair trial)[14] has caused particular annoyance to the Government, not only because they have given it particular political prominence but also because it is an expression of a political philosophy of which the Government claims the Human Rights Act itself to be a part.

Another expression of the same theme is the Government's proposal that social security benefits should be withdrawn from offenders who do not observe the requirements of community sentences. This proposal is difficult to justify on the basis of any evidence that it will reduce crime, the first aim of the criminal justice system, but the Government attempted to justify it 'on the basis of a contract between the citizen and the state, whereby rights to benefits and responsibilities to society are closely linked ... Benefits are conditional on the fulfilment of responsibilities to society' - a clear expression of the conditional and exclusionary view of citizenship is described in *Chapter 4*.[15] Lord Windlesham and others contested that view in the House of Lords;[16] Lord Windlesham did so more fully in his article 'Loss of Benefit: A Misplaced Sanction' and Amitai Etzioni has criticised it in his paper *The Third Way to a Good Society*.[17]

A third example is the benefits which are increasingly available to offenders who admit their guilt - the prospect of a police caution, or a reprimand or final warning, or under the Youth Justice and Criminal Evidence Act a referral order, rather than a possible conviction or sentence; or in more serious cases a reduced or 'discounted' sentence. Even after a sentence of imprisonment, offenders who continue to deny their guilt are at a disadvantage because they are seen as not having 'come to terms with their offence' and are liable to have their release delayed on that account. There is an underlying assumption that to deny one's guilt is to aggravate the offence, rather than to exercise a citizen's right to put the prosecution to the test; and despite the continuing evidence that miscarriages of justice can still occur, there is no acknowledgement that a person might be wrongly convicted.

The three examples reflect the limited conditional and exclusive view of citizenship which has been described in *Chapter 2* and which is considered again in *Chapter 10*.

LANGUAGE, STYLE AND ATTITUDE

Three other points can be made about the Government' s language, style and attitude.

The Government continues to use the language of warfare - a war on crime, a fight or even a 'crusade' (with all its moral but historically unfortunate overtones) against crime, victory and defeat. This is the language of exclusion and of an instinct which treats offenders as enemies. It is consistent with the limited or qualified notion of citizenship already described: offenders who disqualify themselves from citizenship, can - and perhaps should - be denied its benefits, and deserve to be cut off from ordinary social relationships. Not only that, but the language of warfare implies a call to unity against a common external enemy - an enemy which has to be defeated with whatever means the country has at its disposal, including some which would be unjust or illegitimate in ordinary times. It encourages feelings of hatred, suspicion and fear. Accompanied by an instrumental and managerial view of criminal justice, it suggests that the objective to be achieved justifies the means of achieving it. Such language could thus be seen as justifying a lack of sympathy for suspicious or unsympathetic individuals, an attitude of superiority towards suspects or convicted offenders, and in more extreme cases the use of intimidation or the falsification of evidence. It suggests the 'positivist' view of crime and criminals, associated with Lombroso and described in *Chapter 6*.

The language of warfare is not appropriate for discussion of how to prevent crime or how to treat offenders, and the Conservative Government was careful to avoid it during the ten years or so before 1992.

Secondly, and consistent with the first point, the word 'punishment' appears constantly in government publications. It is as if the 'defeat' of the enemy is not complete until he or she has been not only defeated, but also 'punished'. It does not take into account the ways in which situations arising from criminal offences (or acts of disorder) can be resolved by other means, including the restorative measures which the Government itself supports, without resorting to punishment (see *Chapter 10*). And some of the community-based methods which the Government seems to regard as punishment would not be seen as such by many people who are not familiar with them - or indeed by many of those who are.

The dilemma faced the Conservative as well as the Labour Government. It is politically convenient to give the impression that anyone convicted of an offence is punished for it, and therefore to describe as punishment anything that the court orders after a conviction. But to do that raises expectations that whatever the court orders will be retributive, and in some way painful or unpleasant. Those expectations then have to be met, at least in the case of community-based penalties, by increasing their punitive content. There is no point at which this process can be halted on the basis that the public will then be satisfied, but there is quite soon a point at which it becomes no longer practicable, or damaging to any intended outcome in terms of the offender's likelihood of re-offending. Logically, punishment is part of the language of retribution; once the model, or the paradigm, is changed to a utilitarian model of reducing crime, its use is potentially confusing and sometimes out of place. Of course the word cannot (unlike the language of warfare) be removed altogether from the criminal justice vocabulary, but it needs to be used with caution and without raising false expectations.

Thirdly, the Labour Government (like its predecessors in the early 1960s) sees part of the solution to the problem of crime as an advance in the development and application of new technology. The most prominent examples are in communication systems; the collection and retrieval of information, especially criminal records; methods of overt and covert surveillance and monitoring (closed circuit television, electronic monitoring of offenders, the interception of communications, various devices for keeping suspects under hidden observation); and an expansion of DNA testing of suspects and offenders and the maintenance of a DNA database. Of course technology has its place in the prevention and detection of crime and in the treatment and, where necessary, control of offenders. It should be developed and used wherever it is useful and appropriate. Few applications can be ruled out altogether on the grounds of principle (human rights or civil liberties). But they all raise questions of accountability and professional integrity in their use, some of which are considered in *Chapter 17*, and experience in the 1960s suggests that it would be unwise to have extravagant expectations of their success.

The Government claimed in its White Paper *Criminal Justice: The Way Ahead*[18] that its strategy had three 'core components' - social policies to tackle the causes of crime; 'targeting' of those types of crime which cause the greatest concern - burglary, car crime, street robbery and alcohol related disorder; and as already mentioned a comprehensive overhaul of the system to 'lever up' performance in dealing with offenders. The first deserves general applause, although it is still easier for the Government to take credit for the money it is spending than for the results it has achieved. The second also deserves approval, subject to some reservations about the methods which might be used and which are discussed in *Chapter 17*. The third raises serious questions about the Government's underlying values and expectations, about the expansion in the role and scope of criminal justice which seems to be implied, and about the evidence on which its policies would be based.

Talk of a DNA database which will hold 'virtually the entire criminally active population', and of 'catching, prosecuting and sentencing the 100,000 hard-core persistent criminals' shows an attitude of mind which perceives 'criminals' as a distinct class of people who can be identified, targeted, perhaps reformed but otherwise controlled and coerced, and to whom the normal rights of citizenship do not apply. Apart from any ethical concern about this attitude, it is one which does not recognise the extent to which crime and criminality are related to the values, conditions and experience of society as a whole, or the limited effect which the criminal justice process can achieve on its own (as has been shown by attempts to control the misuse of drugs). Even to talk of targeting the '100,000 most persistent hard-core criminals' is to ignore the fact, acknowledged in Appendix B to the White Paper, that the 'active offender population is not static' and different individuals will be involved at different times. Attempts to reform or rehabilitate offenders through programmes of education, training and resetttlement are admirable in themselves, but there must still be questions about the ability of the Prison and Probation Services to provide them on an adequate scale and to a satisfactory standard in present circumstances; and about the effectiveness of those programmes in changing behaviour if offenders return to or remain in the same social situations.

The Government recognises the need for social and criminal justice services to work together: the danger is that instead of doing so in a common endeavour to promote responsible citizenship and social stability and well-being, they will see themselves as working with different classes in society, and with different classes of citizen.

ENDNOTES for *Chapter 9*

[1] Home Office, *Reducing Offending*, London, Home Office Research Study 187, 1997.
[2] *The Review of the Crown Prosecution Service: A Report* (Chairman the Right Honourable Sir Iain Glidewell), Cm. 3960, London, HMSO, 1998.
[3] Home Office, *Joining Forces to Protect the Public: Prisons – Probation; A Consultation Document*, London, Home Office, 1998.
[4] Home Office, *Criminal Justice: The Way Ahead*, Cm. 5074, London, Stationery Office, 2001.
[5] Joint Statement by the Home Secretary, Lord Chancellor and Attorney General, *Joint Planning Structures*, London, Home Office, 21 July 1998.

[6] The two aims and eight objectives are set out, with measures, targets and a commentary, in *Criminal Justice System: Annual Report 1999-2000*, published jointly by the Home Office, the Lord Chancellor's Department and the Law Officers' Department in February 2001. The aims, as indicated at the head of this chapter, are to reduce crime and the fear of crime and their economic costs, and to dispense justice fairly and efficiently and to promote confidence in the rule of law. It is clear from the report that measures and targets are easier to find for objectives under the first aim - for example percentage reductions in rates of crime - than they are for those under the second, except for example where they relate to the time taken from arrest to sentence. Work is in hand to extend the range of measures and targets and to make them more sophisticated: but the dangers of a 'target driven' approach, and of an assumption that the criminal justice system can by itself achieve prescribed reductions in levels of crime, are discussed in *Chapters 6, 17* and 22.

The Home Office itself has a more detailed set of seven aims, four of which relate to criminal justice and three to other Home Office responsibilities. There are references to 'effectiveness' but the only reference to 'fairness' is in the aim which is concerned with race equality and human rights. Each aim has a senior official who is the 'aim owner', and a set of performance measures and 'targets and milestones'. Some targets have a surprising degree of precision (for example 14 per cent reduction in the level of recorded robbery in principal cities by 2005), and similar assumptions are made. See the *Business Plan 2001-2002*, Home Office 2001.

[7] Barry Loveday, 'Measuring Performance in Criminal Justice' in Marco Ferri and Philip Langbroek (eds.), *The Challenge for Judicial Systems*, Amsterdam, IOS Press, 2000.

[8] The Government had stated in reply to a question by Lord Dholakia in the House of Lords on the previous day (18 July 2000) that £1 million spent on building and running more prisons would result in approximately 180 recorded offences being prevented annually; the corresponding figure for drug treatment programmes in prisons was 500.

[9] Roger Hood, 'Penal Policy and Criminological Challenges in the New Millennium: An Address to the Annual Conference of the Australian and New Zealand Society of Criminology', *Australia and New Zealand Journal of Criminology*, (forthcoming).

[10] John Graham and Ben Bowling, *Young People and Crime*, Home Office Research Study 145, London, Home Office, 1995. Peter Goldblatt and Christopher Lewis (eds.) *Reducing Offending*, Home Office Research Study 187, London, Home Office, 1997.

[11] Paul Wiles, 'The Contribution of Research to Policy', London, *Criminal Justice Matters*, 1999-2000, No. 38, Winter, pp. 35-7.

[12] Jack Straw, *Building a Human Rights Culture*, Address to a Civil Service College Seminar on 9 December 1999, London, Home Office.

[13] Available on the Number 10 website.

[14] Article 6 of the European Convention On Human Rights (right to a fair trial) only applies to those charged in 'criminal proceedings'. Breach of the new anti-social behaviour order is a criminal offence, but the order itself is obtained through civil proceedings where the safeguards provided for by Article 6 do not apply. See Andrew Ashworth 'Is the Criminal Law a Lost Cause?', *The Law Quarterly Review*, Vol. 116, 2000, pp. 225-56.

[15] Baroness Hollis, House of Lords, *Hansard HL*, Vol.612, col. 529, 17 April 2000.

[16] Speaking in the same debate, Lord Windlesham objected to the principle of using social security legislation to serve criminal justice purposes. He drew attention to the mandatory, and therefore arbitrary and discriminatory, nature of the proposals and to their vulnerability under the Human Rights Act 1998. For a fuller account of the ill-considered and populist nature of the proposal, see Lord Windlesham 'Loss of Benefit: a Misplaced Sanction', *Criminal Law Review*, August 2000, pp. 661-6. The Bill was subsequently modified to provide that the withdrawal of benefit would only take effect after the breach of conditions had been determined by the court, but the broader objection of principle remained.

[17] Amitai Etzioni, *The Third Way to a Good Society*, London, Demos, 2000.

[18] See n. 4, above.

PART III Crimes and Criminals

CHAPTER 10

Punishment, Shame and Restorative Justice

All punishment is mischief: all punishment in itself is evil.

Jeremy Bentham, 1789

Two words which have become increasingly prominent in the political vocabulary are 'punishment' and 'shame'. Both words can be, and are, used in ways which have different meanings in different context or to different people, with resulting ambiguity and opportunities for confusion and exploitation.

THE MEANING OF PUNISHMENT

In ordinary language, punishment is an act which causes a person to suffer because of an offence which they have committed. Loss of liberty or payment of a fine is clearly a punishment. A requirement to do something which the person would not do otherwise, or to refrain from doing something which they would like to do, may be seen as a punishment if the person can be seen to suffer as a consequence. The less the person is seen to suffer, the less 'real' the punishment is likely to appear. Punishment has to be deserved because of the nature of the offence, and the culpability of the offender; and no more severe than is proportionate to the seriousness of the offence. Otherwise the punishment is unfair. There may however be room for mercy or mitigation, so that the punishment need not be so severe, or may not be needed at all. It has to be administered by a person or an institution which has legitimate authority to do so (see *Chapters 5* and *11*). If these conditions are not satisfied, the act is not one of punishment, but of oppression, bullying or abuse.

Punishment can be administered in several settings - at home, at school, at work or through the criminal justice system. Different kinds of punishment are available in those different settings (for example 'grounding', detention or dismissal). At school, punishment may be for offences like running in the corridor or talking in class; offences such as bullying, cheating or stealing may be too serious for ordinary school punishment and have to be dealt with in other ways. In criminal justice, punishments include the obvious examples of imprisonment and fines, but also other sentences or sanctions such as community punishment and community rehabilitation orders (to use their new titles under the Criminal Justice and Court Services Act 2000), together with curfew orders, compensation orders, and suspended sentences of imprisonment; anti-social behaviour orders and numerous other orders made under the

Crime and Disorder Act 1998; referral orders and other orders made under the Youth Justice and Criminal Evidence Act 1999, and disqualification, exclusion and drug abstinence orders made under the Criminal Justice and Court Services Act 2000. All these are made by the courts.

Not all of these would appear at first sight to be 'punishments' in the sense that they cause suffering, and some of them contain a threat of future punishment rather than, or as well as, an immediate sanction. And yet all of them, certainly those which are imposed as a sentence or order of the court, are likely to be described politically or by practitioners as 'punishment' in some sense. They are so described because of what seems to be an implicit assumption that any wrongdoing must always be visited with punishment. Not only that, but there is an increasing political assumption that they must on that account cause some suffering to the offender. It was in this spirit that the Conservative Government developed the rhetoric of 'punishment in the community', and the Criminal Justice Act 1991 imposed restrictions on the use of suspended sentences (because the offender was not actually 'punished'), and made the probation order a sentence of the court instead of, as previously, an alternative to a sentence.

Confusion and ambiguity

The present pre-occupation with punishment contains a number of confusions. It was for a long time taken for granted that the punishment for an offence was the sentence of the court, and whatever was necessary to give effect to that sentence. It was not the function of the prison or probation services to continue the punishment into the treatment which the offender received while in custody or under supervision, for example through deliberate acts of collective or individual humiliation. Such acts have not generally been accepted as part of prison regimes and when they have taken place, they have generally been treated as breaches of staff discipline. There have however been attempts from time to time to intensify the degree of punishment involved in prison regimes (for example the short-lived 'short sharp shock' regime in the early detention centres in the 1950s and its revival in the early 1980s); and talk of it in programmes of supervision (for example by requiring offenders undertaking community service to wear distinctive uniforms). The Government has abandoned its proposal that the Probation Service should be re-named the 'community punishment and rehabilitation service', but is determined that punishment should still be seen as part of the service's function. The confusion becomes greater if programmes of rehabilitation which require the offender's co-operation, goodwill and commitment - for example for education, or treatment for addiction to drugs or alcohol - themselves come to be seen as punishment, imposed without consent and with a strong emphasis on coercion and sanctions such as imprisonment for failure to comply. Further complications arise if the programme depends on a partnership with an organization which is not a part of the criminal justice system and which does not see an involvement with 'state punishment' as part of its role.

Attempts to intensify punishment in these ways have usually been abandoned quite quickly[1] (see *Chapter 6*). There comes a point where either staff or offenders no longer comply, or they develop a collusive and ultimately corrupt relationship in which both manipulate the system for their own or each other's benefit. But there is a different and perhaps greater danger in a situation where a government invests its political credibility and resources in punishment, namely that there is no point at which the demand can be reasonably satisfied. If punishment is seen as an 'answer' to crime, if it is regularly described as 'effective' in reducing crime, and still more if it is seen as a 'weapon' with which to 'defeat' it, there will be an unsatisfied demand for more punishment so long as crime exists.

In most situations where people have experience of receiving or administering what they would see as punishment - families, schools, even the armed forces - there is a continuing and reciprocal relationship of love, care or loyalty which may be temporarily suspended but which all the parties hope and intend to restore as soon as possible. That relationship both mitigates the severity of the punishment that is likely to be imposed, and prevents the alienation or exclusion which might otherwise result from it. Harsh or erratic punishment is one of the experiences which are strongly related to offending in adolescence or later life; and what is claimed as punishment, especially physical punishment, may sometimes amount to abuse. But generally speaking, once the punishment is over, the matter has been dealt with, the person has 'paid the price', and they can return to their situation and relationships, perhaps a little wiser, but able to continue as normal.

No such relationship exists, and no such protection is available, for crimes which are dealt with and punished through the criminal justice process. It used to be said, and it is sometimes still said, that offenders who have completed their sentence have paid their debt to society and are entitled to the same consideration and opportunities as anyone else. But to say that is no longer realistic, if it ever was. Convicted offenders carry the stigma of the conviction with them; and under recent legislation, practice and systems of keeping and gaining access to records, they are increasingly the object of suspicion and sometimes surveillance. Part of their dignity and status as citizens is withdrawn from them. How punishment for wrongdoing can be reconciled with a continuing status of citizenship, as the Home Secretary seemed to hope in his Constitution Unit Lecture (see *Chapters 3* and *9*), is a major challenge to the country's political and professional leadership.

Punishment and social order

Further considerations arise if a person is punished, or is punished more severely, not for what they have done but for what it is thought they might do. These considerations arose in connection with the provision in section 2(2)(b) Criminal Justice Act 1991 which permits the courts to impose more severe sentences for serious violent and sexual offences (more severe than any which would be justified for the seriousness of the actual offence) in order to protect the public (see *Chapter 12*). Other examples are the practice of extending the term to be served in prison under a life sentence, or of refusing parole, to a prisoner who is considered still to present a risk; the provisions in the Crime and Disorder Act 1998 for extended sentences for sexual and violent offences, and the Government's proposals for the indefinite detention of persons suffering from severe personality disorder. The protection of the public may sometimes – but not often – justify extended terms of detention beyond the period which corresponds with the seriousness of the offence, but such terms should not be regarded as part of the 'punishment', their imposition should be subject to special safeguards and procedures, and their operation should be subject to regular and independent review. They should not be served in prisons if prisons are to be regarded as places to which people go as punishment. Questions of prison administration and regimes are discussed further in *Chapter 19*.[2]

SHAME AND REMORSE

'Shame' is another word which has come into more frequent use, especially as a transitive verb and almost as a synonym for 'punish'. 'Naming and shaming' is an expression used to describe the public identification and criticism, not only of offenders but also of 'failing' services, institutions and individual public servants. When used in that way it is part of the culture of blame which is discussed in *Chapters 5* and *8*; when applied to offenders it can be used negatively to generate either an expression of public opprobrium and humiliation, or more positively a sense of personal remorse. The former may be seen as having some value in the sense of purging the feeling of public anger or as a possible deterrent to others, but it is likely to have a damaging effect on the individual concerned. The latter may provide a starting point from which the offender might start to rebuild his or her life to restore a positive relationship with the family and others around them. This is what the Australian criminologist John Braithwaite had in mind when he wrote of 'reintegrative shaming',[3] although 'remorse' may be a better word than 'shame', and 'shame' may not be a suitable word at all if it is used transitively in that context. Whatever the language used, there are important implications for the development of 'restorative justice', as noted later in this chapter.

The ambiguity in the ways in which 'punishment' and 'shame' are used in public debate reflects at best an unconscious confusion in the way in which legislation, policy and practice are developed; and occasionally, at worst, a cynical attempt to manipulate the argument. Punishment and shame both have their place in human behaviour and relationships, whether for individuals, for institutions or for the state. Whether they are used constructively or destructively - to support or to damage personal relationships, individual commitment and social stability - depends on situations, circumstances and the methods used. The purpose and intention should always be made clear, and the setting and the requirements should be designed accordingly. It is not enough to specify who is to do what without showing how it will contribute to the purpose to be achieved.

Both punishment and shame have limitations as a means of controlling behaviour, and other means of motivating individuals, expressing disapproval and creating conditions to support honest or considerate behaviour will often be more suitable. Crime and anti-social behaviour should never be ignored or condoned, but prosecution and punishment are not the only or in some cases necessarily the best forms of action to be taken. Other forms of action, such as the various types of restorative justice, are also available; and even if an offender is prosecuted and convicted, the sentence or outcome need not always be characterised and justified as punishment. It should be recognised that some outcomes can be accepted which cannot in ordinary language be described as punishment, in the sense of causing suffering. A distinction should be made between punishment, which is essentially about what has been done in the past; and reform (or restoration or rehabilitation) which looks to the future and is about progress and change. Others besides the offender will then be involved, and agents of change will include not only the offender's remorse and determination to improve, but also the compassion and where possible the forgiveness of others. All these influences can then be combined to allow the opportunity for atonement and reconciliation, and the offender's return to full citizenship and membership of society.[4]

PUNISHMENT AND CITIZENSHIP

In his article 'Punishment and Conditional Citizenship',[5] Barry Vaughan traces a connection between ideas of citizenship and approaches to punishment as they have developed over the last two centuries. In particular, he makes a link between approaches to punishment and the feelings of the middle-class once it had begun to emerge and become influential (in today's circumstances one might refer to the feelings of 'Middle England'). His historical analysis is not always easy to follow, but he makes the interesting point that when the middle-class feels insecure or threatened it is likely to see those it thinks of as presenting the threat as less than full citizens, and to demand protective, and therefore, punitive, measures against them without much regard for any rights to which they may be entitled. The threat may at different times come from the working-class, the 'undeserving poor', or single parents, immigrants, refugees or members of other minority groups. Because they are not seen as qualifying for 'full' citizenship, the state need not provide the full standard of care or protection that it would give to others, and although injustice or abuse may not actually be justified, they are not so serious as they would be for citizens who properly 'belong'. Vaughan sees attitudes to citizenship as one of the primary cultural influences on punishment, and an ambivalent or conditional attitude to citizenship as an explanation for the persistence of inconsiderate or, at worst, brutal treatment. The sense of 'lesser eligibility' may continue after the punishment has ended, through the socially and economically disabling effect of a criminal conviction. There is a special ambiguity about the position of those who have not been convicted of any offence but who may be subject to one of the restraining orders - for example the anti-social behaviour order - which courts can impose under the Crime and Disorder Act 1998 (see *Chapters 9* and *18*).

In the more heterogeneous society described in *Chapter 2*, those whom so-called 'Middle England' is inclined to see as threatening its stability are more diverse and difficult to classify than they were in earlier times, although the instinct to stereotype and demonise seems just as strong. Seen from this perspective, it may be easier to understand the present political appetite for punishment which aims first to secure conformity and compliance, and when that 'fails', to impose a more severe exclusion from citizenship in the form of imprisonment. The resulting policies can become an example of the loss of liberalism which Desmond King describes in *In Defence of Liberalism*[6]. As Barry Vaughan puts it . . .

> the state's current punitive stance is a peculiarly modern phenomenon in that it is a response, despite its archaic vestiges, to its failings to make good the promise of social rights . . . Punishment in the modern era has always been ambivalent but it is losing whatever sense of inclusiveness it has as the exclusiveness of citizenship becomes more evident.

David Garland, in his article on 'The Limits of the Sovereign State', discusses some of the reactions which governments have given to what he calls the predicament of crime control in late modern society.[7] He describes, among other things, the denial of British and other governments of the fact that crime does not readily respond to punishment, and their readiness to adopt punitive policies which they can represent as 'an authoritative intervention to deal with a serious, anxiety-ridden problem' - an assertion of power and an expression of what Mick Ryan and Stuart Hall have termed 'authoritarian populism'.[8] Such an attitude to punishment is an indication of political weakness which governments try to disguise as a show of political strength.

RESTORATIVE JUSTICE

The approach known as restorative justice has come into prominence in western societies only during the last ten years. Its origins can be found partly in dissatisfaction with the operation of the adversarial system of justice in common law countries, which coincided with increased recognition of its neglect of the circumstances and feelings of victims of crime and its failure to require offenders to engage with the seriousness and consequences of their offences. They can also be found in different religious and cultural traditions in various parts of the world. Writers in the Christian tradition approach restorative justice from their ideas of punishment, reconciliation, redemption and atonement.[9] John Braithwaite has developed an alternative to the adversarial system which he calls 'reintegrative shaming'.[10] It draws on Maori systems of resolving disputes and conflict arising from criminal activity: the central feature is a 'family group conference' bringing together the offender, the victim, and members of their families or other supporters. The procedure was first applied in practice, in different ways and using different terminology, in New Zealand and Australia. A rather similar process is followed in the children's hearings which are the standard method for dealing with juvenile offenders in Scotland. Procedures of this kind, described variously as family group conferences, children's hearings, restorative cautions, restorative conferences and restorative justice, are now being applied in several other countries in Europe and North America.[11]

In England, there were some limited attempts to develop procedures for mediation between offenders and victims during the 1980s, and the Home Office funded four experimental schemes. Mediation in criminal matters did not make much progress at that stage, partly because the process was time-consuming and laborious, partly because it was difficult to accommodate in cases where a prosecution was also in prospect, and partly because it did not attract sustained political support.

By the early 1990s, the writing of John Braithwaite and the family group conferences in New Zealand and Australia were becoming known in England, and attracted the attention especially of Charles Pollard, Chief Constable of Thames Valley Police. Thames Valley Police began to develop conferencing as a method of dealing with young offenders in conjunction with a caution and as an alternative to a prosecution, and there were similar initiatives in other areas. Conferencing attracted the attention of the Labour Party while it was still in opposition; it gained the Labour Government's approval when the new government came into office; and it the basis for the referral order for which provision was made in the Youth Justice and Criminal Evidence Act 1999. The order is to be brought into national effect during 2001. James Dignan gives an account of the present situation and the recent history in his article 'The Crime and Disorder Act and the Prospects for Restorative Justice'[12].

The term restorative justice can be used loosely to describe several different programmes or provisions. In the sense of 'giving something back to the community', it can refer to almost any activity ordered under a community service order, or community punishment order as it is now to be called, with an unfortunate change of emphasis away from its restorative aspect. In the sense of 'repaying the victim' it can refer to the requirements of a compensation order, or of a reparation order or action plan order - two of the new types of order introduced under the Crime and Disorder Act 1998 - as well as the 'contract' to be drawn up by youth offender panels established under the Youth Justice and Criminal Evidence Act 1999. It can therefore refer either to the requirements of various orders made after an offender has been convicted by a court under the traditional adversarial process; or - as in the Thames Valley and as seems to be intended for the referral order - it can refer to a quite different process, the whole point of which is to provide an alternative to the adversarial system.

Restorative conferences

The restorative conference has a number of features which make it an especially interesting innovation. In the Thames Valley version those present at the conference will include the offender, accompanied by his or her family or other supporters; the victim, also accompanied by supporters; and a police officer as facilitator. Professionals such as a social worker, probation officer or the police officer in charge of the case may sometimes also be present. A conference is quite difficult to arrange and prepare, not only in the sense of bringing the various participants together at a suitable venue (usually but not necessarily a police station) but also in making sure that the facilitator and the other participants are suitably prepared. It is especially important for participants to know what the conference is about and what to expect from it. The facilitator needs to have been thoroughly trained.

The purpose of the conference is to repair the damage caused by the offence, so far as it is possible to do so, and to enable the offender, the victim, and others who may have been affected by it (typically their families) to put the offence behind them and move on in their lives. It is for the benefit of both parties, and both have something to gain and something to contribute. The purpose is not for the offender to be lectured or humiliated, or for the victim to be exploited for the benefit of the offender, or to be conscripted into the process on behalf of the state or the police. A successful conference will be one in which the offender is given the chance to understand the effect of what he or she has done; to explain how he or she came to do it and to accept responsibility for it; perhaps to resolve genuinely to change something about themselves and the pattern of their lives; and, where this feels right, to apologise to the victim. The victim has the opportunity to explain the material or physical damage caused by the offence and how it has affected them; may feel reassured that they will not suffer from that offender in the same way again; and have an opportunity to accept the apology. The offender, the victim and their supporters - not the facilitator or other professionals - should do most of the talking. An understanding may emerge from the conference that the offender will pay for the damage or perform some service for the victim, and certainly that the offender will do better in other aspects of his or her life: but these understandings are not enforceable conditions and should not be represented as if they were. The conference cannot expect the victim to forgive the offender, but if forgiveness is possible it is, of course, to be welcomed.

No victim should ever feel under pressure to take part in a conference, and although the victim's presence and involvement are usually desirable, a conference can still take place without him or her. Institutional victims, such as businesses whose goods or property have been stolen or damaged, can be represented by a member of their staff. A conference can obviously take place only if the offender has admitted the offence.

Understandings and expectations

The process of restorative conferences is open to various interpretations and misunderstandings. It is not a form of punishment, it is not a confrontation, and the offender should not be treated as a 'criminal' in the sense of being a person who is of any less value than the others who are present. It should not be threatening. The focus should be on the prospect of better things in the future as well as what has happened in the past. As already indicated, John Braithwaite has described the process as one of 'reintegrative shaming', but shame should not imply humiliation or loss of self-respect. 'Remorse' may be a better word. Its purpose is not primarily to prevent re-offending (though the hope is obviously that it will have that result) but rather to provide a better way of dealing with the situation which the offence has caused. Tests of its success therefore include questions like

- do victims benefit from the process?
- do offenders 'play the system' by saying what they think people want to hear?
- does the process bring home to offenders the effects of their actions?
- does it help to integrate offenders and their victims back into their 'communities of care'?
- are the restorative justice process, and any outcomes of the process (perhaps embodied in a written agreement), perceived as fair?
- are reparation agreements honoured?

as well as whether it reduces the incidence, frequency and nature of offending.

From an English perspective, restorative conferencing represents a radical new approach to dealing with those who commit crime and those who suffer from it. The process is still at an early stage of its development, and its implications and its potential have still to become clear, especially to those - including ministers and Members of Parliament - who have not been closely involved. Questions to be resolved include professional or technical matters relating to best practice in the preparation and operation of conferences, the training required, the means of monitoring and evaluating the process (the Thames Valley scheme is being evaluated by the University of Oxford Centre for Criminological Research, with funding from the Joseph Rowntree Foundation), and the eventual cost. More immediate is the question of the procedures to be followed in respect of the new final warnings and referral orders, and in particular whether they are to be modelled on the Thames Valley scheme of restorative conferences. The Act provides that where an offender is prosecuted and goes before a youth court, the court is required to make a referral order on any offender, aged under 18, without previous convictions, who admits his or her guilt and who does not require a custodial sentence. The referral is to a young offender panel drawn from the local community and facilitated by the local youth offending team (see *Chapter 14*). The indications are that a restorative approach will be applied to both final warnings and referral orders, and that some form of conferencing will be adopted for referral orders.

The current debate

There is at present no single pattern or model to which all restorative justice programmes in England and Wales attempt to conform. Among the organizations and individuals concerned with restorative justice, there are differences of view about whether its procedures should operate as part of a judicial process, based in a criminal court; as an adjunct to such a process; or as an alternative to it. There are further differences about whether or not it should be regarded as including a punitive or retributive element; whether it should be operated by the police, by other statutory services, or by voluntary organizations or individuals; whether it should be confined to juveniles and minor offences or whether it could be extended to adults or more serious matters; whether it can be applied in cases where the person complained about wishes to deny his or her guilt in court; whether those taking part could or should have legal advisers present and if so whether they should qualify for legal aid; whether the process is sufficiently accountable, including whether there should be formal channels for appeals or complaints; whether it should be subject to a code of standards and if so how it should be enforced; and various other matters. It is not yet clear whether the process will prove to be swift and economical, or long drawn-out and expensive; or what training or preparation will be needed for facilitators or others taking part.

The Restorative Justice Consortium, comprising a number of organizations concerned with promoting restorative practices and representative organizations of some of the relevant statutory bodies, has produced a set of standards.[13] Some members are concerned that practices which do not comply with those standards will bring the idea into disrepute. But there is at present no general agreement to those standards and they do not cover all the issues which are still unresolved. An attempt to impose standards and guidelines prematurely would risk bureaucratising the process and stifling the spontaneity, creativity, flexibility and local enthusiasm which are its strengths.

The way forward

Reflecting on the development of restorative justice in the United States, Michael Smith[14] has drawn attention to the variety of its interpretations and origins - religious, cultural, political, spiritual and practical - and the fact that its consensual and voluntary nature makes it difficult to fuse with existing law and practice on sentencing. He also sees difficulty in reconciling restorative justice with what have come to be seen, after years of neglect, as the proper status and rights of victims and with their individualised and often unpredictable expectations - which do not normally include any sense of obligation towards the offender. Other concerns relate to what he sees as the divergence of aims between a restorative process which is often backward-looking and focused on the offender, the victim and what has happened in the past, and an increasing concern with forward-looking assessments of risk and danger to the public. He also fears that the language and practice of restorative justice will fall short of the political and managerial demands of the evidence-based practice and quantified measures of performance and results.

Tim Newell and Mike Nellis are more optimistic.[15] They have developed a notion of 'community justice' which combines the ideas of restorative justice and community safety (see *Chapter 18*). Some people will associate community justice with the 'exclusionary' ideas of communities which was described in *Chapter 2* - independent-minded, self-reliant groups of people, not dependant on the state and taking responsibility for dealing with the trouble-makers and criminals who come into their midst.[16] Examples range from an idealised view of small-time America and other close-knit communities, through local activists or vigilantes and the community or workplace tribunals which were a feature of the Soviet Union, to beatings administered by para-militaries in Northern Ireland and lynchings when they took place in the United States. The action against supposed paedophiles, stimulated by the campaign in the *News of the World* newspaper during the summer of 2000, is a recent example.

For Mike Nellis and Tim Newell, community justice is something very different. It is closely linked with the ideas of inclusive citizenship and civil society which were the subject of *Chapter 2*. Mike Nellis quotes Jock Young[17]

> The solution lies not in the resurrection of past stabilities, based on nostalgia and a world that will never return, but on a new citizenship, a reflexive modernity that will tackle the problems of justice and community, of reward and individualism, which lie at the heart of liberal democracy.

He criticises the 'liberal' view of society and criminal justice for placing too much emphasis on individual rights, and not enough on the social context and responsibility, and he contrasts it with the communitarian's emphasis on social circumstances, mutual interdependence and responsibilities towards the common good. He sees community safety as a 'step towards community justice' and hopes to see the current initiatives in community safety and community sentences brought together in a combined 'movement' and a range of practical initiatives informed by the principles of restorative justice. Civil society, including voluntary organizations, would have a role to play both in promoting the movement and in giving practical effect to its ideas.

Tim Newell proposes a similar programme of development, with community service having a central role and becoming the core element of a new sentence of the court. He gives examples of the types of processes and the kinds of outcomes which might form part of such a programme, and sees prisons as being included within it.[18] In a different setting and from a different perspective, Michael Smith and Walter Dickey have argued in the United States for a new framework for corrections which would emphasise 'the power of naturally occurring forces in the community to create and maintain public safety and invite corrections to form relationships with them'.[19]

Both Mike Nellis and Tim Newell see a continuing role for punishment, including imprisonment, but they would hope to displace it from the central position which it occupies at present. The associated ideas of sin and guilt would be joined and perhaps overlaid by ideas of reparation, penance, forgiveness and reconciliation. Restorative conferences would be one of the mechanisms for achieving a cultural shift but others would be developed from existing programmes and initiatives[20].

It is hard to tell whether or how far the ideas of restorative or community justice will transform the present system and practice of criminal justice. So far as restorative conferences are concerned, the way forward is probably to allow, encourage and support the developments which are already in progress, with careful monitoring and evaluation, but not to attempt to force any particular pattern, targets, expectations or limitations on those developments at present. But enough is known already to show that those developments will not succeed if they are carried forward in the expectation - among the public, practitioners or offenders and victims themselves - that the process is a form of punishment which is deliberately intended to be humiliating and unpleasant for the offender; or if it begins to appear that victims are being exploited, either as agents of punishment on behalf of the state, or as instruments for the offender's rehabilitation or reform. Nor will they succeed if they are judged only on their 'success' in reducing rates of re-offending, without regard to other considerations such as the satisfaction of victims or the confidence of communities or the public. Despite the danger of bureaucratisation, there may eventually need to be an acknowledged and authoritative framework of principles and safeguards, and of standards and accreditation, if restorative conferences are to be seen as accountable and legitimate. The arrangements will probably need to include a more formally constituted forum, with an independent and suitably qualified chair and requirements to publish reports, and with provision for a separate mechanism to deal when necessary with appeals and complaints.

Other forms of restorative or community justice could be developed and applied in different parts of the system and at different stages in the process. Examples are offences against prison discipline, instances of rowdy and inconsiderate behaviour, and complaints against members of the criminal justice services, especially the police, and including complaints about racist behaviour. In some instances the restorative element will be incorporated into the process (for example discussion with victims and families); in others it will be incorporated into the outcome (apology, some form of compensation, reconciliation; and in some it may be in both. Remorse and the prospect of reconciliation may be a reason for a court to show compassion in sentencing or, in the traditional terminology, may be a mitigating factor. But it is hard to see how both restorative and adversarial elements could be combined in a single form of procedure; or how the outcome of a restorative process could properly be regarded - by the state, by the parties or by the public - as having the same status of a conviction and sentence, arrived at through the traditional process of law. Nor can restorative or community justice be made accountable through the same mechanisms or with the same authority, especially if the 'ownership' of restorative justice rests in some sense with communities rather than the state.

Some dangerous forms of community justice have already been indicated. Those forms favoured by the proponents of restorative justice come from different cultures and societies. No satisfactory means have so far been found for dealing restoratively with cases where the facts are in dispute. The political environment seems, even more than in the 1980s, to favour naming, blaming, shaming, punishing and excluding rather than restoring, reconciling and including. Some of the applications of restorative conferencing and other forms of community conferencing can however be identified and developed, and the opportunities for them can be expanded. It is difficult at present to perceive and design a process by which they can be moved from the margins to the mainstream. Frustration at the limitations of the traditional adversarial system of justice, and the eventual realisation that those limitations are not so much failings that can be corrected by greater efficiency in management and severity in punishment but are inherent in the system, may lead in time to the change in culture and the 'new paradigm' for which the supporters of community justice are hoping. The transformation will need patience and skill, political and professional courage, and calm judgement. There are examples and encouragement to be drawn from experience in other western societies, including Canada. Australia, New Zealand and the United States. Necessary conditions for success are honesty, clarity of purpose and integrity in putting programmes into effect. Programmes must not be presented as reducing crime, or as providing a new service for victims if they are in reality just another means of dealing with offenders.

ENDNOTES for *Chapter 10*

[1] Leon Radzinowicz and Roger Hood, *A History of English Law and its Administration from 1750 Volume 5: The Emergence of Penal Policy*, London, Stevens and Co., 1986, pp. 221-87.

[2] Tim Newell, *Forgiving Justice, A Quaker Vision for Criminal Justice*, London, Quaker Home Service, 2000, pp. 75. Newell suggests that detaining a person on grounds of dangerousness should become a civil matter (in the sense of the person's status while being so detained) and writes: 'If we can see this detention as "protective" of the rights of the person detained, rather than purely "preventive" then the emphasis upon every person as a member of a community who is entitled to respect can be reflected within public policy'.

[3] John Braithwaite, *Crime, Shame and Reintegration*, Melbourne, Cambridge University Press, 1989.

[4] See Tim Newell, *op. cit.*

[5] Barry Vaughan, 'Punishment and Conditional Citizenship', *Punishment and Society*, 2000, 2(1), pp. 23-39.

[6] Desmond King, *In the Name of Liberalism: Illiberal Social Policies in the United States and Britain*, Oxford, Oxford University Press, 1999.

[7] David Garland, 'The Limits of the Sovereign State: Strategies of Crime Control in Contemporary Society', *British Journal Of Criminology*, 1996, pp. 36/4.

[8] Mick Ryan, 'Penal Policy Making Towards the Millennium: Elites and Populists; New Labour and the New Criminology', *International Journal of the Sociology of Law*, 1999, 27, pp. 1-22; Stuart Hall, *The Drift to a Law and Order Society*, London, Cobden Trust, 1980.

[9] See for example Tim Gorringe, *God's Just Vengeance*, Cambridge, Cambridge University Press, 1996; Jim Considine, *Restorative Justice: Healing the Effects of Crime*, Lyttelton NZ, Ploughshare Publications, 1994.

[10] John Braithwaite, *op. cit.*

[11] JUSTICE, *Restoring Youth Justice*, London, JUSTICE, 2000.

[12] James Dignan, 'The Crime and Disorder Act and the Prospects for Restorative Justice', *Criminal Law Review*, 1999, pp. 48-60.

[13] The Restorative Justice Consortium, *Standards for Restorative Justice*, London, Restorative Justice Consortium, 1999.

[14] Michael Smith, 'What Future For Public Safety and Restorative Justice in a System of Community Penalties?', Paper for the 24th Cropwood Conference, Cambridge Institute of Criminology, 2000, (forthcoming).

[15] Tim Newell, *op. cit.*, n. 2; Mike Nellis, 'Creating Community Justice' in Scott Ballintyre, Ken Pease and Vic McLaren (eds.), *Secure Foundations*, London, Institute for Public Policy Research, 2000, pp. 67-86.

[16] Amitai Etzioni favours restorative justice as part of his vision of confident self-reliant communities. See *The Third Way to a Good Society*, London, Demos, 2000.

[17] Mike Nellis, *op. cit.*, n. 15, pp. 42-66; Jock Young, 'Writing on the Cusp of Change: A New Criminology for an Age of Late Modernity' in Paul Walton and Jock Young (eds.), *The New Criminology Revisited*, Basingstoke, Macmillan, 1998.

[18] Tim Newell, *op. cit.* p. 70. See also Martin Wright, *Restoring Respect for Justice*, Winchester, Waterside Press, 2000.

[19] Michael Smith and Walter Dickey, 'Reforming Sentencing and Corrections for Just Punishment and Public Safety' in *Sentencing and Corrections: Issues for the Twenty-first Century*, Washington DC, National Institute of Justice, September 1999.

[20] Tim Newell, *op. cit.*, n. 2, p. 110. He lists six principles which will 'assist in forging a way forward which is recognised in current good practice':

- Criminal justice should have a well-defined and limited role to play in any democratic society.
- Civil justice is based on the principle of restitution and therefore is more in keeping with our theme.
- De-penalisation should be the aim for all societies.
- Private, for-profit prisons are likely to lead to pressure to increase the use of imprisonment and therefore should be opposed.
- Respect for human rights should be asserted to include all members of the community.
- Criminal justice systems should work to include women and ethnic minorities working at all levels of their operation.

CHAPTER 11

Crimes and the Scope of the Criminal Law

The end of law is not to abolish or restrain, but to preserve and enlarge freedom.

John Locke, *Second Treatise of Civil Government*, 1690, Ch. 6 Sect. 57

Society cannot live by law alone. It needs our common commitment to the common good.

Jonathan Sacks, 'Law, Morality and the Common Good' in *Juvenile Delinquency in the US and the UK*, 1999

There is no simple statement of the purpose of criminal justice – of why there is a system of criminal law, an apparatus for its enforcement and for the trial and punishment of those who offend against it, and services or institutions which perform those functions. *Chapter 6* has described various approaches to questions of crime and criminal justice, from which it could be inferred that the purpose is to condemn and punish acts of wrongdoing (on the classical or retributivist approach), or to prevent crime and protect the public (on the utilitarian approach). The Conservative Government set out the objectives of its own strategy for the criminal justice system (see *Chapter 7*), and the Labour Government set out what it sees as the objectives of the system itself - namely *to reduce crime and the fear of crime, and their social and economic costs; and to dispense justice fairly and efficiently, and to promote confidence in the rule of law* (see *Chapter 9*). Statements of this kind are very much in the spirit of modern government and management, but they are of little help in indicating the kind of policies which might be adopted to achieve them, or in resolving the conflicts which inevitably arise within them. Even so, the way in which a modern state conceives the purpose of its criminal justice system, the standards and beliefs which inform its criminal justice arrangements, and the attitudes of its citizens towards crime and those who commit it, are both an expression of, and a powerful influence upon, the character of their society.

Increase in the number of criminal offences

Most people would probably agree that for an action (or omission) to be made a criminal offence, it should be one which is generally perceived to be wrong, either because it is morally wrong in itself or because of its likely effects. Other considerations arise from the practicability of detection and enforcement; from the construction of the offence itself (for example whether it should be an absolute offence or require evidence of criminal intent, or whether any statutory defence should be available);

and from any other evidential requirements which may need to be satisfied.

The scope of the criminal law has been greatly expanded in recent times. JUSTICE calculated in 1980[1] that there were at that time about 7,200 different criminal offences, but no official count had ever been made. Andrew Ashworth has suggested that by 2000 the total had probably reached 8000.[2] In a Parliamentary Question on 18 June 1999, Lord Dholakia asked the Government

> How many criminal offences have been created or are currently proposed in (a) public legislation and (b) private acts since 1 May 1997.

Lord Williams replied

> Although the Home Office is responsible for scrutinising proposals for new offences in both public and private legislation, no comprehensive records are kept centrally of all new offences created in public legislation.
>
> The Crime and Disorder Act 1998 creates two new offences: breach of anti-social behaviour orders and breach of sex offender orders. It also creates nine racially-aggravated offences, but these are based on existing offences and do not render unlawful behaviour which would otherwise have been lawful. All these measures have been implemented.
>
> The Data Protection Act 1998 creates four offences, which have yet to be implemented.
>
> The following proposals for new offences are currently before Parliament:
>
> - the Immigration and Asylum Bill: 12 new offences;
> - the Sale and Breeding of Dogs (Welfare) Bill: ten new offences (of which four apply only in Scotland);
> - the Youth Justice and Criminal Evidence Bill: four new offences; and
> - the Football (Offences and Disorder) Bill: one new offence.
>
> Among Private Bills/Acts
>
> - The City of Westminster Act 1999 contained eight new offences.
> - Four private Bills proposing the creation of new offences are currently before Parliament:
>
>> Kent Council Bill: 23 new offences;
>> Medway Council Bill: 23 new offences;
>> City of Newcastle upon Tyne Bill: 13 new offences; and
>> London Local Authorities Bill: 14 new offences.
>
> The 23 offences proposed in the Kent Council Bill are identical to those in the Medway Council Bill.

In a similar Answer on 1 February 2001, Lord Bassam indicated that a total of 139 new offences had been created in legislation passed during the Parliamentary session 1999-2000, and the process seems likely to continue indefinitely at a similar rate.

Types of criminal offence
Criminal offences now comprise, broadly

- those acts which are regarded as morally wrong in most societies and cultures - for example murder, robbery, assault, burglary, fraud and theft - although cultural differences may be reflected in their definitions or in attitudes towards them;
- regulatory offences relating to the consumption and supply of drugs and alcohol, road traffic, public health or safety, trading standards and a range of other matters which may need regulation in a complex modern society;
- a range of sometimes controversial offences which fall between those categories, relating for example to public order, unfair forms of discrimination, sexual behaviour or cruelty to animals, and perhaps including some of the new forms of 'cyber-crime';
- increasingly, absolute offences of failing to comply with orders or instructions issued under legislation designed to promote social control, for example those created by the Criminal Justice and Public Order Act 1994, the Prevention of Harassment Act 1997 and the Crime and Disorder Act 1998.

The Government's Answers to Lord Dholakia make clear that new offences are constantly being created, especially in the last three categories. Their intention and effect is both to make the criminal law more severe and to extend its scope by bringing within it new forms of action, omission or behaviour. Governments regularly use expressions like 'strengthening the law' or 'making the law more effective' to describe proposals of this kind.

Particular difficulties arise over those actions or types of behaviour which some sections of society regard as repugnant on social, moral or religious grounds - abortion, certain forms of sexual behaviour, the use of drugs - but which others regard as tolerable or even normal. The former will regard any weakening of the criminal law as a threat to society's social and moral order, and may sometimes call for the law on these matters to be strengthened; the latter may evade the law or ignore it altogether. The law itself may be selectively enforced (or hardly at all). These are traditionally the areas where political parties allow Members of Parliament a free vote, and members have to make difficult judgements when such issues come to be debated. Changes in the law can have a powerful symbolic, or declaratory, as well as a substantive, effect and they should not be undertaken lightly. But laws which are unenforceable, or which are widely disregarded or regarded as oppressive, do not do much for the authority of the state. And just as the criminal process can by itself have only a limited effect in preventing crime, so it is a weak moral code which has to rely on the criminal law for its observance and enforcement.

The Terrorism Act 2000 created a number of offences which are punishable by sentences ranging from six months to life imprisonment. Terrorism is broadly defined to include an action or threat of action which is 'designed to influence the government or to intimidate the public or a section of the public' if it involves serious violence, serious damage to property, endangers life, creates a serious risk to health and safety of the public or a section of the public, or is designed to interfere with or seriously disrupt an electronic system. A person commits an offence punishable by 14 years' imprisonment if (among other things) he or she 'uses money or other property for the purposes of terrorism'; and (with some qualifications) an offence punishable by five years' imprisonment if he or she does not disclose a belief or suspicion that another person has committed such an offence. These are draconian provisions, perhaps justifiable if they are related to acts of terrorism as the term is ordinarily understood, but they are capable of being applied to almost any act of public protest under the definition as it stands. The Government claimed that the police and the Crown Prosecution Service would use their discretion sensibly, but discretion in these circumstances is a matter of political rather than professional or operational judgement. It is not a judgement which the police should be expected to make, and it does nothing for the rule of law to have in force a statute which is rarely enforced, or if it were generally enforced would be an instrument of political oppression.

Well-known arguments relate to the Misuse of Drugs Act 1971, and to proposals that the possession of cannabis should cease to be a criminal offence, presumably with parallel amendments to the law on supplying the drug so that it could be legally supplied through channels which could be suitably approved and regulated. This chapter will not attempt to rehearse those arguments, except to point out that the criminal law is only a small and not particularly effective part of the array of measures which are needed to deal with the problems associated with the abuse of cannabis and other more dangerous drugs – problems which are themselves perceived by different people in very different ways. The structure, content and operation of the Misuse of Drugs Act should therefore be kept under regular and dispassionate review, and proposals for adjustment should be considered calmly and on their merits. Demands for increased penalties and for more rigorous enforcement or decriminalisation are not the only arguments which deserve to be examined. The Police Foundation's Independent Inquiry into the Misuse of Drugs Act put forward a total of 81 recommendations, only one of which concerned the re-classification (not de-criminalisation) of cannabis.[3] Others concerned, for example, the creation of a new offence of dealing; the redefinition of certain other offences; the statutory defences which might be put forward in various circumstances; the features which should be treated as aggravating factors; adjustment to maximum penalties; and proposals on how penalties should be imposed or enforced, including the introduction of out of court fines (see *Chapter 12*) and the creation of a new agency to manage the confiscation of assets.

The Inquiry is an example of the kind of review of the criminal law and its enforcement which should be taken on a more regular and systematic basis. Such reviews are the proper business of the Law Commission, which should normally be the body to undertake them; but the Inquiry was able to look beyond the provisions of the Misuse of Drugs Act to the wider questions of treatment for addiction and abuse, and their relationship with other parts of the criminal law, in ways which would have been difficult for the Law Commission with its present composition and terms of reference.

Criteria for creating a criminal offence

In a second Parliamentary Question, also on 18 June 1999, Lord Dholakia asked Her Majesty's Government

> What principles they observe, and what considerations they take into account, when proposing the creation of new criminal offences and the maximum penalties which they should attract.

Lord Williams replied

> The Government are mindful that the criminal justice system is a scarce resource and take the view that new offences should be created only when absolutely necessary.

> In considering whether new offences should be created, factors taken into account include whether:

> - the behaviour in question is sufficiently serious to warrant intervention by the criminal law;
> - the mischief could be dealt with under existing legislation or using other remedies;
> - the proposed offence is enforceable in practice;
> - the proposed offence is tightly drawn and legally sound; and
> - the proposed penalty is commensurate with the seriousness of the offence.

> The Government also take into account the need to ensure, as far as practicable, that there is consistency across the sentencing framework.

The two replies suggest a degree of insouciance on the Government's part in asking Parliament to restrict citizens' liberty by creating new criminal offences. It is remarkable that the first constraint which they acknowledge is the cost of enforcement, rather than the need to justify encroachments on personal freedom. There is no mention at all of the social consequences of criminalising an increasingly wide range of actions or behaviours, of giving increasing numbers of individuals a criminal record, or of the stigmatising effect of doing so. There has been no recent study of public attitudes to convictions or to people with criminal records. But a statement of any convictions is increasingly required in connection with applications for insurance, banking or mortgage facilities or rented accommodation, and those with criminal records are increasingly at risk of being refused or of having to pay higher charges. An expansion of the behaviours which are classed as criminal, especially if it extends to behaviour which is not in itself thought to be harmful or morally wrong, may also lead to a reluctance on the part of the police to charge or the courts (especially juries) to convict, and to a more general loss of respect for the criminal law and a weakening both of its authority and of its deterrent effect. As Andrew Ashworth has said

> There is little sense that the decision to introduce a new offence should only be made after certain conditions have been satisfied, little sense that making conduct criminal is a step of considerable social significance.[4]

One reason for the increase in the number of criminal offences is the increased complexity of modern life, including the problems presented by drugs and alcohol, the danger of racial and other forms of discrimination, and the need to regulate activities which have been made possible by the growth of technology and the opportunities it has provided. But another is the difficulty of sustaining prosecutions and obtaining convictions for 'ordinary' criminal offences such as those associated with disruptive or anti-social behaviour, or of controlling behaviour which cannot itself easily be made criminal. The obvious examples are the public order offences created by the Criminal Justice and Public Order Act 1994 relating to noise, parties ('raves'), squatters and demonstrations; the offences of harassment created by the Prevention of Harassment Act 1997; and those created by the Crime and Disorder Act 1998 to which Lord Williams referred in his Answer to Lord Dholakia. Further examples are the offences created or re-defined by the Terrorism Act 2000, and the classification as 'terrorism' of offences which most people would regard as ordinary, even legitimate, acts of protest. From a human rights perspective, it is no consolation for the Government to say that prosecutions will be used sparingly, at the discretion of the police: that amounts to saying that there will be no effective protection against their use in ways which are arbitrary or haphazard unless there is a breach of the European Convention On Human Rights.

This expansion of criminal law is central to the Government's view of social responsibility and the duties of citizenship. But Andrew Ashworth has pointed out that it raises questions of compatibility with the Human Rights Act and the European Convention On Human Rights,[5] and the creation of new offences needs careful scrutiny and constant vigilance. A more principled approach is encouragingly to be found in the consultation paper which the Home Office issued in August 2000 on the law on sex offences.[6] The review which produced the consultation paper took careful account of the European Convention On Human Rights, especially the articles concerned with the right to a fair trail, to private life and to non-discrimination in the enjoyment of ECHR rights. The Law Commission was associated with the review, and contributed its own report on consent in sex offences.

The review established two principles. The first was that society's judgement of what is right and wrong should be based on an assessment of the harm done to the individual, and through the individual to society as a whole. The second was that the criminal law should not intrude unnecessarily into the private life of adults. The review also assumed that any application of the criminal law must be fair, necessary and proportionate; and thought it was vital that the law should be clear and well understood. These are sound principles, which should be generally applied.

Problems of complexity and scale

The problem of creating offences for regulatory purposes, and of criminalising actions which are not seen as particularly wrong in themselves, led JUSTICE and others to propose a 'middle' system of law[7] with a clear distinction between 'crimes' and 'contraventions', with 'contraventions' generally being enforced by administrative measures or penalties, although with the possibility of a reference to a magistrates' court in the event of a disagreement. Under such a system a range of what are now criminal offences would be taken out of the criminal law and dealt with administratively by financial penalties or orders to carry out certain works or pay compensation for damage or loss. There would be provisions for appeals to a court or another suitable tribunal, and for the enforcement of penalties which might for some exceptional purposes include imprisonment. The view within government at the time was that some progress in this direction could be made by extending the use of fixed penalties - as has been done, especially in relation to road traffic offences - but that the apparatus which would be needed for a complete new system of enforcement and adjudication would be too expensive, and the practical benefits too limited, for any further development to be justified. This view will no doubt continue to prevail, but the problem of 'over-criminalisation', of the disabling social consequences of a conviction, and of the possible effect on respect for the criminal law, remain unresolved and should be re-examined.

More recently, Andrew Ashworth[8] has argued that the law of tort should not be seen only as a system for securing compensation for people who have been wronged, and that it also has a more public function of discouraging certain forms of behaviour. He does not go on to argue that the scope of the criminal law might be cut back and proceedings in tort allowed to take its place - the perceived ineffectiveness of civil proceedings and the delays involved were among the reasons for some of the criminal offences which have been created in recent years - but it does have the attraction, in modern political circumstances, of focusing attention on the interests of the victim and the harm which the victim may have suffered. Ashworth's own conclusion, resembling that of JUSTICE 20 years before is that

A fine solution would be to create a new category of 'civil violation' or 'administrative offence' which would certainly be non-imprisonable and would normally attract a financial penalty; procedures would be simplified but would preserve minimum rights for defendants, such as access to a criminal court.

Ashworth does however point out that the inter-relationship of punishment and compensation is becoming more complex and the boundaries blurred, especially in criminal cases. He is particularly critical of attempts to combine civil and criminal procedures as a means of by-passing the normal protections of the criminal process, for example in the provisions relating to the anti-social behaviour order in Section 1 Crime and Disorder Act 1998. The situation is likely to become even more complex, the distinctions even more blurred, and the protection of the criminal law perhaps more enfeebled, if legislation to promote the interests of victims in criminal proceedings is pursued without full consideration of the implications and consequences. It is also likely to become more complex if the criminal law comes to be seen primarily as an instrument of crime prevention and social control, for which on all the evidence it is not particularly successful or well-suited - as distinct from resolving, so far as possible, the situation created by harmful and unacceptable behaviour.

Problems of a different kind arise from the number of criminal offences, and from the complexity which results both from their number and from their different origins in common law and in statute law. Some offences, such as theft, vary enormously in their character and seriousness, and a maximum penalty of, say, five years (in the case of theft, having been reduced from seven years in the Criminal Justice Act 1991) may be out of all proportion to most of the offences which are prosecuted under the relevant provisions. The problems have led some reformers to call for the formulation and enactment of a unified criminal code. Arguments in favour of a code include not only simplicity, but also certainty, and savings in cost. Most other European countries have a unified criminal code, and the Law Commission proposed in 1989 that a code should be adopted in England and Wales.[9] Further reports from the Law Commission put forward a draft for the section of the code which would deal with assault and other offences against the person, involuntary manslaughter and corruption.

The Law Commission and others supporting the adoption of a code acknowledged the Parliamentary and political difficulty of its enactment under the present procedures and conventions - the amount of Parliamentary time which would be occupied and the draft's vulnerability to detailed and time-consuming amendment. But it would be disappointing if a modernising government, ready among other things to reform the House of Lords, were not prepared to ask Parliament to examine those of its procedures which prevent it from enacting measures of law reform. Such measures might reasonably be expected to form part of any programme for 'modernisation' as it applies to the criminal law. It is interesting that in its White Paper *Criminal Justice: The Way Ahead* published in February 2001,[10] the Government says it will consider 'reform of the criminal law to provide a consolidated, modernised core criminal code, covering evidence, procedure, substantive offences and sentencing'. This would be an ambitious programme, needing effort, experience and skill, probably over a number of years. It would be a welcome and worthwhile project. But it would have to be approached with the aim not only of improving the system's efficiency and effectiveness in achieving more convictions and doing so more rapidly, but also of improving standards of justice and of promoting the rights and responsibilities of citizenship by making the law more intelligible and accessible.

Whether or not the Government is disposed to re-open discussion on a 'middle' system of law, or to give any serious consideration to the enactment of a criminal code, the Government and Parliament should be rigorous in scrutinising proposals for the creation of new criminal offences.

The Government should ask the Law Commission to review the criteria for the creation of new criminal offences which Lord Williams indicated in his Answer, together with the boundary between the criminal law and the law of tort. The Government should then propose, and Parliament should approve, a revised and up-to-date set of principles and criteria; and in scrutinising future legislation Parliament should rigorously test any proposals for new criminal offences against those criteria and an assessment of the social consequences. The approach which the review of the law on sex offences adopted for the reform of that area of the criminal law, and the principles which it established, provide an excellent model and starting point.

ENDNOTES for *Chapter 11*

[1] JUSTICE, *Breaking the Rules*, London, JUSTICE, 1980.

[2] Ashworth argues that in the majority of instances there are important issues of how the criminal law ought to be shaped, of what its social significance should be, and of when it should be used, which are simply not being addressed. 'Is the Criminal Law a Lost Cause?', *The Law Quarterly Review*, 2000, Vol.116 pp. 225-56.

[3] Police Foundation, *Drugs and the Law*, Report of the Independent Inquiry into the Misuse of Drugs Act 1971, London, Police Foundation, 2000.

[4] Ashworth states that the contours of English criminal law are 'historically contingent', in the sense that they are not the product of any principled inquiry or consistent application of certain criteria, but largely dependent on the fortunes of successive governments, on campaigns in the mass media and on the activities of various pressure groups. Ashworth's opinion is that governments often take the view that the creation of a new crime sends out a symbolic message that 'may get them off the hook'. *Op. cit.*

[5] Ashworth, *op. cit.*

[6] Home Office, *Setting the Boundaries: Reforming the Law on Sex Offenders*, London, Home Office, 2000.

[7] JUSTICE, *op. cit.*

[8] Ashworth, *op.cit.*

[9] Law Commission, *A Criminal Code for England and Wales*, Vol. 1 and 2; *Report and Draft Criminal Code Bill*, Law Commission Report No. 177, 1989.

[10] Home Office, *Criminal Justice: The Way Ahead*, Cm. 5074, Stationery Office, 2001.

CHAPTER 12

The Sentence of the Court

It is excellent to have a giant's strength, but tyrannous to use it as a giant.

Isabella in Shakespeare's *Measure for Measure*, Act II, Scene ii.

The aims of sentencing

The traditional aims of sentencing, to which most judges and magistrates would probably still subscribe, are those of retribution (on the classical model), and of prevention, deterrence and rehabilitation (on the utilitarian model). The need to find a suitable balance between them in particular cases is one of the acknowledged difficulties in the criminal justice process.[1] As *Chapter 7* has described, a sense that the balance was not being satisfactorily achieved, and that sentencing was inconsistent and sometimes unnecessarily severe, was one of the reasons which led to the passage of the Criminal Justice Act 1991. Another reason was the need to achieve some correspondence between sentencing practice and the availability of prison accommodation. Further influences on the Act were the evidence from research that an increase in the severity of sentencing has in general little deterrent effect;[2] and doubts whether the rehabilitative effect of imprisonment (which some critics had been inclined to deny altogether) could ever justify a longer sentence than could be justified on the grounds of retribution alone. In a more general sense, there was widespread scepticism about the actual or even potential effectiveness of sentencing - and especially of custodial sentencing - in achieving utilitarian or instrumental aims of the kind for which earlier reformers had hoped. Other concerns related to the criteria and procedures for early release on parole, or for release on licence from sentences of life imprisonment.

The 1991 Act accordingly established the 'seriousness' of the offence as the principal justification for the severity of the sentence: 'so serious' that only a custodial sentence could be justified, and 'serious enough' to justify a community sentence - although with an exception for cases where a longer custodial sentence might be justified to protect the public from serious violent or sexual offences. The sentences themselves were similarly graded, with a clear distinction between imprisonment, community sentences, and financial penalties (fines and compensation orders). The Act thus imposed a structure on the sentencing process, and it reinforced that structure by a requirement for the court to give reasons for its sentencing decisions.

Chapter 8 has described how the 1991 Act was subsequently modified both by amending legislation and also, in effect, by the Court of Appeal. In particular, the Crime (Sentences) Act 1997 provided for mandatory sentences of imprisonment for certain repeated offences - life sentences for those convicted for a second time of serious sexual or violent offences, seven years for those convicted for a second offence of manufacturing or supplying class A drugs, three years for those convicted for a third time for burglary. More recently, the Labour Government has imported further considerations into what it sees as the aims of sentencing - the protection of the public; the need to maintain public confidence; a renewed if unsubstantiated belief in deterrence (expressed for example through its endorsement of mandatory sentences); and more positively an increasing interest in 'reparative' or 'restorative' justice.

The considerations which governments, and possibly the public, expect the courts to take into account have therefore become even more complex since the passage of the 1991 Act. At the same time, the problems of inconsistency, and of what is seen as unnecessary severity in some cases and undue leniency in others, are just as intractable,[3] although it is only undue leniency that seems to give rise to public or political concern. The problems seem to be more acute, and to have more serious consequences, for members of minority ethnic groups (see *Chapter 16*) than they do for other offenders; and the report of the Prison Reform Trust's Committee on Women's Imprisonment has shown that they may also do so for women.[4] The Government, and the public, are also concerned about the rates at which offenders are convicted of further offences, and about the lack of attention which is paid to victims.

The Sentencing Advisory Panel

Section 81 Crime and Disorder Act 1998 requires the Lord Chancellor to constitute a Sentencing Advisory Panel, with duties to advise the Court of Appeal on the framing or revision of the sentencing guidelines which the Court has a statutory duty to consider under section 80 of the Act. In doing so, the Court must have regard to, among other things, the need to promote consistency in sentencing, the cost of different sentences and their effect in preventing re-offending, and the need to promote public confidence in the criminal justice system.

The appointment of the Sentencing Advisory Panel is a welcome development. It has the potential to generate a more principled and more coherent or 'joined-up' approach to sentencing, as Andrew Ashworth hoped when he first put the idea forward (in a rather different form) in the early 1980s.[5] Its statutory authority - and the Government's, and the courts', own expectations so far as they can be ascertained at this stage - do not as yet require it to look beyond the detail of anomalies which may arise in particular types of case, or beyond offences to the circumstances and characteristics of the offenders. The Police Foundation's Independent Inquiry into the Misuse of Drugs Act 1971[6] recommended that the Panel should propose guidelines for drugs offences, and especially for the aggravating factors relating to trafficking offences. The Committee on Women's Imprisonment has made some valuable suggestions for expanding the Panel's role and scope,[7] and specifically recommended that it should consider those mitigating factors which may be of particular significance to women. Similar considerations apply to members of racial or cultural groups. The hope must be that the role and influence of the Panel will be progressively extended, so that it can make an increasingly dynamic contribution to the sentencing process. *Chapter 21* considers a possible structure for strategic planning more generally.

Review of the sentencing framework

The Government announced on 16 May 2000 that it was setting up a review of the sentencing framework, to be led by John Halliday. In a leaflet explaining that decision it said

> Public confidence in our system of justice is too low. There is a feeling that our sentencing framework does not work as well as it should and that it pays insufficient weight to the needs of victims. Too many offenders are returning to court on too regular a basis. There is insufficient consistency or progression in sentencing practice and sentencers received insufficient information about whether their sentencing decisions have worked. The sentencing decision itself focuses too much on the offence and not sufficiently on offenders and their future behaviour...
>
> Some steps to improve consistency and progression have already been taken. Minimum mandatory sentences for repeat serious sexual and violent offenders, drug dealers and burglars have been introduced. The Crime and Disorder Act established a Sentencing Advisory Panel which is already doing valuable work. But the current legal framework established in the Criminal Justice Act 1991 remains, and this appears now to be a contributory factor to inherent problems of sentencing - based as it is on the principle of 'just deserts' by which the sentence imposed is tied to the seriousness of the offence, taking little account of offenders' propensity to re-offend. It also offers little opportunity to take into account how offenders respond to measures taken during the sentence which are designed to reduce their re-offending, nor the need for some form of reparation to society.

It went on

> In the light of the Government's objectives to protect the public by reducing crime and re-offending, and to dispense justice fairly and consistently, the terms of reference of the review are:
>
> To consider:
>
> - what principles should guide sentencing decisions;
> - what types of disposal should be made available to the courts in order to meet the overarching objectives;
> - the costs of different disposals and their relative effectiveness in reducing re-offending;
> - what changes therefore need to be made to the current sentencing framework, as established by the Criminal Justice Act 1991, so as more effectively to reduce re-offending, including any transitional and consequential arrangements; and

- the likely impact of any recommendations in terms of costs and the effects on the prison population.

In particular, the review will identify and evaluate new more flexible frameworks for sentence decision-making and sentence management, which join up custodial and community penalties, in ways which maximise crime reduction, sustain public confidence, protect the public, and take full account of the interests of victims, as cost effectively as possible.

In a speech to the Central Probation Council on the day of the announcement[8] the Home Secretary, Jack Straw, said

I would like to see whether a different framework would be more supportive of what we are trying to do. One which encourages the prison and probation services to work even more closely together to reduce re-offending and protect the public. One that is based on evidence as well as principles. A framework which takes account of the relevance of re-offending risks to the sentencing decision. One which allows us to develop new sentences which embrace part custody, part community elements. And one which allows for new ways of taking into account changes in the risk of re-offending during the sentence.

One obvious question is whether the new forms of sentencing – the Government indicated such ideas as a 'custody plan', 'variable custody', 'suspended custody' and 'day custody'[9] - would be introduced as additions to the sentences already available, or whether they would form a new framework into which existing sentences would be absorbed. At one extreme, all existing community sentences could be incorporated into the new arrangements as conditions of a suspended sentence of imprisonment, leading to an increased and possibly arbitrary use of custody for those who 'failed'. At the other, the new arrangements might be used as a method of accelerated release for large numbers of prisoners who would serve substantially shorter periods in custody than they do at present. They could thus lead to a substantial fall in the prison population.

The Government's thinking and explanation

The Government's explanation of the Review begs a number of questions. Public lack of confidence in the criminal justice system is not focused exclusively or even especially on sentencing: people will often say that sentencing in general is too soft, but Home Office surveys have shown that in relation to a range of typical cases public opinion seems to correspond broadly with existing sentencing practice.[10] Public concern is much more generalised. Similarly, there are good reasons for saying that the system as a whole does not pay enough attention to the needs of victims, but it is much less clear that victims' needs can or should be taken more fully into account in the sentencing process (see *Chapter 15*). And although the extent to which sentencing should focus on the offence or the offender is open to debate, it is still arguable (to say the least) that justice requires the starting point to be the seriousness of the offence - the harm done and the culpability of the offender - rather than the offender's character and personality. The reference to mandatory sentences as a means of achieving 'consistency and progression' in sentencing implies an arbitrary and mechanical approach which is potentially unjust. So far from achieving consistency, mandatory sentences will result in identical sentences for offences which may be very different in their character and seriousness. The whole approach, especially the words 'whether their sentencing decision has worked', implies an empirically and conceptually misguided view of sentencing which sees it as an instrumental process similar to the prescription of a drug or a repair to a piece of machinery. In a situation of such political confusion about the nature, purpose and principles of sentencing, a review which starts with the principles which should guide sentencing decisions is timely and welcome.

The Government's emphasis on consistency, progression and flexibility in sentencing clearly marks a significant and deliberate change of direction from the approach adopted in the Criminal Justice Act 1991. It reflects a move away from the classical or retributive view of sentencing which informed the 1991 Act, and towards a utilitarian and instrumental view of the kind which had been prominent in the 1960s. There are similar references to courses and programmes which will change an offender's behaviour and to sentencing decisions which will 'work' or 'do the trick' in turning an offender away from crime. There is a similar faith in scientific or 'evidence-based' methods which will produce recipes or remedies for changing human behaviour (although the methods are now based more on technology and actuarial accountancy than on social science). The language of 'progression' also recalls the attempts to deal with the 'habitual criminal' which were made in the 1860s, and later through the sentence of preventive detention (see *Chapter 6*); and 'flexibility' suggests a return to indeterminate sentences such as borstal training, or to a more flexible form of parole or conditional release (see *Chapter 13*). Both were eventually found to be unjust. 'Progression' had a disproportionately severe effect on those whose offences were relatively trivial; 'flexibility' was open to manipulation and abuse by institutional staff.

Questions and concerns

The fact that previous attempts to achieve progression and flexibility in sentencing were eventually abandoned is obviously not, in itself, an objection to reviving them. It is reasonable to take a more optimistic view that 'some things work' (or may work) than was fashionable in the 1970s and 1980s. But more evidence still has to be assembled and tested, and the discovery that 'some things work' owes as much to the political imperative for successive governments to find some things that the public think will work as it does to the actual discovery of new empirical evidence. The Home Office Research Study *Reducing Offending*[11] reviewed the evidence on 'what works' to prevent crime, and showed that only a small contribution can be expected from changes in sentencing policy and practice. It did however make the point that the cost of achieving a reduction in crime of around 0.6 per cent through increases in the prison population alone would be about £380 million a year, whereas a similar reduction could be achieved through a targeted programme to reduce burglary in high risk areas at one tenth of the cost. The Government should satisfy itself, and the country, that previous failures and disappointments will not be repeated.

Principles of sentencing
As well as questions about the empirical evidence to support whatever reforms the Government decides to introduce as a result of the review, there are concerns about the coherence and perhaps even the legitimacy of the principles involved. 'Consistency' for the Government seems to mean consistency in relation to the statutory (or occasionally common law) offence of which a person has been convicted, for example through the application of mandatory sentences which deny or severely restrict the courts' discretion. The courts on the other hand have usually thought of consistency as related more to the seriousness of the offence as actually committed, the harm done, and the culpability of the offender and the impact of the sentence on him or her. More controversial applications of consistency would relate it to the circumstances of the offender, or his or her family, or the situation and feelings of the victim. Whether or not the court decided to take these considerations into account in a particular case, its discretion to do so has usually been seen as a necessary part of justice.

Similar considerations apply to 'proportionality'. Proportionality is usually judged in relation to the same criteria, and it is an important feature in the jurisprudence of the European Court of Human Rights. It has not usually been linked to judgements about the character of the offender. A person's previous record may be relevant to the court's judgement of the seriousness of the offence, or of the culpability of the offender, but it is hard to see how it could justify treating the latest in a series of small thefts from shops as equivalent to an offence of armed robbery. It is equally hard to see how such an outcome could be justified by an assessment of the actuarial probability of the person's re-offending, based on risk factors over which they may have no control.

A related principle is 'parsimony' - the punishment or interference with a person's life should be the minimum that is possible in the circumstances of the case. The Prison Reform Trust's Committee on Women's Imprisonment argued for this principle. It did not seem to appeal to the Labour Government, but many judges and magistrates would accept it as a necessary part of justice, even though they might disagree about its application in particular situations.

A fourth principle is the avoidance of improper discrimination and, more arguably but in the spirit of the Race Relations (Amendment) Act

2000, the need to promote racial equality. This principle is discussed in *Chapter 16*.

Persistent and dangerous offenders

Andrew Ashworth has considered the problems which have been associated with attempts to predict the frequency or type of offences which a person might commit in the future, and therefore with proposals to frame sentencing provisions which are claimed to give the public special protection from particularly troublesome or dangerous offenders. Such proposals are likely - and have been found in the past - to be both ineffective and unjust. He has drawn particular attention to the provisions of section 2(2)(b) Criminal Justice Act 1991 which, contrary to the general framework of the 1991 Act, allows courts to impose longer sentences than would be justified by the seriousness of the particular offence in order to protect the public from serious offences of a sexual or violent nature.[12] He writes

> The power to impose a longer-than normal sentence granted by section 2(2)(b) of the 1991 Act is fundamentally unsatisfactory. The legislative scheme is inadequate, incorporating few procedural safeguards (particularly a medical report) against the imposition of what is, in plain terms, an extra sentence. The Court of Appeal deserves considerable credit for adopting a more critical approach to these enhanced sentences in some decisions, but this cannot conceal the underlying flaws of the power. Section 2(2)(b) is presented as if the criminological evidence of the fallibility of predictions of dangerousness did not exist. It is also presented as if no further or stronger justification is required for imprisoning these offenders for longer than normal. The theoretical weaknesses stem from its origins in political compromise - a counterweight to what was intended to be a reduction in the use of custody for less serious offences - but their significance remains fundamental.

The outcome of the review was still unclear at the time of writing. But it seemed clear that the report would include a strong emphasis on programmes and procedures to reduce re-offending, which would be in some way incorporated into the sentence itself; and on measures to protect the public from persistent or dangerous offenders, probably by some form of 'loaded' sentence related to the offender's record and an assessment of risk. Both would include provisions for the conditions of the sentence to be varied to take account of the offender's progress or circumstances - to be moved into or out of custody, to take part in or be withdrawn from a programme of training or resettlement, to be subjected to or released from a condition of residence or electronic monitoring. A new type of 'review court' might be established to take or supervise those decisions.

Putting reforms into effect

In acting on the review, the Government will need to take into account the capacity, culture and dynamics of the services which have to administer progressive or flexible sentences, both in custody and in the community; the resources and good will on which statutory services and civil society are able to draw in providing support for offenders in local communities; the perceived fairness and legitimacy of the sentence; and the consequences of that perception both for offenders and for those who work or are involved with them. One relevant consideration will be the operation of any process or risk assessment, especially if decisions are made on a basis of previous record and statistical probability which the individual can do nothing to change, rather than individual assessment of the offender's intentions, prospects and character. Problems of fairness and legitimacy will be particularly acute if the methodology of its application are open to question - for example if it is perceived to have a discriminatory effect against black people or women.

It is difficult to see how a traditionally constituted court, operating within an adversarial system of justice, could start the sentencing process otherwise than by asking 'What is the offence that the person has been proved to have committed?', 'How serious is it?' and 'How culpable is the offender?'. The answers to those questions should then set the boundaries within which the sentencing decision has to be made. The answers will in the normal case determine the amount of punishment which can be imposed - loss of liberty, demands on the person's time or restrictions on their movements, still very often a fine. *Chapter 10* has however argued that courts should not feel obliged to impose retribution or punishment in every case, and that there will be some cases where an opportunity to make amends through various forms of restorative justice will be sufficient.

There will be occasions for mercy and compassion, even if these words are nowadays not often used. It should only rarely be necessary for the courts to use the full weight of the authority or the powers that are available to them, and never to do so without considering other possible means of resolving the situation that has been presented. Judges and ministers should ponder the dialogue between Isabella and Angelo in Shakespeare's *Measure for Measure*,[13] quoted at the beginning of this chapter, where Angelo argues that Isabella's brother must be executed to uphold the law and satisfy the public 'which a dismissed offence would after gall'. Isabella famously replies 'Oh it is excellent to have a giant's strength, but tyrannous to use it like a giant', and she then goes on to scorn '... proud man, dress'd in little brief authority, most ignorant of what is most assured ....' Angelo speaks in the language of public confidence and mandatory sentencing; Isabella in the language of compassionate and restorative justice.

While the seriousness of the offence should set the upper limit for any loss or curtailment of liberty or the amount of the fine it must probably be accepted, despite the problems already mentioned, that the limit may sometimes have to be exceeded for the protection of the public. If so, the justification should be rigorously tested by the parties in court and the court's decision should be fully explained. Where the outcome is a disproportionate period in custody, special restrictions on movement, or a prolonged or intrusive form of surveillance, the courts and the criminal justice service should not regard those measures as punishment, and as argued in *Chapter 13*, their imposition and subsequent operation should be subject to special conditions, safeguards and mechanisms for review. Whatever the conclusion of the sentencing process, the reasons, including the weight which has been given to the considerations the court has taken into account, should always be explained in open court. The discipline of this practice can also help to guard against any actual, or appearance of, discrimination or prejudice, and to support the authority and legitimacy of the sentencing process. It is now, in effect, a requirement under the Human Rights Act.[14]

Impact of sentences

Whatever loss or curtailment of liberty has to be imposed, the sentence should still allow offenders the greatest possible opportunity to retain or restore their links with their family and community, and with society more widely (or sometimes to establish them for the first time). They should be enabled, and expected, to exercise their rights and responsibilities as citizens, and to make some form of reparation where that is practicable, either to the victim or to the wider community.

The Prison Reform Trust's Committee on Women's Imprisonment argued

> ... the criminal justice system should be designed so as to foster respect for the rights and responsibilities of citizenship and to provide for the potential realisation of those rights to the greatest extent compatible with a similar possibility for all other citizens. The reciprocal obligations of citizenship both inform the justification of punishment and set limits to penal practice; crime violates duties of citizenship and hence demands censure, yet society's response to crime must itself be consistent with offenders' status as citizens and must aim to foster social inclusion.

They go on to say that criminal justice policy, and penal policy in particular, must serve broad social goals and observe social principles. Courts should seek and reconcile the objectives of 'reprobation, reparation and re-integration', and they should observe the principles of 'parsimony, non-discrimination and accountability'. The Committee's recommendations include a wider role for the Sentencing Advisory Panel (as mentioned above), consideration of the re-introduction of unit fines, more extensive and mandatory use of pre-sentence reports, an extension to adults of the restorative measures now available for young offenders, and the repeal of the provisions of the Crime (Sentences) Act (1997) which relate to mandatory sentences. They support the policies underlying the Criminal Justice Act 1991, but argue that it needs a fresh interpretation; that there should be a new, formal statement of the underlying principles; and that there should be a stronger emphasis on a structured, step-by-step approach to sentencing decisions. The review of the sentencing framework, and the Government's conclusions on it, should take these arguments into account.

A distinction should be made between the aims which the courts can properly and realistically expect to achieve in the sentences they impose, and those which the executive agencies - principally the prison and probation services - should try to achieve in giving effect to those sentences. It should be made absolutely clear that punishment is a function of the courts, not of the prison or probation services (or for that matter of the police). It is unfortunate that the Criminal Justice and Court Services Act 2000 made 'the proper punishment of offenders' a function of the reformed Probation Service (though it is not at all clear what that could mean in practice), and that it renamed 'community service' as 'community punishment'.[15]

Courts have to handle questions of guilt or innocence; intention, aggravation and mitigation; seriousness and proportionality, including the effect on victims; equity and fairness; and many others. They have to do so in a context of law and precedent. Their intended outcome is a just resolution of the case. The services have to handle questions of behaviour, attitude, relationships and safety within a context of professional integrity and discipline, and of management structures and procedures. Their intended outcomes are the successful completion of the sentence, the prevention of re-offending, and if possible a more stable and responsible pattern of life for the offender in the community to which he or she returns. This is an important distinction, which would be obscured if a government sought to impose a unified objective on the criminal justice system as a whole in the interests of so-called effectiveness or managerial efficiency.

The extent to which the courts consider themselves to be accountable to the public in sentencing matters - or accountable at all except through the processes of appeal - is an interesting and difficult question. The courts certainly feel that they have to respond to public opinion, usually by imposing severe sentences in types of cases about which they think there are strong public feelings. And yet, as already mentioned and as Lord Bingham himself pointed out as Lord Chief Justice, there is considerable evidence that the public are not as punitive as has sometimes been supposed,[16] and the courts would deny that public or media pressure could ever by itself justify an exceptional decision in a particular case.

Mandatory sentences

Both Conservative and Labour Governments have favoured mandatory sentences of imprisonment for offences about which they believe the public to have strong feelings. The mandatory life sentence for murder emerged from the debates on the abolition of capital punishment, on the argument that the special nature of the offence distinguishes it from all other offences. In 1995 the Conservative Government proposed the introduction of mandatory sentences for a second serious violent or sexual offence (life imprisonment); for a third offence of trafficking in class A drugs (seven years); and for a third offence of burglary (three years). The arguments on that occasion were the supposedly deterrent effect of mandatory sentences, the protection which the public would gain from further offences not being committed while the offender was in prison, and the inconsistency, and supposed leniency and unreliability, of the judges' sentencing practice. The new measures were duly enacted in the Crime (Sentences) Act 1997. The commencement of those relating to burglary was delayed because of their effect on prison overcrowding, but the Labour Government brought them into operation at the end of 1998.

None of this makes for a happy story. The mandatory sentence for murder was an awkward political compromise, the argument for which does not stand up to scrutiny when the actual definition of murder and the range of circumstances in which it can be committed are taken into account. It has given trouble ever since (see *Chapter 13*). The arguments justifying the Crime (Sentences) Act 1997 similarly appealed more to political opportunism than to rational argument or to any claim to justice or sentencing principle. The judges, especially the Lord Chief Justice, Lord Taylor, opposed them strongly, the fundamental objection being their injustice in preventing the judge from taking account of the circumstances of the offence and the offender unless there were genuinely exceptional circumstances. Other arguments concerned their possible effect in discouraging guilty pleas, encouraging plea bargaining, and the lack of empirical evidence for their supposed deterrent or protective effect. Ian Dunbar and Anthony Langdon give an account of the arguments in *Tough Justice*.[17]

The Labour Government sought to extend the scope of mandatory sentences in its proposal for a presumptive sentence of three months' imprisonment for a second breach of the conditions of a community sentence. Lord Windlesham, Lord Dholakia, Baroness Stern and Lord Ackner spoke powerfully on the subject in the House of Lords[18] and the Bill as finally enacted in the Criminal Justice and Court Services Act 2000 gave a little more flexibility than the Government had originally proposed.

Mandatory sentences are fundamentally unjust and are likely to have a distorting effect on the criminal justice process. It is still too soon to judge the effects of the provisions contained in the Crime (Sentences) Act 1997, but if the review of sentencing does not lead to their repeal - as properly it should - there should at least be no further extension of mandatory sentencing until their effects have been properly assessed.

In a carefully considered judgement in *Regina v. Offen* and other cases, published on 10 November 2000, the Lord Chief Justice, Lord Woolf, held that section 2 Crime (Sentences) Act 1997, which requires a life sentence to be imposed on a defendant who had committed two previous serious offences, was not incompatible with the European Convention On Human Rights because its purpose was to protect the public. On the other hand, if the offender did not constitute a significant risk to the public, that would constitute an exceptional circumstance which would under the Act justify a court in not imposing an automatic life sentence. If the two offences were of a different kind, or if a long period had elapsed between the offences during which the offender had not committed other offences, that could be a very relevant indicator as to the degree of risk to the public that an offender constituted. It is too soon to tell how the jurisprudence on that section of the Act is likely to develop.

The special case of the mandatory life sentence for murder is discussed in *Chapter 13*.

Fines and fixed penalties

Governments have paid little attention to the fine since the 'unit fine' was introduced by the Criminal Justice Act 1991 and hurriedly abolished soon after it came into effect (see *Chapter 8*). And yet the fine is probably the simplest, most straightforward, longest established and most economical of all penalties. The decline in its use during the 1980s was a matter of concern to government at the time (hence the attempt to introduce the unit fine) and the decline has continued under both governments since then.[19] Whether or not the Labour Government's lack of interest is due to its preference for more intrusive measures which 'do something' to offenders or which can be represented as helping victims, may be a matter for speculation. But the fine should not be neglected.

Two possibilities are available. One is to restore the unit fine, on a full statutory basis. Memories of 1993 may still be too fresh for that to be an easy option, but the mistakes made in the method of its introduction under the 1991 Act need not be repeated and a successful scheme could now be devised.[20] The other is for courts to develop a similar system, on a discretionary basis but with guidance from the Magistrates' Association to ensure consistency. There are encouraging signs that courts are increasingly ready to adopt the approach: a statutory system may then become a logical and natural development.

Both the Government and the Conservative Party have favoured an extension in the use of fixed penalties. As was argued in *Chapter 11*, there is quite a good case for some limited expansion in the use of fixed penalties for actions which are a nuisance, or potentially dangerous, but which would not normally be regarded as especially serious, or as 'criminal' in any but a technical sense. Dropping litter and smoking in prohibited places are examples which might be added to the existing range of situations – mostly involving road traffic or travelling on public transport without a ticket – in which fixed penalties or the equivalent, a penalty fare, can be imposed. Such penalties probably provide an effective deterrent in the circumstances in which they are used, but cost, speed and certainty of enforcement are the most obvious benefits. Many fixed penalties are operated by commercial companies, and the police and the courts are not usually involved.

In September 2000 the Government published a consultation paper proposing that fixed penalties should be introduced for offences of drunkenness and public disorder.[21] Proposals based on the consultation paper were included in the Criminal Justice and Police Bill which was before Parliament at the time of writing. The paper discussed various matters relating to scope and procedure, and the practical questions which might arise, but it did not address the question of principle, namely the point at which fixed penalties cease to be appropriate or legitimate for the type of conduct concerned or the consequences which might be involved. In fact it marked a significant departure from the principles which have governed the use of fixed penalties in the past, in the sense that they were to be applied, for the first time, to offences which involve significant social or moral disapproval for the person concerned and to which the Government itself wishes to attract greater disapproval. Some of them are also offences which might be committed in circumstances where there is argument about degrees of responsibility; or where it might be practicable for the police to issue fixed penalty notices to only a few of those involved, the others having disappeared from the scene. Fixed penalties of £10, £40, or even £60 are unlikely to be beyond the means of a motorist or a passenger on public transport; a fixed penalty of £100 (as the Government proposed) could well be beyond the means of some of those accused of public order offences, especially if the provisions are to apply to people as young as 16. The consultation paper is silent on whether acceptance of a fixed penalty is to count as a conviction for the person's criminal record; if so it could have serious practical implications for their future employment, or access to services such as insurance or finance.

One answer to considerations of this kind is that the person would always have the option of going to court. But it would still be important to ensure that the person is not intimidated or cajoled into accepting a fixed penalty without being aware of the consequences and alternatives; and that the court has full discretion to impose a lower fine or a conditional or absolute discharge, as well as to dismiss the case. The accused person must be able to plead mitigation or hardship as well as innocence. The danger that 'too many' people might then prefer to go to court is one that should be accepted.

Necessary safeguards for any extension of fixed penalties to more serious cases are an understanding that the acceptance of a fixed penalty does not count as a criminal conviction or form part of a person's criminal record, and that they should be enforced as civil debts. The Government accepted the first of the safeguards in the proposals which it put to Parliament, but not the second.

A more promising alternative might be a system of 'out of court' fines, to be offered by the Crown Prosecution Service to defendants who admit the offence as an alternative to a full prosecution. For the range of offences for which it might be appropriate – small thefts, minor criminal damage, some drug offences and various regulatory offences – it would be simpler, cheaper and more proportionate than a prosecution. Published guidelines would set the criteria, procedures and safeguards to be observed and the case could always be taken to the magistrates' court in the event of a disagreement or at the request of either of the parties. An out-of-court fine might not be suitable if an individual victim was involved. A similar system operates in Scotland as the 'fiscal fine', and the Royal Commission on Criminal Justice and subsequently the Police Foundation's Independent Inquiry into the Misuse of Drugs Act 1971 recommended its adoption in England and Wales.

Chapter 21 considers a possible role for the Crown Prosecution Service in the sentencing process.

Sentencing and strategic planning

Sentencing is an example of a cross-cutting issue with ramifications which extend throughout the criminal justice system, and beyond it to social policies which are concerned with social services, health, housing, education and employment. It affects not only offenders themselves, but also their families, households and dependants. And yet the Government has so far chosen, as a matter of conscious political judgement, to distance itself from any consideration of the social and economic issues of sentencing, and especially of imprisonment. It has done so on the grounds that sentencing is 'entirely a matter for the courts' and that it is not for the Government to tell the courts what sentences to impose. And yet it has not only left in place those provisions of the Crime (Sentences) Act 1997 which were already in force when it came into office, but has also brought into effect the mandatory minimum sentences of imprisonment for repeated offences of burglary. In an Answer to a Question in the House of Lords from Lord Windlesham on 3 February 1999, the Attorney General Lord Williams gave as the reason the fact that the latest long-term projections of the prison population were lower than previously, and the Government hoped that the Prison Service would now have the capacity to cope with the resulting increase.[22] The Government claimed to have taken into account and to have made provision for the extra prison places which mandatory minimum sentences will demand, but it has never acknowledged the effect which such decisions, and its political stance as a whole, can have on sentencing practice more generally. In its strategic and business plans, the Government's policy on prison accommodation is in effect based on the principle of 'predict and provide' which has been so thoroughly discredited in all other areas of public expenditure. It is interesting to note that mechanisms for bringing sentencing practice and accommodation in prisons into closer alignment are now being explored in the United States[23].

Chapter 21 considers the structures and mechanisms by which sentencing should be brought within the Government's strategic planning process.

Prospects for sentencing reform

Sentencing is therefore a 'black hole' to which little or no principled thought so far has been given since the passage of the Criminal Justice Act 1991. The correct view - and fundamental principle - that the sentence to be imposed in particular cases is for the courts alone, as a matter of judicial rather than political or administrative judgement, was distorted to justify the Government in withdrawing from its proper responsibility for promoting the legislation and establishing the administrative structures and procedures through which principles can be formulated and practice can be developed and reviewed. The report of Lord Woolf's Inquiry into the prison disturbances in April 1990[24] shows that he, Sir Stephen Tumim and their assessors recognised the point, and addressed it in their proposal for the formation of a national Criminal Justice Consultative Council and area criminal justice committees. The government of the day accepted their proposals, and the Council and the area committees have been established and are still in existence - the area committees having been re-formed as local strategy committees. They have more or less the right composition to enable them to contribute to the formulation of principles (which Parliament should ultimately endorse), and to develop and review practice, although a great deal depends on the quality of their chairmanship and administrative support. But they have never developed the strategic role that the report intended.

Despite this rather gloomy analysis of the present situation, a solution - at least in terms of administrative structures and procedures - is not hard to find. The Criminal Justice Consultative Council should be revitalised and integrated with the Government's own machinery for strategic planning and 'joined-up policy' across the criminal justice system. More systematic procedures should be developed for consultation; for research, not only into the effectiveness of sentencing and penal treatment (typically in terms of re-offending), but also into the wider social and economic ramifications of sentencing practice; and for connecting discussion of sentencing practice more directly with discussion of the resources (of all kinds) needed to give effect to sentencing decisions. The Sentencing Advisory Panel could also be an important element in the procedures for making those connections.

For the courts themselves important questions are how far their sentencing practices, and the individual sentences they impose, are open, accessible, intelligible, and arrived at through a process which is seen as fair and consistent. That is another reason why all sentencing decisions should be made through an orderly, structured process, with due regard to the principles and considerations indicated in this chapter. Reasons for decisions should be explained fully in open court, and should if necessary form grounds for appeal. They should help the sentence to be better understood not only by the offender and his or her family but also by the victim, and the local community, including the media. The situation and feelings of the victim should where possible be acknowledged in the court's explanation of the sentence, but without any implication that one sentence has been chosen rather than another in deference to the victim's views. Sentencing considerations should be argued more openly in court, including by the prosecution although without going so far as to 'demand' a particular sentence in the style of district attorneys in the United States. Defence lawyers should be better informed, and able to argue more effectively, about matters of sentencing as well as matters of guilt or innocence. The provisions for a community legal service and a criminal defence service in the Access to Justice Act 1999 have great potential if they are used to improve standards and not just to reduce the cost of legal aid.

Other important developments may follow from Lord Justice Auld's review of the Criminal Courts.

Features of principled sentencing

It is probably a fair criticism of the present sentencing framework that the Criminal Justice Act 1991 did not make adequate provision for the 'forward looking', utilitarian or instrumental aims of sentencing which the courts, the public, and governments inevitably expect to be taken into account. Those aims have been re-introduced into the sentencing framework by subsequent legislation and jurisprudence, mostly as a result of *ad hoc* and sometimes opportunistic political or judicial decisions. The problem of finding some coherent and principled means by which the courts can resolve the conflicts between those aims in particular cases, which the 1991 Act tried to resolve on a basis of retribution and just deserts therefore remains. Michael Tonry has described a similar situation in the United States.[25]

This chapter has suggested an approach by which the court would set the 'amount' of the punishment on the basis of the harm done, the seriousness of the offence and the culpability of the offender, and the 'forward looking' aims would be achieved by the measures taken under the authority of the sentence or included within it. The nature and scope of those aims – the rehabilitation and reform of the offender, the protection of the public or the victim – would be set out in statute, together with the principles in accordance with which they would be applied – proportionality, parsimony, equity and respect for diversity, transparency, accountability. The judge or bench would be required to explain in open court which aims were to be achieved by a particular sentence, and how the principles were to be applied. In this way the reasons for the sentence and its purpose would be better understood, not only by the offender, the victim and the wider public, but also by the services which give effect to the sentence. The significance for those services is discussed in the next chapter.

Whatever the conclusion of the Government's review of sentencing may be in detail, they should preserve or establish the following features:

- The classical or retributivist tradition should be maintained in the sense that the sentence or punishment should be related to the seriousness of the offence and the culpability of the offender. No sentence should be more severe than the offender deserves on those grounds.

- There should be recognised and possibly structured provision for courts to show compassion or mercy by withholding, suspending or mitigating punishment when that is justified in the circumstances of the case.

- Punishment is a function of the court, expressed and given effect by the sentence. It is not a function of the services whose task is to administer the sentence, and the conditions under which the sentence is served should never be made deliberately humiliating or degrading.

- Those serving sentences of imprisonment or who are being supervised in the community under orders of the courts should still be regarded as full citizens entitled to consideration and respect, and to services which are the same as or equal to those available to other citizens. They should also be enabled, and expected, to discharge their responsibilities as citizens to the fullest extent possible consistently with the purpose and nature of the sentence imposed.

- Within the terms of the sentence imposed by the court, the administration of prison or community sentences is a matter for the professional judgement of the services concerned. It is in itself not a matter either for judicial or for political judgement. Where the sentence is in effect to be varied, for example by decisions for early release, extended detention or removal or recall to custody, the decision should be taken in accordance with due process by a suitably constituted body with a judicial element.

- All mandatory sentences of imprisonment should be abolished.

- Statements by victims may be relevant to the sentencing process to the extent that they bear on the seriousness of the offence and the culpability of the offender. Their feelings or opinions should not be relevant, but courts and services having responsibility for the administration of sentences should be sensitive to those feelings or opinions in the way in which the sentence or its effect is explained to victims, both at the time of sentence and if necessary in the period during which it is being served.

- If the need to protect the public makes it necessary to extend the period of a person's detention, or to impose restrictions on their freedom of movement, beyond the limits of proportionality and what the person deserves for what they have done, special rules and procedures should apply. The decision should be made by a properly consistituted authority, with judicial and professional membership; the decision should be subject to appeal and regular review; and restrictions on the person's freedom should be no more onerous than the minimum that will achieve the protection that is needed. (Proportionality is a consideration which courts will have to take into account in interpreting the European Convention On Human Rights and the Human Rights Act 1998.)

- The Government should learn from past experience with the Criminal Justice Act 1991 that the legislation should be neither so convoluted in its drafting that it is difficult to comprehend, nor so complicated in its content that it is difficult to apply in practice.

Alternative procedures based on the principles of restorative or community justice should be encouraged and developed (see *Chapter 10*). Their eventual scope and character is unclear at present, but they might in time replace or complement the traditional process of trial, conviction and sentence in a substantial number of cases. If they do, suitable principles and safeguards will need to be established. Restorative and traditional procedures should not be confused in an attempt to amalgamate the two processes, and experiments or developments carried out in the name of restorative justice should not be allowed to comprise the principles set out in these paragraphs, for cases which continue to be dealt with under the adversarial system.

ENDNOTES for *Chapter 12*

[1] For a full discussion of the issues relating to sentencing, see Andrew Ashworth, *Sentencing and Criminal Justice*, third edn., London, Butterworths, 2000. Chapter 3 considers sentencing aims, principles and policies. See also Lord Bingham of Cornhill, *Crime and Punishment: Four Propositions for the New Millennium*, Vista, 2000, 5/3, pp. 200-9. The four propositions were:
- There is no simple, straightforward answer to the problems of sentencing;
- There is no single solution;
- No one can win the war on their own; and
- A fair and effective penal policy must be underpinned by public understanding and support.

[2] Andrew von Hirsch, Anthony Bottoms, Elizabeth Burney and P. O. Wikstrom, *Criminal Deterrence and Sentence Severity*, Oxford, Hart Publishing, 1999.

[3] See Nigel Walker, *Aggravation, Mitigation and Mercy in English Criminal Justice*, London, Blackstone Press, 1999.

[4] Prison Reform Trust, *Justice for Women: The Need for Reform*, London, Prison Reform Trust, 2000.

[5] Originally in a lecture as part of a series organized by NACRO in 1983; see also Andrew Ashworth *Sentencing and Penal Policy*, London, Weidenfeld and Nicolson, first edn., 1983.

[6] Police Foundation, *Drugs and the Law*, Report of the Independent Inquiry into the Misuse of Drugs Act 1971, London, Police Foundation, 2000.

[7] Prison Reform trust, *op. cit.*, n. 4.

[8] Jack Straw's speech to the Annual Meeting of the Probation Council, 16 May 2000.

[9] The Home Secretary explained these ideas as follows:

- 'custody plus' - a sentence starting with a fixed period in custody, followed by an element in the community which would be subject to sanctions depending on behaviour;
- 'variable custody' - a sentence starting with a fixed minimum period in custody, extendable subject to assessment and proper procedures, and completed in the community;
- 'suspended sentence plus' - a suspended custodial sentence, overhanging a community sentence. The custodial element could be activated depending on the offender's behaviour;
- 'day custody' - a requirement for offenders to be at a day centre for fixed periods, keeping them off the streets and out of trouble and possibly incorporating programmes to reduce re-offending.

[10] Mike Hough and Julian Roberts, *Attitudes to Punishment: Findings from the British Crime Surveys*, Home Office Research Study 179, London, Home Office, 1998.

[11] Peter Goldblatt and Christopher Lewis (eds.), *Reducing Offending*, Home Office Research Study 187, London, Home Office, 1997; see also JUSTICE, *A Review of the Sentencing Framework: A Response by JUSTICE*, London, JUSTICE, 2000.

[12] Andrew Ashworth, *op. cit.* n. 1, p. 188.

[13] In Act II, scene ii.

[14] JUSTICE, *op. cit.* n.11.

[15] See criticisms in the House of Lords during the debate on the second reading of the Bill for the Criminal Justice and Court Services Act 2000, *Hansard*, 3 July 2000.

[16] Lord Bingham of Cornhill, *loc sit.*, n. 1; Michael Hough, *op. cit.* n. 10.

[17] Ian Dunbar and Anthony Langdon, *Tough Justice: Sentencing and Penal Policies in the 1990s*, London, Blackstone, 1998.

[18] During the debate on the second reading of the Bill for the Criminal Justice and Court Services Act the Attorney General, Lord Williams of Mostyn, stated that '. . . after all, a community sentence in a sense is an alternative to imprisonment. If it is to be an alternative, it has to be a serious alternative. It is not to be regarded as not a sanction by way of punishment' (col. 1339). The implication seems to be that the Government regarded imprisonment as the standard or normal penalty for any offence which could not be dealt with by a discharge, fine or compensation order; that a community sentence should be considered in some way exceptional and as needing some special justification; and that the conditions under which community sentences are served should be assimilated as closely as possible to those of imprisonment itself. If so, the Government had set aside not only the thinking which informed the Criminal Justice Act 1991 but also 30 years of progress in the development of community sentences. See also JUSTICE, *op. cit.* n. 9.

[19] Claire Flood-Page and Alan Mackie, *Sentencing Practice: An Examination of Decisions in Magistrates' Courts and the Crown Court in the Mid-1990s*, Home Office Research Study 200, London, Home Office, 2000.

[20] Lord Windlesham, *Responses to Crime* Vol. 3, *Legislating with the Tide*, Oxford, Oxford University Press, 1996; Prison Reform Trust, *op. cit.*

[21] Home Office, *Reducing Public Disorder: The Role of Fixed Penalty Notices*, London, Home Office, 2000.

[22] *Hansard*, House of Lords, 3 February 1999.

[23] Michael Tonry, 'Reconsidering Indeterminate and Structural Sentencing' in *Sentencing and Corrections, Issues for the Twenty-first Century*, U. S. Department of Justice, September 1999.

[24] Lord Justice Woolf, *Report of an Inquiry into the Prison Disturbances of April 1990*, Cmnd. 1456, London, HMSO, 1991.

[25] Michael Tonry, *op.cit.*, n. 23.

CHAPTER 13

Administering the Sentence: Conditions, Enforcement and Release from Custody

History . . . reminds us that in the field of criminal justice, the final word belongs, more often than not, to social rather than penal policy.

Leon Radzinowicz and Roger Hood, *A History of English Criminal Law*, Vol. 5: *The Emergence of Penal Policy*, 1986.

Questions of sentencing cannot be separated from consideration of the conditions which may be attached to a sentence, the enforcement of those conditions (for sentences served in the community), and of release from or recall to custody (for sentences of imprisonment). The Government's ideas for flexibility in sentencing will clearly strengthen the connection between the various procedures as well as, probably, reducing the relative significance of the original sentence.

CONDITIONS ATTACHED TO COMMUNITY SENTENCES

Sentences served in the community must by their nature involve conditions or requirements - to report to the supervising probation officer, to carry out the required form of community service, to attend courses or day centres, to live in an approved hostel. Their nature and scope was transformed by the introduction of community service in the early 1970s, when courts became able to make orders requiring offenders to undertake demanding programmes of work which would also enable them to make some reparation to the community. The Criminal Justice Act 1982 added to the range of requirements which could be imposed under a probation order, for example to attend a day centre, and the Criminal Justice Act 1991 created the combination order which in effect allowed the requirements available under a probation order to be added to those of a community service order. Failure to comply with any of the orders could result in action for 'breach' under which the defaulter could be returned to court to be fined or re-sentenced for the original offence. Centrally imposed standards defined what was meant by an 'unacceptable breach' and set targets for compliance which services were required to meet.

The Criminal Justice and Court Services Act 2000 took the development a stage further. It provided new powers for courts to make exclusion orders, excluding the offender from specified places; to add 'drug abstinence requirements', with compulsory testing, to community sentences in a range of situations; and to add electronically monitored curfews to community sentences.[1] Breach of the conditions of a community sentence could result in the loss of social security benefits (see *Chapter 9*), and a second breach in a term of three months' imprisonment, although the Government moderated the rigidity of its original proposals in response to criticism in the House of Lords (see *Chapter 10*).

The Act also renamed probation, community service and combination orders as community rehabilitation orders, community punishment orders and community punishment and rehabilitation orders respectively. The reason was to make clear what the orders were about, but the changes to probation and community service orders were criticised in the House of Lords[2] as unnecessary and in themselves confusing, and the loss of any expression of service to the community was thought especially unfortunate (see *Chapter 12*). The gradual, and more recently, rapid expansion in the court's powers to impose conditions or requirements was intended to serve two purposes. One was to make the order more 'demanding' so that the courts and the public would see it as a credible 'punishment' and therefore suitable as a sentence for a relatively serious offence without the need for imprisonment. The other was to improve the rehabilitative effect of the sentence so that the offender would be less likely to commit further offences. How far those measures have been or are likely to be successful in achieving either of these purposes is open to debate. Changes in the sentencing environment, and especially in political and public opinion, made it difficult to judge their success in achieving the first; and the lack of reliable evidence, and the methodological problems involved in obtaining reliable evidence, have so far made it difficult to judge their success in achieving the second. But the Government, and the Probation Service, are deeply committed to them.

In deciding on the conditions or requirements to be imposed, the court has to consider how far to regard them as relating only to the character and circumstances of the offender, and therefore as incidental to its judgement of the seriousness of the offence and the severity of the sentence which is appropriate or proportionate to it; and how far to regard them as a factor which increases its severity, and which therefore needs to be taken into account in relating the sentence to the seriousness of the offence. The second question has become more significant with the wider range of potentially burdensome and in effect punitive requirements, including the penalties for a breach of those requirements, which the court is able to impose under the Criminal Justice and Court Services Act. It is clear that the Government's intention for the longer term is that courts should be free, encouraged, and perhaps required to make full use of their powers or to impose additional requirements if they are thought justified in order to protect the public or to prevent re-offending, regardless of whether the offender 'deserves' the loss of freedom involved, or whether it is proportionate to the offence or the breach of conditions of which he or she has been convicted. It will be interesting to see how that intention is addressed in the report of the Government's review of sentencing; how it is translated into legislation; and in the meantime how the existing legislation is applied in practice and with what results, including any challenges under the Human Rights Act. Possible, but not necessarily successful, challenges might arise under Article 5 (right to liberty), Article 6 (right to a fair trail) or Article 14 (freedom from discrimination) of the European Convention On Human Rights, although it might be argued the right of other people to security of person (Article 5) justifies the detention of 'dangerous' persons for their protection. In any event, the situation should be carefully monitored.

Technological devices such as increasingly sophisticated forms of electronic monitoring will be able to restrict a person's liberty to a degree which is virtually equivalent to the loss of liberty which is caused by imprisonment. Challenges to their use may arise under the Human Rights Act 1998 and Articles 3 (inhuman or degrading treatment), 5 (right to liberty) or 8 (right to respect for private and family life, which might include a person's home), including challenges based on whether their use is proportionate in any particular case. Whatever challenges may arise, and however they may be decided, some understanding will be needed on which devices are legitimate to use and which are not; and what applications, for what duration and with that intensity, are acceptable for what purposes and in what circumstances.

ENFORCEMENT OF COMMUNITY SENTENCES

Arguments about the enforcement of community sentences were transformed by the Labour Government's discovery that standards of compliance with the conditions of community sentences - and of their enforcement - were sometimes so low that community sentences could be seen as neither effective nor credible. This was a matter to which the Conservative Government had paid little or no attention, perhaps because it felt no great commitment to community sentences in the first place. But there should be no surprise that National Probation Standards and the Criminal Justice and Court Services Act should between them demand much higher standards of compliance and much more rigorous practices on enforcement.

It is hard to predict how the provisions for new requirements to be added to orders, and the new rules for enforcement, will work out in practice. The Government's hope is obviously that they will succeed in achieving their two objectives of giving community sentences greater credibility as a form of punishment and in improving rates of re-offending. There was some anecdotal evidence, even before the new legislation came into force, that the new standards had improved attendance at probation programmes and rates of compliance more generally. There was also some evidence that electronic monitoring had helped some offenders to adopt more settled and responsible patterns of life, and that the monitoring process and its equipment could help to improve offenders' contact with supervisors and access to advice at critical moments. On the other hand, concern has also been expressed that offenders will regard burdensome requirements as punishment rather than a source of help and support, and fail to derive benefit from them or even to comply. They may see rigid procedures for enforcement as unfair and illegitimate, and their behaviour may suffer in consequence. If burdensome demands are sustained over a long period, the offender is likely to give up or try to escape from them by going 'underground'.[3] The withdrawal of social security benefits or the experience of imprisonment for breach may drive them further into alienation and criminality, especially if they regard the decision as unfair or the prison regime to which they are subjected as having no positive content.

Related questions concern the nature of the programmes in which offenders are required to take part, and their validity and legitimacy - as well as their effectiveness - for the purposes which are intended for them. They will have to be carefully designed, using the best available experience and expertise, and they will have to be tested as thoroughly as circumstances permit. Figures can be provided to show the percentage by which they are expected to reduce an offender's likelihood of re-offending. The Home Secretary, Jack Straw, has indicated that offenders will be subjected to careful 'electronic' assessment of their risk of re-offending, and their suitability for the course. But the assessments and predictions will be statistical or actuarial rather than clinical or individual; there will inevitably be false positives and false negatives; and courses may not always be provided on the scale or to the standard of quality that are expected. Offenders who 'fail' may do so for a variety of reasons relating to the quality or availability of the course, or to circumstances in their own lives, which could not be regarded as their 'own fault'. Automatic return to prison in these situations would be oppressive and unjust, but procedures for representation and appeals would be time-consuming, expensive and contrary to the spirit in which the new procedures have been introduced. Again, there may be questions about the application of the Human Rights Act, or about any disproportionate effect on cultural minorities (see *Chapters* 12 and 16).

The Government has been inclined to argue that a community sentence is in some sense a 'contract' between the offender and the supervisor, or perhaps between the offender and the state. To describe the - deliberately unequal - relationship in these terms is misleading and disingenuous, especially since the requirement for the offender to consent to the order was removed by the Criminal Justice Act 1991. An act of punishment by the state can hardly be regarded as a contract entered into by the other party. The situation could however be improved if the National Standards were expanded to include duties and obligations on the part of the supervising authority towards the offender for whom it has responsibility, or better still a set of statutory duties such as those which the Children Leaving Care Act 2000 places upon local authorities in respect of such young people. Those duties include an assessment of needs, a 'pathway plan' which has to be prepared and kept under review, and arrangements for each child to have a personal adviser. Local authorities must also maintain contact and provide material support, including cash, if it is needed. Such support should be regarded as a reasonable expectation of citizenship for offenders who are serving or who have completed their sentences, just as it is for children leaving care.

Another difficult and important question in relation to enforcement, as in sentencing, policing, and many other areas of criminal justice and public administration, is the extent to which supervising officers or the courts should have discretion. Mandatory provisions under which procedures are automatic, with no flexibility or exceptions, put the offender in a position where he or she can know exactly what to expect, and the supervisor in an arguably strong position because there is no room for concessions or argument. The objections are that situations and individuals are varied and complex, and rigid procedures are arbitrary and potentially unfair and unjust. They reflect a lack of confidence and trust. They can create resentment and may invite evasion or collusion. Different individuals will react in different ways, but those who think of themselves as victims may regard such provisions as illegitimate and consider themselves entitled to disregard them or to resume offending.

The Government presents its policies on enforcement, like its other criminal justice policies, as having the essentially utilitarian purposes already described. But they also appear to be based on ideas of retribution and punishment, a sense that a person who 'fails' is of little value as a human being, and not fit to be a full citizen or member of society. They again reflect an exclusive rather than an inclusive view of citizenship. There are no compensating rewards for achievement, whether in completing the sentence successfully, in overcoming difficulties in other aspects of the person's life, or in not re-offending. On the contrary, the person still has the disadvantage and the stigma of a criminal conviction, and unless society can offer something more to hope for the most accessible rewards may seem to be those of a return to crime. The scope for a system of recognition and reward for success, as well as punishment for failure, should be seriously considered.

No government or public service could tolerate or justify the lax procedures on enforcement which the Labour Government appears to have found on taking office. The policies it has introduced may for some offenders have the salutary effect of inculcating a stronger sense of personal discipline and responsibility and a greater respect for the law; for others the provisions on enforcement may drive them further into criminality. Punishment is not incompatible with rehabilitation, certainly not if it is accompanied by a sense of remorse and reconciliation as proponents of community justice would argue. But the other two aims may be difficult to reconcile in particular circumstances or for particular individuals, especially in a setting where all the emphasis is on guilt, blame and personal failure. There is as yet no reliable evidence on which those policies can be justified as 'evidence-based', or on which they can be criticised for any damaging consequences they may have. They are essentially based on political conviction and belief, but also on a pessimistic view of human nature, an instinct for blame and social exclusion, a conditional view of citizenship, and a lack of trust in public services. They have the potential to be discriminatory in their operation. They may be vulnerable under the Human Rights Act, as Lord Windlesham has argued in relation to the withdrawal of social security benefits. They should be kept under rigorous scrutiny, and should be formally reviewed in three to five years from the date when the Act came into effect.

Review by the court

In setting up the review of the sentencing framework, the Government clearly contemplates a more flexible form of sentence in which the restrictions or demands imposed by the sentence might be varied to take account of an offender's progress and of any changes in their situation or the risk they are thought to present to the public. Requirements which the court has set at the start of the sentence could be reviewed as the sentence proceeds. If the outcome is to vary the original order of the court, or to impose any additional restrictions on the offender's liberty, the mechanisms would need to include some reference back to the court or some other judicial element (in the latter instance to comply with the Human Rights Act and the European Convention On Human Rights). Questions of legitimacy might arise if decisions are taken on the basis of actuarial rather than individual assessments of risk, as already indicated in *Chapter 12*.

Chapter 12 has already referred to the possibility that the review of the sentencing framework might recommend the creation of a review court. Apart from the need to comply with the Convention, some form of independent authority must be established to ensure that decisions are not manipulated to serve institutional purposes, especially in prisons or for the benefit of institutional staff. Experience with the intermediate sentence of borstal training showed how the procedures for promotion through the 'grade' system and for eventual release could be manipulated and sometimes abused for these purposes; and that any procedure for individualised assessment became difficult if not impossible to operate once the system came under pressure from rising numbers and shortage of accommodation. But the significance of the court's involvement could extend far beyond a procedural requirement or formality. Judicial and professional or operational judgements should never be confused, but earlier chapters have argued that public services should be made more effectively accountable through channels which extend beyond management control, political direction and the government's accountability to Parliament. *Chapters 19* and *20* argue that the prison and probation services should be made more accountable to their local communities: that accountability could be made more effective if it included an element of oversight by the local courts. This oversight would extend beyond the detention, supervision or release of individual offenders. It would not extend as far as any managerial or operational responsibility for the prison or probation services. But it would include a duty to consider the quality and availability of the programmes on which offenders were placed in accordance with the court's orders, the conditions and degree of supervision under which they served their sentences, and for custodial sentences the adequacy of their preparations for release. The courts will typically operate by calling for reports and by submitting their own report to the relevant authorities. Visiting committees of local magistrates had similar responsibilities, not always effectively discharged, in relation to their local prisons. A new and more dynamic relationship would come to be established, which could also help to promote a greater sense of responsibility and involvement on the part of local communities (for example through developments in the role of the magistrates). But there would be important questions of training, familiarity, expertise and continuity, which courts would have to consider while at the same time preserving their independence.

Michael Smith and Walter Dickey have described some comparable developments in the United States.[4]

PAROLE AND DISCRETIONARY CONDITIONAL RELEASE

Any system of discretionary release from the sentence of a court is a sensitive matter, to be scrutinised carefully for evidence of executive interference with judicial discretion. The system of parole always had to be handled carefully from this point of view, from its introduction in 1967 onwards. Changes to the system which the Government introduced in 1983 caused deep resentment among the judiciary when their effect became evident (carefully differentiated sentences from 12 months to two years might result in virtually the same period being spent in custody), and led to the Carlisle Committee's review of parole which reported in 1988[5] (see *Chapter 7* for an account of the Committee's recommendations). The report largely resolved the tensions with the judiciary, and its recommendations were given statutory effect in the Criminal Justice Act 1991.

Even so, the purpose and rationale for parole were always to some extent open to question - whether the aim was to improve prisoners' chances of resettlement by releasing them at the point when their outlook and motivation made them ready to accept the responsibility involved in release; whether it was a device for reducing the number of people in prison, or whether it was more simply an act of mercy towards those for whom imprisonment no longer served any rehabilitative or protective purpose. Even by the 1970s the first view was becoming hard to sustain, and a similar idea which had for many years been applied to the indeterminate sentence of borstal training was becoming discredited. It was however the view on which the parole system had been largely constructed, and which was the principal justification for the apparatus and procedures of the Parole Board. The second view has always been present to some extent, but could never be openly acknowledged. The third had by the 1980s become, in effect, the main purpose and rationale for the parole system, but it had by then become institutionally well established and the main arguments were not so much about its purpose but about the means of making it acceptable, fair and legitimate as it appeared to the courts, to the public and to prisoners themselves.

Roger Hood and Stephen Shute have described the subsequent history of parole in a series of research reports, culminating in 2000 in *The Parole System At Work: A Study of Risk-Based Decision-Making.*[6] The Carlisle Committee's hope had been that under the arrangements they proposed, more prisoners would have the benefit of parole, or conditional discretionary release as it came to be called in the 1991 Act, at some point in their sentence unless they presented a risk of committing a further serious offence. Otherwise, the Parole Board's decision should take into account 'the benefit both to him and the public of his being released from prison back into the community under a degree of supervision which might assist his rehabilitation and thereby lessen the risk of his re-offending in the future'.[7] The terms of the 1991 Act, which set the framework within which the Secretary of State gives Directions to the Parole Board, were consistent with that approach.

In the event, however, the proportion of prisoners released under the new system was only about 48 per cent compared with 70 per cent of those released under the old one, so that the rate of parole or discretionary conditional release declined by about a third. Discretionary conditional release, when granted, was also for a shorter period. Roger Hood and Stephen Shute discuss the reasons, which included the Parole Board's more cautious approach to the consideration of risk, both under the statutory Directions which the Home Secretary had issued to them, and especially the revised Directions issued in 1996; and also because of their own tendency to exaggerate the risk which individual prisoners might present if released, and their lack of confidence that prisoners would complete any offending behaviour courses if they were left to do so outside prison. A further conclusion from the research was that a very high proportion of the Parole Board's decisions could be predicted in advance on the basis of information which was already recorded, so raising questions about the 'added value' which formal meetings of Board members brought to the process. Prisoners for their part welcomed the greater openness which the new system had provided, but felt some resentment at what they saw as the unfairness of some of the Board's decisions, especially when they related to an aspect of the prisoner's history which had occurred some time in the past and which he could do nothing to change.

A wider implication of the study is that considerably more prisoners could be released without any increased overall risk to the public, with substantial savings in cost, and with benefits to prisoners and their families. Whether that change should be adopted is a matter for political judgement by ministers in the first instance, in the light of the public reactions they expect to it, but also for professional judgement by probation officers who would have to take responsibility both for their advice to the Parole Board (or any new authority which might take its place) and for any offences which might be committed by offenders under their supervision. In a political climate of general hostility towards offenders, and in a professional and managerial culture of blame and recrimination, such a decision would need some courage and support. But it is a decision to be taken so far as possible dispassionately, with careful examination of the evidence, and so far as possible with some confidence that it will then be respected and not misrepresented or distorted for the sake of opportunist political advantage.

PROGRESSIVE AND FLEXIBLE SENTENCES IN OPERATION

Looking further ahead, progression and flexibility in sentencing and the establishment of a review court would have obvious implications for the work of the Parole Board and the operation of discretionary conditional release in its present form. Decisions affecting an offender's liberty will need to be taken within the legitimate authority established by the original sentence of the court, or on the new authority of a fresh court decision. Those decisions should normally ensure that any restriction of liberty, including demands on offenders' time and limitations on their freedom of movement, are proportionate to the seriousness of what the offender has done, but there can be plenty of flexibility within these limits so long as fairness and due process are maintained. Traditionalists may argue that the distinction between custody and sentences served in the community should be rigidly maintained in order to preserve the status of custody as an extreme sanction to be used only in the last resort. There is much to be said for this argument, but modern technology and the conditions of modern life allow equally exclusionary, and therefore if abused oppressive, sanctions to be applied without actually admitting a person to prison. It is difficult to contest proposals to 'join up' the administration of custodial and community penalties on grounds of principle.

Practical difficulties will however continue so long as the prison system remains overcrowded and centralised, prisoners are sent a long way from their homes, and it is difficult for programmes for prisoners to be individualised or arranged at short notice. There may for example be no objection in principle to day or weekend imprisonment, but it is difficult to see how day or weekend prisoners could be accommodated in existing prisons, or how a system of new institutions could be built and managed (even under the Private Finance Initiative) except at disproportionate cost. These are the reasons for which the Conservative Government decided not to pursue similar proposals when it considered them in the early 1980s. It is also difficult to see how, in the present condition of the prison estate, short terms of imprisonment for breach of community orders, or as an intervention in a new form of 'joined-up' sentence, could have any but a deterrent and punitive effect - for which there is at present no empirical evidence of any benefit in terms of reducing re-offending.

Whatever the legislative structure within which new forms of sentence operate, it seems unlikely that a place could logically be justified for parole, or discretionary conditional release, in its present form. The functions of the Parole Board might be restricted to life sentences and to any extended terms of detention which might be ordered for the protection of the public, for example under a new form of sentence or a modified verson of section 2(2)(b) Criminal Justice Act 1991 introduced as a result of the review of the sentencing framework. More effective arrangements will however be needed to make sure that prisoners eligible for any form of discretionary or flexible release are not 'lost' in the system because arbitrary transfers have interrupted their courses, their records have been mislaid or procedures have been overlooked. And the structure for managing prisons and probation may need to be less centralised than the Prison Service is at present or the Probation Service is likely to be under the new structure introduced by the Criminal Justice and Court Services Act. *Chapters 19* and *20* make suggestions for how those systems might eventually be organized.

THE MANDATORY LIFE SENTENCE FOR MURDER

A subject which is usually on the margins of debate about sentencing, but which comes into prominence every two or three years when there is a controversial case, is the mandatory life sentence for murder. Some of the arguments are those which apply to mandatory sentences generally and which were discussed in this previous chapter, but special difficulties arise over the procedures for determining the period to be spent in custody and for deciding on a life sentence prisoner's release. The case for reform has been argued, mostly in the courts and in the House of Lords, at various times since the early 1980s.[8] The subject is closely linked with the - quite broad - definition of the offence of murder itself (an act is one of murder even if the intention was not to kill but only to cause serious injury).

The mandatory life sentence has its origin in a concession, made at the time when capital punishment for murder was abolished, and intended to mark the unique gravity of the offence. With the passage of time, it has become clear that not all murders are of equal seriousness, or necessarily more serious than acts which may be charged as manslaughter or other offences. Cases which have attracted sympathy - but also, usually, controversy - have included a soldier on patrol in West Belfast (Private Clegg), a doctor who gave a lethal dosage to a terminally ill patient (Dr Cox), a woman who killed her allegedly violent abusive husband (Sara Thornton), and a farmer who shot at an intruder with an illegally held firearm (Tony Martin). All except Dr Cox were convicted of murder; all had supporters who claimed that the conviction and resulting life sentence were, or would have been, unjust - although in each case there were others who took the opposite view. Whatever the merits of the particular cases (and at the time of writing Tony Martin's case may still be subject to appeal), there is a strong argument that courts should be able, as a matter of natural justice, to distinguish between the seriousness of different cases by imposing different penalties. The argument for mandatory sentences for serious offences is their supposed deterrent and declaratory effect: experience with the mandatory sentence for murder shows that their result is more likely to be rigidity and injustice. Similar arguments apply to the mandatory sentences created by the Crime (Sentences) Act 1997 (see *Chapters 8* and *12*).

The procedures for determining the period to be served and for taking decisions on release from a life sentence (or for juveniles a sentence of detention at Her Majesty's Pleasure) have been the subject of a series of cases in the European Court of Human Rights and in the domestic courts. The outcome so far has been that procedures for prisoners serving 'discretionary' life sentences - that is those not serving sentences for murder - are effectively controlled by the courts and the Parole Board, while those for prisoners serving sentences for murder are controlled by the Home Secretary. Decisions on the former are taken on the basis of a judicial judgement, those on the latter are a political matter. The supposed justification is again the unique gravity of the crime of murder, and the need therefore for decisions on length of custody and release to be politically accountable. But it has already been argued that the 'unique gravity' of the offence of murder, as it is legally defined, cannot be sustained. The claim that decisions on release have to be made on political grounds, endorsed by successive Home Secretaries from David Waddington onwards (although Kenneth Baker subsequently changed his mind) is exactly what makes the practice objectionable in principle. The European Court of Human Rights has ruled in the cases of *Thompson* and *Venables* that it is unacceptable in cases where a person has been sentenced as a juvenile, and the Criminal Justice and Court Services Act has introduced a new procedure in which responsibility rests with the courts and the Parole Board as it does for non-mandatory life sentences under provisions introduced in the Criminal Justice Act 1991.

The European Court has not so far challenged the practice as it applies to offenders sentenced as adults, but it seems unlikely that the practice can much longer be sustained.

Attempts to find a new definition of murder which preserve its 'unique gravity', and so justify its special status, are unlikely to be successful. And the objections in principle, both to mandatory sentences and to political decisions on release, would continue to apply. Two powerful statements of the arguments, in addition to the passages in Lord Windlesham's *Responses to Crime*, are contained in the reports of the House of Lords Select Committee on Murder and Life Imprisonment,[9] and of the Prison Reform Trust's independent committee on the Penalty for Homicide.[10]

As already indicated, the present law and practice and the present sentence for murder are a survival from a compromise reached at the time of the abolition of capital punishment. They are now out of date and unjust. Successive governments have held back from proposing any change, partly because of their reluctance to do anything which might re-open the question of capital punishment itself; partly because a change might be seen as 'weakness' on crime generally; and partly because cases, when they arise, are usually controversial and those who engage in the controversy - especially newspapers - are likely to take different sides according to the nature of the case and their sympathy for the defendant. There is a strong case for change, but any review in today's circumstances would open up difficult questions such as the part which the families of victims might have in any new procedure (see *Chapter 15*). It would be understandable if governments continued to defer action on this contentious subject until there is a greater prospect of agreement.

Whether some form of restorative justice can be imported into decisions about release from life sentences, or about release from imprisonment more generally, is a difficult question to which no clear answer can be given at present. The suffering caused to the family of a victim of murder, or of any premature death, is of a kind which can affect, even dominate, the rest of their lives. It deserves, and usually receives, public sympathy. For some people it may inspire a lifetime of charitable work; others may have feelings of bewilderment, anger or a desire for revenge which they express in public whenever they are given the opportunity to do so. Everything possible should be done to help them find some peace in their lives, and restorative justice may have some contribution to make. But the outcome of restorative justice must be reconciliation rather than revenge, and it is not at all clear that a formal place in the decision-making process of the state is a means by which reconciliation can be achieved (or would even be intended). Restorative justice should certainly be explored and developed in the ways indicated in *Chapter 10*. It may have something to offer on an individual and informal basis for the families of the victims of murder. But the country is still some way from understanding how it could be formally and systematically applied in cases of that kind. Support for those families, and for victims generally, must always be as much a matter for civil society as it is for the state.

CRITERIA AND CONDITIONS FOR SUCCESS

The various arrangements considered in this chapter have in common the ostensible aim of protecting the public, and of doing so either by promoting opportunities for the offender's rehabilitation, or more often by imposing restrictions or controls on the offender's movements (including the threat or extension of a period of imprisonment) which ensure his or her attendance at programmes and give early warning of any prospect of re-offending. Their success will be measured, reasonably enough, by rates of known re-offending. The absence of known re-offending is not however the only test of their success and only one of the criteria of good citizenship. For offenders to become good citizens should be the aim both of offenders themselves, and of those who have responsibility for their progress and rehabilitation.

Good citizenship is the outcome of a range of processes and influences, of situations and circumstances, and of opportunities and temptations, among which an offender's experience of the criminal justice system will be a significant but still relatively small part. The criminal justice system must do all it can, but the country should not have unrealistic expectations of the system and what it can achieve. It should not focus its attention so narrowly on the working of the system that it neglects the social and economic context in which crime can be encouraged or prevented; or the wider responsibilities of citizenship and civil society which have been discussed in earlier chapters. It should not automatically treat re-offending, when it occurs, either as a failure of the system, or as a matter for which the offender should be irretrievably condemned. Above all, it should not react irrationally by demanding a continuous escalation of coercion and punishment. The state's relationship with offenders should include reciprocal responsibilities in both directions. The state's responsibilities towards offenders should include recognition and support, similar to those which it owes through local authorities to children who have been in care, and they should be embodied in legislation on the lines of the Children Leaving Care Act.

ENDNOTES for *Chapter 13*

[1] The statutory provisions for exclusion orders, drug abstinence requirements and electronically monitored curfews, as originally proposed, included powers for the Secretary of State to increase by order the terms for which the orders would remain in force. The House of Lords Select Committee on Delegated Powers and Deregulation, session 1999-2000, Second Report, HL Paper 83 argued that these provisions, which would have increased the severity of the orders' effect without the need for any statutory authority from Parliament, should be omitted from the Bill, or failing that

should be subject to affirmative rather than negative resolution procedure. The Government accepted the second proposal but not the first.

2 *Hansard*, House of Lords, 3 July 2000, cols. 1294 and 1306-8. Speeches by Lord Windlesham, Lord Ackner and Baroness Seccombe.

3 Michael Smith points out that in the United States '[a] substantial portion of probationers [are] carried in the "absconder status" on the books of probation agencies. Arrest warrants may or may not have been issued, but the absconders are quietly retained in the caseload without any attempts to find them – without even a phone call to the last known residences – until they show up for initial appearance on new charges.' 'What Future For Public Safety and Restorative Justice in a System of Community Penalties' , Paper for the Twenty-fourth Cropwood Conference, Cambridge, 2000, Cambridge Institute of Criminology, forthcoming

4 Michael E. Smith and Walter J. Dickey 'Reforming Sentencing and Corrections for Just Punishment and Public Safety' in *Sentencing and Corrections: Issues for the Twenty-first Century'*, No. 4, Washington DC, National Institute of Justice, September 1999.

5 Lord Carlisle of Bucklow, *The Parole System in England and Wales,* Report of the Review Committee, Cmnd. 532, London, HMSO, 1988

6 Roger Hood and Stephen Shute, *Parole in Transition: Evaluating the Impact and Effects of Changes in the Parole System. Phase One: Establishing the Base-Line,* University of Oxford Centre for Criminological Research, Occasional Paper No. 13, 1994; Roger Hood and Stephen Shute, *Evaluating the Impact and Effects of Changes in the Parole System. Phase Two: Paroling with New Criteria,* University of Oxford Centre for Criminological Research, Occasional Paper No. 16, 1995; Roger Hood and Stephen Shute, 'Parole Criteria, Parole Decisions and the Prison Population: Evaluating the Effect of the Criminal Justice Act 1991', *Criminal Law Review,* 1996, pp. .77-87; Roger Hood and Stephen Shute, *The Parole System at Work: a Study of Risk-based Decision Making,* Home Office Research Study 202, 2000.

7 See paragraphs 321-2 of the report.

8 Lord Windlesham gives what is probably the most complete account of the debate in Volumes 2 and 3 of *Responses to Crime,* Oxford, Clarendon Press, 1993 and 1996.

9 HL, 78/1, HMSO, 1989.

10 *The Penalty for Homicide,* London, Prison Reform Trust, 1993.

CHAPTER 14

Children and Young People

> Juvenile justice shall be conceived as an integral part of the national development process of each country, within a comprehensive framework of social justice for all juveniles . . . contributing to the protection of the young and the maintenance of a peaceful order in society.
>
> UN Standard of Minimum Rules for the Administration of Juvenile Justice
> (Beijing Rules), 1985

The country's attitude to its children and young people contains a number of contrasts, contradictions and ambiguities. Children are to be cherished and protected from danger - from traffic accidents, disease, drugs, violence and abuse. Events which damage children evoke a special degree of tragedy, horror or revulsion. But children are also seen as a source of trouble. They are often unwelcome as neighbours, and viewed with dislike or suspicion in public places. Juvenile crime is presented by the media as growing and widespread, and attributed to loss of discipline and respect for authority, the irresponsibility of parents, and the influence of 'liberals'. At the same time, as the Social Exclusion Unit's Policy Action Team 12 has pointed out in its report,[1] a large minority of young people experience a range of acute problems, including illiteracy, homelessness and mental illness, often leading to drug addiction and serial offending; many of the problems have become worse over the last 20 years; and many of those indicators show the situation is worse in Great Britain than in other comparable nations. Members of minority groups are disproportionately affected.

Different approaches and attitudes

For some purposes children are treated as people in their own right, entitled to their autonomy and respect for their own feelings and wishes; for others they are treated as the possessions of their parents and subject to their control. When things go wrong, people are unsure whether to blame the children or the parents. Or more positively, courts, teachers and social workers may decide that it is unhelpful to argue about blame, and more productive to look for solutions in the wider context of the child's situation, opportunities and relationships. The social and economic changes described in *Chapter 2* and in the Policy Action Team report have made the transition from childhood to adult life more complicated and difficult, especially for young men. Many of the opportunities for independent discovery and adventure which were taken for granted in the 1950s have become too 'dangerous' or have largely disappeared. The guidance, and the dignity and respect, which young men found from wiser colleagues when they started work in the older - often dangerous - industries, have been lost with large parts of those industries themselves. Poor prospects of employment and limited access to social benefits compel many young people to stay longer at home living with their parents: beneficial for some but disastrous for others. The legal landmarks - age of majority, ages at which it becomes legal to marry, buy tobacco or alcohol, drive a car, vote, join the armed forces, together with the age of criminal responsibility - are all different and appear to have no logical relationship to one another or to the circumstances of young people themselves.

A lot is said about teaching children to tell right from wrong, to accept discipline, and to respect authority. It is often suggested that this should be done by restricting what children are allowed to do; sometimes by physical punishment or by fear. It is a sad and barren approach for children who are probably living very restricted and poverty stricken lives already, and it shows a confused understanding of what punishment should be for and what it can be expected to achieve. Much has been written on that subject, some of it in *Chapter 10*, but for the present purpose it may be enough to say that children are not taught right from wrong by being put down and humiliated. Nor will much progress be made by simply telling them that stealing, bullying and telling lies are wrong; and that doing as they are told, working hard at school and being polite to other people are right. To say this is not to argue for 'moral relativism': it is simply to recognise that children have to learn to cope with situations, influences and conflicts which cannot be resolved in simple terms, in ways which they can see make sense for them. They need parents and other adults who will listen and understand, who will explain and set an example, who will have time to do all these things, and whom they respect. They need other children with whom to share their experience. And they need to develop a sense of the boundaries of acceptable behaviour, and a set of guiding principles with which to shape their lives. All this is part of the idea of citizenship, civil society and social responsibility which were discussed in *Chapter 4*. As Baroness Warnock has put it, 'We need most urgently to teach children to understand, to feel in their gut (or in their conscience) what it is to do wrong ... This lesson will not be taught by threats or aggression or savage punishment. It can be taught ... only by conversation and example, far more difficult, time-consuming and laborious'[2]

THE ROLE OF CRIMINAL JUSTICE

The criminal law and the criminal justice process have an undoubted part to play in preventing criminality, both generally and among young people. But it is only one of the many influences which will be at work. Children need to grow up with the knowledge that society, or the state, fixes boundaries and is prepared to enforce them. They need to accept that those boundaries and the process of enforcement are legitimate; to respect them; and to believe that the forces of the state stand ultimately for fairness and justice. They will not have that respect if they see that the law is widely disregarded, whether by their contemporaries or by those in positions of power or authority; or if they perceive it to be arbitrarily, capriciously or oppressively enforced. But just as important - perhaps more important - than respect for the law is their own sense of duty and responsibility. That sense has to be learned from the inspiration, guidance and example of others, and young people must be prepared in time to set an example themselves.

The idea of the young offender as someone who needed, or deserved, special consideration and treatment was largely a Victorian invention. Under the common law, a child could not be convicted of a felony below the age of seven, and was presumed *doli incapax*, or 'incapable of crime', unless it could be proved (which was not usually difficult) that he or she had acted with malice. Otherwise, children were treated like adults, with the full force of the criminal and legal system.

Historical background
Moves to provide a different form of treatment for children began with the establishment of separate institutions in which children could be detained away from the hulks and the adult prisons (although at one time in hulks of their own). The aim was on the whole reformative rather than punitive, but was often seen as a preparation either for transportation or for service in the armed forces, especially the navy. But by the 1850s, through the influences of reformers like Mary Carpenter, such institutions had been put on a statutory footing as industrial schools and reformatories.[3]

Special institutions for children were first developed as a humane alternative to the appalling conditions in early nineteenth century prisons. They came to be used on a large scale as a response to public fears about the tide of juvenile crime and depravity which was thought to be about to overwhelm the country in the middle years of the nineteenth century. They were on the whole considered to have been successful in turning back the tide, and juvenile crime was far less of a problem in the 1870s and 1880s than it had been 30 or 40 years before, but it is hard to judge how far the change was due to the institutions themselves or how far it could be attributed to other forms of social progress during that period. Accurate statistics or reliable records of children's progress were hard to obtain. By the end of the century these institutions were coming under criticism both from the abuses which were coming to public notice, and also for the large numbers of children who were detained in them and for the cost of their operation. And children were still being sent to prison, in smaller but still significant numbers, if only for short periods of time.

As already explained in *Chapter 6*, the Children Act 1908 introduced for the first time a separate court system - the juvenile court - for juvenile offenders and other young people in trouble, with its own separate, less formal accommodation and procedures and not open to the general public. It also placed severe restrictions on the imprisonment of children. Industrial schools and reformatories continued but under closer supervision from the Home Office whose Children's Department was established in 1914. They were reformed to become approved schools under the Children and Young Persons Act 1933, with a tighter statutory framework of inspection and control. After a number of further scandals during the 1950s they were eventually abolished under the Children and Young Persons Act 1969. Some of the facilities were taken over by local authorities as community homes or secure accommodation.

The 1933 Act also broke new ground by introducing the notion of 'welfare' into the proceedings of the juvenile court, making it a statutory requirement for the court to have regard for the welfare of the child appearing before it. This requirement remained virtually unchallenged for 40 years, and its spirit was reinforced by the Children and Young Persons Act 1969, and the transfer of the Children's Department of the Home Office and its Inspectorate to the Department of Health and Social Security in the following year; and by further efforts to reduce the use of custody for young people and to substitute programmes of 'intermediate treatment' in the community during the 1980s. Finally, section 1 Children Act 1989, which among other things gave effect to the United Nations Convention On the Rights of the Child, stated that courts should have paramount regard for the welfare of the child.

Recent developments

The 1989 Act had however the effect of separating the family jurisdiction of the magistrates' courts from their criminal jurisdiction, so that the functions of the old juvenile court were split between the new family proceedings courts and youth courts, with separate membership of the panels from which members of the two courts were drawn. The youth court became as a consequence more criminally or 'justice' oriented, and the Criminal Justice Act 1991 placed a requirement upon youth court magistrates to focus, in all cases, on the 'seriousness' of the offence in ways which could not obviously be reconciled with the welfare of the individual child or young person. A tension, never far below the surface, began to emerge between a 'welfare' approach to juvenile justice in which courts and social workers were expected to know what was in the child's best interests and act accordingly; and a 'justice'approach by which children were expected to take responsibility for their actions and if necessary to be punished for them.

Other developments were taking place at the same time. Michael Cavadino, Iain Crow and James Dignan give an account in *Criminal Justice 2000*.[4] As already described in *Chapter 8*, and despite the statistics and Home Office research indicating that crimes attributed to juvenile offenders were falling[5] a belief was gaining ground that large parts of the country were being overrun by serious and persistent juvenile offenders - children who were out of the control of their parents and whom the police and the courts were powerless to prevent. The demonising of children and some of the language used to describe them was reminiscent of the 1850s (see *Chapter 5*). The country was deeply shocked by the abduction and murder of two-year-old Jamie Bulger by two ten-year-olds; an appalling but isolated event, although one which was made to appear characteristic of a state of affairs in which large numbers of children were both wicked and out of control. What could be seen in effect as a 'positivist' view of crime and criminality, and an 'exclusionary' view of society, were becoming more influential. Results could be seen in the increased penalties for children and young persons and the provisions for secure training orders for children aged 12-14 which were contained in the Criminal Justice and Public Order Act 1994; and a rapid increase in the numbers of children and young people detained in prison establishments, both under sentence and on remand.

There was and is still a lot of debate about the extent to which there is amongst young people a hard core of persistent juvenile offenders who are responsible for a disproportionate amount of crime in particular areas and at particular times.[6] Newspapers will report cases where a young man has committed, or is suspected of committing, offences which may run into hundreds, but such cases are far less common than they were made to appear. The police will sometimes claim that if the known persistent offenders were removed from circulation, the level of crime in the area would significantly decrease. So it might, but other offenders will soon take their place. These claims were the reason for the secure training centres and secure training orders introduced under the Criminal Justice and Public Order Act 1994. The persistent juvenile offender becomes much harder to identify when the task is to create a system for dealing with him (or occasionally her). It is not clear how many persistent offenders there are, and different definitions will identify different individuals. The Victorians found similar problems in giving effect to the Habitual Criminals Act 1869, and in devising suitable criteria or regimes for the indeterminate sentence of preventive detention. Individuals identified today will probably not be the same as those identified three months ago or in three months' time. Even if they can be identified in advance, it is not clear what the criminal justice process could do with them. They cannot justly be punished for what they have not yet done, and it is hard to justify 'privileges' which are not available to others who may be thought equally or more deserving. Many young people will share similar characteristics but not become offenders.

What will usually be true is that most persistent offenders will have chaotic and often tragic lives; parents and schools will have had little influence; and they will have reached a point where notions of honesty, decency or consideration for others take second place to day-to-day survival - not in terms of life or death, but of managing and coping in a complex, difficult and, as it often seems to them, hostile world. Policies aimed at inequality, poverty and deprivation are likely to have a far greater long-term impact on juvenile crime than any measures which can be taken through the criminal justice system, but these were not part of the Conservative Government's programme.

Legislation and joined-up policies
The change of government in May 1997 brought a radical new approach. The Audit Commission's report on Misspent Youth had recently been published,[7] drawing attention to the inefficiency and ineffectiveness of the system of juvenile justice as it had developed over the previous five or ten years. There were long delays in bringing cases to court; court proceedings were often incomprehensible to the young people and others involved; the adversarial system encouraged denials of responsibility; lawyers and their clients were trying to manipulate the process by putting forward spurious excuses or arguing about technicalities; far more was being spent on processing cases through the system than on an attempt to prevent crime or on serious work with offenders themselves; victims felt excluded and dissatisfied; too little attention was being given to developing, managing, communicating and evaluating good practice. There was no sense of coherence or common purpose. Similar criticisms could have been made about other aspects of the criminal justice process, but they were considered particularly serious when applied to youth justice. It is probably fair to say that 'justice' as distinct from the 'welfare' aspects of work with young people had been seen as relatively unimportant since the transfer of the Home Office Children's

Department and its responsibilities to the Department of Health and Social Security 27 years before. Juvenile crime and juvenile justice had featured only marginally in the Conservative Government's efforts to improve co-operation and co-ordination in the criminal justice system as a whole during the 1980s. Whether or not juvenile crime had been increasing in volume and was becoming more serious - and the Audit Commission thought the evidence was inconclusive on this point - the administration of youth justice clearly needed the new Government's urgent attention.

The Labour Party had been impressed by the Audit Commission's report while it was still in opposition; it had worked hard to prepare and publish its own proposals before coming into government; and it was ready to proceed quickly with its own plans. They were announced first in the White Paper *No More Excuses,*[8] and then embodied in the bill which became the Crime and Disorder Act 1998. Further measures were contained in the Youth Justice and Criminal Evidence Act 1999.

The measures themselves were summarised in *The Government's Crime Reduction Strategy*, published at the end of 1999.[9] They consisted principally of the following:

- Administrative measures to halve the time it takes to deal with persistent young offenders from arrest to sentence.
- The abolition of *doli incapax* - the rule that required the prosecution to show that an offender under 14 knew that the act was wrong.
- Legislation to establish 'new, more demanding types of punishment for young offenders with much greater emphasis on reparation and victims'. They include *final warnings by the police; reparation orders, action plan orders, referral orders* and *detention and training orders*. These are in addition to the existing supervision orders under the Children and Young Persons Act 1969.
- Greater emphasis on the responsibilities and involving of parents, including *parenting orders* which require parents to attend courses of instruction.
- The formation of a national Youth Justice Board to promote national and local measures to prevent offending, including advice on standards and best practice and arrangements to pilot, monitor and evaluate programmes, and to act as the commissioning authority for secure accommodation.
- Local *youth offending teams*, bringing together a range of agencies and skills, devising and delivering community-based programmes of intervention with convicted young offenders and promoting other programmes to prevent offending.

- *Youth offender panels* to draw up 'contracts' with young offenders making their first appearance in court, and their parents, to tackle the causes of their offending.
- A new approach to the custody of young men under 18 involving a new range of institutions (or an 'estate') 'providing secure accommodation and new regimes.
- A common statutory 'principal aim' of the youth justice system to prevent offending by children and young persons.

Just as important for their effect on levels of juvenile crime and criminality were the Government's legislation, policies and programmes on wider aspects of social policy - poverty, education, health, employment, housing, social security.

There is clear evidence[10] that offending is commonly associated with:

- low family income;
- poor housing;
- an unstable job record (the offender's or his parents);
- failure or exclusion from school;
- delinquent family or friends;
- a remote father (not necessarily an absent father);
- harsh and erratic discipline (at home or at school);
- abuse of drugs;
- mental disturbance; and
- previous experience of violence or abuse.

Relevant programmes included those to raise standards in education, especially for those with low levels of achievement or attention; to reduce truancy and exclusions from school and social exclusion more generally; to improve the quality of healthcare and public health more generally; to tackle the abuse of drugs and the misuse of alcohol; programmes such as Sure Start for children under four and their families; New Deal for helping young people into work; the Connexions Service for providing social support; and the duties towards those leaving care which local authorities have to undertake under the Children Leaving Care Act 2000. Within the criminal justice system, but separate from youth justice, were the provisions in the Crime and Disorder Act 1998 for anti-social behaviour orders, sex offender orders, child safety orders, child curfew orders, and local strategies to counter crime and social disorder (see *Chapter 18*). The Policy Action Team report, already mentioned, considered how well the existing range of policies and services work for young people at risk. It suggested that more should be done to emphasise prevention, especially through work with families; to recognise the specific needs, circumstances and aspirations of young people at risk; and to ensure that services are not provided haphazardly or on a restricted basis. It concluded that there is a big gap, on several dimensions: at the national and local level, in the evidence base for policy, and in the lack of machinery for bringing policies and service delivery together. The Team believed that there are hugely damaging consequences, socially for individuals, their families and communities; and economically in the waste of resources. But 'the greatest cost is to the vulnerable young people who fall through the hands of countless agencies with the young person's problems never being tackled effectively.' Work with and for young people needs to be fully co-ordinated, nationally and locally on the ground; services need to communicate effectively with one another and it is important that the need to communicate should not result in too many new structures, distractions and frustrations. And despite the range of new initiatives which have been or are being put in place, children's mental health is still an area of comparative neglect where there remain too many gaps in provision.[11] With important implications for youth justice, the Policy Action Team's report set out a number of principles and themes underpinning good programmes for young people. They include not only a robust understanding of risk and protective factors and 'joined up' policy and practice, but also:

- The best programmes are planned, focused and persistent, with early intervention, intensive action at key transition points, sustained following through, and ways back offered to those who have gone off track.
- The best programmes use data and local knowledge to target action and monitor their success.
- Some of the best programmes are innovative and proactive, making use of 'non-professional' resources, for example communities, families and young people themselves.

Later chapters in the report make recommendations for structures and mechanisms for co-ordination at national and local levels, for action in various specific areas of social policy, and consultation and funding. An annex analyses the problems faced by young people from ethnic minority groups.

WHAT IS NEW IN YOUTH JUSTICE?

Notable features of the present Government's approach to youth justice include:

- Recognition that juvenile crime and criminality have to be dealt with by social measures outside the youth justice system as well as through the youth justice system itself.
- A deliberate and systematic attempt to construct policies and programmes which are based on empirical evidence, and to monitor and evaluate those policies and programmes in terms of their intended outcomes.
- Declaratory legislation to give a sense of progress, direction and commitment, although without provision for enforcement.
- An entirely new administrative structure, comprising a national Youth Justice Board and local youth offending teams, established by statute and having executive and advisory functions which cut across those of established departments and agencies.
- Persistent use of the language of punishment to describe requirements and activities which are essentially educational, restorative or rehabilitative in their nature.
- The start of a movement away from an adversarial towards a more consultative and restorative but also inquisitorial process, with pressure on offenders to acknowledge and 'face up to' their offence and its consequences, but with potentially serious effects for anyone who may be intimidated or wrongly accused.
- A wider context of public service reform, with an emphasis on performance management and measurement, and of a changing relationship between the state and the citizen based on a combination of rights and responsibilities.

Innovation, tension and conflict - turning principles into practice

Like the measures being developed a hundred years ago, the Government's policies represent an eclectic approach which draws on a number of criminological and penological traditions and ideas - positivist, socialist, classical or retributivist, utilitarian. They draw on all the three strategies which Michael Cavadino, Ian Crow and James Dignan identify in *Criminal Justice 2000*[12] (see *Chapter 6*). They thus raise a number of potential conflicts and contradictions which will ultimately need to be resolved on a day-to-day basis by practitioners on the ground. Conflicts are likely to arise over public expectations of what is meant by punishment or remorse; victims' attitudes or expectations of restorative procedures, for example in young offender panels; the extent to which protection should be given to vulnerable defendants or those who deny their guilt; and the difference between the degree of responsibility and culpability which can be attributed to an adult as compared with a juvenile, for example if a juvenile is less able to foresee the consequences of his or her actions, now that the presumption of *doli incapax* no longer applies.

The new arrangements for youth justice attempt to bring together a wide range of approaches, skills and organizations. They do so more comprehensively than previous legislation on children and young people and they deserve public and professional support. But it is important to be clear how much is involved, and how much is required of those who have to put them into effect and those who have to monitor and judge their success.

The philosophy is that many, perhaps most, young people are at some risk of getting into trouble during their formative years; that quite a number actually do so; and that the task is to prevent them from getting into more serious trouble as they grow older. For this purpose the Crime and Disorder Act and the Youth Justice and Criminal Evidence Act have set up a range of mainly preventive measures for young people, and their parents, who are at risk and who are not yet serious or persistent offenders. Many of these draw on the ideas of restorative justice, and enable those ideas to be further developed. For those who continue to offend, there is a graduated range of penalties, culminating in the detention and training order of up to two years, part of which will be served in custody (or for extremely serious offences, a longer period of custody under section 53 Children and Young Persons Act 1933).

Within all these provisions, there is a requirement that cases should be dealt with quickly, and that the various procedures will compel offenders to control their behaviour, understand its effect on their victims, and not make excuses. They all have the overarching, statutory aim of preventing re-offending.

All this is fine in theory, and it should in most cases be fine in practice. But some cases will be complicated, messy and will have more than one side to the story. The facts will sometimes be disputed. Some facts may be admitted, others not. Degrees of culpability, sometimes relating to a young person's maturity and understanding, will still have to be considered. Co-defendants and multiple offences will sometimes be involved, with different attitudes on the part of families, victims and the defendants themselves. Questions of race, ethnicity and culture will sometimes be in the background, or in the foreground if the offence has a racial aspect. Local feeling, sensitivities and sometimes publicity may have to be considered. The process of taking all these considerations into account may need time, which will conflict with the requirement for speed, or resources which cannot easily be found among hard-pressed police officers or the busy members of a youth offending team.

There are other grounds for concern. Most of the preventive or positive aspects of the new arrangements require an admission of guilt, with an assumption that a denial of guilt is somehow a failure to accept responsibility which itself deserves punishment. For many of the procedures there is no provision for legal representation or legal aid, again on the assumption that to expect it is a denial of responsibility. Vulnerable young people may be placed under pressure to make admissions in order to 'get it done with' or to avoid more serious consequences. Those who are convicted after a plea of 'not guilty' are likely to move quickly 'up tariff' and gain the status of serious offenders, even 'criminals'. Ministers have spoken of the need to end the 'culture of non-prosecution', with the expectation that fewer cases will be dropped by the police or discontinued by the Crown Prosecution Service on 'public interest' grounds - triviality or lack of conclusive evidence. They have also spoken as if the whole purpose of the various procedures, and their outcomes is to 'punish' the offender, although what is seen as punishment may not be easy to reconcile with the overarching aim of preventing re-offending, or with other aims such as reparation to the victim or re-integration into the community.

The ending of the presumption of *doli incapax* implies that more young children, even as young as 10 or 11, will be brought into the system. Even an admission of guilt carries with it a criminal record, and although the intention is that the conviction should in some cases be regarded as 'spent' for the purpose of the Rehabilitation of Offenders Act 1974 it still remains on the books and can be disclosed, for example to prospective employers, in certain circumstances. The involvement of victims, though admirable in its intention, and probably in most cases in its results, raises the questions which *Chapter 10* considered in the context of restorative justice more generally. The courts and youth offending teams have an almost bewildering array of orders which are available to them, but very little flexibility or discretion to deal with special circumstances in particular cases. The role of the youth court; its relationship with youth offending teams and youth offender panels; and the status of contracts and reparation or action plans raise further questions about whether the orders are seen as punishment imposed by the court or as agreements which are negotiated by offenders, victims and their families. Experience with restorative justice so far, certainly in the form of restorative conferencing (see *Chapter 10*), suggests that success, certainly in the sense of acceptability and respect for the process, requires the 'ownership' and commitment of the parties and is likely to be compromised if it is seen to be imposed 'from above'.

A restorative approach is consistent with the three principles by which youth offender panels are to be guided - making reparation to the victim, achieving re-integration into the community, and taking responsibility for offending behaviour. It is in a broad sense consistent with the aim of preventing re-offending. It is not so easily reconciled with an aim of 'punishment', unless punishment is understood in the vaguest terms as anything which happens when a person has been found out.

How the various working relationships are developed, and how the status of contracts and orders is perceived, raise important questions for their acceptability and effectiveness, and ultimately for their authority and legitimacy.

JUSTICE's report *Restoring Youth Justice: New Directions in Domestic and International Law and Practice Retaining*[13] provides a valuable comparative study of restorative practices in youth justice in various parts of the world. It generally supports the initiatives which the Government has taken in this country, but it expresses concern on certain aspects - the role of the courts, access to legal advice, the role of victims, the position relating to criminal records, the danger that cases will be dealt with hastily or superficially because of pressures of time or lack of resources, the lack of clarity about the specific aims to be pursued in particular cases. It emphasises the importance of training, monitoring and evaluation. It also points out that some of the procedures raise questions about the situation under the Human Rights Act and the European Convention On Human Rights, under the United Nations Standard Minimum Rules for the Administration of Juvenile Justice (the Beijing Rules) and the International Convention On the Rights of the Child.

Accountability

The new arrangements are an innovation not only in their penal, restorative and preventive aims, but also in the administrative structures and working methods which are needed to put them into effect. They rely on enthusiasm, commitment and goodwill which are all available in abundance at the present stage of their development, but relationships may become less cordial and co-operation may become harder to obtain when difficulties or disagreements arise. Sensitive but critical relationships at national level are between the Youth Justice Board, ministers and their political advisers, Parliament, and officials in the Home Office and other departments. At local level they are between the youth offending teams, their local authorities including elected members, and the various services and organizations which comprise their statutory or non-statutory partners and stakeholders. Restorative justice, in particular, relies on local confidence and goodwill, on the understanding and co-operation of local communities, and on their 'ownership' of the procedures and the outcomes which result from them. They depend on the value of citizenship and the support of civil society as described in *Chapter 4*. The structures and dynamics of its accountability are therefore essential for its success.

The Youth Justice Board and local teams can be held publicly to account through the publication of reports, statistics, data on performance and the processes of inspection and audit, and information will therefore be available from which the public can judge how the new system is doing. The Home Secretary is the responsible minister accountable to Parliament. But elsewhere in the structure it is not always clear who is accountable for what and to whom; whose responsibility it is to take action in complex situations or when things go wrong; or how responsibilities, for example to supply suitably qualified staff to be members of teams, to restore conflicts over priorities or to overcome difficulties over confidentiality, can be enforced if they are not willingly discharged.

Team managers are accountable to the chief executives of their local authorities (sometimes directly, sometimes through another officer). But it is not clear how far teams, or chief executives, should or do in fact regard themselves as accountable to the chair or elected members of the local authority; to their local communities (direct or through elected members); to central government; to the Youth Justice Board; or to the courts. Most teams have a strong sense of responsibility towards the public or their communities, but it is not as yet clearly focused or expressed in ways which are generally recognised or respected. Members of different professions have different assumptions and expectations, use different language, judge themselves and their colleagues according to different criteria, use different methods of evaluation and are accustomed to different working systems and policies. There is no formal structure of accountability for youth justice within those professions, or of accountability to local communities. Arrangements for that kind of accountability will have to be constructed locally, pragmatically, and probably by trial and error.

The main point of concern about youth justice by the end of 2000 was the increase in the number of juveniles whom the youth courts had committed to custody on remand or sentenced to custody under the new sentence of a detention and training order, the resulting overcrowding in Prison Service establishments, and the conditions which young defendants and offenders were having to suffer as a consequence. There were also wide variations in sentencing practice in different geographical areas. The Youth Justice Board became responsible for commissioning and purchasing all places for under 18 year olds in April 2000. Some of the places available were secure units provided by local authorities or in secure training centres provided by the private sector, but most were still in former young offender institutions or even in adult prisons. Conditions in Feltham and Portland were acknowledged to have been a national disgrace, although improvements were taking place, and even the better establishments were suffering from pressure of numbers and shortage of staff and facilities. The Youth Justice Board was committed to seeking a reduction in the number of juveniles in custody, on remand or under sentence, but had evidently not anticipated the courts' increased use of custody since the detention and training order became available. In March 2001 the Board announced a new strategy for the 'juvenile estate'[14] which involved reducing its reliance on Prison Service accommodation, more use of places provided by the private sector (400 new places by 2005), a better geographical distribution of places across the country, and new arrangements for young women. The need for an expansion in the number of places was a matter for regret, but the intention to improve standards was clearly welcome – although the programme stopped short of withdrawing all responsibility for juveniles from the Prison Service, which must be a clear and urgent objective (see also *Chapter 19*).

CONCLUSION

The new arrangements for youth justice are a bold innovation which deserves to succeed. They have some features - the creation of the Youth Justice Board, the application of restorative methods - which could well be adopted for other parts of the criminal justice system. There are some aspects which critics will regret, especially the prominent place which custody still holds in youth justice; and rather more, such as those which JUSTICE have identified, where things may go wrong if the potential difficulties are not identified and anticipated. But the task is to acknowledge and deal with those difficulties, not to be defeated by them or use them as a reason for criticism. Success will depend on the actual or perceived effect on the volume and character of crime committed by young people; and on the efficiency, fairness and legitimacy of the procedures themselves. The two should be, but are not necessarily, connected. The Labour Government undoubtedly found the youth justice system in a state of administrative confusion and neglect when it entered office in May 1997, with justified and well documented complaints about delays, waste of time and money, and ineffectiveness in terms of the impact it was making on young people who became involved with it. Whether it was also facing a surge in juvenile crime, as distinct from a number of well publicised individual cases and public reactions to them, is harder to tell. There can be no doubt that young people were responsible for a large volume of crime, and that everything possible should be done to reduce it, for the sake of the victims, the wider public and young people themselves. But it will be harder for measures such as those to which the Government rightly committed itself to be credible if they are put into effect in a context of sensational reporting and opportunist political criticism or in a culture of punishment and blame. The Government itself must not allow itself to seek spurious popularity by bidding against that kind of criticism and blaming public servants for their supposed failure. Public servants themselves must work together, and with their communities, on a basis of confidence and trust, of professional expertise, of openness and accessibility, and of public understanding and goodwill. These must be established from the beginning and carefully maintained thereafter. They are much harder to create once confidence has been damaged.

Juvenile justice, more than any other part of the criminal justice system, is an area where the arrangements for dealing with suspects and offenders have to be related to other services for children and young people. If they are not connected to the ordinary services for education, health - especially mental health - and social services, including child protection, or if young people are growing up in poor housing or serious poverty, the juvenile justice process will at best have no impact and at worst it will reinforce the young person's criminality and propensity to offend. Shortcomings in those services, many of which have been identified and acknowledged in numerous reports from government, statutory and charitable sources, similarly increase young people's likelihood of offending and the difficulty of dealing with their offending when it occurs. The shortcomings are particularly acute for young people who have been in care.[15]

The state and civil society have special obligations towards the nation's children, and through them to its own future. Supporting those obligations is one of the most important responsibilities of citizenship, whether through the work of children's charities, organizations which provide or support opportunities for young people, or voluntary effort such as the work of school governors. For children leaving care, the responsibilities of the state have now received statutory expression in the Children Leaving Care Act 2000. *Chapter 13* has suggested that similar statutory provision should be made for the resettlement of offenders: the case is especially strong in relation to children and young people. But the responsibility for preventing criminality among young people, and for dealing constructively with those who commit it, belongs not only to the state but to its citizens as a whole.

The longer term concern must be that once children or young people become identified as troublesome, responsibility for dealing with them will pass from civil society to the state, and not only to the state but to the criminal justice system. Other services then begin to lose interest; the child or young person comes to be seen and treated (however humanely) as a criminal; and the aim of 'reducing offending' takes priority over other aspects of his or her development. The hope for the future must be that provision and responsibility for juvenile offenders will be progressively integrated with the arrangements for young people more generally, with an increase in the age of criminal responsibility,[16] and with a stronger and more unified focus in central and local government. The Policy Action Team's report points logically to the formation, not of the Ministerial group which has now been established (welcome though that may be), but to a separate government department covering education, the youth service and children's social services as well as youth justice. No-one would wish to recreate the old approved schools, but they were at least meant to be schools rather than penal institutions.

ENDNOTES for *Chapter 14*

[1]   Cabinet Office, *National Strategy for Neighbourhood Renewal: Report of Policy Action Team 12: Young People*, London, Cabinet Office, 2000.

[2]   Baroness Warnock, 'A Prayer for our Children', *Observer*, 24 December 2000.

[3]   For a general account see Leon Radzinowicz and Roger Hood, *A History of the English Criminal Law, Volume 5, The Emergence of Penal Policy*, London, Stevens and Sons, 1986.

[4]   Michael Cavadino, Iain Crow and James Dignan, *Criminal Justice 2000*, Winchester, Waterside Press, 2000.

[5]   *Police Report of Notifiable Offences Cleared up Following Arrest Report by Age, Gender and Offence*, Home Office Statistical Findings, February 1996.

[6]   Ann Hagell and Tim Newburn, *Persistent Young Offenders*, London, Policy Studies Institute, 1994.

[7]   Audit Commission, *Misspent Youth: Young People and Crime*, London, Audit Commission, 1997.

[8]   Home Office, *No More Excuses:*, London, Home Office, 1997.

[9]   *The Government's Crime Reduction Strategy*, London, Home Office, 1999.

[10] For a study of the extent, frequency and nature of self-reported offending among 14-25 year olds see John Graham and Ben Bowling, *Young People and Crime*, Home Office Research Study 145, London, Home Office, 1995.

[11] Mental Health Foundation, *Bright Futures, Promoting Children's and Young People's Mental Health*, London, Mental Health Foundation, 1999.

[12] *Op. cit.*, n. 5.

[13] JUSTICE, *Restoring Youth Justice: New Directions in Domestic and International Law and Practice*, London, JUSTICE, 2000.

[14] *Youth Justice Board News*, Issue 7, March 2001.

[15] Sir William Utting, *People Like Us: the Report of the Review of the Safeguards for Children Living Away from Home*, London, Department of Health and Welsh Office, 1997.

[16] For a discussion on the age of criminal responsibility, see JUSTICE, *Children and Homicide: Appropriate Procedures for Juveniles in Murder and Homicide Cases*, London, JUSTICE, 1996, and Sula Wolff and Alexander McCall Smith, 'Children Who Kill', *British Medical Journal*, Vol. 322, 13 January 2001. Although prompted by the case arising from the murder of Jamie Bulger, the arguments apply to the responsibility of children generally. In the cases of *T and V v. United Kingdom*, the European Court of Human Rights recommended that the age of criminal responsibility in England and Wales (among the lowest in Europe) should be reconsidered.

CHAPTER 15

Victims of Crime

Public wrongs, or crimes and misdemeanors, are a breach and violation of the public rights and duties due to the whole community, in its social aggregate capacity . . . since besides the wrong done to the individual, they strike at the very being of society.

William Blackstone, *Commentaries on the Laws of England*, 1765

I want victims to feel that they are at the heart of the criminal justice system.

Jack Straw, 2000

Victims of crime received little or no effective recognition in England and Wales until the Government established the Criminal Injuries Compensation Scheme in 1964. The Probation of Offenders Act had made provision for courts to impose compensation orders on offenders as long ago as 1907, but courts had made little use of that power. The Scheme, and the Board which administered it, were originally set up on a non-statutory basis and were expected to operate on a small scale, very much at the margins of criminal justice policy and practice. It is perhaps not too cynical to say that the intention at that time was more to divert attention away from rising crime and falling rates of detection than to provide a new service or to respond to any recognised, legitimate or coherent demand. It was another 25 years before the government, or the criminal justice services, came to recognise that victims had other reasonable needs or expectations - for information, help and support; sometimes for protection; and perhaps for a voice or certainly some recognition in the criminal justice process itself.

As late as the early 1980s, ministers thought and spoke as if compensation was what most concerned victims themselves, and as if an acceptable compensation scheme were all that victims could reasonably expect from the government or the state. Compensation was certainly important to victims, but the focus of their attention, in Great Britain and abroad, had for several years been moving towards support and services, and towards recognition and a possible role for victims in the criminal justice process itself.

SUPPORT AND SERVICES FOR VICTIMS

The organization now known as Victim Support had its origin in a scheme in Bristol sponsored by the National Association for the Care and Resettlement of Offenders (NACRO, now known simply as Nacro) in the mid 1970s. Ten years later, victim support schemes covered virtually the whole of England and Wales; they were co-ordinated by the National Association of Victim Support Schemes, which later became Victim Support, and NACRO was no longer involved. Schemes were entirely voluntary; each scheme had a management committee, a co-ordinator and a number of volunteers who gave help and support to individual victims. Government funding was available for the national office of Victim Support; funding to enable schemes to employ paid co-ordinators gradually became available during the 1980s, although the Government was originally reluctant, fearing that funding for local schemes would lead to a demand for a new, and expensive, paid social service. By 2000-2001, funding amounted to about £18.3 million a year. Other organizations emerged with more specialised interests such as domestic violence, rape, and the families of victims of homicide. Similar, sometimes more militant, organizations were growing up in other parts of Europe, in North America and in Australia and New Zealand. Paul Rock tells the story in his book *Helping Victims of Crime.*[1]

Much of Victim Support's early energy was directed towards the practical aspects of providing the service - the recruitment and training of co-ordinators and volunteers; relationships with the police, the Crown Prosecution Service and the Courts; the development and communication of good practice. But questions of philosophy and principle were never far away. In 1977, the Norwegian academic Nils Christie had written his article 'Conflicts as Property'[2], in which he argued that lawyers, probation officers and other professionals had 'stolen' conflicts, including crimes, which 'belonged' to the people directly involved. The article prompted two lines of argument. One was that victims should in some way be brought into the criminal justice process so that they could have a voice in decisions about how their crime was investigated, and how the offender was tried, convicted and sentenced. The other was that the traditional, and in common law countries adversarial, procedures for trial, conviction and sentence should wherever possible be replaced by a process of mediation and restoration, involving direct contact between the victim and the offender. This kind of process is now often described as 'restorative justice', although it can take several different forms (see *Chapter 10*).

VICTIMS' INVOLVEMENT IN THE CRIMINAL JUSTICE PROCESS

Victim Support, and to some extent successive governments, have been cautious about approaches which involve victims in the criminal justice process (otherwise than as ordinary witnesses), or which involve direct contacts between victims and offenders. An understanding has emerged that victims should have all the help, information and support that can reasonably be provided (though views may differ on what counts as reasonable), but closer involvement presents a risk that victims might be exploited by schemes which are intended primarily to benefit the offender (for example so that he can 'confront his offending behaviour', or show remorse which a court might subsequently regard as a mitigating factor). Or the victim might take the opportunity, or might even be encouraged, to show anger or distress in order to influence the process against the offender. Different victims will in any event react to similar crimes in different ways but the crime will not necessarily be more serious, or the offender more culpable, on that account.

By the early 1990s a broad agreement had developed that victims are entitled to information about the important decisions which may be taken during the progress of the case - arrest, identity of the suspect, offence charged, decisions on bail, verdict, sentence, the terms of any orders such as probation or community service, and in some instances the date of the offender's release from prison and his or her subsequent destination. Victims are also entitled, and may often be expected, to provide factual information which is relevant to these decisions, both about the nature of the crime and the damage it has caused, and to express any concerns which the victim may have, for example about his or her safety. This information may be needed to inform decisions about the offence to be charged, the seriousness of the offence and hence the sentence to be imposed, and also about any conditions which might be attached to a grant of bail, a community sentence, or release on licence. It will also inform any order for compensation. The victim is not however entitled to demand a particular sentence, and the victim's feelings or behaviour are not in themselves a reason for the offender to be treated more or less seriously than would be justified on the facts of the case. Information provided by victims should be open to challenge and cross-examination by the defence but victims' privacy should be respected. They should be protected from attempts to humiliate them in cross-examination and from pleas in mitigation which unnecessarily attack their character or credibility.

A committee of JUSTICE has expressed these legitimate expectations as follows:[3]

- appropriate acknowledgement of the role and responsibilities of the victim within each criminal justice process and by each institution, agency or individual involved in those processes, including, where relevant, timely consultation on decisions, without expecting victims to take responsibility for decisions which are properly the remit of a criminal justice institution or agency;
- support and assistance for victims in relation to the effects of the offence and in discharging all responsibilities placed on them in relation to criminal justice;
- information and explanation as to what is happening to the case;
- means to ensure timely and accurate provision of information to relevant criminal justice institutions and agencies about the offence and its effects on victims;
- being made aware of what is expected of them at each stage (when they will be needed, where they go, what will happen);
- making the safety of victims and those close to victims a major factor in relation to decisions in criminal justice and, where relevant, civil justice processes; in particular, provision of a safe

environment for victims on the premises of all criminal justice institutions;

- minimisation of further damage or harm to victims through criminal justice procedures;
- compensation and alleviation of the effects of the offence, as well as minimisation of cost to victims in assisting criminal justice.

Victims' rights and expectations

The reasonable expectations of victims have been to some extent codified in the *Victim's Charter*, first issued in 1990 (and then described rather misleadingly as a statement of 'rights' but without any mechanisms for their enforcement) and revised in 1996. In some respects it is a typical document of the period, especially in its revised form - plenty of quantified standards and targets, but reflecting a rather authoritarian, top-down, statement of what the services think they can deliver rather than an expression of what victims themselves have said they would like to have provided. The charter has been criticised for being too limited in its scope and too mechanical in its operation; and especially for failing to provide any special procedures by which victims could make complaints, apart from those - sometimes bureaucratic and inaccessible - procedures which apply to the courts and the criminal justice services in general. But the charter has served to raise awareness and to generate a genuine commitment to improving the treatment of victims.

Victim Support itself believes that victims are entitled to five fundamental rights:[4]

- to be free of the burden of decisions relating to the offender - we believe that the responsibility for dealing with the offender lies with the state and should not be placed upon the victim;
- to receive information and explanation about the progress of their case - victims should have an opportunity to provide their own information about the full financial, physical and emotional consequences of the crime and this information should be taken into consideration whenever decisions are made about the case;
- to be protected in any way necessary;
- to receive compensation; and
- to receive respect, recognition and support.

Standards set out in the revised charter require the police to respond rapidly to reports of incidents, to supply victims with any information they may need, including information about the progress of the case, and to do their best to catch the person responsible for the crime. Victim Support itself is charged with sending a letter to the victim, or arranging for a volunteer to visit, within four working days of a report of a crime; and with offering support to witnesses in the Crown Court (since extended to most magistrates' courts). Much of the current work on victims' issues relates to the application and development of the charter standards and other aspects of service - a Victim Support helpline; developing the service for witnesses at court; work with children and young people with special attention to their situation and circumstances; work with victims of domestic and sexual violence, of murder and manslaughter, and of racially motivated crime.

PROTECTION OF WITNESSES

Other issues concern the protection of vulnerable and intimidated witnesses, and action to follow up the Government's report on *Speaking Up For Justice*.[5] Measures taken as a result of that report include:

- screens to ensure that the witnesses cannot see the accused;
- the delivery of evidence by live television link;
- clearing the courtroom of public and press to allow evidence to be given in private;
- allowing a video-recorded interview to stand as evidence-in-chief;
- allowing pre-recorded cross-examination as evidence;
- allowing children and those suffering from physical or mental impairment to communicate through an intermediary;
- restricting the defendant's right to cross-examine personally a witness in certain circumstances;
- restricting the allowability of evidence or questioning about previous sexual history in trials for rape and other sexual offences;
- restricting the publication of information which might lead to the disclosure of certain witnesses' identity; and
- changing the definitions of who is competent to give evidence.

Several of these measures raise questions about the accused person's right to a fair trial, and the victim's right to privacy, under the European Convention On Human Rights.

THE STEPHEN LAWRENCE INQUIRY REPORT

A third set of issues arises from the report of the inquiry into the death of Stephen Lawrence,[6] in particular the need for

- improvements in police family liaison, and improved training for police officers in racial awareness;
- Victim Support and police to make more active use of local contacts in minority ethnic communities to help in liaison with families;
- the formulation of new guidelines for the handling of witnesses and victims, particularly in the context of racist incidents, and leading to amendments to the *Victim's Charter*; and
- the possible introduction of the victim as a 'civil party' to criminal proceedings, as is done in some continental European countries.

The first three of these may involve difficulties in practice, but there should be no problem over the principle. The last is more complex, and it is questionable whether victims in countries where they are able to appear as 'civil parties' are in practice likely to be treated more favourably or more fairly than they are in Great Britain.[7]

VICTIMS IN COURT

Two troublesome questions in any discussion of victims' rights and expectations concern the extent to which victims should be able to make statements to the court about their experience of the crime which has been committed against them; and whether and if so how they should be enabled to contest derogatory remarks made about them in pleas in mitigation.

The *Victim's Charter* (revised version) provided for a pilot project in which victims were invited to make 'victim personal statements' describing the impact which the crime made upon them. The project has been evaluated to establish why victims chose or did not choose to make statements of this kind, and also the uses which courts and other criminal justice services made of the statements which were provided.[8] Such statements resemble the 'victim impact statements' which are commonplace in the United States and some other countries, but they have been viewed with suspicion in Great Britain. One reason is the fear that they would be used prejudicially against the defendant, with the possibility that an emotional appeal by an exceptionally distressed victim might affect the court's view of the defendant's credibility, or of the seriousness of the offence and therefore the sentence. Another is a fear on behalf of victims themselves that they might be placed under pressure and feel themselves to be exploited or put at risk, for example if their statements were likely to be challenged by the defence. There are also various procedural questions - when the statements are to be made; to whom they should be communicated, when and by what means; what use is to be made of them and what purposes they are intended to serve.

The results of the evaluation were not particularly encouraging. The initiative raised expectations which could not easily be realised; victims were less enthusiastic than might have been expected and sometimes actually disappointed; the objectives were unclear and needed to be clarified; and they seemed to have little practical effect. The victim's experience in terms of loss or injury is clearly relevant to the seriousness of the offence and therefore to the sentence which might be imposed on a defendant or an offender as a condition of bail, a community sentence, or release on licence. There had been no training to guide services on how the statements might be used, and there was obvious confusion about their purpose. But more thought needed to be given to the best ways of obtaining this information and placing it before the court.

The Home Secretary announced in May 2000 that a 'Victim Personal Statement Scheme' was to be introduced in England and Wales 'to give victims of crime a greater say in the Criminal Justice Process.' It was to be 'rolled out' between December 2000 and March 2001, and evaluated over a period of 12 months after that. Victims will be given the opportunity to make a voluntary statement at the stage when the police take a witness statement, and subsequently a further statement describing its longer term effects. Matters which might typically be covered include the victim's wish to have more information about the progress of the case, any fears about vulnerability or victimisation, and whether he or she is seeking compensation. It did not appear that the statement was intended as an opportunity for the victim to express views on the sentence which the court might impose, but a later statement on 12 October 2000 indicated that it would be read out in court, and taken into account in sentencing.

A critical question, still unresolved at the time of writing, is whether victim personal statements are to be used like victim impact statements, as a contribution to the sentencing process; or whether, as Victim Support would prefer, they will be taken and used at a much earlier stage to alert the police and the Crown Prosecution Service to the victim's legitimate needs and interests. They would then be relevant in the large number of cases which do not result in a conviction or sentence.

Some procedures already exist, for example in the Bar Council's Code of Conduct, to prevent or deal with derogatory assertions made in pleas in mitigation, but they are not always followed or effective and they are not easy to apply when the defendant pleads guilty. Further possibilities would be to require pleas in mitigation to be disclosed in advance, or to give the prosecution a right or duty to reply. Either of those would be likely in practice to add to delays and costs, and possibly to invite argument and recriminations from which nothing would be gained. A more radical proposal would be for the prosecution to have a formal role in sentencing (see *Chapter 21*). Although controversial, it is probably the most promising line of development if the issue is to be pursued.

COMPENSATION FOR VICTIMS OF CRIME

While Victim Support and its services were becoming established, the demands on the Criminal Injuries Compensation Scheme, the sums paid in compensation, and the administrative arrangements needed to operate the scheme, grew beyond all expectations. Those demands, and the difficulty of meeting them, led during the 1980s and early 1990s to criticism of delays, and to long running arguments about the purpose, cost and character of the scheme. The arguments focused principally on four questions. The first was whether the scheme should continue to operate on its original basis of individual assessment, with awards related to those which courts might make for civil damages for similar injuries; or on a 'tariff' basis of published rates for different types of injury. The second was the cost of the scheme and the means of controlling it, typically achieved at that time by manipulating the minimum level of award below which less serious injuries would fail to qualify for payment; and the number of staff whom the Board was allowed to employ and therefore the rate at which payments could be made. The third was the practice, in many cases, of withdrawing social security benefits from those who received awards; and the fourth concerned the exclusions from the scheme, for example the disqualification or reduction in awards for those with criminal convictions at some time in the past. An independent working party set up by Victim Support expressed its concern about all these points in a report published in 1993.[9]

The Committee's 24 recommendations included the following:

- The purpose of a state compensation scheme for victims of crime should be to recognise on behalf of society the experience which victims have suffered; and to help the victim to recover from it and live as normal a life as is possible in the circumstances.
- Victims of violent crime should receive compensation awards for pain, suffering and loss of amenity. Entitlement should extend not only to those who have been the victim of a crime of violence, but also to those who have experienced psychological injury as a result of other offences, such as domestic burglary or those having a racial aspect. Additional payments should be available where the physical or psychological effects of the injury persist over a long period which could not have been foreseen.
- Payments to provide a continuing long-term level of income should be assimilated to the structure of social security benefits and paid by the Department of Social Security, but without being dependent on national insurance contributions or means tests.
- Compensation for loss of earnings above this level should not be a matter for the government but employers. They should provide suitable insurance cover or the equivalent, especially for those in high risk occupations, for example police and fire fighters. Payments from the Department of Social Security should not be affected by any benefits of this kind.
- Financial support should also be available, under separate arrangements and on a basis of need, to victims of property crime who suffer serious hardship. Payments should again be made by the Department of Social Security; they should be treated as grants and not recovered as loans.
- The bereavement award for relatives of victims of homicide should be increased and made more widely available; dependants should be eligible for a bereavement pension.
- Compensation awards should be based on a fixed scale; the payment for each type of injury would include an amount for pain, suffering and loss of amenity, based on the average payment for that type of injury under the current scheme.
- The minimum level of award, currently £1,000, should be abolished. Compensation should be available for all injuries which are more serious than minor cuts and bruises, and the psychological equivalent.
- No one should be excluded on grounds of character as indicated by previous convictions or unlawful conduct.

- Payments should be made without any deduction for social security benefits, and benefits should not be stopped or reduced because a person has received compensation.
- Compensation should be paid without discrimination on grounds such as race, gender or class, and payments should be monitored accordingly.
- The government and the insurance industry should make further efforts to ensure that flexible and affordable insurance is available in high crime areas.

There was a separate argument that the scheme ought as a matter of financial propriety and Parliamentary accountability to be placed on a statutory basis. Legislation for this purpose had been included in the Criminal Justice Act 1988 but had not been brought into effect because of the cost.

In the event, the Government paid little attention to the working party's report, and sought to introduce a new scheme of its own.[10] It resembled the working party's proposals in that it was based on a 'tariff', but it left untouched most of the other points of concern. But because the earlier provisions of the Criminal Justice Act 1988 had not been repealed, the new scheme was challenged by way of judicial review and the House of Lords eventually found its introduction to have been unlawful and an abuse of power.[11] The outcome was a new Act, the Criminal Injuries Compensation Act 1995, which prescribed a 'tariff' basis for the assessment of awards, and at last placed the scheme and the board on a proper statutory footing. The new scheme made under the Act kept the limit for awards at the relatively high level of £1,000, and confirmed a wide range of disqualifying criteria, although the board had some discretion in how they were applied. No change was made in the arrangements regarding social security benefits.

Compensation for victims of crime has not been a prominent issue since the passage of the Criminal Injuries Act in 1996. The House of Commons Committee of Public Accounts has however drawn attention to the fact that about half of those applying for compensation do not receive an award because they do not meet the Scheme's criteria, and that there are wide variations in the level of applicant relative to recorded violent crimes in different parts of the country.[12] The concerns which Victim Support's working party expressed in 1993 have not however been resolved, and the operation of the criminal Injuries Compensation Scheme reflects in many respects the exclusive or conditional view of citizenship described in *Chapter 4*.

STRUCTURES AND ACCOUNTABILITY

The report for JUSTICE from its committee on the role of the victim in criminal justice already mentioned included an interesting chapter on Criminal Justice as a Public Service. The Committee recommended the creation of a new Victims' Board, with formal responsibility for co-ordinating the procedures for work with victims and negotiating standards; more systematic and accessible mechanisms for complaints; and the appointment of a Commissioner for Victims of Crime who would:

- be the ultimate point of reference for complaints;
- be able to undertake thematic review of professional practice and victims' experience;
- have statutory duties to examine standards, rules and working procedures, and to monitor their practical application;
- examine legislation and legislative guidance and to make recommendations; and
- report annually to Parliament.

These proposals, if acted upon, would raise the profile of victims and victims' issues still further, both politically and operationally with the services concerned. They would also introduce a degree of tension into the criminal justice system, which would have been potentially uncomfortable not only for government and the criminal justice services but also for the organizations representing victims' themselves. The Government announced in October 2000 that it intended to appoint a victims' ombudsman, but gave no details of the functions which that person would perform or of the powers which he or she might possess.

The 'rights' which Victim Support advocates for victims are generally acknowledged as reasonable expectations on the part of victims and as responsibilities on the part of the criminal justice services who have contact with them. But they are not for the most part enforceable in any legal sense, or included among those to which the Human Rights Act might apply. The JUSTICE committee thought that victims' groups should make more use of judicial review to create a body of rules and acceptable practices in relation to victims, but accepted that a comprehensive code of rights enforceable by litigation was unlikely to be of practical benefit for most victims. Some statutory recognition may however be needed to deal with questions, for example, of confidentiality and data protection; and the statute might include authority for the Secretary of State to issue standards of service on matters of practical detail. The Home Office has suggested[13] that the time is now right to introduce statutory rights for victims, but they would be confined to 'headline' rights – to dignity and respect, to protection, help and support, compensation, information and an opportunity to make a victim's statement – and it does not seem to contemplate any mechanism for enforcement.

The implications of the Human Rights Act and the European Convention On Human Rights are difficult to predict at this stage. Much will depend on the courts' interpretation of the right to a fair trial, to liberty, to privacy and to freedom, from cruel or unusual treatment. But it should certainly not be supposed that all the protection provided by the Act will go to defendants and offenders. The Articles relating to privacy and cruel treatment, in particular, should also benefit victims and witnesses, for example in protecting them from intrusive enquiries and questioning on behalf of the defence. The police and other parts of the criminal justice system probably have an obligation to protect a victim's 'security of person' (Article 5) against a known threat from an offender. Victims should also benefit from the culture of rights which the Act may help to create (see *Chapter 4*).

VICTIMS AS CITIZENS

There is a wider sense in which victims of crime can become a focus of the ideas of citizenship. Victims are regarded as having rights, or certainly an entitlement, to consideration, respect and support in the ways already discussed and as set out in the charter. Those rights, or that entitlement, are usually seen as applying to their treatment by the state, as represented by the criminal justice system and the Criminal Injuries Compensation Scheme. They also apply to their treatment by Victim Support - an interesting example of the government's conscription of a voluntary organization into its own service (see *Chapter 4*). But their practical application is to a large extent confined to cases where there is a defendant or a convicted offender. Many cases do not reach that stage. And even when the offender has been found, convicted and sentenced (whether or not to the victim's satisfaction), there may be consequences of the crime, such as financial loss or disruption to the lives of the victim's family, which are beyond the victim's acknowledged entitlement to consideration and support. Those affected by the crime will then need to look to others - the health service, the children's teachers, employers, religious institutions, a bank or insurance company, family, friends, and neighbours. Help in this situation is not a matter of victims' rights, but of public or professional duty, civil society and citizenship. Victim Support's working party on compensation, and JUSTICE's working group, both approached these questions, from rather different perspectives, but with similar conclusions. They deserve more serious attention from government and the statutory services. Victim Support and other voluntary organizations working with victims are themselves an important part of civil society, and as such they have had a powerful influence on successive governments and on the statutory public services with whom they work.

Victims are also regarded as having responsibilities and duties of their own - to report the offence, to co-operate with police enquiries, to give evidence in court. A failure to carry out those responsibilities might well disqualify a victim from compensation and victims who were regarded as unco-operative, who were suspected of having committed offences of their own, or who did not conform to 'normal' expectations in dress or appearance, might not receive from the statutory services the standard of service which the charter would lead them to expect. Victim Support would not however discriminate on these grounds, and has always been ready to work with offenders who become victims or who do not conform to conventional stereotypes. Victims do not at present have any obligation to make 'statements' of the formal kind indicated in the charter, or to take part in restorative conferences. Both are matters of personal choice: they are perhaps better regarded as acts of good citizenship, and with a strong obligation to be reasonable and responsible in the way in which this right or this opportunity is used.

Questions affecting victims of crime raise a wide range of social and political issues: gender, race, culture, and disability, as well as contrasting views of rights, responsibilities and citizenship. Women who are victims of rape or domestic violence attract public sympathy and, sometimes, the sympathy of their friends and families, but also raise questions of prejudice and stereotyping in the way in which cases are investigated and prosecuted. Complaints are usually from women's groups against the allegedly male-dominated system, or against writers or researchers who do not share their assumptions. Sometimes they are against the 'feminist' prejudices of those who make such complaints and demands. Similar issues arise in relation to race, and have been brought into prominence by the death of Stephen Lawrence and the findings of the subsequent inquiry. And satisfaction for victims has sometimes been claimed politically as a justification for harsh penal practices as if increasing the suffering of offenders could somehow improve the victim's situation.

THE VICTIM, THE OFFENDER AND THE STATE

The relationship between the victim, the offender and the state is complicated. Nils Christie's article, already mentioned, illustrated its complication. In modern societies, the state has taken to itself the responsibility for detecting and prosecuting offenders, and punishing them when necessary, on the argument that crimes are an offence not just against an individual but against society as a whole (see Blackstone's statement at the beginning of this chapter).

It follows that individuals have no right to private vengeance, or to take the law into their own hands. It probably follows that they have an obligation to co-operate with the state in the ways indicated. The state for its part has an obligation to protect its citizens from crime, to whatever extent is reasonably possible. Until the Human Rights Act 1998 came into force, the strength of that obligation was largely a matter of political judgement or operational discretion, and the means of enforcing it was a matter of political rather than legal action. And no action by the state can prevent or control the feelings which victims will inevitably feel towards offenders who have affected their lives. Some writers who approach the subject from the perspective of restorative justice might of course reject Blackstone's argument altogether and seek to construct an entirely different system and a different set of relationships (see *Chapter 10*) but few people would take this argument that far at present.

The treatment of victims of crime inevitably involves conflicting considerations and arguments. Total consistency may be hard to achieve. The conflicts cannot be resolved by 'changing the balance' in favour of the victim and against the offender. Nor can they be resolved by continually providing more services for victims, or more opportunities for them to make their views heard, although there is more that could usefully be done. Solutions must be sought not only within but also outside the criminal justice system, through a process of patient enquiry and negotiation and in a spirit of compassion, public service and inclusive citizenship. As Victim Support's working party wrote in their report

> Policy and practice on compensation should not be considered in isolation from policy and practice relating to other forms of recognition. Not all of these are matters for the state or the government: they are also matters for individuals, employers, providers of services, and statutory and voluntary organizations of many kinds. The government does however have important responsibilities which include not only funding and providing for the administration of a state compensation scheme, but also promoting an awareness of victims' issues in all the services and for which it has responsibility (health and social services and social security as well as the various criminal justice services), providing support and funding for victims' services, and overseeing the legislative and administrative framework in which the relevant functions are performed. None of these should be neglected or overlooked.
>
> Victims of crime should not be seen or portrayed as 'belonging' to the criminal justice system, as people whose needs and expectations can be fully satisfied by the criminal justice process, and neither they nor the voluntary organizations which support and represent them should be conscripted into the system as agents of the state in the action it takes against offenders. The state and civil society have much wider responsibilities towards victims of crime, and of other misfortunes, which will be neglected if that view prevails.

VICTIMS AND THE GOVERNMENT'S BUSINESS PLAN

The Government's *Business Plan for the Criminal Justice System for 2000-2001* had a good deal to say about 'meeting the needs of victims and witnesses'. It indicated a further increase in funding for Victim Support, and reported an extension of Victim Support's service to witnesses so that all courts would be covered by the end of 2001-2002. The Crown Prosecution Service was piloting a scheme in which they gave victims an explanation of any decision to discontinue cases or substantially to alter the charge. Victims' statements, as announced in the *Victim's Charter*, were to be introduced nationally: they 'will be taken into account by the police, prosecution and courts to inform decisions such as bail, compensation claims and sentence', and 'they will also help to identify any support victims might require through the prosecution of the case'; but briefing on the announcement seemed to make clear that victims would still not be given an opportunity to state the actual sentence which they think the court should impose. There were to be improvements to the Criminal Injuries Compensation Scheme, based on an earlier consultation exercise, but the indications from that exercise were that the 'improvements' were as likely to extend the grounds for disqualification as to increase or add to the benefits which are available. The *Victim's Charter* was again to be reviewed, and the Government published a consultation paper for that purpose in February 2001.[14]

These are mostly sensible measures which should be generally welcomed. They reflect a cautious, conservative approach, rightly so while victims' issues have to be considered within a predominantly adversarial and retributive system of justice. A more radical approach, if one is to be adopted, should not involve giving victims substantially new procedural rights within the existing system, but the construction of an alternative system based on restorative principles. That has been discussed in *Chapter 10*. Such an approach would also need to discuss more systematically the question of rights, responsibilities and citizenship, including the application of the Human Rights Act, which have been indicated earlier in this chapter.

CONCLUSION

As Paul Rock has said in an address to a Home Office conference[15]

The outcome is something of a mélange of different policies, emphasising different ideologies and different images of the victim and victimisation. The victim is at once a citizen and representative of the community; a consumer in an individualising, neo-liberal marketplace of services; a greater, but certainly not a full participant in criminal justice procedures; and a member of particularly exposed groups in a politically-charged hierarchy of vulnerabilities. Policies for victims themselves have largely been propelled by external events that have been mediated and diffused by ever more tightly cohesive networks, working in the name of 'joined-up government', that are ever more susceptible to a rights talk once considered alien to legal processes in England and Wales, but a talk which is bounded by entrenched notions about the limits to which reform can at present go and by the contradictory ideological themes which suffuse the current politics of the victim. No doubt some of those contradictions and ambiguities will be resolved in the years to come, but, in the throes of so much urgent activity, there is not much evidence of a master intelligence orchestrating a new synthesis.

ENDNOTES for *Chapter 15*

[1] Paul Rock, *Helping Victims of Crime*, Oxford, Oxford University Press, 1990.
[2] Nils Christie, 'Conflicts as Property', *British Journal of Criminology*, 1977, pp.1-15.
[3] Joanna Shapland, *Victims in Criminal Justice, Report of the JUSTICE Committee on the Role of the Victim in Criminal Justice*, London, JUSTICE, 1998.
[4] Victim Support, *The Rights of Victims of Crime*, London, Victim Support, 1995.
[5] Home Office, *Speaking Up for Justice*, London, Home Office, 1999.
[6] Sir William Macpherson of Cluny, *The Stephen Lawrence Inquiry*, Cm. 4262 London, Stationery Office, 1999.
[7] Discussed in *The Role of Victims in the Criminal Justice Process*, Report of a Criminal Justice Conference held on 13-15 September 1999, London, Home Office, 1999.

[8] Carolyn Hoyle, Rod Morgan, Ed Cape and Andrew Sanders, *Evaluation of 'One Stop Shop' and Victim Statement Pilot Projects,* University of Bristol Department of Law, 1998. The findings were inconclusive but the Government nevertheless decided to proceed with the general introduction of victim statements.

[9] Victim Support, *op. cit.*

[10] Home Office, *Compensating Victims of Crime,* Cmnd. 2434 London, Home Office, 1993.

[11] Lord Windlesham tells the sorry story in Chapter 11 of *Responses to Crime, Volume 3, Legislating with the Tide,* Oxford University Press, 1996.

[12] Committee of Public Accounts, *Compensating Victims of Violent Crime,* Thirtieth Report, Session 1999-2000, HC 472.

[13] Home Office, *A Review of the Victim's Charter,* London, Home Office, 2001.

[14] Home Office, *op cit.,* n. 13.

[15] Home Office, *loc. cit.,* n. 7.

CHAPTER 16

Racism, Discrimination and Diversity

One of the most important lessons of this century, as it nears its end, is that racism must not be allowed to flourish . . . The message must be received and understood in every corner of our society, in our streets and prisons, in the services, in the workplace, on public transport, in public houses and clubs, that racism is evil. It cannot co-exist with fairness and justice. It is incompatible with democratic civilisation . . . The Courts must do all they can, in accordance with Parliament's recently expressed intention, to convey that message clearly by the sentences that they pass in relation to racially aggravated offences.

From Lord Justice Rose's judgment in *R v. Saunders*, CLR 2000, 1 CAR 458

EARLY ATTEMPTS TO RECOGNISE AND PREVENT DISCRIMINATION

Criminal justice services, and the courts, were slow to acknowledge the influence of racism and the possibility of discrimination for which they might themselves have some responsibility. Direct discrimination in services like housing, or in employment, came to be recognised in the 1960s and was dealt with (though not of course eliminated) in the Race Relations Act 1976. The police had become well aware of difficulties in their relationship with minority communities by the early 1970s[1], and other services and the courts became aware of them a few years later. But even after the disturbances in Brixton and the Scarman report in 1981[2], it was some time before these services came generally to realise that the problem might need more than better communication and understanding, some token training and the appointment of a few race relations officers, and that it might be due to discriminatory practices of their own.

For their part, members of minority groups had for a long time recognised that they were disproportionately likely to become victims of crime; that some of the crime committed against them had a racist aspect; and that when they reported a crime to the police, the police often appeared unsympathetic and seemed to have difficulty in appreciating the racist aspect if there was one. White society seemed to have little understanding of the especially hurtful nature of crime that is motivated by hatred and especially by racism, or of the resentment caused by the fact that racist crime was not statutorily distinguished from other offences (although courts could and did treat it as an aggravating factor at common law and as a matter of discretion).

People from minority groups who came into contact with the criminal justice system as suspects, defendants, offenders or witnesses, especially if they were black, had for a long time been conscious of racist attitudes among police and prison officers, and sometimes among the judiciary; and had observed differences between their own treatment and the treatment received by white people. Their experience of the police was described in the report of Lord Scarman's Inquiry in 1981, and in David Smith's research on the Metropolitan Police.[3] In prisons, the disproportionate number of black people had by the 1980s become obvious not only to prisoners themselves and to prison managers and staff, but also to visitors and to other observers and commentators. Nor could the differences in treatment, for example in allocation to workshops or in matters of discipline and control, any longer be ignored.

NACRO's Race Issues Advisory Committee, established in 1983, published a series of reports - in 1986, 1989, 1992 and 1993 - which demonstrated the ways in which the criminal justice process treated black people differently from those who were white; and which showed how young people, especially young black people, had become cynical and alienated from it. Elaine Genders and Elaine Player gave an account of discriminatory practices in prisons in *Race Relations in Prisons* and Eric Smellie's *Black People's Experience of Criminal Justice* showed that among those he interviewed many more black than white people thought they had been sentenced unfairly, or were generally dissatisfied with their treatment.[4]

Solutions favoured during the 1980s and 1990s were to prepare policies or statements on equal opportunities; to provide training in race relations, or more often simply information about cultural minorities and non-Christian religions; to try to recruit more staff from minority groups; to create designated posts carrying special responsibility for race relations matters; and to introduce some ethnic monitoring. At their best, these measures were seen, and quite enthusiastically supported, not only as helping to prevent discrimination, but also as providing new insights into the dynamics of the criminal justice process, and into the nature of justice itself. They were measures from which all those involved in the process could benefit, whatever their cultural background and whatever the nature of their work or their engagement with specifically racial or cultural issues. But they were also seen (and sometimes ridiculed) as additional and often burdensome requirements to deal with what was regarded as a self-contained and unnecessary problem – one which could best be resolved, if it was thought necessary to resolve it at all, by the passage of time. Some staff found them professionally or personally threatening.[5]

Successive governments consistently opposed any extension to the criminal justice system of the Race Relations Act 1976, and any application of the procedures and safeguards which the Act provided in respect of other services, transactions and relationships. Apart from a reluctance to expose the criminal justice services, and the government itself, to any statutory form of discipline or accountability, it was thought to be impossible, by definition, for the courts to be guilty of discrimination or prejudice of any kind. The case for statutory safeguards was raised in the context of the Bill which became the Criminal Justice Act 1991[6], and especially of the increased scope for discrimination which provisions such as the greater use of pre-sentence reports and the emphasis on the 'seriousness' of an offence were thought to provide. The Government continued to oppose an extension of the Race Relations Act, but the clause which became section 95 was added to the Bill as a compromise. Section 95 requires the Secretary of State each year to publish 'such information as he considers expedient for the purpose of . . . facilitating the performance of . . . persons [engaged in the administration of justice], of their duty to avoid discrimination against any persons on the ground of race or sex or any other improper ground.'

The country was slow to recognise the special character of racist crime as an offence not just by one individual against another, but as an assault on a person's identity because of their membership of a particular racial, ethnic, cultural or religious group. The legally correct argument that any racism aspect could (and still can) be dealt with as an aggravating factor of an ordinary offence at the discretion of the court was accepted as adequate until sections 28 to 32 Crime and Disorder Act 1998 gave statutory force to racism as an aggravating factor for a range of offences under the Offences Against the Person Act 1861, the Criminal Damage Act 1971, the Public Order Act 1986 and the Prevention of Harrassment Act 1997.[7]

The Criminal Justice Consultative Council did however make race one of the first issues which it considered after its formation in 1993. It commissioned a report from a sub group on race issues, which put forward 50 recommendations. The Council and its area committees worked to put those recommendations into effect during the years which followed. The Judicial Studies Board also made questions of race an important focus of its work during the early 1990s, especially after the publication of Roger Hood's study on *Race and Sentencing*.[8]

Experience of minority groups
The main facts about the experience of members of minority groups are as follows:[9]

- Members of minority groups are more likely than white people to be victims of crime, and more likely to be in fear of crime.
- The police are less likely to identify a suspect if the victim is black.
- Black people are six times more likely than whites to be stopped by the police.
- Black people are more likely than white people or members of other ethnic groups to be dealt with by arrest rather than summons, and by prosecution rather than a caution; and to be remanded in custody rather than on bail.
- Black people are more likely than whites to be charged with indictable-only offences and therefore to be tried in the Crown Court; to elect trial at the Crown Court rather than the magistrates' court for either-way offences; and to plead 'not guilty'. They are less likely to be the subject of a pre-sentence report. They are more likely to be acquitted, but all these factors expose them to the possibility of a more severe sentence if they are convicted.

- The Crown Prosecution Service discontinues a higher proportion of cases against black defendants on evidential grounds.
- Members of minorities, but especially black people, are disproportionately represented in the prison population. Black people represent ten per cent of males and 16 per cent of females in prison, although they comprise only about 1.7 per cent of the general population over ten years of age. In total, and if foreign nationals are included, almost one prisoner in five is from a minority group.
- Disparities between the treatment of minorities and of white people are less marked among those of South Asian or Chinese origin.
- Minority groups are under-represented among the staff of most criminal justice services, especially in senior posts. Numbers are gradually increasing, especially in the magistracy, the Probation Service, and the practising legal profession, but they are still very low among senior officers or the higher judiciary.
- The number of racial incidents reported to and recorded by the police rose by two-thirds between 1997/98 and 1998/99.
- 15 per cent of complaints against the police were made by people from minority groups.
- Members of minority groups are less satisfied than white people with their treatment after reporting an offence or incident to the police.
- Services most poorly rated for recognising different needs by users from minority groups include the courts, police, local councils (especially as regards housing), and the immigration service.

It is difficult to say conclusively or precisely how far this information constitutes evidence of discrimination or prejudice; or how far if at all it reflects a higher rate of offending among (especially) black people. As David Smith has pointed out in his chapter 'Ethnic Origins, Crime and Criminal Justice'[10], the evidence is uncertain, complex and open to different interpretations.

Crude figures for arrests and convictions may at first sight suggest that black people commit proportionately more crime than white people or Asians. But figures of arrests and convictions are not a reliable or consistent indication of the number of offences that are actually committed. Nor do comparisons based on total populations take account of factors which are associated with higher levels of criminality, such as age, social and family background or economic circumstances, regardless of racial or ethnic background: see *Chapter 9*. The Social Exclusion Unit's report *Bringing People Together: A National Strategy for Neighbourhood Renewal*[11] recognised that members of ethnic minority groups are more likely than the rest of the population to live in poor areas, be unemployed, have low incomes, live in poor housing, have poor health and be victims of crime. Higher rates of criminality are only to be expected[12]. The only reasonable conclusion is that black people do not appear to commit more crime than white people from similar social or economic backgrounds or in similar circumstances (although Asians may commit less).

Differences in the treatment or experience of black people at the various stages in the criminal justice process have a variety of explanations. Decisions on bail, assessments of risk, and recommendations in pre-sentence reports are all influenced by criteria based on social background and circumstances which are again racially correlated. Sentencing decisions are influenced by decisions taken at earlier stages in the process. It is hard to find evidence of direct discrimination at any of those stages in individual cases, but many people would regard their cumulative effect as one of indirect or institutional racism. However that may be, there can be no doubt that many members of minority ethnic groups feel a deep sense of injustice at the way in which they consider themselves to be, and are in fact, treated by the criminal justice system. What can certainly be said is that the situation is the result of a complex range of social and cultural factors, and that it has enormous implications for the integrity and legitimacy of the criminal justice process. An analysis and understanding of those factors, and some practical conclusions drawn from them, are likely to be more productive than an instant and simplistic reaction which attempts to attribute blame for discrimination on the one hand, or for criminality on the other.

Stephen Lawrence and the Inquiry's report

The debate on racism in the criminal justice system, and public understanding of the problem, was transformed by the murder of Stephen Lawrence, by Sir William Macpherson's Inquiry into the way in which the murder was investigated by the Metropolitan Police, and by his finding that the Metropolitan Police was 'institutionally racist'.[13] These events taught the country two painful lessons. One was that a 'colour blind' approach to justice and social policy - symbolised for the courts by the blindfold figure at the Old Bailey - so far from guaranteeing fairness and equality, will actually conceal discrimination and promote injustice. The second was that legislation, policy and practice must move beyond preventing discrimination to promoting equality to respecting and valuing diversity.

The report defined racism and institutional racism as follows.

> 'Racism' in general terms consists of conduct or words or practices which advantage or disadvantage people because of their colour, culture or ethnic origin. In its more subtle form it is as damaging as in its overt form.

> 'Institutional Racism' consists of the collective failure of an organization to provide an appropriate and professional service to people because of their colour, culture or ethnic origin. It can be seen or detected in processes, attitudes and behaviour which amount to discrimination through unwitting prejudice, ignorance, thoughtlessness, and racist stereotyping which disadvantage ethnic minority people.

The expression 'institutionally racist', as used in the Stephen Lawrence Inquiry report to describe the Metropolitan Police, has been variously criticised from political, journalistic and academic perspectives as unfair to individual police officers who were not themselves racist, and damaging to the Service's reputation and morale. As example of the academic criticism, Gurchard Singh's 'The Concept and Context of Institutional Racism'[14] refers back to the use of the expression in the United States in the 1960s and in the Scarman report in 1981, and to the ambiguity and confusions associated with it, including the complex relationships between intention, outcomes and black disadvantage. Singh's conclusion is that although the expression has been widely adopted by the Government and the police, it is little more than a slogan. It has had some power in catching public attention and galvanising support for the report's recommendations, but it may not have enough precision to sustain them in the longer term. In particular, there is no clear empirical test of whether institutional racism is or is not present in a particular service or situation, or of whether or not it has been or is being removed.

The report made a total of 70 recommendations, almost all of which the Government and the police service have accepted. The Government published an immediate Action Plan for implementing the recommendations, including a Ministerial Priority 'that the trust of minority ethnic communities in policing (and the criminal justice system) should be increased'; and undertook to publish an annual report on progress. It published the first annual report in February 2000[15] and a second report a year later. The Government, and the services themselves, were able to claim that action on all the relevant recommendations was well in hand. The Criminal Justice Consultative Council revived its sub-group on race, with new terms of reference and a new programme of work to be put into effect through the newly reconstructed area strategy committees. Others, for example Michael Mansfield QC, were more sceptical[16], and *Chapter 17* refers to the hostile reaction which the report of the Inquiry prompted from certain sections of the media who portrayed it as undermining the authority of the police and encouraging crime and the criminal classes. There was a similar reaction to the report of the Commission on the Future of Multi-Ethnic Britain when the report was published in October 2000.[17]

A later Home Office publication *Race Equality in Public Services: Driving up Standards and Accounting for Progress* set out 'what the Government has achieved in promoting race equality and . . . where more needs to be done'. It stated that the Government would develop a 'basket of indicators', including a combination of 'attitudinal' and quantified data, as its 'key overall measure on race equality'. The 'basket' would include data about sentencing outcomes, with information about the prosecution and sentencing process to test the contention that members of minority groups are less favourably treated. The Home Office published a progress report in February 2001.[18]

Most importantly, the Race Relations (Amendment) Act 2000 extended the provisions of the 1976 Act to virtually all of those public authority functions not already covered by the Act, and placed a general duty on listed public authorities to be proactive in promoting race equality. More specific duties would be imposed by secondary legislation. Codes of practice, prepared by the Commission for Racial Equality, would give guidance to public authorities on how to fulfill their general and specific duties. Consultation on implementing the Act, specifically on extending the range of public bodies to which it should apply and on the duties to be imposed by secondary legislation, was taking place at the time of writing.[19] The Act is a major advance, but attention needs to be given to other aspects of diversity – ethnicity, culture and religion – as well as race.

An agenda for reform

Most of the immediate agenda for reform, as the Government saw it, was set out in the Inquiry's report, and in the Government's Action Plan. *Chapter 17* considers some of its implications for the police. Although addressed primarily to the police, many of the recommendations can and should be applied equally to other services - as Sir William Macpherson himself emphasised. Apart from those which are specific to the Metropolitan Police, they fell into four main groups - the recruitment, retention and promotion of staff; training; the reporting, recording, investigation and resolution of racist incidents; and the monitoring of all significant aspects of the services provided.

Public appointments

Recruitment, retention and promotion or appointment to senior posts are clearly of crucial importance for all public service positions. Their importance is not seriously disputed, and the issues are not about the principle but about methods, commitment and the working culture and environment. They are closely connected with questions about the reputation, standing and perhaps above all legitimacy (see *Chapter 5*) of the service or institution concerned. Neither 'positive discrimination' nor less controversial methods such as affirmative action or the setting of targets will succeed for long unless people who work for a service feel that it is an honourable occupation; that their colleagues appreciate them and they are treated fairly; and it is one in which they will have the respect of their families and communities. Much has been written on the subject, for example in the report of the *Commission on the Future of Multi-Ethnic Britain*. Action which is narrowly focused on achieving a numerical target will result in disillusion and frustration if these wider considerations are not taken into account.

Awareness and sensitivity to cultural differences, together with a commitment to promoting racial equality, should be an element in all appraisals of staff and criteria for promotion. Staff making those assessments should themselves be suitably qualified, and assessment procedures and centres should be suitably validated.

As well as the criminal justice services themselves, the judiciary and the practising legal profession, there is a large and increasing number of appointed authorities and advisory bodies, some of them with considerable powers, which are not directly accountable to Parliament or to any elected authorities. They include the Youth Justice Board, the Legal Services Commission and its Consultative Panel; police authorities and - of critical importance - the new police authority for London; probation boards set up in a new form under the Criminal Justice and Court Services Act 2000; the Criminal Cases Review Commission; and longer established bodies such as the Police Complaints Authority and prison boards of visitors. All these bodies will in future have a positive duty under the Race Relations (Amendment) Act to promote race equality. The Commission on the Future of Multi-Ethnic Britain has pointed out that they must also be seen as able, and determined, to act on behalf of society as a whole and all its diverse communities. The Commission has recommended that the criteria for appointment to all public bodies, especially those set up under recent legislation, should include a requirement for their composition to demonstrate the organization's ability to understand and act in the best interests of all sections of the communities for which it has responsibility; and that such organizations should be required to include in their reports the action they have taken to promote equality.

Of particular concern is the need for a visibly independent, transparent and accountable way of appointing judges (see the case for a judicial appointments commission: *Chapter 21)* and Queen's Counsel.

Training
Training in what has usually been termed 'race relations' has been of variable quality and has produced different results. To be successful it has to involve more than factual information about so called 'minority cultures'. Training has too often been of this limited kind, usually because of the sensitivity of the subject and fear of the reactions which a more penetrating, and therefore inevitably more provocative, treatment of the subject might produce. An example of a successful, and courageous, approach to the subject has been the work of the Ethnic Minorities Advisory Committee, now the Equal Treatment Advisory Committee, of the Judicial Studies Board. All training programmes should be thoroughly and independently evaluated.

The Commission on the Future of Multi-Ethnic Britain has set out the features which it believes should be incorporated in all effective training, under nine headings - curriculum content; materials and methods; new insights and skills; participants; community-based trainers; evaluation; training the trainers; status; and re-entry when the training has been completed. The last is often overlooked. Those who have been on a training course should be expected to share their experience with colleagues, and an assessment should be made of the difference it has made to them individually and collectively. Training on race and ethnicity should not be confined to specialised courses, but be included in courses and materials on other aspects of professional development.

Reports and complaints
All services must encourage people to report racist incidents and to complain about instances of direct or indirect racist behaviour. The

procedures for them to do so must be welcoming and accessible. All reports must be accurately recorded, with a note of the action which has been taken on the report or complaint in a form which enables the action to be inspected and reviewed. The action will often include an investigation, and if the report or complaint is substantiated, prosecution or disciplinary action against the person responsible. But as well as acting on a complaint, it is important to listen to the person making it; to understand what lies behind it, and the context in which it is made; to make clear that it is taken seriously; and if prosecution or disciplinary action are not justified, to explain the reasons and to indicate if appropriate that action will still be taken to prevent the cause of the complaint from being repeated. It should not be supposed that prosecution or disciplinary action are the only outcomes which make the report or complaint worth considering: conciliation, a better understanding of the situation, or a fair and sympathetic hearing may be just as worthwhile.

There will be occasions when the courts, an employer, and the public including members of minority groups, will feel - rightly - that an example has to be made of an individual who is conspicuously to blame. But in matters of racial equality as for other issues of public accountability, the situation will often be complicated, with several individuals involved, perhaps over quite a long period of time and with different degrees of responsibility. Exemplary action against one or two of them may not always be practicable, or fair. A culture of blame and defensiveness may itself have a damaging effect on trust and confidence, on the development of a proper sense of responsibility, and on the determination to do better in future. The police, the Crown Prosecution Service and the courts should bear similar considerations in mind in applying the sections of the Crime and Disorder Act which relate to racially aggravated offences. Those sections are no substitute, and increase the need, for education and understanding in communities so that the nature and consequences of racist behaviour are properly recognised and appreciated. The Howard League's programme on Citizenship and Crime is one example of a programme which has this as one of its aims. [20] Attention to these matters should never be ridiculed as 'political correctness'.

Complaints may come not only from those who have suffered from racist behaviour, but also from people who object to what they see as favouritism towards minority groups or of what they may describe disparagingly as 'political correctness'. Such complaints may reflect prejudice, ignorance or misunderstanding; or they may sometimes be justified. They deserve a fair hearing and explanation, including if necessary an explanation that what may appear as 'political correctness' to one person may be no more than common courtesy to another.

Racist incidents may occur in situations where members of staff are not directly involved but for which they have some responsibility - for example in prisons, in community service programmes, in education classes or rehabilitation programmes, or at court. Where staff have that responsibility, they must have the training and skills to deal with them effectively. And all reports or complaints should whenever possible be used constructively so that they can help to improve confidence, relationships and practice.

The Code of Practice on reporting and recording racist incidents which the Home Office issued in response to the Stephen Lawrence Inquiry Report in April 2000, including its references to multi-agency working, monitoring, use of reporting centres, practice in schools, and the treatment of victims and witnesses, should be generally welcomed.[21]

Ethnic monitoring

Ethnic monitoring has been a regular practice in most criminal justice services since the 1980s. But it has often been resisted and its scope, sensitivity and accuracy have been limited. It was the subject of industrial action in the Probation Service during the 1980s, and prison staff have been consistently reluctant to record their own background. There is a lot more to be done to extend the scope of monitoring to areas which are not adequately covered (for example sentencing); to refine the categories according to which people or situations are classified, so that they correspond to the ways in which people think of themselves; and to make sure that staff understand the monitoring requirements and comply conscientiously with them. The information needs to be regularly and systematically analysed, both internally by local managers and independently by inspectors and auditors, and an understanding of the diversity, complexity and sometimes ambiguity of the situations which may be involved. Skills need to be developed for that purpose. The information should be made available for inspection and audit, and should be systematically assessed in the course of those procedures. As an immediate step, the inspectorates for the prison and magistrates' courts' services and the Crown Prosecution Service should carry out thematic inspections of the three services, co-ordinated with one another and with the work which has already been done or is in hand with the Inspectorate of Constabulary and the Probation Inspectorate.[22]

In the longer term, there is a strong case for some form of monitoring of judicial decisions, so that the influences on those decisions and their impact can be better understood (see also the section on *Race and Sentencing* below).

Implications for government policies

There are important implications for many of the new policies which the Government has proposed or introduced. Examples include the array of new orders (especially the anti-social behaviour order) made available to the courts under the Crime and Disorder Act; the measures to reduce crime and disorder; the new arrangements for youth justice; the measures in the Criminal Justice and Court Services Act to intensify the effect and tighten the enforcement of community sentences; the application of targeted and intelligence-led policing; the various procedures for assessing, managing or avoiding risk, for example in connection with pre-sentence reports or discretionary release from prison; and the changes in sentencing which will follow from the review of the sentencing framework (see *Chapter 12* and below). Those policies have in common a deliberate shift of emphasis away from due process, proportionality and the situation and culpability of the individual, and towards protecting the public, managing risk and actuarial assessment. To the extent that they succeed in their avowed overall aim of protecting the public, the public as a whole, including members of minority groups, should benefit. But to justify their possible effects on that ground alone is to follow the 'colour blind' approach: the approach which Governments and services - and perhaps the Labour Party in Opposition - were inclined to accept but which the Stephen Lawrence Inquiry and the Commission on the Future of Multi-ethnic Britain have shown to be inadequate. There is a danger that if the criteria for the various judgements required by the new policies are racially correlated, for example if they relate to personal or social situations in which minorities are disproportionately represented, they could be perceived as racially discriminatory in their effect. The evidence on which the criteria are established, and on which programmes are evaluated, is therefore critical.

Much will depend on the spirit in which the new measures are put into practical effect; the spoken and unspoken assumptions which are made about individuals and situations; the conscious and unconscious expectations which are brought to critical situations and events; and the professional culture within which the courts and operational services go about their work. All those will in their turn be influenced by public opinion - or perhaps rather by what public opinion is perceived to be; by media reporting of individual incidents, and the media's general coverage of crime and justice; by dramatic and high-profile events; and by the quality and style of the country's political leadership. They will also be influenced by day-to-day experiences of professionals and practitioners throughout the criminal justice system, and by their relationships and interactions with each other. Rigorous monitoring and constant vigilance will be necessary to ensure that actions flowing from the new initiatives do not reflect and perpetuate racist stereotypes.

A NEW CONCEPTION OF DIVERSITY AND JUSTICE

This chapter has so far been concerned with the forms of discrimination which have been, or are still, taking place in the criminal justice system, and with the measures which have been, or are now being, taken to prevent them. These two questions have always been the natural focus of any discussion of race or ethnicity and criminal justice. But just as the debate in society as a whole needs to move on from preventing discrimination to working with and valuing diversity, so it must in the criminal justice system. The task has both a legislative and administrative aspect.

On the legislative aspect, an independent Review of the Enforcement of UK Anti-Discrimination Legislation has argued that the present framework is inadequate because it 'places too much emphasis on state regulation and too little on the responsibility of organizations and individuals to generate change . . . [It] adopts an incoherent approach to different manifestations of inequality . . . equality not simply on avoiding negative discrimination but on the active participation of all stakeholders, on training and improving skills, developing wider social networks and encouraging adaptability'.[23] The report makes a number of detailed recommendations for the structure and content of a single Equality Act, for its principles and definitions, and for mechanisms which seek to change organizational policy and behaviour and 'to encourage an inclusive, pro-active, non-adversarial approach to achieve fair participation and fair access'. There would be three interlocking mechanisms: internal scrutiny by the organization itself; the participation of interest groups in the process of change; and an Equality Commission to provide a 'back-up' role of assistance and ultimately enforcement where voluntary methods fail.

Further recommendations are designed to make procedures and remedies more effective, especially in matters of employment. The Act would apply to all forms of unlawful discrimination, in all situations where statutory regulation is needed. It would extend far beyond criminal justice, but the approaches suggested earlier in this chapter would be reinforced if such an Act were in place.

The administrative aspect relates to 'mainstreaming'. In central and local government, and importantly in Northern Ireland, there has been much emphasis on the need to 'mainstream' considerations of equality - to ensure that they are embedded from the outset in the development of legislation, policy and professional practice. 'Mainstreaming' should apply both to management processes and to the evaluation of outcomes. A pamphlet *Race and the Modernisation of the Public Services*[24] sets out the key principles of mainstreaming as follows:

- Equality issues are built into the planning and design of all policies and programmes and are not an add-on.
- A conscious effort to identify systematically the differential impact of policy issues on different groups, such as ethnic minorities, and then adjusting policies accordingly.
- Locating responsibility and accountability with management at all levels and not with equalities specialists – although they are still needed to provide advice and support. This requires that the competencies of all political and administrative managers are developed and improved.
- Increasingly, working with delivery agencies and partners to make sure the right issues are addressed and overcoming the weakness of equalities issues being lost during the procurement process.
- Monitoring outcomes, setting appropriate targets, and using available levers to encourage remedial action where necessary - because mainstreaming must secure results.

The pamphlet goes on to point out that mainstreaming has to be:

- established with clear guidance
- driven politically and adminstratively
- systematic and universal in implementation, and
- sustained over a long period.

This is wise advice. But even mainstreaming cannot operate in a working culture which still thinks the task is one of preventing discrimination against those who are somehow separate rather than one of working with and valuing diversity. All public servants, including and perhaps especially those who work in the criminal justice system, must always be alive to the fact and possibility of discrimination, and the measures to prevent it must remain firmly in place and must be extended as necessary. But managers and staff, judges, magistrates and practising lawyers, should not think of 'ethnic minorities' as a separate, distinguishable (and therefore too easily stereotyped) group within the population with whom they work, different from the 'majority' but similar to one another. In some parts of the country it is already becoming clear that the 'majority' and 'minorities' cannot be distinguished in this simplistic way. In those areas, and even more where 'difference' is still perceived and felt, it must become a natural part of any professional judgement to recognise and value people for who they are rather than how they appear or the group to which they may belong.

A comprehensive programme

The fact that the police received most of the attention, and the criticism, resulting from the Stephen Lawrence Inquiry was no reason for other services to feel complacent. They have generally acknowledged that institutional racism is just as likely to be found in the Prison Service, the Probation Service, the courts and the Crown Prosecution Service, although its manifestations will be different and perhaps more easily concealed. Racism in the Prison Service came tragically to the surface with the murder of Zahid Mubarek in Feltham Young Offenders Instution in March 2000, and was at the time of writing the subject of a formal investigation by the Commission for Racial Equality. This chapter has already referred to the reports from NACRO's Race Issues Advisory Committee. In June 1999 the Committee produced a new report[25] which set out a comprehensive programme of action, with recommendations covering the work of the Criminal Justice Consultative Council and the local strategy committees; research and monitoring; employment and training; the treatment of suspects and defendants; work with sentenced offenders in prison or under the supervision of the Probation Service; and action to prevent crime, including racially motivated crime, and to support its victims. Specific points for attention not already mentioned in this chapter included effective communication and consultation with minority groups and their representation on boards and committees; the preparation and use of pre-sentence reports; the provision of hostels and other accommodation; vigorous application of the RESPOND programme in the Prison Service[26]; work by the prison or probation services with the perpetrators of racially motivated offences; and energetic action to promote equality, understanding and commitment in the legal profession.

The report concludes with a series of 'action points', all of which deserve serious attention and energetic action. There could be added to the list a rigorous programme to implement the recommendations of the report of HM Probation Inspectorate's thematic inspection *Towards Race Equality*, already mentioned.[27] NACRO's 'action points' also include a recommendation for a similar thematic inspection of the Prison Service by HM Inspectorate of Prisons – a recommendation which is repeated in the report of the Commission on the Future of Multi-Ethnic Britain. The Probation Inspectorate's report found that 'despite the promise of the work undertaken in the 1980s and early 1990s, so little had been achieved', and made a series of 19 specific recommendations covering broadly the areas discussed earlier in this chapter. The Prison Ombudsman's Annual Report for 1999-2000[28] includes a section on race in which he describes a prisoner's complaint of racial harassment which he concludes had not been properly investigated because of institutional racism in the prison. He comments that 'on paper, the Prison Service has developed admirable anti-racist policies. Like other institutions, it has to work at making these policies a reality'.

Unlike the situation in the police, there has until recently been relatively little reliable information about the state of racial equality in the Probation and Prison Services. HM Probation Inspectorate's review has helped to correct that situation for the Probation Service; the investigation by the Commission for Racial Equality should help to correct it for prisons; but the serious action needed to turn policy into practice can only be taken by the services themselves. The information needed is likely to extend well beyond the facts and figures required for performance indicators and to include more qualitative judgements of attitudes, impressions, beliefs and relationships. Obtaining that information, sharing it and acting on it is a crucial part of a service's management system and accountability.

Race and sentencing

The possibility of racial discrimination in sentencing has always been a difficult subject. The disproportionate number of black people in prison suggests that some discrimination might be taking place. Roger Hood's study of the sentences imposed in three Crown Court centres in the West Midlands in 1989-90 showed that some element of discrimination appeared to exist, although most of the difference in the sentences imposed on different groups of offenders could be explained by the greater number of black defendants who appeared for sentence and by the nature and circumstances of the offences of which they were convicted.[29] It was limited to three centres in one part of the country; and it did not consider magistrates' courts. But that study is now several years old. Much attention has been given to the subject since then, including the extensive programme of judicial studies and magistrates' training. There is a compelling case for a fresh study on a larger scale. But two more immediate questions are whether enough is being done not only to prevent discrimination but also to promote equality under the present sentencing framework; and what action might be taken to ensure that any new legislation resulting from the Government's review of the sentencing framework (see *Chapter 12*) is not discriminatory in its effect.

This chapter has already argued the need for public services to move on from 'preventing discrimination' to the more ambitious aim of 'promoting equality' as required by the Race Relations (Amendment) Act 2000. The judiciary are not a 'public authority' to which the new Act applies and sentencing is not a 'public authority function'. But the judiciary could reasonably be expected to observe the spirit of the Act, not only by avoiding improper discrimination, but also by working proactively to promote race equality.

The tension between the desire for unity and respect for diversity in public service generally corresponds with the tension between consistency and individualised justice in sentencing. The tension in sentencing has usually been resolved by references to consistency of approach, or of impact, as distinct from consistency of outcome. It takes on a special significance when applied to questions of race and culture. But a more developed understanding of consistency is needed for the purpose of the review and of any legislation to put its conclusions into effect. It must include consistency in looking at the circumstances of the offence and of the situation of the offender, and in the weight which is given to the seriousness of the act, the degree of harm done and the culpability of the offender. Of these, for the purpose of preventing discrimination and promoting equality, culpability is probably the most important.

Whatever discrimination there may or may not be at present, if the new legislation once in force were followed by a disproportionate increase in the number of black people - or members of any other racial groups - receiving prison sentences, or if one element in the new array of sentencing powers appeared to be used disproportionately against them (for example any provision for extended sentences for offenders considered to be dangerous), then an accusation of discrimination or even 'institutional racism' might have to be answered. In particular, the European Convention On Human Rights requires that the right to a fair trial, like other rights in the Convention, must be exercised without discrimination. Obvious requirements are a judiciary and a court system which are properly representative of the country as a whole; for the courts' use of the powers to be rigorously monitored and analysed; and to make sure that procedures for risk assessment cannot be criticised as discriminatory.

This chapter has accepted that the main thrust for preventing discrimination and promoting equality in criminal justice has to start from the post-Macpherson agenda - programmes for recruitment and training; comprehensive monitoring; and rigorous analysis of the results. The success of the sentencing reforms in promoting public confidence, especially among minority groups, will depend to a large extent on the skills, understanding and credibility of judges and magistrates; on those of the operational and administrative staff in the various services; and on the culture, dynamics and relationships of the services and institutions. Within the sentencing framework itself, American experience has shown that rigid frameworks tend to be discriminatory in their operation. The most important features will be the degree of flexibility and discretion which decision-makers have available to them, and the use they make of it within the statutory structure and the guidelines is clearly essential. There is a strong case for some monitoring of decisions by individual sentencers - not to hold them up to public criticism but as a basis for constructive discussion and comparison among judicial colleagues, and as a basis for academic research.

Conditions for success

To recognise the inadequacy of a 'colour blind' approach, and to move on from preventing discrimination to promoting equality and valuing diversity, require changes in outlook and attitude, and in personal and professional behaviour, which extend not only to the whole of the criminal justice system but throughout society. Reactions to the report of the Stephen Lawrence Inquiry show how such changes can be resisted and ridiculed. But they are consistent with and part of the ideas of citizenship and social responsibility, of public service, and of accountability and legitimacy, which have been discussed in other chapters. The task is especially important, and especially difficult and demanding, in criminal justice. In many places and in many communities the changes are already taking place, quietly and unobtrusively, but they need to be consistently sustained, promoted, and brought to those places where progress is still slow or obstructed.

The task demands not only the practical measures described earlier in this chapter, but also at the strategic level

- unambiguous political leadership, not compromised by opportunist appeals to prejudice against groups such as refugees or travellers;
- rigorous monitoring of all significant criminal justice functions, according to a common set of classifications which so far as possible reflects how people think of themselves rather than administrative convenience;
- inspection, audit and research which are focused on the dynamics and outcomes of the various processes and relationships, and which makes assessments of the attitudes which inform them, the confidence and trust which they generate, and hence of their legitimacy and integrity (see *Chapter 9* for a discussion of research more generally);
- energetic efforts to promote communication and consultation with all sections of all communities, with suitable representation on executive and advisory bodies, and hence a spirit of mutual responsibility, trust and confidence, recognising that this is an

immensely difficult task which can easily become opportunistically selective and degenerate into superficiality and tokenism;

- systematic attention to the effects of policy and practice in terms of equality and social inclusion, both at the stage when policy and practice are being developed and when they are reviewed.

These measures and procedures will for the immediate future be seen as having special relevance to those who are conventionally thought of as belonging to minority ethnic groups, especially those who are distinguishable by their appearance. But just as it is no longer enough to classify those groups in simple terms as 'black' or 'Asian', so it will in time become harder to think in terms of minority groups as people who can be defined by their race or ethnicity. Other sources of prejudice and markers of disadvantage may become equally or more significant as power, influence and wealth become differently distributed; as family relationships extend across more cultures and countries, in Europe and beyond; as patterns of migration change under the influence of the global economy or of local conflict in different parts of the world; or as different sections of society find themselves excluded from the skills and benefits of new technology; and perhaps as different religions or different religious groupings become more or less influential. The skills and techniques, the habits of mind and the values which are needed to deal with today's manifestations of discrimination, prejudice and injustice are of universal importance in any modern, changing and diverse society.

ENDNOTES for *Chapter 16*

[1] HM Inspectorate of Constabulary had promoted an early, but very crude, form of ethnic monitoring in 1971.

[2] Lord Scarman, *The Brixton Disorders 10-12 April 1981. Report of the Inquiry by the Right Honourable Lord Scarman OBE*, Cmnd. 8427, London, HMSO,1981.

[3] David Smith, *People and Police in London*, London, Policy Studies Institute, 1983.

[4] Elaine Genders and Elaine Player, *Race Relations in Prisons*, Oxford, Clarendon Press, 1989. Eric Smellie, *Black People's Experience of Criminal Justice*, London, NACRO, 1991.

[5] Both the Probation Service, and in the voluntary sector Victim Support, found difficulty in gaining acceptance for ethnic monitoring which some of those involved regarded as degrading and stigmatising.

[6] For example at a conference in Stafford which the Home Office convened on possible discriminatory aspects of the Bill in October 1990. Conclusions and recommendations in pre-sentence reports can be influenced by assessments and evaluations made of an offender's social background and circumstances. If the social background and circumstances of a person correlate to their race this will result in a person's race indirectly affecting their possible range of sentences.

[7] Drawing on the work of S. A. Marshall and R. A. Duff, 'Criminalisation and Sharing Wrongs', *XI Canadian Journal of Law and Jurisprudence*, 1998, 7. Andrew Ashworth has noted the argument that 'crimes are public wrongs because even those that consist of attacks on the body or property of an individual might be seen as wrongs against the community to which the individual belongs'. They might also be seen as wrongs

committed by the community to which the offender belongs. Ashworth, 'Is the Criminal Law a Lost Cause?', *Law Quarterly Review*, 2000, 116, pp. 225-56.

[8]   Roger Hood, *Race and Sentencing*, Oxford, Clarendon Press, 1992.

[9]   The principal sources are the annual Home Office publication, *Statistics on Race and the Criminal Justice System* and the annual *Prison Statistics*. Others are Roger Hood, *Race and Sentencing*, op. cit n. 8; Home Office Statistical Bulletin 6/98, *Ethnicity and Victimisation*; Home Office Research Study 85, *A Survey of Police Arrests and their Outcomes*; and the Home Office Bulletin *Ethnic Differences in Decisions on Young Defendants Dealt with by the Crown Prosecution Service* by Gordon Barclay and Bonny Mhlanga, Section 95 Findings, 1999, No. 1. Much of the material has been usefully summarised in reports from NACRO's Race Issues Advisory Committee. The Commission on the Future of Multi-Ethnic Britain has argued, on the basis of a study by Mary Hickman and Bronwen Walter (*Discrimination and the Black Community in Britain*, London, Commission for Racial Equality, 1997) that the experience of the Irish is similar to the experience of black people.

[10] David Smith, 'Ethnic Origins Crime and Criminal Justice', in Michael Maguire, Rod Morgan and Robert Reiner (eds., *The Oxford Handbook of Criminology*, Oxford University Press, 1997.

[11] Social Exclusion Unit, *Bringing People Together: A National Strategy for Neighbourhood Renewal*, Cmnd. 4045, London, Stationery Office, 1998.

[12] A Home Office study of self-reported offending amongst young people found little difference between those who were white and those who were of African or Afro-Caribbean origin in the numbers who admitted having offended in the last year, although the study did not cover the number of offences which individuals had committed. (Benjamin Bowling, John Graham and Alice Ross in J. Junger-Tas, G. J. Tarloun and M. Klein (eds.), *Delinquent Behaviour Among Young People in the Western World: First Results of the International Self-Report Delinquency Study*, Amsterdam, Kugler, 1994.

[13] Sir William Macpherson of Cluny, *The Stephen Lawrence Inquiry*, Cm. 4262, London, Stationery Office, 1999.

[14] Gurchard Singh, 'The Concept and Context of Institutional Racism', in Alan Marlow and Barry Loveday (eds.), *Policing After Macpherson*, London, Russell House, 2000, pp. 29-40.

[15] Home Office Action Plan and Annual Report, February 2000; Second Annual Report on Progress, February 2001.

[16] NACRO, 'The First Anniversary of the Stephen Lawrence Inquiry Report: A Challenge for the new Millennium', *Race Policies into Action*, 20, London, NACRO, 2000.

[17] Report by the Commission on the Future of Multi-Ethnic Britain, *The Future of Multi-Ethnic Britain*, London, Profile Books, 2000.

[18] Home Office, *Race Equality in Public Services: Drawing up Standards and Accounting for Progress*, London, Home Office, 2000; *Race Equality in Public Services*, London, Home Office, 2001.

[19] Home Office, *Race Relations (Amendment) Act 2000: New Laws for a Successful Multi-Racial Britain*, London, Home Office, February 2001.

[20] Materials on the programme are available from the Howard League.

[21] Home Office, *Code of Practice on Reporting and Recording Racist Incidents in Response to Recommendation 15 of the Stephen Lawrence Inquiry Report*, London, Home Office, April 2000.

[22] HM Inspectorate of Constabulary has published a series of reports, of which the most recent at the time of writing was *Winning the Race: Embracing Diversity*, London, Home Office, 2000. See also HM Inspectorate of Probation, *Towards Race Equality*, London, Home Office, 2000.

[23] Bob Hepple, Mary Coussey and Tufyal Choudhury, *Equality: A New Framework*. Report of the Independent Review of the Enforcement of UK Anti-Discrimination Legislation, Oxford, Hart Publishing, 2000.

[24] Judith Hunt and Sarah Palmer for the Local Government Association, the Employers Organization and the Improvement Development Agency, *The Stephen Lawrence Inquiry and Home Secretary's Action Plan: Initial Guidance for Local Authorities*, London, Local Government Association, November 1999.

[25] NACRO, *Let's Get it Right: Race and Justice 2000*, London, NACRO, 2000. Also *Race and the Criminal Justice System: Joining Up to Promote Equality and Encourage Diversity*, a report by the Criminal Justice Consultative Council Race Sub-group, London, Criminal Justice Consultative Council, 2000.

[26] In December 1998 the Prison Service adopted a new programme 'RESPOND: Racial Equality for Staff and Prisoners'. It has five strategic aims:

- Confronting racial harassment and discrimination;
- Ensuring fairness in recruitment, appraisal, promotion and selection;
- Developing and supporting ethnic minority staff;
- Ensuring equal opportunities for ethnic minority prisoners; and
- Recruiting ethnic minority staff.

Each of the aims has a set of outcomes, targets, means of measurement and key actions for 1999-2000. A race equality advisor has been appointed to take the programme forward.

[27] *Op. cit.* n. 21.

[28] The Prison Ombudsman's Annual Report 1999-2000, London, Home Office, 2000.

[29] Roger Hood, *op. cit.*, n. 8.

PART IV Running the System

CHAPTER 17

Police and Policing

> The police operate not as agents of government ... but as citizens representing the rest of the community, their powers resting on the support, both moral and physical, of their fellow citizens.

> From the Report of the Departmental Committee on the
> Police (the Desborough Committee), 1920

Aims of policing

Like other parts of the criminal justice services, the police have a complex role, and police traditions have different, sometimes conflicting, elements. A tension which has been present for most of the history of English policing has been between the prevention of crime and the detection and prosecution of offenders. As long ago as 1829, Sir Richard Mayne and Colonel Rowan, the first Commissioners of the Metropolitan Police, distinguished between the prevention of crime and the detection and punishing of offenders as complementary but separate functions when they wrote:

> The primary object of an efficient police is the prevention of crime; the next that of detection and punishment of offenders if crime is committed. To these ends, all the efforts of the police should be directed. The protection of life and property, the preservation of public tranquility, and the absence of crime, will alone prove whether these efforts have been successful, and whether the objects for which the police were appointed have been attained.

They later said

> It should be understood, at the outset, that the principal object to be attained is 'the prevention of crime'. To this great end every effort of the police should be directed.

In practice, the police themselves, most of the general public, and often the government (especially during the mid-1990s) have seen the primary task as being to detect and arrest offenders, or to 'feel collars' and 'lock up villains'. They have seen this, together with sentencing, as the principal means by which crime is prevented and the public are protected. The 'enforcement' aspect of the policing tradition is reinforced when terrorism becomes a serious problem, or when organized crime is seen to threaten the country internally or from abroad. It is also reinforced when modern technology is seen as providing new and more effective methods of detection - easily described as 'weapons' with which to 'win the war' on crime. This is how it was seen during the

1970s, when the weapons were cars, radios and computers, and again in the 1990s when they were DNA, CCTV, and electronic devices for tracking and surveillance. That view is further reinforced in a world of modern management which insists on targets, performance measures, and comparisons and competition between areas ('league tables') to show which areas have the 'best' performance. Arrests, detection rates and numbers of successful prosecutions are much easier to count than crimes which have been prevented or the extent to which people feel safe in their homes or on the streets. In its White Paper on Police Reform, published in 1993,[1] the Conservative Government said

The main aims of the police should be

- to fight and prevent crime;
- to uphold the law;
- to bring to justice those who break the law;
- to protect, help and reassure the community;
- in meeting these aims, to provide good value for money

and that *the main job of the police is to catch criminals.*

Even so, the police and successive governments have for most of the last 20 years recognised that arrests and prosecutions - or the sentences imposed on those found guilty - are not enough to prevent crime, and that other forms of preventive work deserve equal respect (see *Chapter 18*). They also acknowledge that the police cannot be successful in preventing crime, or even in detecting and arresting offenders, if they do not have the confidence and the support of the communities they serve, or if their authority is not accepted as legitimate. The police cannot behave like an occupying force, which was sometimes the tradition of colonial policing (in Ireland as well as further afield - the tradition which many of the nationalist community still associate with the Royal Ulster Constabulary today).

The over-arching purpose of the police service issued by the Labour Government is closer to the service's earlier traditions, and to the role which most police officers, certainly most senior police officers, see themselves performing

To build a safe, just and tolerant society, in which the rights and responsibilities of individuals, families and communities are properly balanced, and the protection and security of the public are maintained.

The changing context of policing, the challenges to policing, and the underlying questions of ethics, leadership and human rights, are the subject of an important analysis by Peter Neyroud and Alan Beckley, *Policing, Ethics and Human Rights*, already mentioned in *Chapters 2 and 5.*[2]

Police culture and relationships

At the level of day-to-day policing and contact with the public, the traditionally respectful and comfortable relationship which the police enjoyed with the middle-classes has come under strain as more confrontational situations developed over such matters as road traffic, demonstrations and public disorder. The public has demanded a more active and at the same time more sensitive approach to offences of domestic and sexual violence and sexual abuse. And there is a serious problem of confidence in the police service's relationship with minority groups.

The police have accordingly developed a range of preventive, supportive and consultative practices, some of which have been associated with terms such as 'community policing' or 'quality of service'. Such practices received special emphasis and prominence as a result of Lord Scarman's inquiry into the disturbances in South London in 1981[3] and in the Police and Criminal Evidence Act 1984 (for example the use of consultative committees and the introduction of lay visitors to police stations); and again as a result of the report of Sir William Macpherson's inquiry into the death of Stephen Lawrence, published in 1999.[4]

The police are increasingly working with other authorities and agencies, for example local authorities, in partnerships to prevent crime and disorder, and with health, education and social services in youth offending teams. Even so, there remains among some police officers, and among some of those who identify themselves with the police service, a propensity to regard the police as in some way protecting society against the dangerous forces which are threatening to damage or destroy it - the 'other' which was described in *Chapter 2*. They see these as forces which are outside and somehow alien to the society they think they know, and represented by individuals who have to be identified and then removed or neutralised so that the threat is eliminated. That view may be reinforced when they hear Ministers speak of a 'war on crime', or sometimes by the influence of colleagues and what has been described as the 'canteen culture'. It is misguided, unprofessional, and damaging to the police themselves, for them to think of themselves as 'fighting' another section of the society of which they are a part, to associate what is familiar with what is safe or right, or to associate what is unfamiliar with what is dangerous or wrong. But it is sometimes an understandable human reaction when police see the effects of a particularly unpleasant crime on those who are its victims, or when the 'system' is for whatever reason unable to deal in their view adequately with an offender whom they 'know' to be guilty, perhaps of a succession of similar offences. It is also understandable in a service whose officers rightly have wide discretion in the way in which they deal with the people and situations they encounter, and whose judgement of what is safe or dangerous may sometimes, if only rarely, become a matter of life or death for themselves, their colleagues or members of the public.

These reactions help to explain, though they do not excuse, what has been described as 'noble cause corruption' (when officers may for example fabricate evidence to ensure a conviction), or 'institutional racism' as defined in the Stephen Lawrence Inquiry report.

The police find themselves being drawn - or propelled - in different directions. They are on the one hand being pressed - and are trying - to improve their relationships with minorities and vulnerable groups, to work with communities, and to form partnerships with other statutory services and voluntary organizations in programmes to reduce crime and to prevent offending, especially among those who might be at an early stage of a criminal career. Those programmes are described in more detail in *Chapters 14* and *18*. The police are also involved in programmes of restorative justice - see *Chapter 10*. But they are at the same time developing the technology and the techniques to 'target' both serious offenders - those concerned with terrorism and other forms of organized crime or especially dangerous individuals - and other troublesome but less dangerous offenders such as persistent burglars, thieves and those involved in crime with or against vehicles. The police are also being urged - by local opinion, the media and even by the Government - to target beggars, 'travellers', prostitutes and their clients, troublesome neighbours, and others whose behaviour is a nuisance but may not actually be criminal. In its extreme form, this is the controversial and sometimes provocative style of policing which has come to be termed 'zero tolerance'.

There is nothing inherently contradictory about an attempt to reduce crime through partnerships and problem-solving, community-based methods, and simultaneously to enforce the law more vigorously against those who are suspected of breaking it and to use police powers to reduce nuisances and incivility. Both are needed. But 'soft' policing, which is focused on preventive and protective work in communities, involves different skills and different types of relationship - perhaps even a different culture - from 'hard' policing which focuses on law enforcement and on finding, convicting and imprisoning offenders. And the second is liable to compromise the first if the two are applied in the same place at the same time. The tensions over the operation of 'stop and search', and the offence it can cause to those who feel themselves to be 'targeted' because of their appearance or background, are an obvious example.

The pressures, and the reactions to them, which have been described in the last four paragraphs demonstrate both the importance of ethics, integrity and leadership in the police service, and the complexity of the situations in which values have to be communicated, sustained and applied to police operations on the ground. Robert Reiner, John Alderson, Peter Neyroud and Alan Beckley are among those who have written on this subject. All argue for principles which are about more than efficiency or effectiveness, or the utilitarian ideal of the greatest good for the greatest number. John Alderson links those principles with the values of the society in which the police operate, including those of the government; Peter Neyroud and Alan Beckley argue for a formal code of ethics; and all three focus their principles on human rights and on the European Convention as applied in the United Kingdom through the Human Rights Act 1985. [5] These arguments must be taken seriously at a time when professional ethics are at risk of being undermined by modern managerialism; and when police performance, often seen in the most simplistic terms, is increasingly treated as an issue over which political parties compete for public approval.

Central direction

Central government, in effect the Home Office, is now directing the content of police work to an extent which would have been thought inconceivable 20 years ago. Carefully phrased and deferential circulars and letters, with expressions like '... chief officers may wish to consider ... , and 'the Secretary of State would be grateful if ... ', have given way to firm, even peremptory, demands for information and, by implication, specific action. Perhaps the most powerful vehicle for Home Office direction is the array of performance indicators, including targets for reductions in crime now set in the statutory context of 'Best Value' (under the Local Government Act 1999) which also applies to local authorities generally and is being progressively extended to other public services.[6] The police now have a set of Best Value Performance Indicators, covering subjects which range from staff sickness and running costs to the number of crimes reported and detected, and the public's sense of safety and satisfaction with the police service. Although targets are formally set by police authorities, with the agreement of chief officers, they are in effect chosen to satisfy a political demand from ministers. Figures for reported and detected crime are now collected, and published, down to the level of 'basic command units' so that levels of crime, and the performance of the police, can be compared between different areas. Similar requirements, including reductions in crime, are placed on local authorities.

This process is certainly laborious for the police services and local authorities concerned, and crude figures of recorded crime will need a good deal of explanation and interpretation if they are not to be misleading. Their limitations will need to be recognised. They are as much an indication of police activity as they are of crime itself. Some of the figures will be open to manipulation, and their reliability will depend on the integrity and understanding of those who assemble them. The Government, and the police themselves, recognise that a rise or fall in the level of recorded or surveyed crime, or in the level of the public's fear of crime, depend not only on the action taken by the police but on a range of social and economic factors which are nothing to do with the police and are outside their control. But the use and presentation of the figures will inevitably suggest that changes in levels of crime or the fear of crime are evidence of the police service's own success or failure. And because the inputs and outputs (though not the outcomes) of 'hard' policing are easier to measure than those of 'soft' policing, the process may tend to promote 'hard' rather than 'soft' police methods. Some of the targets may also prove to have been unrealistic, for example reductions of up to 40 per cent in burglary and car crime in some areas. Of course police practice can influence rates of actual and still more recorded crime, but not in the calibrated, mechanical way that seems to be supposed. Similar considerations apply to rates of re-offending, or re-conviction, by those who have received prison or community sentences.

The Government clearly believed that this approach, backed up by inspection and audit, would drive up standards across the country as a whole. Some critics may believe, or may even hope, that the process will prove too cumbersome and will eventually fall into disuse; or fear that it will have a distorting and therefore damaging effect on the quality of the service which the police provide. Peter Neyroud and Alan Beckley describe a 'vicious cycle' leading to the 'crime fighting' approach and potentially to corruption and scandal. [7] Drawing on evidence from the report of HM Inspector of Constabulary, Barry Loveday has argued that although the attempt to impose a 'performance culture' should in theory have the effect which the Government and senior police officers intend, it still runs counter to the culture of much of the police service. It is often resented or ridiculed. And it is difficult to reconcile with the emphasis on quality, relationships and local ownership and consultation which are essential for successful policing. As Barry Loveday has argued and the Inspectorate of Constabulary has feared, it may even damage the service's integrity in recording information. It is too soon to tell what the outcome will be, but it is politically a high risk approach. The consequences of apparent failure would be serious - for the police, public confidence and the Government's own credibility.

Success in achieving targets and standards will, rightly, be a matter for celebration, by the Government and the police themselves. Disappointing results will, rightly, prompt questions about the reasons and possible remedial action, or about the validity or realism of the targets or standards themselves. They may also prompt questions about who is to blame. These may often be useful and sometimes important questions, but it will be rare for any individual to be uniquely responsible; and if a whole service, or a whole 'command unit', comes to be seen as 'failing' the responsibility for that situation, and for dealing with it, will usually go beyond the service or unit itself. The government itself will often become involved, and the action required will usually involve more than the appointment of a new chief officer or local commander. In real life, a 'failing' organization is more likely to be identified by public events, such as the handling of the death of Stephen Lawrence and the subsequent inquiry, than by any success or failure in achieving targets or standards. Targets and standards have their place, but their importance should be kept in proportion, and they should not be used to create a culture of blame (see also *Chapter 5*).

Accountability and legitimacy

Targets and standards are part of the larger question of accountability, and legitimacy, discussed in *Chapter 5*. The police can be said to be accountable

- to the general public, through Parliament and the Secretary of State;
- to the local public, through the police authority;

- to those with whom they come into direct contact, through the law (proceedings for damages or judicial review) or through internal procedures for dealing with complaints, or through the Police Complaints Authority.

Police accountability can also be described in other ways - financially to the Police Authority, and ultimately to central government; legally to the courts; and democratically through Ministers to Parliament and the public - although there is a tension between that form of accountability and the important principle that police in the United Kingdom are not supposed to be subject to political direction.

The mechanisms through which these forms of accountability are made effective are numerous and of different kinds. *Chapter 5* has discussed some of the considerations as they apply to public services as a whole. The mechanisms include the targets, indicators and standards set by central government as already indicated; the procedures for inspection and audit; the publication of reports; various forms of consultation at national and local level, including consultative committees, surveys and focus groups; the investigation of complaints internally and by the Police Complaints Authority; the role of the Crown Prosecution Service in reviewing cases for continuing prosecution; the function of the courts in ruling on issues such as the admissibility of evidence; the commissioning and use of research; and various others. It can hardly be said that the police are not accountable.

And yet accountability remains a contentious issue. Three fundamental questions present themselves concerning:[8]

- the balance between central and local (or regional) direction and control;
- how far accountability for the police should be democratic, and if so by what means, or how far it should be a matter of professional management and expertise;
- the extent to which the police should be operationally and politically independent.

The Royal Commission on the Police which reported in 1962[9], and the Police Act which followed in 1964, provided an answer to the three questions in the form of the tripartite structure consisting of central government, or the Secretary of State; the police authority, comprising (originally) elected members of the local authority and magistrates; and the chief constable. That structure soon came under strain. Reasons include the financial constraints of the 1970s and pressure for police budgets to be cash-limited; tensions in some areas between assertive police authorities and strong minded chief constables, especially on Merseyside and in Greater Manchester during the 1980s; and a decline in public and to some extent political confidence in the police. The decline was partly a reaction to the rise in crime. But it was also a result of the police handling of the disturbances in Brixton and elsewhere, brought out in Lord Scarman's report; the evidence of various instances of police corruption and malpractice during the late 1970s and early 1980s, leading to a further Royal Commission[10] and the passage of the Police and Criminal Evidence Act 1984; the miscarriages of justice in cases such as the Guildford Four and the Birmingham Six which were brought dramatically to light in the late 1980s; and long-running dissatisfaction with the system for dealing with complaints. Distrust of the police was particularly strong among members of minority groups.

Politics and management

From a government perspective, there were pressures for more central direction, principally in the interests of efficiency, economy and effectiveness, but also politically in order to reduce the influence of local (and especially left-wing) politicians. And from a professional police perspective, there were calls for greater centralisation to deal with the changing character of police work, especially in relation to Irish terrorism, improved co-operation with police in other countries, and the use of technology. The pressure for more central direction was therefore associated with a managerial rather than a democratic view of accountability, and a combination of those views led to a declining emphasis on the independence of the chief constable. There was no serious challenge to the principle that the chief constable and his officers must be able to take decisions on whom to arrest or prosecute without political interference. Nor was the principle denied on such matters as how to deal with terrorist threats or incidents or with large scale demonstrations. These can however be politically sensitive occasions on which ministerial as well as professional police reputations can be put at risk. Ministers may well arrange for their views on how such situations should be handled to be made known to the officers in operational command, for example in situations like the coalminers' strike in 1984-1985 and various incidents of terrorism. There was nothing new about this - Churchill and Harcourt had done the same 70 and 100 years before - and it can be argued that the doctrine of operational independence did not emerge until well into the twentieth century. But the occasions for ministerial intervention have perhaps become more frequent than they were in the past.

The consequence of these pressures have been a gradual increase in central direction and managerial influence throughout the 1980s and 1990s, a corresponding decline in the influence of police authorities, and an increasing subordination of any views which chief officers might have on their local priorities or interests to the political will of central government. It has been a continuous and gradual process, but significant steps were the issue of Home Office Circular 114 of 1983, on Manpower, Efficiency and Effectiveness in the Police Service[11] and the passage of the Police and Magistrates' Courts Act 1994. The Bill for the Act was amended in several important respects during its passage through the House of Lords.[12] In its final form it reduced the size of police authorities and the proportion of elected members and provided for the appointment of 'independent' members approved by the Home Secretary. The Act also enabled the Home Secretary to set national objectives, with which local priorities and objectives must be consistent; it introduced for the first time a cash limit on each service's expenditure, but with greater freedom for the police authority and the chief constable to decide how to allocate funds within the cash limit; and it empowered the Home Secretary to instruct police authorities about measures needed to improve efficiency and effectiveness.

This chapter has already described how the powers enacted under the Police and Magistrates' Courts Act 1994 came to be exercised enthusiastically by the Labour Government. There is however a difference between the Labour Government's use of those powers and their use by the previous Conservative administration. The previous administration introduced and used them primarily as a means of improving efficiency and accountability in a managerial (as distinct from a democratic) sense, and of promoting a generally 'consumerist' approach. The Labour Government has used them more openly to impose its own political priorities. There was nothing that was in itself especially controversial about the particular priorities which the Government set for the police, but it was clear that they overrode any which police authorities or police services might themselves wish to set for policing their own communities or which might emerge from their own processes of consultation. The Government's priorities did not exclude other more local concerns, provided that they were consistent with those priorities, but the single-minded attention which the Government demanded from the police restricted the energy and resources which could be devoted to them.

Another example of the Government's political agenda was its concern to see some of the provisions of the Crime and Disorder Act 1998, especially the anti-social behaviour order and the child curfew order, used on a large scale in order to demonstrate the success of the Act and of the Government's achievement in bringing it forward. Both were controversial, both prompted doubts over their effectiveness as a means of reducing crime and over the fairness of the procedures involved, but both are now available for the police or local authorities to use in suitable circumstances. The police and local authorities should clearly not take local decisions that they would never use those orders in any circumstances; but they are entitled, and it is their duty, to exercise their own careful judgement about what are the circumstances in which orders should be sought and any procedures which should be followed or conditions which should be satisfied. It was therefore surprising that the Home Secretary should have been so insistent in seeking to impose the Government's view of what it thought should be local policing priorities, especially in seeking anti-social behaviour orders to deal with inconsiderate or unruly behaviour (see *Chapter 18*).

Serious organized crime

An aspect of policing which can usually be separated from the prevention of crime, and from the detection and arrest of 'ordinary' offenders, is the action which has to be taken against serious, organized crime. Examples are terrorism, the importation and distribution of (especially class A) drugs, and large scale fraud. These types of crime are distinguished by the damage they cause, and the sophistication and resources of those who organize them, often on an international basis. Special techniques of investigation, including the interception of communications, electronic surveillance and the use of informers, may be needed to detect the offenders; and special rules of evidence and procedure may be needed to bring them to trial and obtain convictions. Two important conditions have to be observed: the techniques, which may have to be used in secret, must be applied in ways which can be held effectively to account; and their use, and the use of any special procedures to gain convictions, must be strictly controlled and restricted to those cases which are exceptionally serious and in which there is no alternative. In the language of the European Convention On Human Rights, they must be proportionate to what is necessary and just in a democratic society.

The first condition is to a large extent satisfied by the passage of the Regulation of Investigatory Powers Act 2000 which provides for new commissioners, usually High Court judges, to oversee the use of those techniques. In this respect it is a welcome measure, which should ensure that covert policing is compatible with the European Convention On Human Rights,, although JUSTICE have expressed regret that the Government did not take the opportunity to bring more coherence and consistency into the arrangements by introducing a unified statutory regime.[13] There are also other criticisms of the Act, for example the intrusion which it allows into private communications and matters of professional confidence.

The second condition has been the subject of argument for 25 years, most of it focused on legislation for the prevention of terrorism. The Terrorism Act 2000 places that legislation on a permanent basis but extends its scope to include not only terrorism connected with Northern Ireland and international terrorism, but also domestic action in Great Britain (see also *Chapter 11*). It covers actions to further political causes, but also those with an ideological purpose; and extends not only to acts which injure people but also those which damage property or create a serious risk to the health or safety of the public. As *Chapter 11* has argued it treats as 'terrorism' a number of acts or expressions of protest which could not conceivably be regarded as 'terrorism' in any normal sense, and which could be used to treat the citizen's ordinary use of the right of protest as if it were a threat to the security of the state. The police may in their discretion use the new powers with restraint, but their existence could place the police under pressure to use them when practical or commercial interests appeared to be threatened. As with other legislation designed to curb protests or nuisances by means of special procedures, rules of evidence or penalties - for example the public order provisions of the Criminal Justice and Public Order Act 1994 or the Crime and Disorder Act 1998 - the use made of those powers will need careful judgement and vigilant scrutiny. Peter Neyroud and Alan Beckley argue for systems of ethical control within a framework of human rights which positively protects the rights of citizens.[14]

The Government, and the police, must also resist any political or commercial pressure, for example from continental Europe, for a more routine deployment of firearms.[15]

The Stephen Lawrence Inquiry report

The most painful experience for the police in recent times, and the most dramatic expression of public lack of confidence in police work, has undoubtedly been Sir William Macpherson's inquiry into the death of Stephen Lawrence.[16] The report demonstrated a serious operational failure on the part of the Metropolitan Police themselves, and a state of what it described as institutional racism. It is discussed in more detail in *Chapter 16*. The report and the reactions to it also revealed an apparently irreconcilable difference of attitude between those who felt appalled and even betrayed by the whole sequence of events - the murder itself, the conduct of the police investigation and the action taken or not taken as a result of the inquiry (for example the Home Secretary's decision not to demand the resignation of the Commissioner of the Metropolitan Police); and those who saw the report as an act of political and intellectual weakness, if not a conspiracy, whose effect was to undermine the authority and credibility of the police, if not of the state itself.[17] The report of the Commission on the Future of Multi-Ethnic Britain[18] also gives disturbing examples of how the two attitudes were expressed, and of the anger which many black people have independently expressed over their own experience of contacts with the police, and it received a similar reaction.

Responding to Sir William Macpherson's report, the Home Secretary published an Action Plan on the way in which the report's recommendations were to be implemented, and the first of what was intended to be a series of annual reports on progress. Another was published a year later (February 2000).[19] The Government accepted virtually all the 70 recommendations in the report, and the progress reports indicate that action is being taken to put almost all of them into effect. The report has important implications not only for the police but also for the criminal justice system, and indeed the public service, as a whole; those which are especially important for the police are concerned with the recruitment, retention and promotion of police officers; with training; with the reporting and investigation of racist offences and incidents[20]; with liaison with families and communities; and with inspection and performance indicators. Other recommendations are specific to the Metropolitan Police.

Some scepticism was expressed about the rate of progress, and the extent of the Government's commitment and that of the police themselves. More optimistically, the hope for the long term must be that the report, taken with other influences on the work and culture of the police service, will confirm and accelerate the changes in attitude, culture and outlook, many of which are already taking place - not only as regards cultural diversity but also in the service's relationships with other agencies and institutions, with civil society, and with the citizens whom it serves.

Principles and accountability

The most recent and authoritative statement of the issues and principles which apply to modern policing, including especially the questions of accountability and legitimacy, is in the Report of the Independent Commission on Policing for Northern Ireland.[21] The report says

> ... we can find plenty of examples of police services wrestling with the same sort of challenges. How can the police be properly accountable to the community they serve if their composition in terms of ethnicity, religion and gender is vastly dissimilar to that of their society? How can professional police officers best adapt to a world in which their own efforts are only a part of the overall policing of a modern society? How can the police ensure that their practices recognise and uphold human dignity and the rights of individual citizens while providing them with effective protection from wrongdoing? How should human rights standards and obligations be reflected in the delivery of policing on the streets? How can police services reorient their approach so that, in the words of the founder of first Irish and then British policing, Sir Robert Peel, their main object becomes once again the prevention of crime rather than the detection and punishment of offenders?

The report continues

> ... we have seen our approach as restorative, not retributive - restorative of the values of liberty, the rule of law and mutual respect ... It is their task to uphold the rule of law, exercising their independent professional judgment in doing so. That independence is rightly prized as a defence against the politicisation of policing and the manipulation of the police for private ends. The police do not serve the state, or any interest group; they serve the people by upholding the law that protects the rights and liberties of every individual citizen. But the proper assertion of independence should not imply the denial of accountability.
>
> Accountability places limitations on the power of the police, but it should also give that power legitimacy ... policing is a matter for the whole community, not something that the community leaves to the police to do. Policing should be a collective community responsibility; a partnership for community safety. This sort of policing is more difficult than policing the community. It requires an end to 'us' and 'them' concepts of policing ... It has implications for the structure of the police which should become more decentralised; for the management style, which should become more open and delegated; ... oriented towards active problem-solving and crime prevention, rather than more traditional, reactive enforcement.

The Northern Ireland Agreement of April 1998 (the Good Friday Agreement), in accordance with which the Commission was established, itself states

The participants [in the negotiations] believe it essential that policing structures and arrangements are such that the police service is professional, effective and efficient, fair and impartial, free from partisan political control; accountable, both under the law for its actions and to the community it serves; representative of the society it polices, and operates within a coherent and co-operative criminal justice system, which conforms with human rights norms.

The report makes a total of 175 recommendations, some of which are relevant only to Northern Ireland. But many of them, and all the principles and general approach, are equally relevant to other parts of the United Kingdom and to other countries in the world. In particular the report acknowledges the need for legitimacy as well as accountability (see *Chapter 15*); it emphasises that policing has to be carried out in a spirit of inclusion, respect and common humanity and citizenship; and it affirms that the police 'do not serve the state'. The last statement is slightly puzzling, given that the police are themselves in a real sense one of the institutions of the state, and the only institution which in normal times can legitimately use force, if necessary lethal force, against members of the public within the state's boundaries. But bearing in mind the confusion which has now developed between the state and the government of the day - see *Chapter 2* - the point being made is perhaps that the police do not exist to serve the government of the day as distinct from the country, or its citizens, as a whole. That must be correct, as indeed it should be for public services more generally (see *Chapter 5*), and the structure and accountability of the police must make sure that a proper degree of independence from the government is guaranteed. The possibility that their independence might be compromised - critics would say that it was in fact compromised - was in the minds of many police officers during the coalminers' strike in 1984-85.

The function of policing

Attention needs to focus not only on the police as an institution but also on policing as a function. Policing is increasingly being carried out in different ways by different organizations. Examples of those organizations include not only the 'non-Home Office' or 'non-Police Act' services - Transport, Parks, Ministry of Defence and others - but also private security companies operating under contract from central or local government, or from private companies or other interests. Staff with security functions are also employed, directly or under contract, by some public service organizations. There has been an expansion in the amount of privately owned space - shopping centres, supermarkets, car parks, developments at railway stations - to which the public have access. That space is often protected by sophisticated devices such as closed circuit television, controlled by security staff, or it may be patrolled by security guards. Security staff and those with or for whom they work have considerable power, and opportunity, to exclude or harass people whose appearance they do not like. When this happens, it will usually be for ostensibly good reasons - to prevent crime, to catch suspected offenders after a crime has been committed, to control crowds, to prevent or contain disorder. It will usually be in their own and their employer's public relations or commercial interests to avoid public confrontations or actions which will cause public resentment or offence. They will usually want to maintain good relations with the regular police. They will be subject to the general law. But private security companies and individual security guards are not subject to the same structures of public accountability as police officers. Their accountability is primarily to their clients and shareholders, not to the public or the community at large. And some of the situations in which security guards come into contact with members of the public - for example protesters and demonstrators - have the potential for serious disorder. Those situations need skilled and sensitive handling, in the wider public interest.

The case for regulating the private security industry has been argued elsewhere.[22] The mechanisms should involve a national regulatory authority with the function of setting standards, accrediting those private security companies which conform to the standards, and reviewing their accreditation at suitable intervals. They should also involve a more local procedure to make sure that any use of private security companies is suitable to the particular purposes and circumstances for which they are employed. The Government's decision to introduce legislation in the Private Security Industry Bill 2000 was a welcome development.

Democracy and legitimacy
The immediate agenda for the police service and policing is quite well defined, by the Government and by the service itself. But as this chapter has already indicated, there is a longer term agenda which involves a more fundamental change in police culture and in police organization, structure and accountability. Some of the change in culture will come from events which are already in progress - the follow-up to the Stephen Lawrence Inquiry report, and the service's own responses to its changing social, political and operational environment. Others will need more deliberation and preparation. The separate proposals for a new system of dealing with complaints, published by the Home Office and by Liberty on 17 May 2000, need to be energetically carried forward. They should be designed to combine independence with mechanisms and a relationship with the Police Service which breaks down defensive attitudes, avoids a culture of blame and enables the police to learn from the complaints which are made about them.

There is great potential in the new proposals for training, which the Home Secretary published on the same day, including the new 'centre of excellence' and the 'national core curriculum' - though it is important that police officers should not be trained in isolation from members of other services and it is a pity that the proposals did not include the more broadly-based college for leadership which is discussed in *Chapter 21*. In an address to the Social Market Foundation in February 1999, Ian Blair, now Deputy Commissioner of the Metropolitan Police, said that

> We need to consider whether the separation of the ways of governance of the police service from those used in the rest of local government remains as sensible as it once did ... [and] ... whether police managers need to be trained separately from their colleagues in local government, from senior civil servants, from the fire service, from the ambulance service.

Provisions on training, including the establishment of a Central Police Training and Development Authority, were included in the Criminal Justice and Police Bill 2000.

Longer term changes should include a reconstruction of the relationship between the police, central government and their local communities; and of the relationship between public or 'Police Act' police services and the various forms of private security. In particular, control by central government over the police should be less detailed and prescriptive; police accountability to local communities should be strengthened; and the private security companies should be brought within a regulated framework of public accountability.

Several writers have drawn attention to the need for greater local accountability.[23] They have mostly sought a return to a form of local governance in which elected members were more strongly represented on police authorities, and police authorities had greater powers and more independence from central government. But the solution is not simply to return to the situation as it was before the Police and Magistrates' Courts Act 1994, and none of those writers would defend the situation as it had become at that time.

Democratic control of the police, in the sense of the involvement of elected members, has been recognised as a difficult issue for at least 20 years. On the one hand policy that is wholly controlled by the police themselves, by appointed (or elected but ineffective) authorities, or even by central government, lacks local legitimacy and is open to criticism for being insensitive, complacent, partial, secretive and discriminatory. On the other hand, the involvement of local elected members has been criticised as bringing politics into policing, undermining its independence and allowing a disproportionate influence to sectional interests. It is a frequent criticism of elected members that they give undue attention to immediate issues which are prominent in their own wards, to the exclusion of the wider public interest or any longer-term strategic vision, or that they are extravagant with pubic funds. Part of the problem and one of the results has been the decline in the power, authority and status of local government, and therefore of its attraction to people who might be interested in standing for office. It must be in the national interest to reverse the decline, but it will be a long process which will need to include measures to extend the scope and opportunities for elected members if it is to succeed.

The involvement of elected members is an obvious and necessary, but not the only, means of achieving democratic legitimacy. Legitimacy can also be achieved by effective and inclusive methods of public consultation and participation, and damaged by insensitive or incompetent police actions, as in the investigation into the death of Stephen Lawrence; by corruption; or more routinely in operations such as 'stop and search', 'targeted' policing or attempts at 'zero tolerance', if they are not carefully handled. The Government and the police service are exploring new methods of consultation and forms of participation, and a similar process is taking place in local government under the Local Government Act 2000.[24] The legitimacy of the police will be even more crucial if they receive and exercise the new powers for combatting crime and disorder, and for disclosure of information, seizure of property, detention and arrest, and the taking of evidence which the Government has proposed in the Criminal Justice and Police Bill 2000.

The longer term

A promising way forward is the proposal which Ian Loader has put forward in 'Governing Policing in the Twenty-first Century'.[25] He describes a world of what he calls 'fragmented, plural policing' in which the operation of the market for private security has skewed the distribution of policing towards those affluent consumers who are willing and able to pay for the service, so presenting the danger of new forms of inequity and injustice. He argues for

> the establishment of national, regional and local policing commissions whose task it would be to formulate policing policies and co-ordinate service delivery across policing networks, and to bring to democratic account the various bodies that compromise them. In pursuit of the former, such bodies would concern themselves with developing policing plans for particular localities or regions and deciding upon the police's role in delivering them; they would issue contracts to agencies who might tender to provide services under these plans (something that might beneficially include using public funds to 'buy-in' services for disadvantaged communities). And they would inspect, monitor and evaluate the policing services that are subsequently provided.

This suggestion resembles, but goes beyond, the recommendations of the Independent Commission on the Future of Policing in Northern Ireland. Ian Loader acknowledges that a great deal more work would be needed on the detail. The commissions would clearly replace existing police authorities. But it is not clear that they would be needed at all three levels, or what the relationship would be between them. Questions would include the composition of the commissions, how far the members would be elected, and whether they would be elected separately or appointed from elected members of local authorities. The local commissions might (as in Northern Ireland) cover areas corresponding to those of district or unitary authorities and basic command units; it would be for consideration whether the regional commissions would correspond with the 42 existing police and other criminal justice boundaries or with the larger regions of government. Much would depend on whether a regional tier of elected government is to be introduced for other purposes. Or there might be a single tier of commissions corresponding with existing authorities and services.

A simpler structure might be a statutory national body for co-ordination and advice to government, assuming the corresponding functions of the Association of Chief Officers of Police, together with a national body to register and accredit private security companies. At area level, 42 commissions would replace existing police authorities. They would act as commissioning authorities for public policing functions, and would have responsibility for approving private security operations and co-ordinating different policing activities. At a more local level, there would be local committees of those commissions, covering district and unitary authorities and basic command units, and paying special attention to consultation with local communities and the participation of their members, from all cultural traditions and backgrounds. John Alderson, Peter Neyroud and Alan Beckley are less prescriptive about the kind of organization they envisage, but they are very clear about the need for policing to have an ethical foundation which includes respect for human rights, and strong professional leadership. Peter Neyroud and Alan Beckley describe in some detail the ways in which that foundation might be established, how it might change the character of policing, and the mechanisms - of recruitment, training, funding, accountability and operational and professional oversight - by which it would do so.[26]

Whatever the details, a more devolved, locally accountable structure may now be needed to ensure that policing, in its multiple forms, is effective, equitable and legitimate in the context of a modern diverse society. Whatever the pressures for specialisation, separation, national or international direction and social control, the police should remain 'citizens representing the rest of the community'. And means must be found of reconciling operational effectiveness with ethical standards, and democratic accountability with professional leadership.

ENDNOTES for *Chapter 17*

[1] Peter Neyroud and Alan Beckley, *Policing, Ethics and Human Rights*, Cullompton, Willan Publishing, 2001.
[2] Home Office, *Police Reform: the Government's Proposals for the Police Service in England and Wales*, Cmnd. 2281, London, HMSO, 1993.
[3] Lord Scarman, *The Brixton Disorders 10-12 April 1981 Report of the Inquiry by the Right Honourable Lord Scarman OBE*, Cmnd. 8427, London, HMSO, 1981.
[4] Sir William Macpherson of Cluny, *The Stephen Lawrence Inquiry*, Cmnd. 4262, London Stationery Office, 1999.
[5] Robert Reiner, *Chief Constables: Bobbies, Bosses or Bureaucrats*, Oxford University Press 1991 and 'Policing and the Police' in Mike Maguire, Rod Morgan, Robert Reiner (eds.) *The Oxford Handbook of Criminology*, 2nd edition, Oxford University Press, 1997. John Alderson, *Principled Policing: Protecting the Public with Integrity*, Winchester, Waterside Press, 1998. Peter Neyroud and Alan Beckley *op. cit* n. 1. Drawing on work by Marian Fitzgerald, they write '[she] has demonstrated just how corrosive quantitative approaches have been in encouraging numbers of stops without any proper control over their legality, the way in which discretion was being exercised, the discriminatory outcome or the community's concerns' (p.163).
[6] The Home Office issued a set of 'Best Value Performance Indicators' to chief officers and police authorities with a letter dated 8 February 2000. The Home Secretary announced a new set of crime targets to be included in police authorities' Best Value Performance Plans from April 2000 in a speech at Newham Town Hall on 14 February 2000.

[7] Peter Neyroud and Alan Beckley *op. cit* n. l, pp. 9-10 and *passim*; Barry Loveday, 'The Impact of Performance Culture on Criminal Justice Agencies in England and Wales', *International Journal of the Sociology of Law*, 1999 27, pp. 351-377 and 'Managing Crime: Police Use of Crime Data as an Indicator of Effectiveness', *ibid*, 2000, 28, pp. 215-37; HM Inspectorate of Constabulary, *Police Integrity: England, Wales and Northern Ireland: Security and Maintaining Public Confidence*, London, HM Inspectorate of Constabulary, 1999.

[8] These and other questions were the subject of the report *Accountable Policing: Effectiveness, Empowerment and Equity* produced by the Institute for Public Policy Research in 1993 and edited by Robert Reiner and Sarah Spencer. They were also the subject of chapters on 'Police Accountability' by Tim Newburn and Trevor Jones in *Themes in Contemporary Policing* and of the chapter on 'Police Performance and Accountability' in *The Role and Responsibilities of the Police*, both produced in 1996 by the independent inquiry established by the Police Foundation and the Policy Studies Institute and published jointly by those two organizations. Events have to some extent moved on since those chapters were written, but the issues have not changed and many of the arguments are still relevant. For a more recent account see Peter Neyroud and Alan Beckley *op. cit* n. l, pp. 145-65.

[9] The Royal Commission on the Police, Final Report, Cmnd. 1728, London, HMSO, 1962.

[10] The Royal Commission on Criminal Procedure, Final Report, Cmnd. 8092, London, HMSO 1981.

[11] See Mollie Weatheritt's chapter on 'Measuring Performance: Accounting or Accountability' in *Accountable Policing: Effectiveness, Empowerment and Equity, op. cit.*, n. 8.

[12] Lord Windlesham describes the Bill's passage through Parliament in *Responses to Crime*, Volume 3, *Legislating with the Tide* (see *Chapter 3*). The centralising effect of the Bill's proposals, especially the composition of police authorities and the Home Secretary's power to appoint the chairman, provoked almost universal criticism and the Government was compelled to make a number of important concessions.

[13] JUSTICE, *The Regulation of Investigatory Powers Bill a Human Rights Audit*, London, JUSTICE, 2000. See also *Under Surveillance: Correct Policing and Human Right Standards*, London, JUSTICE, 1998.

[14] Peter Neyroud and Alan Beckley *op. cit* n. l, pp. 189-202.

[15] Peter Squires, 'Firearms and Policing; Driven to it?', in *Criminal Justice Matters*, 38, Winter 1999-2000, pp. 18-19. Drawing on the *International Police Review* he writes: 'The event driven "war on order" scenarios commonly depicted in the *International Police Review* may fall some way beyond the UK's current domestic policing agenda. Yet the violent and dangerous world it represents demands an armed and capable police. The magazine shows "police capacity" developing, not according to some democratic mandate or needs assessment, but as rather more ideologically, technologically or event driven. As one contributor to the magazine argues, special operations units, their weapons and tactics "must be shielded to the highest degree possible from both departmental and public curiosity." As a policy, however, this secret "event driven" world contains no inherent limits; it lacks a public or democratic safety catch.'

[16] *Op. cit.*, n 4.

[17] NACRO, *The First Anniversary of the Stephen Lawrence Inquiry Report : A Challenge for the New Millennium. Race Policies into Action*, issue 20, London, NACRO, 2000.

[18] Report of the Commission on the Future of Multi-Ethnic Britain, *The Future of Multi-Ethnic Britain*, London, Profile Books, 2000.

[19] Home Office, *Stephen Lawrence Inquiry: Home Secretary's Action Plan: First Annual Report on Progress*, London, Home Office, 2000.

[20] Home Office, *Code of Practice on Reporting and Recording Racist Incidents in Response to Recommendation 15 of the Stephen Lawrence Inquiry Report*, London, Home Office, April, 2000.

[21] Christopher Patten, *A New Beginning: Policing in Northern Ireland. Report of the Independent Commission on Policing in Northern Ireland*, London, Stationery Office, 1999.

[22] The case for regulating the private security industry has been argued, for example in the *Report of the Independent Inquiry into the Role and Responsibilities of the Police* established by the Police Foundation and the Policy Studies Institute; and also in Clifford Shearing, 'Public and Private Policing' and in Trevor Jones and Tim Newburn, 'The Regulation and Control of the Private Security Industry' both in *Themes in Contemporary Policing, op. cit,* n. 7. Also their book, *Private Security and Public Policing,* Oxford, Clarendon Press, 1998.

[23] Lawrence Lustgarten in *Governance of the Police,* 1986; Robert Reiner in *Policing a Post Modern Society,* 1992 and 'Police Accountability: Principles, Patterns and Practices' in *Accountable Policing: Effectiveness, Empowerment and Equity, 1993;* Tim Newburn and Trevor Jones in *Themes in Contemporary Policing, op. cit,* n. 7; Barry Loveday in 'Waving Not Drowning: Chief Constables and the New Configuration of Accountability in the Provinces' in *The International Journal of Police, Science and Management,* 1/2, 1998, pp. 133-47. And most recently Peter Neyroud and Alan Beckley *op. cit* n. l, pp. 150-4.

[24] The Government issued what might be thought rather condescending advice in *Involving Users – Improving the Delivery of Local Public Services,* London, Cabinet Office, 1999. A more substantial document was *Preparing Community Strategies: Government Guidance to Local Authorities,* London, Department of the Environment, Transport and the Regions, 2001. This was issued to local authorities to help them carry out this new duty under the Local Government Act 2000 to 'prepare community strategies for promoting or improving the economic, social and environmental well-being of their areas, and contributing to the achievement of sustainable development in the UK'.

[25] Ian Loader, 'Governing Policing in the Twenty-first Century', *Criminal Justice Matters,* 38, Winter 1999-2000, pp. 9-10.

[26] John Alderson, *op. cit.* n. 5; Peter Neyroud and Alan Beckley *op. cit,* n. l.

CHAPTER 18

Community Safety: Preventing Crime and Disorder

Community Safety is an outcome and not a problem or a service: it is about people's sense of personal security, which is the product of multiple factors. A precise definition of Community Safety does not exist. Commentators have offered a number of broad definitions that suggest that it is concerned with more than crime and aims to prevent, reduce or a least contain, the things that are most disruptive to people's quality of life.

Audit Commission, 'Safety in Numbers', February 1999

It is only the mainstream processes of socialisation (internalised morality and the sense of duty, the informal inducements and rewards of conformity, the practical and cultural networks of mutual expectation and independence etc.) which are able to promote proper conduct on a consistent and regular basis.

David Garland, *Punishment and Modern Society*, 1990

The previous chapter has shown how the original aims of the Metropolitan Police emphasised the prevention of crime and treated it as an activity separate from enforcing the law and detecting and punishing offenders. But crime prevention has only become a serious and distinct focus of public attention, government policy and professional expertise within the last 20 years. Although the first Commissioners of the Metropolitan Police put the prevention of crime as the primary object of efficient policing, the main activities for the police over the next 150 years were the detection rather than the prevention of crime, the processing of offenders through the system once they had been arrested, the gathering of intelligence about the activities of known or suspected offenders; the maintenance of public order; and the increasing range of regulatory functions which fell to the police as society became more complex (for example road traffic accidents, accidents and emergencies). Commercial companies developed and placed on sale an increasingly sophisticated range of safes, locks, and other security equipment, and police crime prevention officers could be called to give advice on their use. But crime prevention did not become a 'mainstream' subject for the police or the government in Great Britain until the 1980s. It is now the subject of an extensive academic literature which Anthony Bottoms and Paul Wiles have reviewed in their chapter on 'Environmental Criminology', and which Ken Pease has reviewed in his chapter on 'Crime Prevention', both in the *Oxford Handbook of Criminology*.[1] A more recent analysis is in the collection of papers which make up *Secure*

Foundations edited by Scott Ballintyne, Ken Pease and Vic Maclaren.[2] Andrew von Hirsch, David Garland and Alison Wakefield have assembled some provocative insights in *Ethical and Social Perspectives on Situational Crime Prevention.*[3]

ORIGIN OF PROGRAMMES FOR COMMUNITY SAFETY

Influences in the early 1980s came from three main directions. Research in the United States and subsequently in Great Britain had shown the benefits which could be obtained from 'situational' crime prevention, including Jane Jacobs' *The Death and Life of American Cities*, published as early as 1961;[4] and Oscar Newman's *Defensible Space: People and Design in the Violent City* (1972);[5] and the harm, in terms of increased levels of crime, which resulted from failures to repair damage, remove graffiti or clean up litter – the subject of James Q. Wilson's work with George Kelling on 'Broken Windows' (1982).[6] Work in Great Britain included *Designing out Crime*, edited by Ronald Clarke and Patricia Mayhew (1980)[7], and *Communities and Crime Reduction*, edited by Tim Hope and Margaret Shaw (1988)[8]; and in the United States *The Reasoning Criminal*, edited by D. B. Cornish and R. V. Clarke (1986).[9] Lessons from this research could be directly applied to the large housing estates which had been built in or on the outskirts of many British cities during the 1950s and 1960s and which had become run-down and vandalised, for reasons which were due at least in part to their poor design.

Secondly, organizations such as NACRO were trying to develop an approach to crime which saw solutions in wider terms than measures directed exclusively towards offenders and punishment (support for victims was another example, see *Chapter 15*). From a different perspective, the police were - quite rightly - keen to demonstrate that they could not alone be held responsible for rising crime and could not alone be expected to deal with it. And thirdly, new technology was becoming available, including new forms of electronic alarms, new devices to protect motor vehicles, and especially surveillance by closed circuit television.

At the start of the 1980s, the Government was still inclined to think of crime prevention as being rather like 'meals on wheels' - a useful service to deserving and vulnerable people, but marginal to any serious attempt to reduce crime. During the next few years a substantial programme of work was undertaken to restore run-down estates by a comprehensive range of mostly 'situational' measures directed to making crime harder to commit and easier to detect, and to improve the residents' own sense of safety and security. They included improved lighting, regular maintenance and prompt repairs, the removal or re-design of walkways and passages, the appointment of concierges, changes in housing allocation policy to create more stable communities, and the formation of residents' associations through which residents' views and feelings could be more effectively expressed. The work was typically carried out through partnerships involving local authorities, voluntary organizations such as NACRO, and central government through the Manpower Services Commission.[10].

At the same time the Government and the police were promoting the formation of neighbourhood watch schemes, and conducting publicity campaigns to encourage householders to pay more attention to the security of their possessions and their property. Critics of neighbourhood watch feared that it would either be exploited by the police as an extra source of criminal intelligence, or be used by residents themselves to harass strangers or people whose appearance might attract attention (for example members of minorities groups) - that is to say in the 'exclusionary' way discussed in *Chapter 2*. These fears were not in the event realised to any significant degree, but neighbourhood watch schemes have generally proved most successful in middle-class residential areas. The Government also tried to persuade motor manufacturers to incorporate more effective security devices in the design of their vehicles. This last campaign had little effect in the early stages, but became more successful as owners began to see the benefits.

A change of pace and direction

Events took a new turn at the time of the general election in 1987. The *British Crime Survey* had by then shown that a large volume of crime was not reported to or recorded by the police, and was therefore out of reach of the normal criminal justice process: it was increasingly important to find, and to demonstrate, other means of dealing with it. Not only that, but the methods which had been developed so far, all quite good in themselves, had been applied piecemeal and without any effective co-ordination or strategic planning. In the administration which Margaret Thatcher formed after the 1987 election, John Patten was appointed as minister of state at the Home Office, reporting to Douglas Hurd as Home Secretary, with special responsibility for the Government's overall response to crime. This responsibility included both crime prevention (but not other police matters) and criminal justice policy including probation (but not prisons). His appointment was therefore an early attempt to create what later came to be described as a 'joined up' responsibility to deal with a 'cross-cutting' issue.

Other developments included the creation of a research-based Crime Prevention Unit within the Police Department of the Home Office - an early attempt to promote and institutionalise an evidence-based approach to policy and practice;[11] the formation of the voluntary organization Crime Concern to work in partnership with government; and the 'Safer Cities' programme, through which the Home Office provided a co-ordinator and a small development fund in each of a number of local authority areas. The programme continued for a number of years, and was eventually merged into the Labour Government's wider programmes for urban regeneration.

These developments acknowledged, and demonstrated, that attempts to prevent crime have to be linked with attempts to reduce criminality. A distinction came to be made between 'primary', 'secondary' and 'tertiary' methods of prevention. Primary prevention focused on physical security, improvements in design and 'situational' measures intended to make crime harder to commit or easier to detect. Secondary measures focused on social circumstances and the motivation of those who might be at risk of committing crime, and on what came to be known as the 'risk' and 'resilience' factors which influence them. [12] Tertiary prevention was concerned with the reform or control of known offenders.

It came generally to be acknowledged that primary measures cannot be taken very far unless attention is also paid to secondary measures, and therefore to the character of the local community and the relationships, opportunities and influences which are available within it. The former are a good deal more straightforward, conceptually and operationally, than the latter. They are visible, popular, and they can usually have a demonstrable effect. They are easier to explain, and to evaluate in terms of quantified results. They are also less controversial. The Jill Dando Institute for Crime Science has been formed to study and promote them. But their results will be limited until people no longer want or try to commit the offences they are designed to prevent, or to commit other offences or commit them elsewhere. That is to say, they need to be connected to secondary measures which help to promote healthy, resourceful, resilient and confident relationships - families, households, friends, what are sometimes called 'peer groups', and communities - neighbours, colleagues, local institutions and services. People should be helped and encouraged to be responsible citizens, supported by a strong civil society. Anthony Bottoms has identified four types of influence or mechanisms which he sees as underpinning law-abiding behaviour – those which are instrumental or prudential (incentives or deterrence); constraints, which may be physical or socio-structural (for example most forms of situational crime prevention); normative influences based on belief, attachments or relationships, or legitimacy; and those which are based on habit or routine. He argues that all four are inter-connected; each will need to be supported by any or all of the others; and normative influences are pivotal. [13]

'Social' measures must therefore be developed in parallel with physical or situational measures to deal with the 'risk' and 'reslience' factors which affect the disposition of individuals and neighbourhoods towards criminality. They are typically concerned with influences and relationships (with partners, family, friends, teachers, colleagues at work); achievement and opportunities at school or in employment; accommodation; problems of literacy or mental health; and the consequences of social exclusion more generally. They are also longer term in their objectives, they are complex and difficult to measure, and they need a commitment which goes beyond the Government's or the local authority's electoral term. Problems can be tackled on an individual basis for people identified as being 'at risk', including those who may already have been convicted of offences; on a local basis for particular areas or neighbourhoods with high levels of crime or social deprivation (the two often go together); or on a national basis as a matter of government policy. But it is a characteristic of all of them that they look beyond the individual to the wider social scene and the dynamics at work within it.

The Safer Cities programme was originally intended to bring together 'situational' and 'social' measures in a series of integrated local projects. Its originators also hoped, more ambitiously, that it would lead to a change of outlook, priorities, and relationships, and to a more strategic sense of direction on the part of local authorities, and the police, as a whole.

The programme had some success in demonstrating the validity of its approach; and the individual projects, together with the work of Crime Concern and longer established organizations such as NACRO, developed some valuable techniques and achieved useful benefits in the areas in which they operated. To the extent that some of its results may have been inconclusive or disappointing, the reason was the difficulty which projects and their sponsors found in establishing a clear sense of purpose, and a clear set of aims for which the various stakeholders felt a sufficient sense of responsibility and commitment. Ken Pease has argued that the difficulty was due to their unrealistic attempt to include secondary or social measures as well as the simpler primary - physical and situational - measures[14]; Tim Hope has argued that strong communities are needed to resist crime, with characteristics which call for secondary measures if they are to be created or sustained.[15] The need for strong communities is also one of the conclusions of a study of male juvenile offending in Pittsburg, by Per-Olof Wikstrom and Rolf Loeber, which indicates that even well-adjusted children can become adolescent delinquents if they are brought up in disadvantaged neighbourhoods.[16] Another reason was the distracting effect of local politics and local political agendas. A third was the Conservative Government's difficulty in acknowledging a connection between the incidence of crime and social conditions and social policies - for example on employment, housing and social security - on which it had taken a dogmatic political position. And a fourth was, often, lack of effective co-ordination at local level.

Organization and responsibility

Throughout the period of the Conservative Government, such attention as was given to crime prevention at local level was awkwardly divided between local authorities and the police. Despite increasing interest from central government, neither saw it as being of more than marginal importance for their own services, or as deserving a high priority in comparison with other demands on their attention and resources. An independent working group of the Home Office Standing Conference on Crime Prevention under the chairmanship of James Morgan carried out an important review of crime prevention policies in 1991.[17] Its report recommended that

> local authorities, working in conjunction with the police, should have clear statutory responsibility for the development and stimulation of community

safety and crime prevention programmes, and for progressing at local level a multi-agency approach to community safety.

Local authorities, the police, and the relevant voluntary organizations warmly welcomed the report, and especially this recommendation. But the Conservative Government's relationship with local authorities was such that it could not contemplate legislation which would give them new responsibilities, and no action was taken on the Morgan Report's recommendation until the Labour Government took office in 1997. The report as a whole received a half-hearted response from central government, which took little political interest in crime prevention for the remainder of its term of office.

The report did however stimulate action at local level. Local authorities, police forces, probation services, social services departments and voluntary organizations formed partnerships to promote community safety (as the broader approach to crime prevention came to be called). Some formed new charitable organizations for this purpose, with full time staff (for example the Thames Valley Partnership); others worked in less structured ways. Some had the benefit of guidance from organizations such as Crime Concern, NACRO or the Divert Trust, or of funding from central government through the Single Regeneration Budget or the Safer Cities or other programmes; others worked independently. Some attempted a comprehensive approach; others concentrated on particular offences or groups at risk. Many found it difficult to target neighbourhoods, and preferred a 'scatter gun' approach, with fewer political pitfalls. All found enthusiasm and good will. All found that joint working requires changes of outlook and attitude, including a readiness to share information and influence, among both managers and first line staff. All found difficulty with funding, and especially with the bureaucracy involved in obtaining funds from central government. All found it difficult to make the transition from short-term, specially funded, self-contained - and therefore vulnerable - projects to permanent schemes and ultimately to new methods of work which form a natural part of each service's ordinary programme. The techniques could be difficult and laborious and the outcomes were often inconclusive (or not considered at all). There was however in most areas a strong commitment to continuing the process of change and to developing the techniques of evaluation, but it had to be sustained by consistent professional managerial and political support.

A LEGISLATIVE FRAMEWORK

The Labour Government came into office in May 1997 with a well-developed set of proposals for legislation which were in due course enacted in the Crime and Disorder Act 1998. They included a statutory duty for local councils and chief officers of police to co-operate with one another, and with other statutory agencies, in formulating publishing, implementing and reviewing strategies for the reduction of crime and disorder in their areas. They placed an important emphasis on local plans, consultation and commitment to respond to the needs of groups who were hard to reach. All these needed careful preparation and therefore time and patience.

The Act effectively implemented the recommendation in the Morgan Report six years previously. But its provisions went considerably further in extending the scope of the new duties to include disorder as well as crime; in applying them not only to local authorities and the police but also to probation committees and health authorities (and other persons or bodies who might be prescribed by order); and in setting a range of detailed statutory requirements relating to surveys, publication of reports of surveys, consultation with the public, the formulation of strategies, the setting of long-term and short-term targets, and the monitoring of performance and results. Section 17 of the Act also provided a general duty for local authorities to exercise their various functions 'with due regard to the likely effect . . . on, and the need to do all it reasonably can to prevent, crime and disorder in its area'.

Alongside the statutory provisions for crime and disorder strategies and partnerships, the Act introduced a number of new court orders aimed at reducing not only crime but also acts of social disorder which might not be criminal in themselves but which could be a nuisance to other people. The orders comprised anti-social behaviour orders, parenting orders, child safety orders, local child curfew schemes and sex offender orders. They had in common the ability of the courts to impose requirements on reported trouble-makers or irresponsible parents; or in the case of child curfew orders all parents and children in the area, using the lower civil standard of evidence that disorderly (not necessarily criminal) behaviour might on the balance of probabilities have occurred or be expected, rather than the criminal standard of proof that an individual had beyond reasonable doubt committed a criminal offence. Sanctions were provided for breach of an order, including in the case of anti-social behaviour order a sentence of imprisonment for up to five years.

Elizabeth Burney[18] has described the origin of these orders, including the Labour Party's discussion paper *A Quiet Life: Tough Action on Criminal Neighbours*, published while the Party was in opposition in June 1995 and its proposal for what was then called a 'community safety order' and later became the anti-social behaviour order. Although the title referred to 'criminal neighbours', it became clear that the proposal, like the anti-social behaviour order, was drawn in much broader terms and was intended to apply to conduct which might be annoying or a nuisance but which was by no means criminal. Once in office, the Labour Government took much pride in the legislation, which the Home Secretary, Jack Straw, described[19] as 'A triumph of community politics over detached metropolitan elites'. (For a different perspective on the anti-social behaviour order, see *Chapter 12*.) The claim that the Party, and subsequently the Government, was more in touch with 'the people' than the professions and operational services who worked with them on a day-to-day basis became a regular theme of the Government's political rhetoric.

FROM COMMUNITY SAFETY TO CRIME CONTROL

The passage of the Crime and Disorder Act was followed immediately (in July 1998) by the announcement of a new crime reduction programme, with funding of £250 million to support new projects. The programme was based largely on the results of previous research, which were summarised and assessed in the Home Office paper *Reducing Crime*.[20] A Briefing Note 'Reducing Crime and Tackling its Causes' said

> The Crime Reduction Programme will invest resources in projects which offer a significant and sustained impact on crime. The programme is intended to contribute to reversing the long-term growth rate in crime by ensuring that we are achieving the greatest impact for the money spent and that this impact increases progressively. It will do so by promoting innovation, generating a significant improvement in knowledge about effectiveness and cost-effectiveness and fostering progressive maintstreaming of emerging knowledge about good practice.

> The programme will build on the foundations laid by the Crime and Disorder Act. It will harness the activities of the local partnerships established under that legislation; their crime audits will provide valuable evidence for deciding whether to run some of the programme's local elements to gain the maximum benefits.

In its own Briefing Paper *Safety in Numbers: Promoting Community Safety*, published in February 1999[21], the Audit Commission put forward a number of recommendations to local partnerships and central government. Those addressed to local partnerships were concerned with the mechanics, and dynamics, of local consultation and co-ordination; with leadership, responsibility and reporting mechanisms; and with information, monitoring and systems of learning. Those addressed to government were concerned with supporting and funding local initiatives and identifying opportunities to divert resources from criminal justice to promoting safety and where national approaches could add value. Important passages included the words quoted at the beginning of this chapter. The report went on

> In order to address the community's fears and concerns properly, community safety work must engage fundamentally with the community in a way that goes beyond the scope of traditional crime prevention work. At the national level, a number of general trends can be detected that build the case for public agencies to focus more on the citizen's point of view.

The term 'community safety' is significant. It had been used for some years to imply a sense of local ownership, involvement and responsibility, of citizenship and civil society, and of social inclusion. It was thus closely associated with many of the ideas which seemed to inform the Government's own policies and approach, including the aims of section 17 of the 1998 Act but also its programmes in other areas of social policy such as support for young children (Sure Start), helping young people into work (New Deal), a new youth support service (Connexions), together with work on education action zones, exclusions from school, social exclusion, and several other subjects.

Despite the reference to the Crime and Disorder Act, the Government's Crime Reduction Programme already marked something of a departure from it, certainly from the 'social' aspect of crime prevention and the spirit of section 17. The first projects to be funded under the programme were concerned with domestic burglary and targeted policing; others were to deal with domestic violence, the resettlement of short-term prisoners, exclusions from school, fine enforcement, restorative justice, the information available to sentencers, work with offenders in the community and in prison, vehicle licensing, and the design of products to make them harder to steal. The programme thus placed its emphasis on specific, narrowly defined issues and projects (whose results may be easier to measure), and on nationally determined priorities, rather than the social 'risk' and 'resilience' factors as they occur in neighbourhoods.

In November 1999, the Government published a new document *The Government's Crime Reduction Strategy.*[22] In his Foreword, the Home Secretary recalled the Labour Party's successful political slogan 'tough on crime, and tough on the causes of crime' and wrote

Being tough on the causes of crime means strengthening communities by getting people off welfare and into work, by improving support for families and young children, by improving education, housing and action against truancy. It means proper investment to make our communities safer, getting addicts off drugs and into treatment and making prison work by preventing re-offending and improving the literacy and employability of prisoners.

It was therefore disappointing that, apart from the words in the Home Secretary's Foreword, the *Strategy* itself had so little to say about what would actually be involved in a strategic and co-ordinated approach to the reduction of crime and disorder at local level, or the means by which it could be achieved. There was no response to the recommendations from the Audit Commission. The main references to education and health were to give those services' experience as an example of the value of league tables, targets and the monitoring of performance as a means of raising standards, and by implication to make an unfavourable comparison between those services and the police and the local 'crime and disorder reduction partnerships' (as they came to be called).

The strategy's emphasis was on targets for reducing 'the crimes which most concern the public - vehicle crime, domestic burglary and street robbery'; the submission of progress reports; the creation of a national Crime Reduction Task Force and the appointment of new regional Crime Reduction Directors in government offices for the regions; the publication of crime statistics on a new basis to allow the public to compare rates for individual towns and cities; and a national review of performance by HM Inspectorate of Constabulary, the Audit Commission and the Home Office. There were later references to an extensive programme of support, including training courses, regional seminars, consultancies and a new web-site; and to more support for the police through advances in technology and extra resources.

Later chapters of the strategy described central government's plans for reducing burglary and property crime, for tackling vehicle crime, and for dealing with disorder and anti-social behaviour. All of these included national studies or programmes, for example to make goods or vehicles harder to steal; and specific schemes targeted at local areas. Some of the schemes were for familiar 'situational' or 'physical' forms of crime prevention; others were focused on problems such as run-down or disadvantaged neighbourhoods, truancy and exclusion from school, racially motivated crime, and social exclusion among 13-16 year olds. Other government initiatives, with which schemes for reducing crime had to be co-ordinated on the ground, included Fresh Start, for young children; the New Deal to help young people into employment; the New Deal for Communities aimed at urban regeneration; Action Zones for special initiatives in education, health and housing; and new progammes to provide outdoor activity for 16 year olds.

Each of these schemes or programmes was individually admirable. Each was focused on an area of proven need, and each was designed to make a real difference. Most involved grants of central government funds for specific purposes, in areas which met specified criteria, to be managed by services or partnerships between specified agencies and according to clearly defined objectives, procedures and arrangements for monitoring. Other funds might be made available from the National Lottery or from the European Union. But bids were laborious to construct, and because the process was competitive some of them would always be unsuccessful. A single area or organization might be involved in putting forward several bids, or in managing several schemes, under several different government programmes applying different rules and criteria, all at the same time. The same individual might also be the target of several different programmes.[23] Funds were usually for limited periods of time, and other means of funding the work, or arrangements to absorb it into 'mainstream' programmes, had to be found if it was not to be abandoned at the end of its funding period. Each scheme had to be separately monitored and evaluated, but where several were operating in the same area, or where other changes were taking place in social and economic conditions, opportunities and relationships, it was hard to attribute specific outcomes to specific schemes. In fluid situations of this kind, setting targets for, say, reductions in domestic burglary and vehicle crime, or holding individuals to account for their achievement, becomes an arbitrary and artificial process. Managing a 'crime and disorder reduction partnership' is an extremely complex, confusing, arduous and so far thankless task.

CLOSED CIRCUIT TELEVISION

Closed circuit television has come to be a feature of most police and most local authorities' programmes to prevent crime. It is widely used not only by police and local authorities themselves, but also by public institutions such as schools and hospitals, but also by commercial operators in places such as shops, shopping precincts, car parks, sports grounds (especially football grounds), and railway and 'bus stations. It seems to be almost universally popular, and is claimed to be effective in reducing crime.

The reasons for CCTV's growth, popularity and apparent success are interesting and complicated. Clive Norris and Gary Armstrong have examined them in their book *The Maximum Surveillance Society*.[24] For the public, CCTV gives a feeling of protection and safety in places and situations which can seem potentially threatening or dangerous. Because it uses (relatively) new and interesting technology, it seems modern, innovative and up-to-date. For central and local government and the various 'users', it is a visible sign that 'something is being done'. Its effectiveness is easy to portray (dramatically and tragically when the abduction of Jamie Bulger was shown on national television), and success stories in terms of arrests and recorded crime can readily be produced. There are powerful commercial interests to support the political advantages in promoting its development. Objections based on arguments of civil rights and intrusions into privacy are easily dismissed.

The large-scale presence of CCTV is now taken for granted and almost universally supported. No one who opposes its use or further extension is likely to be taken seriously. But it can be used in different ways for different purposes, and expectations do not always match the reality. It can, most typically, be used to identify individuals who are engaged in committing offences, or who might reasonably be suspected of having done so, and so help to obtain a conviction. It can help to identify potential sources of trouble, and alert police officers or security staff so they can prevent it from happening or deal with it as it occurs. It can provide a source of intelligence by searching for and locating 'wanted' individuals or vehicles. And in a more general sense, it can be used to identify 'undesirables' whom by reason of their appearance or dress the managers might wish to exclude from their premises.

All these purposes, except probably the last, may be legitimate in particular circumstances. In a sense CCTV can be seen as recovering by technological means the knowledge which in smaller communities and in earlier times was taken for granted by people who knew and recognised one another. But the instincts and attitudes behind its use can be those of isolating, controlling and excluding a dangerous or threatening criminal class, with the dangers which earlier chapters have described. Those instincts can often be detected in the language in which CCTV is described and justified.

The issue is not whether the use and development of CCTV - and other forms of technology - should be promoted or opposed, but how they should be managed, regulated and made accountable. Various standards and guidelines already exist, but they are advisory rather than mandatory. They should be reviewed, standardised and placed on a statutory footing, with provision for inspection and enforcement. The use of CCTV raises questions of purpose, professional practice and integrity which are similar to those raised by police powers to stop and search: although the consequences are less public and mistakes are less immediately provocative, similar principles should apply. The aims and purposes of each scheme should be clearly stated, and the results should be rigorously monitored and evaluated against those purposes. Exaggerated claims should be avoided, and corrected if they are made.

Other applications of new technology

CCTV is of course only one of a wide and rapidly increasing range of applications for new technology. Some of them will provide new means of preventing crime or detecting offenders. Some of them will provide new opportunities for committing what are already criminal offences, or new means of doing so; some of them may result in or make possible new forms of social or economic damage which will call for new methods of regulation or the creation of new criminal offences (despite the cautious attitude to new offences which was favoured in *Chapter 11*).

The Crime Prevention Panel set up under the Department of Trade and Industry's Foresight initiative published in March 2000 a consultation document which speculated on the various possibilities.[25] Its most important comment for the purpose of this chapter was as follows

> We are keen to see technology enfranchise people and bring those who might be socially excluded back into the world of employment and opportunity. We cannot. however, ignore the dangers inherent in a technologically divided society where those without access to the technology will suffer in a number of ways. Already certain services are only available through the internet. Not to have access to this, or a bank account, or technology which proves your identity, could significantly damage an individual's ability to function in society. Creating a technologically disenfranchised underclass would further fuel crime and reduce the opportunities for access to mainstream society.

In other respects, however, the language of the document was in terms of an already existing criminal class, separate from the rest of society, which would seek new opportunities and instruments for its criminal activity; and of mainstream or legitimate society which would need to arm itself with new weapons and join forces to defeat its 'enemy'. While it showed considerable ingenuity and imagination in depicting a range of (sometimes alarming) possibilities, the prospects it offered were bleak and discouraging - a shift in theft from material to 'virtual' property (services, information, personal identities, intellectual property), a rise in violence and disorder, an increase in fraud and extortion. The counter-measures it visualised were essentially of a physical and technological kind, because that was the focus of the study and the purpose of the paper: but the most important conclusion to be drawn from it is to be found in the quotation at the beginning of this chapter. The Panel published a full report in November 2000.[26]

PARTNERSHIPS, SKILLS AND EXPERTISE

Establishing and managing a partnership to deal with a 'cross-cutting' issue like crime and disorder requires skills and expertise that are not a natural part of most practitioners' training or professional equipment. Not only that, but the management culture of the last 15 or 20 years has emphasised personal achievement, individual responsibility and competitiveness in ways which have actively discouraged that kind of expertise. Some of the features of the 'new public management' are more associated with the Conservative than the Labour Government, which has consistently emphasised the importance of partnerships and team effort. But much of the 'new public management' survives and has been deliberately, and prominently, carried into the approach described in this chapter. New kinds of expertise and new skills are now needed, for example in supporting new members of staff, preparing them for unfamiliar roles, tasks and situations, giving them the authority and confidence to innovate and take risks, and helping them to be more strategic and less reactive in their attitudes and ideas. But it is not clear how much they will in the end be valued, or how much effort managers or individual practitioners will be prepared to put into developing them.

The Government has put forward, and carried into legislation in the Local Government Act 2000, some rather similar ideas for promoting accountability and the involvement of communities in local government: see *Chapter 5*. Crime and disorder partnerships do not as yet have a well-defined or generally acknowledged structure of accountability. The Strategy reads as if their accountability is exclusively to central government. But members of partnerships must also be accountable

- to the law - they must clearly comply with the Crime and Disorder Act and with the requirements of public law;

- to local authorities, including elected members;

- to police and health authorities, and probation boards;

- to the senior management of their various services;

- to their colleagues in the partnership, and to its stakeholders more generally;

but perhaps above all

- to the communities and citizens whom they serve, who may or may not be direct users of their particular services;

and in the case of voluntary organizations

- to their own supporters, funders and the groups whom they represent.

Some mechanisms of accountability are well established, but mostly on a single-service rather than 'partnership' basis; some are subject to argument and controversy (the roles of focus groups or of elected members of local authorities); some are not yet fully developed, or effective. Managers and practitioners must clearly do their best to set targets and observe priorities which they will share with other services and whose achievement is not directly within their control. But it will not be easy, while the accountability of partnerships is in such a confused, or at least incohate, state, and while partnerships have no collective identity apart from the separate identities of their individual members.

The Government's Crime Reduction Strategy had a good deal to say about local variations, both in levels of crime and in the content of strategic plans, with the implication that relatively high rates of crime or relatively low targets for reductions in vehicle crime or burglary are a reflection on the competence of the police service or local partnership concerned. In interviews and correspondence, Ministers have repeatedly expressed their irritation that local services and partnerships have not so far made many applications for anti-social behaviour orders or child curfew schemes[27], and their annoyance that questions have been asked about whether anti-social behaviour orders might be in conflict with the European Convention On Human Rights and the Human Rights Act 1998.[28]

The Government's irritation could also be seen in changes in its own language and approach. 'Community safety' had been replaced by 'crime reduction'. The original emphasis on a combination of social and of physical and situational measures had given way to an almost exclusive emphasis on the latter, combined with more rigorous detection and enforcement. The change had been accompanied by demands on behalf of ministers for a bewildering array of returns from 'crime and disorder reduction partnerships' in a degree of detail which was difficult to comprehend. The reasons for the Government's change of emphasis no doubt included the perceived lack of immediately visible results, or in their own language the need for 'quick wins'; political anxiety that an increase in recorded crime might affect their Party's prospects at the next general election; and political weakness of the kind which David Garland described in his article on *The Limits of the Sovereign State*[29], and which is discussed in *Chapter 6*. Whatever the reasons, the consequences were potentially damaging.

By the summer of 2000, there were mixed feelings among those concerned with community safety at local level. There was still a sense of optimism based on the opportunity, and to some extent the authority, which were provided by section 17 Crime and Disorder Act. There was still a spirit of goodwill and a willlingness, sometimes a determination, to co-operate. But there was also a sense that the Government itself had moved back from the innovative and progressive approach which that section symbolised, and had retreated into more old-fashioned ideas of law enforcement, crime control and managerialism. Incessant demands for improved performance, in narrowly-defined terms, had become more of a burden than a stimulus; the concentration on burglary and street crime effectively excluded initiatives in other areas and partnerships with those whose interests and potential contributions lay in other directions. Services outside the criminal justice system and voluntary organizations were themselves pre-occupied with the demands imposed by other parts of government, and had little energy or capacity for work which was again made to seem marginal to their core functions and main interests. It was sometimes hard to engage elected members, to draw on their influence, or to 'mainstream' community safety in the ways people had hoped and thought the Government intended. The situation was especially difficult where elected members were politically unsympathetic or where local government's responsibilities were divided between county and district councils. Where energy and interest in community safety could still be found, they seemed to be sustained in spite of, rather than because of, the Government's policies and influence.

The Thames Valley Partnership has shown how an independent organization can act as a mediator and catalyst, generating enthusiasm and commitment, reconciling different professional cultures and attitudes, and promoting and supporting innovative, practical schemes.[30]

APPROACHES AND PRINCIPLES

This chapter has shown how crime prevention came into prominence in the early 1980s as an essentially scientific study of the means of what Ken Pease (1997)[31] has called 'disrupting crime events'. At that stage it was concerned principally with primary prevention; its focus was widened (later in the decade) to include secondary prevention and the broader concept of community safety. On one view, primary prevention which did not consider the social context and motivational factors was unlikely to have more than a limited application or success; it might even have damaging consequences if the effect was to concentrate protection on commercial interests and prosperous individuals, and to exclude or even stigmatise those who were vulnerable or disadvantaged. On another view, many of the potential benefits of primary prevention were dissipated by the political and professional attention which were given to the supposedly less productive and scientifically questionable forms of secondary prevention.

The contrast and tensions between primary and secondary prevention, between crime prevention and community safety, and between exclusionary and inclusive approaches to crime and the means of managing or reducing it, are one of the subjects examined in *Secure Foundations*.[32] Chapter 10 has already referred to Mike Nellis's paper in that collection which develops his notion of community justice, bringing together ideas of community safety and restorative justice in a spirit of shared citizenship and social responsibility, and a strong civil society. A paper by Paul Wiles and Ken Pease suggests that the scope of section 17

Crime and Disorder Act should be extended to the management of risks and hazards more generally, and its application to include all partners in work on crime and disorder (not just the police and local authorities) together with relevant government departments. Other papers deal scientifically with the evidence for what works or does not work, and with practical questions about how to put programmes into operation. The final section looks ahead to the issues which are likely to arise in the future.

In his paper 'Community Safety in the Age of the Risk Society' Gordon Hughes locates the debate in the context of other writing on the ideas of risk, late modernity and community; the argument for a new, radical but inclusive communitarianism; the changing attitudes of and towards government and new modes of government.[33] He writes

> It is now clearly impossible to discuss multi-agency crime prevention and community safety, in the UK and beyond, without engaging in a debate about the changing modalities of state power in relationship to civil society and the public. Indeed, notions of local and central state are themselves becoming increasingly problematic with the risk of the dispersed state or new modes of governance. As a result of these, we are witnessing not a diminution of the state's role but rather an extension of particular forms of state power, although through new and unfamiliar means.

He identifies various dangers in authoritarian, blaming, managerialist, coercive and exclusionary approaches and attitudes; but sees the possibility of a more optimistic 'participatory and democratic' future, a sense of community safety 'as a public good based on citizenship, solidarity and the recognition of difference' with a positive politics which prioritises 'social justice, collective trust, human rights and social inclusion'.

In the final paper 'Democratic Politics and Crime Prevention', Jon Spencer argues the need for secondary as well as primary strategies of crime prevention, but also for them to provide for 'communities with a strong voice in the decision-making process' and to be supported by 'structures that can be seen as being democratically accountable at the local level . . . ' He goes on 'The imposition of a definition of the problem is the one thing that will result in local people abandoning community safety and crime prevention initiatives'.[34]

So far as the Home Office and its expectations of the criminal justice services were concerned, the focus at the end of the 1990s seemed to have returned to primary prevention, but with much greater attention being given at the same time to tertiary prevention, especially through the control of convicted offenders. The Government's programmes which effectively supported secondary prevention remained in place and continued to be developed; public servants charged with promoting community safety at local level continued to take advantage of them when they could; but little or nothing was made of their contribution to community safety in political debate. As elsewhere in criminal justice, the focus was on groups or individuals who were seen as presenting a problem, with an 'exclusionary' pre-occupation with law enforcement, with the identification and control of those who deviate from what is culturally or socially 'normal', for example in terms of family background and patterns of behaviour, with the implication that those who do not conform are part of the dangerous 'other' which needs to be controlled and from which 'ordinary people' need to be protected.[35]

The new orders introduced under the Crime and Disorder Act, described earlier in this chapter and in *Chapter 9* can all be used to reinforce this 'exclusionary' approach. The Government's choice of targets, which it has effectively imposed on local partnerships, seems to be intended to have this result. It does not seem to have much interest in, or give much encouragement to, the kind of social vision which some partnerships have tried to establish to give coherence and inspiration to their work, for example ideas of citizenship, social inclusion, civil responsibility or respect for diversity, or for the painful efforts some local leaders have made to translate them into practical reality.

The impression is of a Government which is impatient with public servants whom it sees insufficiently committed and failing to perform their public duties, and which is determined to shame them if they do not do better. There is no acknowledgement that public servants who have been asked to consult local opinion on their strategic plans might find that local communities see their own priorities in different ways, from each other and from the government, or that public servants might have a duty to respond to those priorities as well as to the demands of central government. There is certainly no suggestion that public servants might have local knowledge and professional experience which might enable them to exercise a more considered judgement of how to deal with local situations and respond to local citizens than ministers who are preoccupied with national targets, figures and political commitments. And there is little recognition that work to promote community safety, if it is to be successful, has to engage the energy, commitment and confidence of local communities, that it therefore has to be democratically accountable at local level, and that elected members of local authorities must not only be involved but also understand and feel some responsibility for what is being done.

Earlier chapters have made the point that preventing crime and dealing with its consequences cannot be left to the criminal justice system. Nor can it be left to the agencies of the state, or treated as a commodity to be bought and paid for by those who can afford it. It involves many kinds of social relationships and support, ranging from individuals 'looking out' for one another to the work of national voluntary organizations. It involves managing and respecting ethnic and cultural diversity. It implies long-term objectives, including support for children in their early years which may not produce results, in terms of lower levels of crime, for another ten or 15 years. In other words, it involves citizenship and civil society. How to develop a suitable framework of local accountability, and how to mobilise civil society in support of the agenda for social support and the reduction of crime, are two of the longer term, more strategic, tasks which the country as a whole has to address. Section 17 Crime and Disorder Act provides a great opportunity which should not be wasted. Given national encouragement and local leadership, the statutory services, the commercial sector and voluntary and community organizations should be able to achieve through partnerships a more productive, responsive and accountable set of social dynamics and professional relationships. And they could provide a practical example of 'putting into action values that go to the heart of the British character: democracy, tolerance, fairness, decency' (as in the Government's Annual Report for 1998-99). There are already models, like the Thames Valley Partnership, which could be followed and extended. But the vision of citizenship, communities and civil society on which they are based must be the inclusive vision described earlier in this chapter and in *Chapter 4*.

ENDNOTES for *Chapter 18*

[1]   Anthony Bottoms and Paul Wiles, 'Environmental Criminology' and Ken Pease, 'Crime Prevention' both in Mike Maguire, Rod Morgan and Robert Reiner (eds.), *The Oxford Handbook of Criminology*, Second edition, Oxford University Press, 1997.

[2]   Scott Ballintyre, Ken Pease and Vic Maclaren, *Secure Foundations*, London, Institute for Public Policy Research, 2000.

[3]   Andrew von Hirsch, David Garland and Alison Wakefield (eds.), *Ethical and Social Perspectives in Situational Crime Prevention*, Oxford, Hart Publishing, 2000.

[4]   Jane Jacobs, *The Death and Life of Great American Cities*, London, Jonathan Cape 1962.

[5]   Oscar Newman, *Defensible Space: People and Design in the Violent City*, London, Architectural Press, 1972.

[6]   James Q. Wilson and Gilbert Kelling, 'Broken Windows: The Police and Neighbourhood Safety', *Atlantic Monthly*, March 1982, pp. 29-38.

[7]   Ronald Clarke and Patricia Mayhew, *Designing Out Crime*, London, HMSO, 1980.

[8]   Tim Hope and Margaret Shaw, *Communities and Crime Reduction*, London, HMSO 1988.

[9]   D. B. Cornish and R. V. Clarke (eds.), *The Reasoning Criminal: Rational Choice Perspectives on Offending*, New York, Springer-Verlag, 1986.

[10]   See for example NACRO, *Crime, Community and Change: Taking Action on the Kingsmead Estate in Hackney*, London, NACRO, 1996.

[11]   There was a good deal of internal discussion about the proper location of the Crime Prevention Unit within the Home Office and its relationship with ministers. It could equally have been located within the Research and Planning Unit, or with the Criminal Policy Department which had the main responsibility for supporting John Patten's new 'joined up' responsibility for co-ordinating criminal policy. The decision to locate the Unit within the Police Department was intended to ensure that the police felt some 'ownership' for crime prevention, and to emphasise the 'soft' or 'social', as well as the 'hard' or 'law enforcement', aspects of police work. The Unit's functions were transferred to what had then become the Directorate of Research, Statistics and Development in 1999.

[12]   Michael Rutter, Henri Giller and Ann Hagell identify and analyse 'resilience' and 'risk' factors, and consider their application to the prevention of crime and delinquency, in *Anti-Social Behaviour by Young People*, Cambridge University Press, 1998.

[13]   Anthony Bottoms, 'Morality, Crime, Compliance and Public Policy', a paper presented to the Leon Radzinowicz Commemoration Symposium in March 2001, Cambridge Institute of Criminology, forthcoming.

[14]   Ken Pease considers the lessons to be learned from the Safer Cities Programme in his chapter on Crime Prevention in the *Oxford Handbook of Criminology*, op. cit. n. 1. He comes to the opposite conclusion, namely that the Safer Cities schemes began to lose impact once they became distracted by attempts to address secondary prevention. But it is not

clear whether he sees secondary prevention as inherently flawed, or only as liable to corruption by a politics which is obsessed by blame, punishment and a need for popular appeal.

[15] Tim Hope 'Community Crime Prevention' in Michael Tonry and David Farrington (eds.), *Building a Safer Society*, Chicago University Press, 1995.

[16] Per-Olof Wikstrom and Rolf Loeber, 'Do Disadvantaged Neighbourhoods Cause Well Adjusted Children to Become Adolescent Delinquents? A Study of Male Juvenile Serious Offending, Individual Risk and Protective Factors and Neighbourhood Context', *Criminology*, 38/4, November 2000, pp. 1109-42.

[17] James Morgan, *Safer Communities: The Local Delivery of Crime Prevention Through the Partnership Approach* (The Morgan Report), London, Home Office, 1991.

[18] Elizabeth Burney, *Crime and Banishment: Nuisance and Exclusion in Social Housing*, Winchester, Waterside Press, 1999.

[19] Jack Straw speaking on the second reading of the Crime and Disorder Bill, House of Commons, 8 April 1998.

[20] Peter Goldbalt and Chris Lewis (eds.), *Reducing Offending: An Assessment of Research Evidence on Ways of Dealing With Offending Behaviour*, Home Office Research Study 187, London, Home Office, 1998.

[21] The Audit Commission, *Safety in Numbers: Promoting Community Safety*, London, Audit Commission, 1999.

[22] Home Office, *The Government's Crime Reduction Strategy*, London, Home Office, November 1999.

[23] The Thames Valley Partnership identified 19 separate schemes or initiatives, all promoted by central government which could help to reduce crime and with which local crime and disorder partnerships might need to be involved; together with five national programmes involving reorganization, modernisation and often new legislation within which work on community safety would have to be accommodated. Thame, Thames Valley Partnership, 2000.

[24] Clive Norris and Gary Armstrong, *The Maximum Surveillance Society: The Rise of CCTV*, Oxford, Berg, 1999.

[25] Foresight Crime Prevention Panel 2000, *Just Around the Corner: A Consultation Document*, London, Department of Trade and Industry, 2000. See also Michelle Rogerson, Paul Ekblom and Ken Pease, 'Crime Reduction and the Benefit of Foresight' in Scott Ballintyne, Ken Pease and Vic McLaren (eds.), *op. cit*, n. 2.

[26] Foresight Crime Prevention Panel, *Turning the Corner*, London, Department of Trade and Industry, 2000.

[27] In letters and meetings with police and local authorities in the late summer of 1999, reported in the *Guardian* 7 September 1999 and the Home Secretary's Address to the Local Government Association on 26 June 2000. See also Elizabeth Burney, *op. cit.*, n. 18.

[28] Andrew Ashworth, John Gardner, Rod Morgan, A. H. T. Smith, Andrew von Hirsch, and Martin Wasik, 'Neighbouring on the Oppressive: the Government's Community Safety Order Proposals', *Criminal Justice* , 16:1, 1998, pp. 7-14.

[29] David Garland, 'The Limits of the Sovereign State: Strategies of Crime Control in Contemporary Society', *British Journal of Criminology*, 1996, 4, p. 36.

[30] Information on the Thames Valley Partnership is available on the partnership's web-site: www.thamesvalleypartnership.org.uk

[31] *Op. cit.*, n. 1.

[32] *Op. cit.*, n. 2.

[33] Gordon Hughes, 'Community Safety in the Age of the Risk Society', *loc. cit.*, n. 2.

[34] Jon Spencer, 'Democratic Politics and Crime Prevention', *loc. cit.*, n. 2.

[35] In November 2000 the Home Office published three briefing papers: Richard Hester, *Crime and Disorder Partnerships: Voluntary and Community Sector Involvement*; Karen Bullock, Kate Moss and Jonathan Smith, *Anticipating the Impact of Section 17 of the Crime and Disorder Act*; Coretta Phillips, Mary Considine and Rachel Lewis, *A Review of Audi[t] and Strategies Produced by Crime and Disorder Partnerships in 1999*.

CHAPTER 19

Prisons and Penal Reform

> It is fundamental to the Prison Service's position as part of the Criminal Justice System that it should ensure that prisoners are treated with justice in prisons.
>
> From the Woolf Report, 1991

> We must not forget that when every material improvement has been made in prisons . . . the convict stands deprived of everything that a free man calls life.
>
> Winston Churchill, speaking in the House of Commons on 20 July 1910

THE REFORMER'S DILEMMA

Penal reformers face a number of dilemmas. Their main aim has always been to reduce the number of people who are sent to prison and the length of time for which they stay there. But there is no objective or universal standard by which it can be said that a country's prison population is too high or too low, and that judgement has to be made by reference to the situation in other comparable countries, to the amount and cost of the accommodation that is available, or to public opinion. Attempts have been made, in Great Britain and in the United States, to justify increases in the use of imprisonment by reference to the number of crimes which would be prevented because more criminals would be off the streets; or reductions in its use, by claiming that crime would not be significantly increased and that it might actually fall. Neither claim can be conclusively, or even convincingly, substantiated for those who are not persuaded already, although it does seem that a significant reduction in crime could only be achieved by a very dramatic increase in the prison population at an arguably disproportionate fiscal and social cost.

Reformers are also keen to improve the treatment of prisoners and the conditions in which they are held, and to promote regimes which will help towards prisoners' resettlement and reduce their re-offending after their release. But the more conditions are improved, the less inclined the courts and public opinion will be to resist the use of imprisonment on a large scale; and the greater the success that prisons are thought to achieve in resettlement and a reduction in re-offending, the more courts and the public are likely to favour their even greater use.

Opponents of capital punishment faced, and in some countries still face, a similar dilemma: the more safeguards that are introduced to prevent miscarriages of justice, and the more the methods of execution are made quick, painless or humane, the harder it becomes to argue for its

The arguments for penal reform are therefore quite complex. Few reformers (though there are some) would argue that imprisonment should be abolished altogether. There is no 'natural' or 'proper' prison population or level of imprisonment to which reformers can appeal, and comparisons with other countries, if the United States is included, can be used to support both sides of the argument. Reformers can properly protest if prisons are overcrowded, but it is more difficult to find arguments of principle, as distinct from cost, with which to resist a programme of new building. They are therefore left with three main arguments. The first is the 'human rights' argument that restrictions on the liberty of citizens should always be imposed as sparingly as possible, and that the conditions of imprisonment should be as humane and civilised as possible. The second is the claim that the aims of resettlement and the prevention of re-offending can be achieved more successfully by programmes based in the community, without the socially damaging effects of imprisonment such as separation from families and loss of employment. The third is the economic argument that prisons are an expensive resource to be used as sparingly as possible.

The three arguments are all powerful in themselves. But the first is difficult to deploy effectively in a climate of hostile political and public opinion. The second relies on empirical evidence which is at present inconclusive, and loses credibility if offenders in the community re-offend in even greater numbers or regularly fail to turn up for their programmes. The third is also difficult to sustain against hostile political and public opinion, and hard to apply in practice when responsibilities for supplying the resources and for committing their use are divided between central government on the one hand and individual judges and magistrates on the other, with not much effective communication between them, and constitutional objections to making the relationship too close. Successive governments' attempts to manage the criminal justice system more effectively at national and local level have been discussed in *Chapters 7* and *9*, and they are considered again in *Chapter 21*.

This book does not attempt to argue for a reduction in the use of imprisonment to any particular level, or for the prison population to be restricted to any particular figure. But it has argued in *Chapter 12* that the arrangements for managing the criminal justice system should be designed so as to bring about a better and more stable alignment between sentencing policy and practice on the one hand, and the resources needed to give effect to sentencing decisions on the other. The underlying principle, applied to both custodial sentences and to sentences served in the community, should be that the state's restrictions on a citizen's liberty should be no greater than is necessary to protect the rights of other citizens; and that in particular cases they should be proportionate to the situation and the objective to be achieved. *Chapter 21* considers the mechanisms for interpreting that principle and applying it in practice.

MANAGEMENT AND MANAGERIALISM

Management and managerialism first arrived in the Prison Service in the 1960s. Before that, the service had seen itself as concerned more with individuals and relationships than with structures and systems. Advertisements for assistant governors emphasised social work and personal intervention with offenders, usually young offenders in borstal. Assistant governors in borstals, and in some prisons, were known as housemasters. Later advertisements referred to 'social work with management' and then to 'management with a social purpose'. By the early 1970s, 'management' stood alone and 'management' began to occupy a separate place in the service's organizational culture, distinct from work with prisoners or staff. Each of the three parties which make up the prison 'community' – governors, officers and prisoners - was potentially in conflict with the other two, and any two of them could collude with one another against the third. Administrative and specialist staff – instructors, teachers, probation officers, psychologists, chaplains – were often treated as outsiders.

The Prison Service was deeply affected by the new public management described in *Chapter 2*, and by the Labour Government's programme for modernising justice services described in *Chapter 3*. Examples included the transition to agency status, the contracting out of prisons and prison functions, and the new management culture of targets and indicators. David Wilson and Shane Bryans, in their book *The Prison Governor: Theory and Practice*[1], describe the practical impact of those measures, and in particular the impact of Prison Department Circular Instruction 55 of 1984 with its statement of the prison governor's responsibilities, on the task of the Prison Service as a whole, on the functions of establishments, and on the mechanisms for the governor's accountability. They describe the 'doctrinal components' of new public management and their application to the Prison Service through recruitment from the private sector, key performance indicators, devolution to governors of responsibilities for personnel and finance, contracting out, performance pay, the development of 'core competencies', and in other ways. They also describe the reaction of some governors to the 'new' values of efficiency and pragmatism which they saw as replacing those of care and humanity. As usual in the Prison Service, the impact of those measures, and individuals' reactions to them, were different in different places and were experienced in different ways by different people.

OPTIMISM AND DISILLUSION: THE POLITICS OF IMPRISONMENT

The Prison Service enjoyed a period of optimism at the beginning of the 1990s. The prison population had been falling, and the Woolf Report (see *Chapter 7*) offered the prospect of a period of stability and progress, based on an active interpretation of the service's mission statement, already quoted in *Chapter 7* and especially its reference to 'looking after prisoners with humanity'. Delivering the Eve Saville Memorial Lecture in June 1992[2], Joe Pilling, the Director General, said that humanity comprised 'five distinct, yet inter-related concepts, respect, fairness, individuality, care and openness'. He went on to describe how each of these concepts could be translated into the management of prisons.

Chapter 8 has described the change of political direction which took place at the end of 1992 and during 1993. The Prison Service suffered the direct consequences of that change in the rise in the prison population, and ministers' different expectations of how prisoners should be treated. There was an increase in suicides and instances of self-harm. Following disturbances and escapes, the service experienced the Woolf, Lygo, Woodcock and Learmont reports.[3] Those reports, and the Government's reactions to them, sent conflicting messages to the service, which was at the same time adjusting to its new status as an executive agency and a different relationship with ministers (see *Chapter 8* and below).

The service nevertheless had some important improvements to its credit. They included an end, more or less, to three-in-a-cell and slopping out; more purposeful activity for prisoners; and the disappearance, from most parts of most prisons, of the stench of urine and stale food. Staff became increasingly skilled at many of the tasks they had to perform. Many of these improvements could be associated with the effects of the new public management.

Under the Labour Government, the Prison Service benefited from a massive increase in funds from the Government's Comprehensive Spending Reviews, and came to enjoy a more relaxed relationship with ministers; but in many other respects its situation remained more or less unchanged. Ministers and the leading figures in the Prison Service made well-intentioned and often liberal speeches but it was noticed that they were still saying much the same things as were being said by their predecessors 30 years before.[4] Energetic policy-making at headquarters still took a long time to show consistent results on the ground. There always (or almost always) seemed to be a brighter future ahead, but it was usually snatched away by some new crisis or turn of events. In the summer of 2000 there was probably a feeling of optimism, and a hope of a more consistent sense of direction, almost as there had been after the Woolf Report eight years before. It was reinforced by the allocation of funds from the Comprehensive Public Spending Review to expand the system's capacity by another 2,660 prison places, and to develop vocational training and preparation for employment after release. And yet, despite the service's generally able and enlightened leadership, and the professionalism and dedication of many of the staff, there were still 'failing' institutions, such as at various times Wormwood Scrubs, Wandsworth, Feltham, Portland and Brixton; chronic lack of provision in services like education and health; and among some members of staff an attitude which was ready to treat prisoners as an inferior and probably dangerous section of humanity. Moments of crisis were dealt with as they arose, but the politics of imprisonment and the dynamics of the prison system seemed to allow the general situation to continue year to year and from generation to generation.

STRUCTURE AND RELATIONSHIPS

Prison reform will never attract many votes. But prison conditions always attract public attention, and because in the end they reflect the values of society as a whole, no responsible government can afford to neglect them - politically or morally. The Prison Service, like the police, needs an ethical foundation for its work, strong professional leadership and a structure which ensures integrity and public accountability.

Successive governments have for a long time - perhaps since the national system was established in 1877 - found difficulty in sustaining a satisfactory relationship between the Prison Service and the central Home Office, ministers and Parliament; or between Prison Service Headquarters and prison establishments in the field. Arguments for greater integration or for greater separation, both between the service and the Home Office and between establishments and headquarters, have ebbed and flowed. Successive reorganizations have been introduced, modified and abandoned with increasing rapidity since the Prison Commission was finally dissolved in 1963 (the change having been argued over for 15 years since statutory provision for the Commission's dissolution was made in the Criminal Justice Act 1948). The arguments were much the same over the years, but they became more intense, and reorganizations have become more frequent (and more disruptive), as the Prison Service gained in political salience and its operational situation became more precarious. Arguments about internal reorganization distracted attention from other, possibly more important, questions affecting the service's culture, dynamics and internal and external relationships. A pre-occupation - it might even be said an obsession - with the 'unity' of the Prison Service led to the weakening of self-confidence and sense of professional identity which had once been characteristic of the women's and young offenders' parts of the service.

The events of the mid-1990s led to another, internal, review of the management arrangements and organizational structure of the Prison Service, which Arthur de Frisching carried out during 1997.[5] The Service's relationship with ministers was clearly a sensitive matter in the circumstances of the time, on which the Home Affairs Committee of the House of Commons had said[6]

> It is not possible to lay down a rigid dividing line between the roles of Ministers and of the Director General of the agency. If the arrangements for running the agency are to work properly there has to be a good relationship between the Home Secretary and the Director General. The Home Secretary must leave proper freedom to the Director General to do his or her job. At the same time, there is no point in Ministers, the Director General, or Parliament, harbouring unrealistic expectations of the extent to which Ministers can be excluded from the operational process; the needs of accountability and responsibility to Parliament will require some measure of Ministerial involvement.

The report of the Management Review made a number of useful but conventional recommendations for asserting and reinforcing Ministerial responsibility for the service; for improving regimes and preparations for release; and for improving the organization's effectiveness, including changes in the training and development of managers and measures concerned with the service's values and culture. Most of those recommendations were put at least nominally into effect or work is in progress. The report also commented

> There is a striking repetitiveness about the findings of these reviews. They give the impression that the Prison Service lacks both the ability and the will to get to grips with key management issues and to see through major change. There is also a preoccupation with structural change as the solution to failings, despite a good deal of material devoted to managerial competence, staff performance and issues of culture and style.

The report was right to draw attention to the limitations of structural change as a solution to failings, and its relatively cautious approach to management change was understandable and appropriate to the circumstances of the time.

Another report, this time from the Targeted Performance Initiative Working Group, chaired by Lord Laming, appeared three years later. Their report *Modernising the Management of the Prison Service* sought to find the means of preventing the shortcomings which HM Chief Inspector of Prisons had identified in certain establishments. It did so by addressing three questions: how is the service managed; how is its performance evaluated; and, how can the range of contacts with outside agencies and the community be improved. The Working Group was struck by the conflicting elements in the organizational structure, including the lack of continuity among prison governors; uncertainty about the responsibilities of area managers; the range of people who can instruct governors; and the lack of co-ordination or compatibility between different initiatives or programmes; and the volume of paper and bureaucratic inertia.

It is a sad reflection that all these impressions would have been shared by any member or observer of the Prison Service at any time in the previous 40 years. The themes which the Group identified - improved communications, clear lines of command, better working relationships, independence from ministers in day-to-day operations - had been repeatedly argued over the same period. What was new and most encouraging about the report was its recognition that local community-based agencies can be a source of strength to a prison establishment, and can have a role both in this identification of failing prisons and in their recovery. But its recommendations for stronger and better co-ordinated links, and a new role and responsibilities for boards of visitors, were left largely as a matter for training, encouragement and aspiration; and in the case of boards of visitors, for a further review.

The report states firmly, and correctly so far as the present structure is concerned, that the Prison Service is not a 'federal' service. But a conclusion which could be drawn from its own analysis, from the earlier analysis in the Prison Service Review, and from the history of earlier reports to which they both refer, is not that fresh efforts must constantly be made to reinforce the existing, monolithic 'command' structure of the organization, but that a new, more devolved, more flexible and, above all, more locally-based organization is now needed.

THE PRISON SERVICE AGENCY

Much has been written about the constitutional significance of agency status in general, and views differ on whether it represents a fundamental change in the machinery of government and even in the nature of the state, with profound constitutional implications; or whether it is simply a clarification of functions, objectives and responsibilities designed to put existing relationships on a more business-like footing (see *Chapter 2*). For the Prison Service, agency status was at first generally welcomed, both by the service itself and by penal reformers, as providing for greater flexibility and protection from political interference in operational matters. It seems nevertheless to have been disregarded under the Conservative Government when ministers thought they had the opportunity to score political points, as Derek Lewis, Director General of the Prison Service during the mid-1990s, has described.[8] However that may be, the separation of the 'purchasing' or 'commissioning' function from the 'producing' or 'providing' function, which was fundamental to the original concept of agency status, was not in the event applied to the Prison Service Agency. The reason was the difficulty in making the corresponding distinction between 'policy' and 'operations' (a difficulty confirmed by the reaction to the escapes from Parkhurst, when an attempt was made to revive it for political convenience), and the result was a deliberate decision to maintain a unified structure - except for establishments contracted out to the private sector - without a corresponding function of 'ownership' in the central Home Office. As a consequence, the 'ownership' of the Prison Service Agency was confined to ministers and the permanent secretary, and the Director General was placed in an exposed and eventually intolerable position. The short-lived 'monitoring unit' did not seem to be a success.[9]

PRINCIPLES OF PRISON SERVICE REFORM

The Government's general position on the reform or modernisation of public services, and on reaffirming the country's social and civil values, has been discussed in *Chapters 3* and *4*. It is worth recalling that policy-making had to be joined up and strategic; that government was to be inclusive and integrated and more forward and outward looking; and that public services were to reflect real lives, with programmes that were citizen-focused, group-focused and area-based. They were to develop a new culture of citizenship, responsibilities and human rights. *Chapter 4* has discussed some of the features of that culture, and *Chapter 5* has examined the principles of values of public service.

Applied to the Prison Service, those requirements might take the following form.

- The Prison Service is not unique among public services, and the Government's approach should apply to the management of prisons as it applies to the management of other public services. Prisons are exceptionally complex institutions, and managing them is an exceptionally complex task, but that is a different point.

- The Government's commitment to fairness, opportunity, inclusiveness and citizenship should apply to offenders as it does to anyone else. Offenders, including prisoners, are still citizens.

- Programmes to reduce re-offending, and to deal with problems such as drugs and alcohol, clearly have an important place in any prison regime. But if the Government is really determined to reduce crime, it must recognise that jobs, homes and families are likely to have more influence on offending and re-offending than any programme which can be provided in prisons.

- Punishment is a matter for the courts, not for the Prison Service. The service is not an agency of punishment, and the content of prison regimes should not be made deliberately unpleasant, still less humiliating or degrading, as a means of reinforcing the sentence's punitive effect (see also *Chapter 13*).

- As citizens and human beings, prisoners are to be regarded as having equal worth as people with other members of society and of the prison community, although their position is necessarily different in terms of authority and status.

- The restrictions of imprisonment should be proportionate to the objectives which have to be achieved and what the public interest requires. As Lord Wilberforce argued in *Raymond v Honey* in 1983, they should be able to function as citizens in the wider community to the extent that they are not prevented by the fact of their imprisonment. The Government should not argue, as Lord Bassam did in the House of Lords on 25 October 1999, that 'those who are convicted and serving a sentence have no moral right to vote'. The test of proportionality will be particularly significant if, as JUSTICE have argued, it comes to be applied systematically under the Human Rights Act.

- Within the law, and the policy as approved by Parliament, the treatment of individual prisoners should be a matter of professional and managerial, and not of political judgement.

The principle of proportionality, developed in the jurisprudence of the European Court of Human Rights, should apply not only to sentencing but also within prisons themselves. Conditions should be no more restrictive than are required for the purposes to be achieved - the prevention of escapes, especially escapes of prisoners who would present a danger to the public; safety of staff, prisoners and others associated with the establishment; order, integrity and mutual respect in its regime and working relationships. But there should be a more positive aspect as well - an attempt to achieve some sense of progress and improvement in the lives of prisoners and staff, and of the communities with which the prison is associated. Prisoners as citizens should be encouraged - and given opportunities - to function or prepare themselves to function as citizens of their communities, with the rights, responsibilities and respect which go with that status. [10] There should be no suggestion, for example, that those who have been convicted and are serving sentences have lost their moral right to vote. [11] Pressures placed on prisons, including pressures of overcrowding, should not be allowed to compromise that principle.

Practical application
The practical application of these principles, and of the Human Rights Act, presents some interesting challenges for prison programmes and regimes, for example in areas such as education, training, contact with families, and preparations for release and subsequent employment.

Programmes and regimes must be varied, individualised, and closely related both to prisoners' personal circumstances and to local conditions. They should be closely integrated with services which are provided in the ordinary community, especially those for health, education, social services and housing. They should be provided by the same authorities or organizations as those which provide them for other local citizens, and to the same standards. It has always been difficult to provide work in prisons which can be done to normal commercial or industrial standards (it could cynically be said that it can rarely, if ever, be done under a democratic government or without some risk of corruption), but work should similarly be placed and managed so far as possible by local firms. On this view, some provisions and programmes can be justified - and required - not only instrumentally as a means of preventing re-offending or maintaining order within the prison, but also in their own right as a matter of decency and civilised treatment. [12] The Social Exclusion Unit's wide-ranging review of measures to reduce re-offending by ex-prisoners, still in progress at the time of writing, has the potential to become a major instrument of penal reform.

Staffing arrangements should be more flexible and allow both for continuity in particular posts and for movement to and from work outside prisons. Consistency and equality of treatment must be maintained within a national legal framework of national standards, but there should be scope for local initiative and innovation at particular establishments, and for local variation to take account both of local opportunities, and of differences in prisoners' age, gender and culture.

s one of the lessons of Sir William Macpherson's inquiry into the Stephen Lawrence. [13]

Accountability and legitimacy

Earlier chapters have argued that modern and public services, especially those which are concerned with crime and criminal justice, are intimately connected with the rights and responsibilities of citizenship. Their lines of accountability must run in several directions. They must run vertically, connecting the services' managers and practitioners with government departments, ministers and Parliament; and horizontally, connecting them with other organizations, and interests (their 'stakeholders'), and the citizens whom they serve. Services should operate their system of accountability positively and enthusiastically in the knowledge that they will ultimately benefit. They should not be defensive, or try to 'get by' with the minimum that will be accepted, but should welcome the opportunities to communicate, to explain, and above all to learn.

A prison, like any other public service or institution, must be not only accountable but also legitimate. That is to say that it must operate on a basis of confidence, trust and mutual respect between all those who make up the prison community - management, staff and prisoners. There must also be a relationship of confidence, trust and respect between the prison and those who have an interest or a stake in how it functions: courts; other criminal justice services; families and friends of those who work in the prison and those who are detained in it; the local community more generally. Staff should not, for example, be ashamed to say where they work; and those who visit prisoners must not be made to feel awkward or humiliated.

Richard Sparks, Anthony Bottoms and Will Hay discuss the notion of legitimacy in some detail in their book *Prisons and the Problem of Order*.[14] Criteria of legitimacy include, but are more than, acceptance and consent. They also include transparency, conformity to rules, and the justifiability of the rules in terms of shared basic beliefs. They include a sense of common humanity. Legitimacy resembles, but is more than, the sense of justice which Lord Woolf emphasised in his report. It is related to the use of power and authority, to the extent to which prisoners - and staff - have some degree of autonomy and self-determination, and to the assessment and management of risk. It is not a matter of appeasement, though the line between humanity and appeasement may sometimes be difficult to draw in practice, especially in situations where it is thought that prisoners might abuse any humanity which is shown towards them.

The command model which has so far prevailed in the Prison Service is now coming to be seen as rather old-fashioned. In the commercial sector it belongs to the era of production lines and smoke stack industries. In most of the public sector it is too rigid to cope with the complexity, diversity and potential conflicts of modern public service. It is certainly not suited to an approach to social problems which is built on the ideas of citizenship and civil society. And it is not suitable for the Prison Service if the Service is to protect the public through programmes of social rehabilitation and resettlement as well as through physical control. A fundamental transformation is needed in the way most prisons operate and the way prison staff perceive their own jobs and responsibilities, so that initiative and responsibility are shared throughout the organization. Prisons should be more closely linked to the communities which they serve and in which they are located. As Tim Newell has written in 'Forgiving Justice'.[15]

> Geographical location and architectural structures emphasise the exclusion of the community and the inward-looking nature of the institutions. Prisoners' families, friends and other visitors often have difficulty gaining access to the prison. This isolation allows the prison to operate as a kind of eternal exile, which in turn allows the community to ignore our responsibility for the existence of the prison system. This can be reinforced by the geographical and social isolation of prison staff. As imprisonment raises issues of social as well as individual responsibility, all of us have to accept social and political responsibility for prisons, and to open them up to community scrutiny and accountability.

The Service must clearly be able to satisfy ministers, Parliament and the public that it is performing satisfactorily, that it is not putting the public at risk, and that it is properly managed. But it must also be flexible, resilient and capable of adapting to changing situations and circumstances. It needs an outward-looking, problem-solving orientation. The service needs skills that extend not only to delivering programmes and enforcing requirements in accordance with centrally imposed standards and targets, but also to generating the will for communities and individuals to play their part in measures to enable offenders to carry out their obligations and responsibilities as citizens. Together with the Probation Service, the service should make a dynamic contribution to the wider aspects of community safety and public confidence. Communities should have some sense of ownership and responsibility for their prisons, as they do for their hospitals and schools.

The service's skills should therefore include those of listening, consultation, and in the broadest sense mediation, so that solutions to problems emerge from the 'bottom up', with the ownership and commitment of those who experience or are affected by them. The solutions need to be holistic and co-ordinated, to be 'joined up' laterally as well as vertically, and to engage all sections of the community so that young people or others who may be seen as the problem can become part of the solution. Those skills and approaches are likely to lead to more successful, accountable and legitimate forms of working than any which could be achieved by a central, prescriptive definition of the tasks to be performed. The introduction of review courts as discussed in *Chapters 12* and *13,* and a right of prisoners to vote in general and local elections, could both help to bring prisons closer to their communities and to strengthen their accountability and legitimacy.

CONFLICTS, TENSIONS AND AMBIGUITIES

The Prison Service must be able to resolve the conflicts, tensions and ambiguities which are to be found in any modern public service. Those which apply particularly to it are between

- political responsiveness and managerial efficiency;
- centralisation and delegation;
- uniformity and diversity;
- certainty and flexibility;
- central direction and local initiative;
- security and justice;
- good order and humanity;
- due process and individual discretion.

Joe Pilling described some of these tensions in his Eve Saville lecture, already mentioned.

Several legitimate interests must therefore be reconciled, both in the formulation of policy and in the ways in which the service conducts its business locally on the ground. That reconciliation should not be just or even primarily a matter of political judgement or ministerial or central direction - a point which is interestingly brought out in the Public Management Foundation's report on *Wasted Values: Harnessing the Commitment of Public Managers*.[16] It needs a stable pattern of working relationships founded on trust and mutual respect; it also requires an organizational structure, and a framework of accountability, which will sustain those relationships and a wider sense of public confidence. That reconciliation was, and perhaps is still, part of the role of the administrative civil servants who have over the years been seconded to the Prison Commission or appointed to the Prison Department. It was their task to interpret the wishes of ministers to the service, and vice versa. The task was always a source of tension, even though the relationship between individuals was usually one of mutual respect, and it may be harder to sustain in modern circumstances. In more recent years, a number of individuals have moved, in both directions, between 'operational' posts in the Prison Service and 'administrative' policy posts in the central Home Office. This may be the pattern for the future. However it is achieved, an intermediate role is needed if the service's relationship with ministers is to be successfully maintained. Even in times of stability and mutual confidence, it asks too much of the Chief Executive or Director General for the relationship to be focused on one individual.

A NEW ORGANIZATIONAL STRUCTURE?

The model which suggests itself is therefore not a national Prison Service with a unified command structure; a single, exclusive, channel of accountability to ministers and Parliament; a large, monolithic, national headquarters; or a traditional and inflexible pattern of permanent careers.

The new structure might be on these lines. A directorate within the Home Office would be responsible for penal policy and legislation; or, as it might now be said, corrections policy and legislation in both its custodial and non-custodial aspects. In the latest re-organization of the criminal side of the Home Office, the Director, Sentencing and

Correctional Policy, already has that responsibility. The directorate would also be charged with co-ordinating that policy - or with 'joining it up' - with other relevant aspects of government policy. In that respect it would be associated with the Criminal Justice Consultative Council and the new Sentencing Advisory Panel, both of which might need to have their functions expanded and formalised. On the directorate's advice, ministers would establish principles, and set national objectives and standards. In consultation with the Treasury, they would set national budgets.

Alongside, but detached from, the Home Office directorate, a commissioning authority would negotiate, enforce and review contracts with a range of 'providing' organizations. It would develop models and guidelines for good practice, support and evaluate innovative programmes and methods, and commission research. It would provide, sponsor, or accredit the service's professional training. It might in some ways resemble the Youth Justice Board; but this is also where, at national level, the Service's inspiration and professional leadership would be primarily located. Its members would be chosen accordingly.

Providing organizations would manage groups of institutions or perhaps, exceptionally, a single institution such as the therapeutic prison at Grendon. Their configuration would need a good deal of thought. Women's prisons and young offender institutions would be two obvious candidates. The Criminal Justice and Court Services Act 2000 abolished the separate sentencing arrangements for young offenders aged 18-21 and the separate statutory designation of young offender institutions (what has come to be called the 'young offender estate'), but ministers indicated in proceedings on the Bill that institutions for young offenders would continue to have a separate identity within the Prison Service. This age range might be extended up to 23 or 25. For men's prisons there might be a combination of locally-based organizations providing a range of facilities for a particular area, and functionally-based organizations providing, say, maximum security or other specialised prisons. Some providing organizations might even manage a combination of custodial and community-based facilities. Institutions for children and young people under 18 would be taken out of the prison system altogether, but would be similarly organized in relation to the Youth Justice Board as their commissioning authority.

A logical extension of these suggestions would be for the commissioning authority to have a similar function in relation to the Probation Services (see *Chapter 20*). Such an arrangement would enable the authority to take a more comprehensive and strategic view of the type of provision and capacity that are required, to make comparisons of the cost, quality and effectiveness of different programmes, and to arrange its commissioning priorities accordingly; it would encourage the funding of a wider range of innovative projects and methods; and it would reduce the scope for perverse financial incentives.

Providing organizations would be corporate statutory bodies, with executive and non-executive directors able to reflect a range of both local and professional interests. They would be charged with providing services to specific standards within an agreed level of cost, and held to account by the commissioning authority on behalf of the Secretary of State. They would also be rooted in, and accountable to, local communities, and communities would be brought to accept some responsibility for the organizations' work and for the services and institutions they provide.

A structure of this kind would be consistent with the Government's programme of Best Value for local authorities, as set out for example in the Department for the Environment, Transport and the Regions Circular 10/99 issued under the Local Government Act 1999, with its emphasis on 'variety of provision and plurality of providers'.

There is no structural reason why some providing organizations should not be commercial companies or voluntary, not-for-profit, organizations. Many commercial companies operate in a complex environment in which the national interest, ethics and public feeling have all to be taken into account. Experience with the privatised railway has however raised questions about the extent to which a commercial company whose accountability is primarily to its shareholders can satisfactorily provide a public service which is of crucial importance to the safety and well-being of the country as a whole. If independent providers were to be included, it should be to introduce new ideas and methods of working, perhaps for particular groups of offenders, and not to provide competition for its own sake or a separate, private, source of capital. (The Private Finance Initiative or Public-Private Partnership raises much wider questions of government finance and economic management which have been mentioned in *Chapter 2*). Above all, use of commercial providers must never be allowed to generate a 'politics of imprisonment', in which their shareholders' interests come to have an insidious effect on policy, legislation or practice, or take precedence over the public or national interest.

The whole structure would continue to be subject to inspection and audit, using the existing Inspectorate, the Prisons Ombudsman, the Audit Commission and the National Audit Office, and supported by a programme of strategic research as well as by short-term monitoring and evaluation. Those arrangements should however be reviewed to see how they could be made better co-ordinated and more coherent and effective. It would also be for consideration whether the role of the Ombudsman could be expanded to become that of an adjudicator, as the Woolf report recommended; and whether the arrangements for audit could take a wider view of the national interest than is implied by their present concentration on financial propriety and cost effectiveness. If review costs are introduced as a result of this review of the sentencing framework (see *Chapter 12*), they could provide an additional and potentially valuable mechanism for accountability. The role, and perhaps even the usefulness, of boards of visitors has now become rather uncertain, but proposals for their future should emerge from this review which was in progress at the time of writing.

Parliament should also exercise more systematic supervision than the divided and rather haphazard oversight that is at present provided by the Home Affairs, Public Accounts and Public Administrative Committees of the House of Commons and by the House of Lords. And the Prison Service is likely to be increasingly called to account in the courts, whether by judicial review or under the Human Rights Act.

CULTURE AND VALUES

The considerations set out in this and earlier chapters require changes not only in matters of programmes, regimes, and prisoners' rights and responsibilities, but also in prison culture and in the patterns of employment of staff. A culture which values diversity and gives equal respect to individuals requires multi-disciplinary teams which are not dominated by any one professional, institutional or cultural background. There should be a positive attitude to the assessment and management of risk, so that the aim is accurate assessment and responsible management, rather than an attempt to eliminate or avoid risk altogether. There should be recognition and respect for initiative, achievement and conscientious effort, rather than a culture of blame and punishment; and investment in expertise, skills, professional confidence and trust, rather than excessive reliance on rules and central directions. Procedures for problem-solving, mediation and conciliation, using the principles of restorative justice which are now being developed not only by Thames Valley Police but also in schools and other institutions, should where possible replace the formal adversarial procedures for discipline and punishment. Staff and prisoners should address one another by name. Uniform, if it is worn at all, should be smart but relatively informal.

As *Chapter 13* has already argued, the release of prisoners serving mandatory life sentences for murder should clearly cease to be a matter of political decision by the Home Secretary; and the present emphasis on risk assessment and public protection raises increasingly difficult questions about the relationship between sentencing and the operation of the parole system. Similar questions arise from the government's proposals for the indefinite detention of persons suffering from dangerous and severe personality disorder. Again, the Human Rights Act may have important implications.

CONCLUSIONS

This chapter has raised some questions about the Labour Government's vision for a modern Britain and its implications for the Prison Service, and has suggested what some of the features of a modern prison service should be. It has not attempted to put forward a fully worked out scheme. What might be practicable in the short term is likely to be severely constrained by overcrowding, and by the nature and geographical distribution of the prison estate. Few of the questions have simple or self-evident answers. Examples of some which do not are

- the balance between uniformity and diversity, and how much diversity in prison conditions or treatment can properly be sustained or tolerated in a legitimate society;

- the arguments between a geographical or a functional form of organization;

- the extent to which prisons can realistically relate to local communities, or adopt a different culture or pattern of relationships from those which prevail at present (it has been argued within the Prison Service that the nature of prison institutions and prison life make this impossible, but this argument seems unnecessarily conservative and to the extent that it has any force the answers may be different for different types of institution);

- the mechanisms of accountability and the balance between political, administrative and legal methods of holding prisons to account;

- how to devise funding arrangements which match the structure of authority and responsibility and avoid perverse incentives.

But those questions should be on the national agenda; and the answers should be informed by a principled and coherent sense of direction and purpose. The increased funding made available to provide 2000 new prison places, announced by the Chancellor of the Exchequer and the Home Secretary in July 2000 should be the starting point for a re-appraisal of the organizational structure of prison establishments, their functions and their geographical distribution; and for a review of the mechanisms for achieving a better alignment between supply and demand. The first should take as its starting point the arguments put forward earlier in this chapter, the second is discussed in *Chapter 21*.

ENDNOTES for *Chapter 19*

[1] Shane Bryans and David Wilson, 'The Prison Governor: Theory and Practice', *Prison Service Journal*, 1998.

[2] Joe Pilling, The Eve Saville Memorial Lecture, 'Back to Basics: Relationships in the Prison Service', in *Perspectives on Prison: A Collection of Views on Prison Life and Running Prisons*, Supplement to the Annual Report of the Prison Service 1991-1992, Cmnd. 2087, London, HMSO, June 1992.

[3] Lord Justice Woolf, *Report of an Inquiry into the Prison Disturbances of April 1990*, Cmnd. 1456, London, HMSO 1991. See also *Management of the Prison Service: Report by Admiral Sir Raymond Lygo KCB*, London, Home Office 1991; *Report of the Enquiry into The Escape of Six Prisoners From the Special Security Unit at Whitemoor Prison Cambridgeshire on Friday 9th September 1994*, (The Woodcock Report), Cmnd. 2741, London, HMSO, 1994 and *Review of Prison Service Security in England and Wales and the Escape from Parkhurst Prison on Tuesday 3rd January 1995* (Report of the Learmont Inquiry), Cmnd. 3020, London, HMSO, 1995.

[4] Jack Straw, 'Making Prisons Work' , Speech to the Prison Reform Trust, 22 July 1998.

[5] Arthur de Frisching, *A Management Review of the Prison Service*, HM Prison Service, 1997.

[6] House of Commons, *The Management of the Prison Service, Public and Private Second Report from the Home Affairs Committee*, Session 1996-7, London, Stationery Office, 1997.

[7] Lord Laming, *Modernising the Management of the Prison Service*, An Independent Report by the Targeted Performance Initiative Working Group, London, HM Prison Service, 2000.

[8] See Derek Lewis, *Hidden Agendas: Politics Law and Disorder*, London, Hamish Hamilton, 1997.

[9] The Management Review included in its report:

> The Prison Service is not a typical agency. Not only is it large, complex and politically sensitive but it is notable for the fact that there is no residual prison department within the Home Office dealing with policy, on the basis that prisons policy and operations are so inextricably linked that responsibility for both must be in the same organization. One result of this is that the role of Director General is heavily loaded. He is the chief executive of a large and complex organization running over 130 prisons holding over 60,000 prisoners employing some 40,000 staff and with a budget of £1.8 billion. He is also the focus for all the issues needing to be put to Ministers and for all Ministerial directives on how the Prison Service should operate. The relationship with Ministers is therefore especially important. There must be a question mark over whether the role of Director General is unfeasibly large.

The review's solution was to recommend that the Director General should be supported by a deputy.

[10] Lord Woolf (*op. cit.*, 14.289) who wrote, 'The European Court of Human Rights has set out succinctly a principle which is part of the law of this country. It is that "Justice does not stop at the prison doors". A feature of this principle is that "in spite of his imprisonment, a convicted prisoner retains all civil rights which are not taken away expressly or by necessary implication".' (See *R v. Board of Visitors of Hull Prison, Ex Parte St Germain* [1979] QB 425, at pp. 454/5 per Sebag-Shaw L. J., and *Raymond v. Honey* [1983] 1 AC 1, at p. 10 per Lord Wilberforce. Tim Newell comments more sceptically: 'The emphasis on "prisoners' rights" in reforming prisons is questionable from a communitarian perspective. It has been argued that prisoners should retain all rights that are not expressly removed through the reality of custody. But as soon as people are incarcerated they are in a powerless position in which the idea of rights is very limited. More fundamental questions should be addressed about the nature of the prison regime and its effects on human autonomy.' (Tim Newell, *Forgiving Justice*, London, Quaker Home Service, p. 123). For an account of the courts' approach to prisoners' rights more generally, see J. H. Schone, 'The Short Life and Painful Death of Prisoners' Rights', *Howard Journal of Criminal Justice*, 40/1, 2000, pp. 70-82.

[11] See Amitai Etzioni, *The Third Way to a Good Society*, DEMOS, 2000, pp. 29-30.

[12] Thomas Mathieson has written:

> As long as we have prisons, prisoners obviously not only have the same rights as other citizens to such services; in view of their background of general poverty and the inhuman prison conditions under which they live, they have the right to more of them. The point is that such services should be given as precisely that; as *rights* which prisoners have and should have, and as a part of a sensible, enlightened and humane policy. The services should not be given on the condition that rehabilitation follows, because if they are, they can all too easily be withdrawn when only marginal results are produced, and they should not and cannot be used as an ideological argument in favour of prison.

Prison on Trial, second English edition, Winchester, Waterside Press, 2000, p. 179.

13 Sir William Macpherson of Cluny, *The Stephen Lawrence Inquiry*, Cmnd. 4262, London Stationery Office, 1999.

14 Richard Sparks, Anthony Bottoms and Will Hay, *Prisons and the Problem of Order*, Oxford, Clarendon Press, 1996.

15 Tim Newell, *op. cit.*, n. 10, p. 123.

16 Jane Steele, *Wasted Values: Harnessing the Commitment of Public Managers*, London, Public Management Foundation, 1999.

LIVERPOOL JOHN MOORES UNIVERSITY
LEARNING SERVICES

CHAPTER 20

Probation

It is very hard for a free society to figure out how effectively to deal with crime rates other than by imprisonment.

James Q. Wilson, quoted in *Criminal Justice Matters*, 25 April 2000

Like the Prison Service, the Probation Service has been deeply affected by the changes in public management which have taken place over the last 20 years. It has been subjected to the usual pressures to demonstrate and increase its effectiveness, and to the disciplines of cash limits and performance indicators and targets. National standards have been introduced for most of the statutory aspects of its work. Inspections have become much more rigorous and detailed. At the same it has had to adjust to the changing social and economic context which has been described in earlier chapters, and to an operational context which has become more complex, more politicised and sometimes more hostile. Far more than the Prison Service, the Probation Service has suffered a series of public and political assaults on its professional identity and values.

BACKGROUND AND CONTEXT

Among the criminal justice services, probation has always been overshadowed by the much larger and more powerful police and prison services. For a short time after the Conservative Government took office in 1979, there was talk of the Probation Service having 'come of age', and of the removal of some Home Office controls in the spirit of deregulation which was current at the time. This talk soon gave way to the pressures of the Financial Management Initiative and to a demand that the service should transform itself not only managerially, but also professionally. It had previously thought of itself as a more or less autonomous group of largely independent practitioners, loosely co-ordinated by benevolent principal probation officers and employed by well-intentioned probation committees composed mostly of lay magistrates. It was now to become a managed, criminal justice service, functioning as part of a managed criminal justice system, working in accordance with nationally determined priorities and contributing to the achievement of the government's objectives. In particular, the service was to help bring down the level of crime through a reduction in the rate of re-offending among those former offenders who were under its supervision, and to contribute to a fall in the prison population by increasing the credibility of its programmes as a form of punishment. The relationship with those under supervision was to be one of authority and control, no longer that of a professional adviser with their client. Probation officers were to become case managers rather than case workers.[1] At the end of the 1980s, there were already suggestions that the service might be re-formed as an executive agency of the Home Office,[2] in parallel with the Prison Service, and even of the service being contracted out to commercial operators, but nothing came of those suggestions at that stage.

All this came as a shock to many probation officers, some of whom felt that probation was no longer the service they had joined or the career they wanted to pursue.[3] But probation managers and in time most probation officers came to support the change and welcomed the increased authority and status which it gave both to managers and to individual practitioners. They approved (mostly) of the aims and principles which lay behind the Criminal Justice Act 1991, and recognised that a successful, influential and publicly respected Probation Service was essential for their achievement.

The service suffered a series of public attacks and humiliations, from both Conservative and Labour governments, after the change of political direction at the end of 1992. Opinions will vary on the extent to which they were deserved or justified, or to which they had a more political purpose - whether to propel the service into changes which could then be used to give the courts or the public more confidence in the use of community sentences, or to demonstrate the Government's own credentials for being 'tough on crime' (or more particularly on 'criminals'). Statistics of re-offending did not show the hoped for improvement, and those for failure to comply with court orders suggested that breaches were too often complacently ignored. Both were represented as evidence that too many officers were 'on the side of the offender' and neglecting their duty to protect the public, and that the service's management was too often ineffective and incompetent. Legitimate, and often well justified, attempts to interpret the statistics in less damaging ways attracted little attention or sympathy. Some of those trying to work with the service, whether from government, other statutory services or voluntary organizations, found it unresponsive, or even obstructive, and were unwilling to accept pressure of work or lack of resources as an explanation. Others, including many judges, magistrates, and managers and practitioners in other services, found the service committed, hardworking, conscientious and often innovative and imaginative. But to the general public it was, and is still, relatively unknown and still less understood.

During the later years of its administration, the Conservative Government put forward several proposals which seemed designed to limit the service's role and change its orientation. They included a proposal to abolish the requirement of probation officers to hold a post-graduate diploma in social work (accompanied by suggestions that the work could be done better by retired non-commissioned officers from the armed forces); and a Green Paper, *Strengthening Punishment in the Community*[4], which proposed amalgamating the various community sentences (probation, community service and combination orders), leaving the courts to decide the requirements to be imposed on the offender in any particular case. By implication, the decision to be ma would become a judicial judgement of the type and severity of punishment to be imposed, rather than a professional judgemen on the needs and circumstances of the individual. The task of the Probation Service would be reduced to one of administering punishment by enforcing compliance with the terms of the order and reporting failure to the courts. Probation officers would need to pay little attention to their traditional aims of rehabiliation and resettlement; and still less to any wider social purpose, such as developing opportunities in the community for offenders to find training, housing or employment, or working with other agencies in broader programmes to promote community safety or social stability.

Probation and the new Labour Government

No action to implement the Green Paper was taken before the Conservative Government left office in May 1997. The incoming Labour Government did not revive those particular proposals, and in 1998 the Comprehensive Spending Review made an extra £127m available to the service over the next three years. But criticism continued, and the Government clearly believed - and made no secret of its belief - that probation was a 'failing service'. A series of reports by HM Inspectorate indicated how the service's performance could be improved, especially in the supervision of offenders but also in other functions such as the preparation of pre-sentence reports. An important report on *Strategies for Effective Offender Supervision*[5] offered 'the service and its many valued partners an opportunity to review and revitalise community penalties and, in increasing their objectiveness, enhance public confidence and reduce offending'. Another on *Evidence Based Practice: A Guide to Effective Practice*[6] distilled some of the thinking behind the report and addressed issues of professional practice, operational management and best practice in monitoring and evaluation. Various programmes designed to reduce offending were developed and evaluated, and a procedure was established for those found to be successful to be given accredited status. National standards were revised to make more stringent the procedure for dealing with failures to comply with the conditions of court orders.[7]

The Government was not however to be satisfied with changes limited to improvements in the service's internal management and professional practice. It clearly believed, probably rightly, that more fundamental changes were required in the service's functions and structure, and in its professional identity, culture and orientation. Unlike its proposals for youth justice, which it had largely made known in opposition, the Government's intentions for probation took some time to emerge. Soon after it came into office, it announced a review of the prison and probation services to identify and assess options for closer and more integrated work between them. The announcement brought a ～~ ~f opportunity and optimism to many probation officers, prison ｜ers and others who hoped for a more positive and ｜ach to crime and the treatment of offenders. The ｜already brought a new emphasis on policies based on ｜intervention and support for those in difficulty. It was ｜a markets and competition, and seemed at first to have ｜nded approach than its predecessor to targets and performance measures. It seemed ready to listen and take advice, to respect the judgement of professionals and practitioners, and to take a reasonably long-term view. It had already introduced imaginative and energetic policies on youth justice and community safety. It was introducing fundamental and forward looking reviews of policy and organizational structure in other areas of government. Talk of principles or values such as fairness or social inclusion was no longer an expression of self indulgence, and it seemed that a new, dynamic concept of citizenship, based on human rights and social responsibilities, was beginning to emerge. There was a sense of a 'new politics' which would be less adversarial, more responsive and more regional or local. Some of this optimism was expressed at a seminar on 'New Politics, New Probation', organized by the Probation Studies Unit at the University of Oxford Centre for Criminological Research in December 1997.[8]

Against this background, there were hopes that the Prison Service might become less monolithic and less carceral in its organization and culture; and that the Government might see the service not only as an agency of punishment and social control, but also as an instrument of social change and renewal, working to strengthen communities and promote social inclusion in partnership with other agencies in the statutory, commercial and voluntary and community sectors.

The Criminal Justice and Court Services Act 2000

The report of the review[9] was a thoughtful document offering a number of possible ways forward. The Government's own approach began to emerge in its publication *Joining Forces to Protect the Public: Prison-Probation. A Consultation Document*[10], from which it became clear that the Government had no interest in any radical reform of the Prison Service and that its objective was a more centrally managed Probation Service with a different culture and attitudes and with the protection of the public as its main aim. A period of discussion followed, involving principally the Home Office, the Association of Chief Probation Officers and the Probation Council (representing probation committees), but there was very little public interest or argument. The outcome was the Bill for the Criminal Justice and Court Services Act 2000 which became law, after a fiercely contested passage through the House of Lords, in December 2000. It provides for

- a single National Probation Service for England and Wales (the Government has not pressed an earlier proposal for it to be called the 'Community Punishment and Rehabilitation Service'), directly accountable to the Home Secretary, with a structure based on 42 local areas whose boundaries will correspond with those of the police and eventually of other criminal justice services;

- a separate Children and Family Court Advisory and Support Service, established as a non-departmental public body accountable to the Lord Chancellor;

- a National Director, appointed by and accountable to the Home Secretary;

- a probation board for each of the 42 areas composed of representatives of the local community, appointed by the Home Secretary (except for a judge who will be appointed by the Lord Chancellor), and acting as the employer for probation staff other than the chief officer;

- a chief officer for each area, also appointed by the Secretary of State as a separate post-holder or Crown Servant, who will be a member of the local board;

- powers for the Secretary of State to give directions to boards, and through them to chief officers, as to how they fulfil their statutory responsibilities;

- powers for the Secretary of State to displace the board and substitute other management arrangements if it is failing to perform its functions or not providing good value for money.

The Act states that the aims of the service are the protection of the public, the reduction of re-offending, and the proper punishment of offenders.

THE CHARACTER OF THE SERVICE AND THE NATURE OF THE TASK

Chapter 5 has pointed out that all public services have to manage and resolve tensions and conflict. The Probation Service has to do so in an exceptionally sensitive and complex working environment. It has to support the Government in its political need to be 'tough on crime', and to acknowledge that measures to deal with crime are politically sensitive in Britain as in most developed countries. Community-based, in the sense of non-custodial, and preventive measures need especially careful handling if they are to carry conviction and credibility. They can always be made to look as if they are a 'soft option', however physically and emotionally demanding they may be in practice.[11] On the other hand there is a danger that if they are made too demanding the offender will be 'set up to fail'. The service has to respond to the Government's management agenda of standards, target indicators and accreditation of demonstrably successful programmes; and to give effect to the new organizational structure as set out in the Act. It also has to put into effect the new requirements on the enforcement of orders; and the new orders and associated requirements for electronic monitoring and testing for drugs. If the service fails to respond, or if its response appears inadequate, it would not be surprising if the Government sought to introduce even more punitive measures based on law enforcement and the use of imprisonment, whether or not they were likely to affect the volume of crime.

At the same time, the service needs to re-establish its own professional pride and identity; to have its own sense of direction and vision for the future; to start to take control of its destiny. Many probation officers have had and still have a strong sense of who they are and what they are trying to do. But the service as a whole has for the last 20 years given the impression that it lacks a sense of professional purpose, and that successive governments have dragged it reluctantly along a badly maintained road towards an uncertain destination. There has been little sense that the service has any clear leadership of its own.[12] And yet it should be making a powerful contribution to a professional debate about how the country can and should deal with crime. It needs its own professional leadership, complementing but separate from the political leadership it receives from ministers, and from the administrative directions and guidance it receives from the Home Office. The Government clearly intends that professional leadership will come from the National Director, and the Service has welcomed Eithne Wallis's appointment and will give her undivided support. But it is open to question how far the structure established by the Act will enable her to provide leadership which is sufficiently professional and therefore politically independent. As usual, the outcome will depend on the relationships and dynamics as they develop, and on the degree of mutual confidence and trust between all those concerned. These may change over time.

Central direction and local identity
Earlier chapters have referred to the tensions between central direction and local identity and responsiveness. Central direction, as proposed in the Act, will give the service a stronger national voice, a higher political profile, and the benefits of consistency and uniformity. Many probation officers have welcomed the new structure for these reasons. But crime still has to be dealt with where it occurs and where offenders and victims make their lives, and the means of dealing with it have to be found in local situations. The opportunities and relationships, and the support available in local communities vary from one area to another. Practices rigidly imposed from the centre will not be equally successful wherever they are applied, and may not be successful at all if they lack a sense of local commitment and ownership.

The attempt to combine central control with an element of local identity has produced some odd results. Chief officers are to have an employment status which isolates them both from the Home Office and from the services they are to lead and manage. Probation boards are to represent local communities but are to be centrally appointed, they are to be the employers of their services and have powers to hold property and enter into contracts, but they must operate in accordance with the directions of the Secretary of State They must prepare an annual plan and submit an annual report, but the Secretary of State can direct them to modify it and give directions about the information to be given in the

report and about the form and timing of its submission. Lord Phillips of
Sudbury described these arrangements as a 'totally counter-productive
set of powers' which could easily become unworkable.[13]

The service's main 'customers' or 'stakeholders' are the courts, but
apart from the appointment of a judge to the local board there is no
formal mechanism which requires the service and the courts to
communicate. The courts for their part may be less ready to
communicate with a service which they see and which is presented, as if
it were almost as an executive arm of government, and the Service's
closer relationship with government may begin to displace its
relationship with the courts.

The Government's Crime Reduction Strategy[14] describes the new
arrangements as providing 'a centrally driven, unified service, aligned to
police boundaries and directly accountable to the Secretary of State'. Its
Business Plan for the Criminal Justice System for 2000-2001 similarly
states that the service is to be 'directly accountable' to the Home
Secretary for its performance.[15] The Home Secretary will in turn be
accountable to Parliament, but in the limited sense of accountability
which has been discussed in *Chapter 2*.

To probation audiences, the Home Secretary, Jack Straw, has
indicated that[16]

> the new service will work more closely with the police and other agencies,
> and with local crime and disorder partnerships. Local probation boards will
> work to deliver their services in a way that serves their locality better .... We
> are... looking to recruit members to the new boards who ... reflect a breadth
> of experience from the local community.

And most importantly that

> . . . one of the key challenges will be to find ways of being accountable to
> local communities for the work of the service and to encourage groups who
> have not previously identified with probation work to become involved.

He might have added that one of the key challenges will also be to
reconcile differences of emphasis, approach and possibly priorities
between those communities and central government.

Other tensions and conflicts
The tension between central direction and local identity and
responsiveness is only one of those which the Government and the new
service will have to resolve. Another is between the demands of
effectiveness, public protection and the management (or avoidance) of
risk on the one hand, and those of justice, equity and social inclusion on
the other.

Problems of injustice could arise in matters of enforcement,
especially from the lack of discretion allowed either to probation officers
or to courts in dealing with breaches of conditions, and the absence of
any distinction between serious and minor breaches. It may, for example,
seem unjust and possibly ineffective for an offender who commits a

second minor breach to be sent to prison when he or she is otherwise doing well and other people, for example, children, are also made to suffer.

Problems of equity could arise in the transition from a process of risk assessment based on an offender's own character, behaviour and background, to one of actuarial assessment based on statistical probabilities relating to groups of offenders of whom the individual may be a member. Rigid procedures, whether on assessment or enforcement, are also difficult to apply fairly in a spirit which respects and values cultural diversity.

A further tension is between professional and (again in a broad sense) political judgement. *Chapter 3* has pointed out that judgements which were once regarded as matters of professional discretion are increasingly becoming matters of political decision, or administrative direction. It must be a matter of concern that the service's political credibility should have come to depend so heavily on success in terms of 'what works' at a time when the evidential base for offending behaviour programmes is still so precarious, the methods by which they are evaluated are so narrowly drawn, and the pressure from performance indicators is to demonstrate the numbers who are accepted onto programmes rather than the quality of the programmes themselves.

The measures contained in the Criminal Justice and Court Services Act 2000 may make some of these tensions more acute. Among the statutory aims of the reconstructed service, it is hard to see how the 'protection of the public' differs from the 'reduction of re-offending', or what the service is expected to do to achieve the first which it would not do to achieve the second. Nor is it clear what is meant by the 'proper punishment of offenders' or what kind of action that might involve - especially when 'punishment' is properly to be regarded as a function of the courts, and as consisting of the sentence itself rather than any specifically punitive action which might be taken under it.[17] The most notable exception - the attempts to impose a 'short, sharp shock' regime in detention centres in the 1950s and again in the early 1980s - came on both occasions to be seen as a mistake.

However that may be, the appearance of 'punishment' as a statutory aim of the Probation Service, but with no mention of it for the Prison Service, is at best confusing and at worst alarming. So is the replacement of the community service order by the community punishment order - both for its use of the word 'punishment' and for the loss of the sense of restoration and 'paying back to the community' which the old title implied. The change also drains 'community' of any positive meaning: combined with punishment - unless it implies that the community is somehow to join in the offender's humiliation - it means no more than 'not served in prison'.

Probation officers must find it ironic that these changes were taking place in their own service at a time when recruitment advertising for the Metropolitan Police depicted the Police as   performing what is essentially a social service.

DYNAMICS AND RELATIONSHIPS

Ministers and the country are right to demand from the Probation Service an organization which will reduce re-offending, and do so more successfully than the Service seems to do at present and which is more visibly well-run and decisive. They are entitled to demand that offenders should not be allowed to disregard the requirements of their orders, and in some instances that offenders should be given a harder time in terms of the obligations - to work, to learn, to discharge their responsibilities as parents or citizens - that are laid upon them. But those requirements demand not only structures, standards, accredited programmes and central direction - important though they are - but also dynamics, relationships, leadership and personal influence, example and integrity. These are all acknowledged in Sir Richard Wilson's Report to the Prime Minister on Civil Service Reform (see *Chapter 3*), but they do not seem so far to have received much attention in the Government's plans for the Probation Service where the overwhelming impression is of the Government's lack of confidence in the service and its procrustean belief that both probation officers and offenders can be forced into compliance by threats of punishment. Mike Nellis's article[18] on 'The New Probation Training in England and Wales: Realising the Potential' and the importance of 'overarching' as well as 'underpinning' knowledge has already been mentioned in *Chapters 2 and 5*.

The Government's general approach to public services and social policy, described in *Chapter 5*, suggests that the Probation Service could have a dynamic and effective part to play, not only in the supervision and punishment of offenders but also in its overall strategy for modernisation and social reform. But to make the contribution of which it should be capable it needs a more flexible, locally responsive and diversified structure than the Government now seems to propose. The considerations which apply to the Prison Service, as described in the previous chapter, apply with even greater force to probation.

Arrangements for offenders need to be individualised, varied and related to local conditions and circumstances. They should be closely integrated with services in the community, and especially with those for health, education, social services and housing. They should have regard to the whole person, including the person's relationships with their families and communities, and where relevant their schools or employers; and they should take account of the interests of victims. Staffing arrangements should be flexible, allow for greater movement between services, and accommodate a wide range of professional experience and discipline. Consistency of treatment should be maintained within a national legal framework, national standards and a consistent approach to sentencing, but there should be scope for local initiative, innovation and development. A proper emphasis on 'what works' and on monitoring and evaluation should not result in a 'single track' approach to supervision, especially while the empirical base for 'what works' still needs more assessment, development and research. An emphasis on accreditation should not discourage probation officers from exploring new ideas or developing new schemes, or prevent them from introducing relevant programmes - for example to deal with racist behaviour and attitudes - because they do not match the criteria. An emphasis on record keeping and the bureaucracy of performance measurement should not drive probation officers into offices and away from the homes, the streets and the places of work or entertainment of those for whom they have responsibility. Programmes should provide opportunities for recognition and rewards for success as well as punishment for breaches of conditions.

Looking beyond its work with individual offenders, the service should have a more general influence in its various communities, helping to generate and support a sense of citizenship and of civil and social responsibility, and to promote the projects, programmes and activities that can give it practical effect. It should help its communities to invest in social capital and to mobilise the resources of civil society. Like other public services, it must be fully accountable, and its lines of accountability must run in several directions - vertically, connecting the services' managers and practitioners with government departments, ministers and Parliament; and horizontally, with other organizations and interests and the citizens whom they serve. Ministers' concern that the service should be accountable to central government and responsive to the national responsibilities which they wish the service to undertake must be matched by the local understanding, support and commitment which are needed if Parliament's legislation, and the Government's own policies, are to be successfully put into effect.

The service should also accept some responsibility for, and some accountability towards those whom it supervises. In particular, there should be formal duties of care and support and standards to which services should conform. The Children (Leaving Care) Act 2000 provides a possible model. To give those duties and standards statutory force would give formal expression to their status as citizens.

Like the Prison Service, a modern Probation Service needs the outward-looking, problem-solving orientation, the skills of listening and consultation, and the ability to manage conflicts, tensions and ambiguities which have been discussed in the previous chapter. It needs to exercise skills not only in relation to offenders under its supervision or about whom it is writing reports, but also in relation to its stakeholders and partners (other services, voluntary or community organizations), communities, and victims of crime.

Future arrangements for the service therefore need not only a sense of identification and understanding between those providing the service and local communities, but also a sense of 'ownership' on the part of those communities themselves. A sense of local ownership and responsibility - of the kind felt passionately, for example, about community hospitals - hardly exists at present. It is needed, not only because it is the means of generating the sense of public confidence which is so important both for the Government and for probation itself; but also because it helps to mobilise the resources of civil society and the sense of civil responsibility which are, or should be, crucial elements in the Government's own thinking. The absence of that sense of ownership and responsibility from the present situation is all the more reason for trying to create a set of arrangements through which it can be actively promoted.

A sense of local ownership and responsibility will be especially important if restorative justice is to be promoted in the ways considered in *Chapter 10*. John Harding has described the role which a modern, reorganized and revitalised Probation Service might play in community, and especially restorative, justice and the conditions which would have to be satisfied for it to do so.[19] David Smith and John Stewart have examined the effects of social exclusion on young people supervised by the Probation Service; they have suggested strategies for more inclusionary and integrative practice; and have considered what local structures might be needed to put them into effect.[20] The Service should carry these ideas forward and use them to inform professional practice: but it needs the space, confidence and encouragement to do so.

Immediate prospects
The hope must obviously be that the Probation Service will move forward confidently and successfully in its new form and structure and with its newly-defined aims and responsibilities. The concerns expressed in this chapter are matters to be recognised and dealt with positively and constructively, not as regrets or predictions of failure (and certainly not as nostalgia for the past). The service must demonstrate its effectiveness, and also its accountability - in the full sense described in this and other chapters - and its legitimacy. It must establish a relationship of confidence and co-operation with its local communities, with the offenders, victims and their families with whom it works directly, and with the citizens whom it serves. Government for its part must provide political leadership, resources and support; and, in holding the service to account, it must accept its own accountability and responsibility in the new form which the Act has established. It must respect the service's local identity, accountability and responsibility, as well as its accountability to central government, and must give them equal emphasis not only in rhetorical but also in practical terms. The new structure, and perhaps the new provisions on enforcement, can be made to work successfully given mutual trust, respect and good will between the Government, the service and the service's local stakeholders. But the situation will be difficult to sustain if things go wrong, if confidence is lost or if trust is broken.

Structures and relationships in the longer term
The immediate task is to make the Criminal Justice and Court Services Act a success. Neither the service nor the Government will want to look beyond it at present. But the situation will continue to evolve, new pressures and opportunities will present themselves, and the service's role, structure and relationships will need to respond to them. As the next stage in a process of continuing development, a new structure could

be devised on lines similar, and parallel, to the structure which was proposed for the Prison Service in the previous chapter.

Under that structure, a single commissioning authority could have responsibility both for prisons and for what is now probation. Providing organizations would run the equivalent of today's probation services. Providing organizations for prisons and for probation would probably remain separate, but with close working relationships, some common procedures, and more freedom of movement for staff. But new configurations might emerge over time, with some providers supplying some local or specialist services both inside and outside institutions. The process would be accelerated if prison sentences became less sharply distinguished from community sentences in the way that is implied in the Government's announcement of the review of sentencing (see *Chapter 12*). In 20 or 30 years a distinctive Probation Service, and a self-contained unified Prison Service, might no longer exist in any recognisable form. There would inevitably be some regret at the loss of the identity and traditions which the two services have represented, and very proper concern if the transition implied a more careless attitude on the part of the state and its agents towards the liberty of the citizen. But there might be some approval if it represented a movement towards a humane and flexible approach to imprisonment in which personal freedom was treated with greater respect and greater efforts were made to prevent or mitigate its loss.

All this is speculation at present. While some people may regret that the Government has not taken the opportunity for a more radical reconstruction of the two services, further reform of the Probation Service is not in the Government's mind. Nor, apparently, is a more sparing use of custody. The thrust of its policies, as expressed in all the legislation it has introduced since it came into office, is to increase the numbers of people convicted and sentenced by the courts, and to intensify the effect of the punishment they receive. On a pessimistic view, the longer term prospect may be that the enforcement aspects of the Service's work will be increasingly automated and contracted out to commercial companies, and that its rehabilitative work will be taken over by voluntary organizations - both of which seem to be possible under the terms of the Criminal Justice and Court Services Act 2000 - and that very little professional probation work will remain. More optimistically, the hope for the Probation Service must be that its new relationship with central government will help it to achieve the confidence, status and professional skills to be more effective in serving the public by helping to change offenders' lives as well as by enforcing the sentences of the courts. It may then have the authority and trust to take on the more dynamic role in social support and intervention which this chapter has suggested.

ENDNOTES for *Chapter 20*

[1] David Faulkner, 'The Future of the Probation Service: A View from Government', Clarke Hall Conference, July 1989, Cambridge Institute of Criminology.

[2] In the Green Paper, *Punishment, Custody and Community*, Cmnd. 424, London, HMSO, 1988.

[3] Mike Nellis has described the history of community penalties and with it the history of the Probation Service itself in the period from 1948 onwards in his paper *Community Penalties, A Historical Perspective*, Cambridge Institute of Criminology, (forthcoming). He includes an account of the resistance of many probation officers to many of the legislative changes and developments in professional practices which the Government pursued during the 1980s, even when the intention and the effect was to give the service a more central and more influential position and to promote its work in supervising offenders in the community.

[4] Home Office, *Strengthening Punishment in the Community*, Cmnd. 2780, London, HMSO, 1995.

[5] Andrew Underdown, *Strategies for Effective Offender Supervision*, London, Home Office, 1998.

[6] Tim Chapham and Michael Hough, *Evidence Based Practice; A Guide to Effective Practice*, London, Home Office, 1998.

[7] *National Standards for the Supervision of Offenders in the Community*, 2000, London, Home Office, 2000.

[8] Seminar on *New Politics, New Probation*, organized by the Probation Studies Unit at the University of Oxford Centre for Criminological Research, December 1997, University of Oxford Centre for Criminological Research, 1998.

[9] Home Office, *Prisons – Probation Review Final Report*, London, Home Office, 1998.

[10] Home Office Consultation Paper, *Joining Forces to Protect the Public- Probation a Consultation Document*, London, Home Office, 1998.

[11] For an account of James Q. Wilson's influence see Andrew Rutherford, *Transforming Criminal Policy*, Winchester, Waterside Press, 1996. From a different perspective Lord Bingham said in his Police Foundation lecture on 10 July 1997, 'Among the public I think that custody is seen as the only true retributive or punitive sentence. Anyone who commits a crime of any seriousness and is not sentenced to custody is generally perceived to have got away with it. This is very unfortunate, because of the inherent drawbacks to imprisonment, which I have just mentioned; because the efficacy of imprisoning offenders is very high, and inevitably absorbs resources which would otherwise be available for schools, hospitals and other facilities of more obvious benefit to the public than prisons; and because the prison system is already bursting at the seams. It is all the more unfortunate because there exists another sentence – community service – which is intended to punish and intended to provide an alternative to custody in cases which would otherwise demand a sentence of custody.'

[12] See the House of Lords debate on the second reading of the Criminal Justice and Court Services Bill on 3 July 2000, *Hansard*, House of Lords, Cols. 1313-1315. In his thoughtful article, 'A Community Justice Dimension to Effective Probation Practice', *Howard Journal*, November 1999, 39, pp. 132-49, John Harding describes the service's 'loss of mission', drawing on writings by Bill McWilliams and Ken Pease, 1990. See also David Garland, 'Probation Practice and an End to Punishment', *Howard Journal*, 1997, 29, pp. 14-24 and 'Probation and Reconfiguration of Crime Control' in R. Burnett, (ed.) *The Probation Service: Responding to Change*, Oxford, Centre for Criminological Research, Probation Studies Unit Report No. 3, 1999 and Mike Nellis, 'Towards the Field of Corrections: Modernising the Probation Service in the Late 1990s', *Social Policy and Administration*, 1999, 33, 302-323. Those writers relate the situation of the Probation Service to the decline in respect for social work and the welfare state, and to the influence of managerialism and actuarial justice.

[13] Lord Phillips of Sudbury speaking in the House of Lords on the second reading of the Criminal Justice and Court Services Bill, *Hansard*, House of Lords, 3 July 2000, col. 1312.

[14] The Government's Crime Reduction Strategy, London, Home Office, 2000.

[15] Lord Chancellor's Department, Home Office and Attorney General's Department, *The Criminal Justice System; Business Plan 2000-2001*, 2000.

[16] For example in his speech to the Annual Meeting of the Central Probation Council, 16 May 2000.

[17] Baroness Stern made this point in the debate on the second reading of the Bill, *Hansard*, House of Lords, 3 July 2000, cols. 1299-1300.

[18] Mike Nellis, 'The New Probation Training in England and Wales: Realising the Potential', *Social Work Education* (forthcoming).

[19] *Op. cit*, n. 12.

[20] David Smith and John Stewart, 'Probation and Social Exclusion', *Social Policy and Administration*, 1997, 31/5, pp. 96-115.

CHAPTER 21

Prosecution, Courts and the Machinery of Government

There are two parties in Europe. One party considers nations to be the property of their governors, the other holds that governments are established for the good of the many.

Lord Palmerston

This chapter deals with those parts of the criminal justice system which have not been discussed in earlier chapters - the prosecution system, the courts and central government. Some of the questions it considers are likely to be examined in the course of Lord Justice Auld's Review of the criminal courts, which was still in progress at the time of writing.

THE CROWN PROSECUTION SERVICE

The Crown Prosecution Service has had a turbulent history during the short time since it was set up following the report of the Royal Commission on Criminal Procedure in 1981 and the passage of the Prosecution of Offences Act 1985. The Royal Commission recommended a prosecution service independent of the police but set up on a local basis, accountable to local combined police and prosecution authorities. The Government preferred a national service which it thought less likely to be influenced by local considerations or relationships. The Government had also been influenced by impressions of the prosecution arrangements in other countries, including the national prosecution service which forms part of the Ministry of Justice in The Netherlands, and it visualised a service which, while retaining its independence in the exercise of its prosecutorial discretion, would also play a part in the development and implementation of national policy and professional practice. Policies immediately in view were those concerned with the efficiency and effectiveness of the system and its co-ordination across different services. Others were at a more speculative stage, but areas for possible development were seen as a contribution to sentencing; responsibilities relating to victims; and diversion from formal prosecution and the criminal justice process, for example a system of 'out of court' fines (see *Chapter 12*), or referral to various forms of care or treatment for mental disorder or addiction to drugs.

In the event the CPS's early years were beset by difficulties arising from its lack of adequate funding; a succession of internal reorganizations; often strained and sometimes acrimonious relations with the police; and dissention among its own members. These difficulties prevented it from achieving its full potential or establishing a sufficient basis of confidence on which imaginative developments in its role could have been founded. The service did however come to have a greater role in sentencing through the provisions in the Criminal Justice Act 1988 which gave the Attorney General power, on advice from the service, to refer apparently over-lenient sentences to the Court of Appeal; and through the Victim's Charter it became more involved in communication with victims.

The Labour Party in opposition had become acutely aware of the long-running criticisms of the quality of the CPS's work and the management style of its headquarters, and one of the new Government's first actions after taking office was to appoint Sir Iain Glidewell to carry out a review. He reported in 1998 with proposals for a further reorganization and a closer alignment of the service's structure with that of the police, on the basis of what were to become the 'standard' 42 areas for all criminal justice services.[1] The new structure was put into effect later that year.

Sir Iain Glidewell's review was essentially a management exercise, which did not and was not intended to address the more strategic questions of the role which the prosecution should take in a modern but still probably adversarial criminal justice process. That role has come to be seen as rather ambivalent, if not actually confused. The Royal Commission and the Government were clear that the prosecution was to be independent of the police and to act in the public interest on behalf of the state. As the interests of victims became more prominent and began to gain greater attention, the question began to be asked whether the prosecution should also act on behalf of victims, defending their interests against any prejudicial comments which the defence or other witnesses might make about their behaviour or character, and perhaps representing their views or feelings to the court. Other questions concerned the extent to which the prosecution, and the police, had a duty to be fair to the defence, for example by disclosing details of the prosecution case or unused evidence, or otherwise ensuring 'equality of arms' in the existing adversarial tradition. Further questions related to the legitimacy of plea or sentence bargaining, where 'deals' are struck to reduce charges (and so shorten trials) in exchange for admissions or co-operation. Academic writers expressed concerns about the structural advantage which the prosecution enjoys, at least in the magistrates' courts; and about the ethics and legitimacy of plea bargaining.[2]

These questions are not easily resolved in a political context of a 'war on crime' and a view which sees all defendants, but especially those who deny their guilt, as unscrupulous and probably dangerous criminals from whom the country needs to be protected. It is true that some defendants may be both those things, as well as having legal advisers who are skilled at manipulating the rules of evidence and the system as a whole; but there are other defendants who are wrongly accused, and many more who are vulnerable, confused, open to suggestion or sometimes intimidation, and whose legal representation may be inadequate for the situation in which they are placed and the charge they have to answer.

These considerations suggest that the Crown Prosecution Service, and the Government, should vigorously defend the service's independent role, continue to respect the possibility that the evidence may not be sufficient to support a conviction, and regard a fair trial and a just verdict - rather than a conviction for its own sake - as their criterion for success. The prosecution could, and often does, have a role in challenging unjustified statements by the defence which are damaging to a victim, and in putting before the court evidence from victims which is relevant to the court's judgement of the seriousness of the offence. But it should not be the role of the prosecution to represent the victim as if he or she were one of the parties in the trial, or to demand satisfaction or revenge, on behalf either of the victim or of the state.

This is not to deny that the role of the Crown Prosecution Service might still be expanded on the lines which the previous government contemplated in the mid-1980s. In particular, although the service' s role in initiating the Attorney General's references to the Court of Appeal seems to have worked satisfactorily,[3] references seem to be more often triggered by complaints in the media or from the victim than by any process of systematic review within the Crown Prosecution Service itself. It is against the English adversarial tradition for the prosecution to advise the court on sentencing, but it could be a helpful practice for the prosecution to indicate, in a dispassionate and non-partisan way, the guidelines, precedents and other considerations which the court could be expected to take into account. The defence could then, if necessary, contest that advice and advance other arguments or suggest a different interpretation. Sentencing would then become a more open, transparent and accountable process, and the offender, the victim, the public and the media would have a better understanding of why the sentence had been imposed. The case would be even stronger if new legislation on sentencing is introduced on the lines discussed in *Chapter 12*, especially if sentencing came (unfortunately) to be based more on an actuarial form of risk assessment, as well as - or even instead of - the usual criteria of seriousness and culpability.

Whether or not the role of the service is deliberately expanded, it will have a profound influence on the quality of justice as the Government's various reforms come into effect and as practice develops around those reforms. The obvious examples are in youth justice, in the protection of witnesses, in the operation of proceedings arising from the Crime and Disorder Act 1998, the Youth Justice and Criminal Evidence Act 1999, and the Criminal Justice and Court Services Act 2000, any legislation which follows the review of the sentencing framework, and - perhaps most importantly - the Human Rights Act 1998.

As for all public services, and especially for those working in criminal justice, the CPS's accountability, and the legitimacy which flows from it, are a complex and sensitive matter which will need constant vigilance and periodical adjustment. The service must be accountable both to the public and to the law. Its public accountability must be partly to Parliament through the Attorney-General; but also locally to the communities it serves on the ground; and to the law through processes of appeal, challenge and review. All three forms of accountability involve complex and multiple mechanisms, and sensitive relationships with 'stakeholders' such as other criminal justice services and institutions, the legal and other professions, and organizations representing victims. Certain limitations are needed to preserve the service's political independence and to protect it from undue sectional or populist interests (for example from the police or the media).

Sir Iain Glidewell's review was probably right to reject at this stage the idea of local accountability to some form of locally elected or representative authority - although this is what the Royal Commission on Criminal Procedure had recommended 15 years earlier. Public accountability through mechanisms which are visible and effective is however a necessary condition for the service to have credibility, authority and legitimacy. One possibility would be the formation of local advisory boards, comprising representatives of other statutory services and local committees. Another would be a stronger role for local strategy committees. Accountability will be increasingly important as the service becomes - inevitably - more visibly involved in decisions affecting the rights, expectations and liberties of individuals, whether as offenders, victims or witnesses or as members of their families or households.

THE CRIMINAL COURTS

The criminal courts have been under almost continuous criticism since the early 1980s. They have been criticised both for inefficiency and for injustice. Criticisms of inefficiency have been concerned mostly with cost and delay: those of injustice have ranged from wrongful convictions (or sometimes failures to convict), through racial prejudice, to inconsistency and excessive leniency or severity in sentencing. Other criticisms have concerned the competence of lay magistrates to try complicated cases; the number and role of stipendiary magistrates (now district judges); the social composition of the judiciary, especially the higher judiciary; their method of appointment; and the composition and competence of juries.

Reforms intended to deal with inefficiency and those to deal with injustice are hard to separate in practice. In principle, they should reinforce one another. Delays in bringing a case to a conclusion are both inefficient and unfair to those involved, including both defendants and victims. Memories may fail, and evidence - for both parties - may become less reliable or harder to collect. Improvements in efficiency should therefore improve the standard of justice. In practice, they are often seen, especially by lawyers, as having the opposite effect - in reducing the time or opportunities available to the defence to prepare their case, or in removing safeguards such as the right to silence (the Criminal Justice and Public Order Act 1994 allowed a court to draw adverse inferences from an accused person's silence in various circumstances). From another point of view, including that of successive governments, reform can be seen as removing opportunities for an unscrupulous defence to exploit the opportunities or safeguards that are available to them, either to escape conviction altogether, or to prolong the trial so that the defendant can continue to enjoy the status of a remand prisoner while in custody. Any discussion of measures which are seen as removing or weakening the safeguards available to the defence will be controversial; and some safeguards, such as the presumption of innocence (which is protected by Article 6 of the European Convention On Human Rights and the Human Rights Act 1998), and the right to trial by jury (which is not) are often seen as fundamental rights which cannot be compromised in the interests of efficiency.

By the autumn of 2000 the courts were still adjusting to the effects of some of the earlier reforms, but attention had come to be focused on two main issues. These were the Government's proposals to restrict a defendant's right of access to trial before a jury; and the review of the criminal courts which the Government had set up under Lord Justice Auld.

The Government had brought forward two bills which would have removed a defendant' s right to insist on a trial before a jury for a range of offences, most importantly burglary, theft and assault, which could also be tried in the magistrates' court more quickly and at less cost. Previous governments had considered a change of this kind at various times during their terms of office, and in one version it had been recommended by the Royal Commission on Criminal Justice, but the Conservative Government had not taken any action on it. The Labour Government argued at one stage that its case rested not on cost but on the need to create a 'more transparent, clear and fair criminal justice system', and it clearly believed that juries were too often inclined to give defendants the benefit of any doubt and were finding too many defendants not guilty. The Government's first bill, the Criminal Justice (Mode of Trial) Bill, included provisions which would have allowed defendants with no previous record and a reputation to protect to continue to have their cases tried before a jury, but this provision was criticised as discriminatory and the House of Lords in effect rejected the Bill. The Government then introduced a second Bill, the Criminal Justice (Mode of Trial) (No. 2) Bill, which would have prevented the magistrates from considering any 'circumstance of the accused', but would have allowed various other considerations to be taken into account and included a right of appeal.

The second bill was also defeated in the House of Lords in the face of arguments that the proposed procedure would be time-consuming and expensive to administer; that the savings in cost were unlikely to materialise; and that its effect would be racially discriminatory.[4] For many opponents, the real argument was one of principle. But it was already clear that the issue would return in the context of Lord Justice Auld' s review.

The Government' s decision to set up a thorough-going review of the criminal courts was timely and welcome. The terms of reference were

A review into the practice and procedures of, and the rules of evidence applied by the criminal courts at every level, with a view to ensuring that they deliver justice fairly, by streamlining all their processes, increasing their efficiency and strengthening the effectiveness of their relations with others across the whole of the criminal justice system, and having regard to the interests of all parties including victims and witnesses, thereby promoting public confidence in the rule of law.

Lord Justice Auld interpreted those terms as including, but not necessarily limited to, the following headings

- The structure and organization of, and distribution of work between, courts.
- Their composition, including the use of juries and of lay and stipendiary magistrates.
- Case management, procedure and evidence (including the use of information technology).
- Service to and treatment of all those who use or have to attend criminal courts or who are the subject of their proceedings.
- Liaison between the courts and agencies involved in the criminal justice system.
- Management and funding of the system.
- The organization and procedures of the Court of Appeal (Criminal Division).

Early speculation about the outcome of the review suggested the possibility of a substantial reduction in the role of lay magistrates and a corresponding increase in the role of stipendiary magistrates or district judges (magistrates' courts as they are now called).[5] It had for a long time been argued that stipendiary magistrates dispose of cases more quickly and therefore more economically, an advantage which was thought to outweigh the saving which comes from the fact that lay magistrates are unpaid. Arguments on grounds of justice are more subtle and complex. Criticisms include lack of consistency, especially in sentencing; and more subjectively a claim that lay magistrates are more 'prosecution minded', more ready to accept uncorroborated police evidence, and more ready to convict. The latter argument is linked to the claim, already mentioned, that trial in the magistrates'court can be racially discriminatory.

Pressure to reduce the role of the lay magistracy was strengthened by the prospect of the passage of the Criminal Justice (Mode of Trial) Bill and the substantial increase in the number of relatively serious offences which would then be tried in the magistrates' court. Further arguments related to deficiencies in procedure which might come under scrutiny as a result of the Human Rights Act. In its briefing on the Bill, JUSTICE identified those deficiencies as including

the relative lack of disclosure, the difficulties for lay magistrates in making decisions on the admissibility of evidence as well as fact finding, and the advantages these trials are seen to confer on the police. These problems would be exacerbated considerably by a new swathe of cases.

The implementation of the Human Rights Act means that magistrates' courts will be under particular scrutiny. For example, magistrates may find they can no longer retire with their clerks in private, denying prosecution and defence the right to hear advice.

Arguments in favour of lay justice are usually linked with arguments for local justice. The claim is typically that local lay justices have a better understanding than professional judges can achieve of their local communities, the nature and effects of crime within those communities, and the social circumstances and cultural background of those who commit it. Variations in practice between different areas can accordingly be accepted and even welcomed. Critics would say that these assumptions are no longer valid in most areas of the country, and that far from improving the standard of justice, they increase the risk of prejudice.

Rod Morgan and Keith Russell have carried out a review of the judiciary in the magistrates' courts to investigate the balance between lay and stipendiary magistrates, the arguments supporting the balance, and whether each type of magistrate is deployed in the most effective way. They summarised the arguments as

- participatory democracy and justice versus consistency and the rule of law;
- local justice versus national consistency;
- open versus case-hardened minds;
- symbolic legitimacy versus effectiveness and efficiency; and
- cost - high or low.

The study assembled and analysed a range of evidence and opinions. Its report did not point to any simple conclusions to the effect that lay magistrates are likely to be more or less cost-effective than stipendiaries, that their decisions are likely to be more or less fair or just, or that they are likely to command more or less confidence among the public. The authors conclude that 'eliminating or greatly diminishing the role of lay magistrates would not be widely understood or supported'.[6]

In a separate study, Andrew Sanders argues that the lower courts should be judged according to the standards of fairness in decision-making; participatory democracy - including legitimacy and the public's involvement as citizens, as discussed in previous chapters; and efficiency. He proposes mixed panels of lay and legally-qualified magistrates in which each would make their own distinctive contribution towards observing the three principles in judicial practices. He argues that both types of contribution are needed if the principles are to be fully observed.[7]

The preliminary conclusions as they began to emerge from Lord Justice Auld's review suggested that he was unlikely to recommend a substantial reduction in the role of lay justice, and that he would argue, consistently with the themes of this book, that there is an important role for local lay justice both as an expression of citizenship and on grounds of local ownership, accountability and legitimacy.[8] Whether the lay magistracy and the system of magistrates' courts can achieve those aims as they are now constituted is however another matter.

Other likely proposals included the creation of an intermediate level of jurisdiction, in which a district judge would sit with two lay magistrates to try what are at present 'either-way' offences - those triable either summarily in the magistrates' court or on indictment in the Crown Court – with powers to impose sentences of up to two years' imprisonment. The Crown Court would continue to try the most serious, indictable only, offences; lay magistrates would keep their existing powers to impose prison sentences of up to six months (or 12 months consecutively). The separate category of 'either-way' offences might be replaced by a category triable only at the new level of jurisdiction, although there would be power to commit aggravated offences in that category to the Crown Court if the new court's sentencing powers were not adequate. With juries still being retained in the Crown Court, an element of lay justice would be maintained throughout the system, but in a new form at the intermediate level where it would be combined with a professional element.

It was not clear at the time of writing whether Lord Justice Auld would consider the formation of specialised courts to deal with offences such as those involving drugs or domestic violence, or to administer a form of restorative justice. Charlotte Walsh has described a tentative movement towards specialised courts in West Yorkshire.[9] Nor was it clear whether he would consider a movement towards 'virtual' courts in which business would be conducted electronically rather than by face-to-face communication. These should be subjects for future debate.

Trial by jury raises similar questions about the tension between efficiency and justice, and about lay and local justice.[10] To substitute a panel of professional judges, or trained or specialised jurors, who would come with some prior knowledge or understanding of the issues to be resolved, has obvious attractions for those whose concern is to promote efficiency. The Conservative Government considered but rejected a proposal for specialised panels to hear complicated fraud trials during the 1980s. The removal of the requirement that verdicts should be unanimous (in 1967), and the removal of the defence's right of peremptory challenge (in 1988), were designed to improve both efficiency and justice in the sense that juries would be less vulnerable to intimidation or manipulation by an unscrupulous defence. The Contempt of Court Act 1981 protects the secrecy of the jury's deliberations in the interests of justice, but also prevents research into how juries function and reach their verdicts - research which might suggest ways in which their efficiency or reliability might be improved. The Royal Commission on Criminal Justice recommended that the restriction should be removed.

Other concerns relate to the composition of juries and the difficulty of achieving a representative cross-section of society (or a suitable proportion of its 'responsible' members), or of including members who share or who are likely to understand the defendant's cultural background. Lord Justice Auld seemed likely to make recommendations which would address these concerns, for example by making it more difficult for (especially middle-class) people to be excused because of the demands of their employment.

A more serious issue relates to perverse verdicts, where the jury returns a verdict of 'not guilty' against what appears to be the weight of the evidence; and to 'jury nullification', where a jury accepts that a person has broken the law but nevertheless returns a not guilty verdict, for example because it believes the law to be unjust or the prosecution to have been oppressive. To prevent such verdicts, it has been suggested that the jury's role could be limited to answering questions of fact, from which the judge rather than the jury would decide on guilt. This is a dangerous line of argument. For many people the possibility of 'jury nullification' is one of the justifications for having juries at all. The point is especially important when new offences, often absolute offences, are increasingly being created for political purposes but whose enforcement depends on the judgement and discretion of the police, and subsequently the Crown Prosecution Service. Examples include the offences created by the Criminal Justice and Public Order Act 1994, the Prevention of Harrassment Act 1997, the Crime and Disorder Act 1998, and especially the Terrorism Act 2000 (see *Chapter 11*).[11]

Several questions arise from any review of the criminal courts. One is the means of ensuring a proper balance between judicial independence; judicial involvement in the management of the system (at national, area and local levels and including any functions contracted out to commercial companies); and judicial accountability (for what and to whom?). How that balance is found affects not just public confidence but also the courts' legitimacy. The pressure for even more efficiency and co-ordination, for common information systems and the most effective use of modern technology, must not result in the courts losing their special role and separate identity in a 'unified' criminal justice system with common, politically determined, aims and objectives and a unified central management. The courts' essential function is to ensure justice and fairness in the operation of the criminal process: they must be able to hear, and if necessary to uphold, challenges to the operational services and to the government of the day, as well as to support them. They must have their own set of objectives – for example to establish the truth and render justice in accordance with the law; and principles such as legality, proportionality, openness and fairness to all parties. Among the institutions of the state, their legitimacy must have a separate foundation from that of the government.

Another question, already discussed in *Chapter 12*, concerns the balance between what a person has done - and has been proved to have done - and what the person might have done or might do in the future, and more generally what kind of person he or she is. *Chapter 12* has argued that proof or an admission of what the person has done, and a judgement of its seriousness and the person's culpability, should in all normal cases be the starting point for a sentencing decision. That principle should also be reflected in rules of evidence and rules of procedure. If extended terms of custody or supervision are to be imposed, not on the principle of proportionality or even following a finding of guilt (as is proposed for those suffering from severe psychopathic disorder[12]) but simply in order to protect the public, then special rules, procedures and safeguards should apply, including a requirement for regular review. All these should be under the supervision of the courts. A clear distinction should be made between matters of judicial judgement (such as the amount of punishment to be imposed in a particular case), and matters of professional judgement (assessments of risk or likely responses to various programmes of treatment), although the propriety or reasonableness of those judgements might be challenged in ways which the courts would have to resolve.

Both the courts and the Crown Prosecution Service would be deeply affected by any serious movement away from what is sometimes described (unfavourably) as 'state' justice and towards a (supposedly more attractive) form of 'community' justice. *Chapter 10* has considered some of the arguments and recent developments, especially in restorative justice. There is a great deal to be said for an 'inclusive' process which involves more people in the arrangements for dealing with crime and administering criminal justice, as a means of generating a wider sense of ownership and responsibility and as part of the obligations of citizenship. Working as mentors, membership of referral panels for juvenile offenders and involvement in consultative procedures, as well as work as lay magistrates and service on juries, are some examples. But 'community justice' could also imply the use of arbitrary or informal (and unaccountable) procedures to target and then humiliate or remove those who are thought to be dangerous, a nuisance or simply do not conform. For the purpose of this chapter, the main point to emphasise is that changes to make the system more 'community-based', 'restorative', 'responsive' or simply more 'flexible', should not be introduced piecemeal into the existing system without serious thought for their implications and consequences. If their effect is to undermine the presumption of innocence, to shift the burden of proof, or to involve other parties such as victims, their families, or representatives of the 'community', then the status, authority and legitimacy of the process, the nature of its outcomes and the character of the institutions which conduct it, will all need to be re-examined.

Whatever the Government's conclusions on the Criminal Courts Review, it cannot continue for much longer to resist the creation of an independent commission for judicial appointments, to widen the field of choice, to ensure a more diverse range of social and cultural backgrounds, and to give more legitimacy to the process. The appointment of an advisory commission in March 2001 is not an adequate substitute. Recent arguments in this sense have come from JUSTICE and from the Commission on the Future of Multi-Ethnic Britain,[13] but the creation of an independent commission had been a Labour Party manifesto commitment in 1992.

CENTRAL GOVERNMENT

Chapters 7 and 9 have described how successive governments have sought closer co-operation between departments and moved towards a more integrated organization and set of procedures. The annual Comprehensive Spending Review, the annual strategic plans and (to some extent) the public service agreements are all welcome developments. The Criminal Justice Consultative Council is becoming a more significant and effective body, with new terms of reference, after a period of neglect by the Conservative Government. The area criminal justice committees seem set to become valuable, possibly powerful, centres for co-ordination and initiative in their new form as strategic committees covering the 42 areas in which all the main services will have boundaries. The Government should consider how it might carry the process further.

Two questions need to be considered, among others. One is the method of budgeting for the prison and probation services, and perhaps more generally for the costs incurred (and paid for) by the taxpayer when a person is in custody or under supervision. The present method of budgeting for the Prison Service has already been described, in *Chapter 9*, as being to 'predict and provide'. It seems extraordinary that this method, discredited throughout the rest of government, should still be tolerated for prisons. The Comprehensive Spending Review should require the Government to decide, as a matter of policy and the national interest, how many people the country needs and can afford to have imprisoned or under supervision and for how long, and what provision should be made for them and at what cost. It should then allocate funds accordingly. Of course the decisions should be made in consultation with the judiciary, and both the government and the judiciary should agree that they are made on reasonable assumptions - for example about levels of crime, numbers of convictions, the number and type of sentences likely to be imposed, and perhaps above all the purposes which sentencing is to achieve. The government should then see that capacity is made available in accordance with those assumptions, without undue overcrowding in prisons or excessive strain on the Probation Service, and the judiciary should accept some responsibility for ensuring that sentencing follows more or less the pattern on which they are based.

The location for this process of consultation could be the Criminal Justice Consultative Council, with contributions from the local strategy committees. It need not be a process in which the government pressed the judiciary to adopt a politically motivated change in sentencing practice, whether towards greater or less severity, and it would certainly not be a matter of the government telling the judiciary whom they should or should not send to prison. The relationship between the government and the judiciary is one of the most important and sensitive in modern governance. The judiciary's independence is critical, but government and the judiciary still have to communicate. In practice, it has sometimes suited both sides to keep their distance from one another, but communication, no less than judicial independence, is necessary in a complex modern state. Without it there is a danger not only of inefficiency but also of injustice. Channels through which it could take place have traditionally included the office of Lord Chancellor and the position of the Law Lords in considering new legislation. Both are now coming under criticism, and are more difficult to sustain in a reformed House of Lords, for the reasons discussed later in this chapter. Meetings can of course take place between judges and ministers or officials whenever they are needed, but there is a strong case for a regular forum, as Lord Woolf recognised. The Council should of course continue to discuss other subjects, as it does at present, of which the implications of cultural diversity and the opportunities and dangers of modern technology. are two obvious examples.

The second question concerns the way in which funding is directed towards particular services, organizations and projects. In order to strengthen central control, and as the government would say to ensure effectiveness and value for money, funding is increasingly being provided specifically for individual projects, often by-passing local authorities and statutory services, and going direct to the partnership or voluntary organization which is running the project (not only of course in the area of criminal justice). Or if funding is paid to local authorities or statutory services, it is 'ring fenced' so that it can only be spent for a specific purpose. The project is then evaluated to see if it is successful. When it announces a funding programme of this kind, the government typically advertises it to those organizations who might be interested; sets out the terms and conditions, which often include a requirement to form partnerships and find matching funds; and almost always for it to be evaluated; and invites bids which then have to compete with one another.

This approach may have made some sense at a time when the previous Conservative Government had for some years shown little interest in innovation, very little funding had been available, and skills in forming partnerships and managing projects were in short supply. As a permanent routine it has serious drawbacks. It is an expression of the Government's lack of confidence in the imagination or competence of local authorities or statutory services; it reduces their confidence and credibility; it assumes an understanding of local conditions and circumstances on the part of central government which it does not always possess; and it is a laborious and time-consuming process for those who make the applications. Applications may sometimes be made more because the money is available than because there is a clear need for the particular project which the applicants put forward; evaluations are sometimes too limited in their depth or quality for reliable conclusions to be drawn from them; and the project can be left in the air at the end of the funding period, or adopted as a model on the basis of questionable evidence.

At the same time, funding for 'mainstream' services and 'core' activities is severely restricted, and the continuous pressure for efficiency savings leaves little room for innovation, or even flexibility, to meet local demands. The situation can be especially complicated, and often frustrating, for anyone dealing with an individual, for example a disturbed adolescent, who needs attention from several services and who has an unsettled lifestyle - moving about the country, not attending schools or keeping appointments for interviews, not registered with a doctor.

Just as there is no single or simple answer to the problems of crime, deprived neighbourhoods or disturbed individuals, so there is no single reform of funding arrangements which will simplify them or remove those frustrations. Public money has to be spent effectively, for the purpose for which it is intended, through procedures which can be properly audited and by people who can be held to account. But the time may have to come when the arrangements should be reviewed, when the government could afford to have more confidence in local authorities and services, and when local authorities and services should be allowed more discretion and given more encouragement,

Earlier chapters have emphasised the constitutive importance of public services as part of a civilised, or it might be said liberal democratic, state. The Government sees them as maintaining the country's social stability and making it successful in competitive global markets. But it has also made the connection between public services and citizenship, and has acknowledged the importance of leadership. Leadership is more than management. It involves vision and inspiration; it looks outwards from the organization beyond its users and stakeholders, or in commercial terms its customers and suppliers, to the wider social, political and ethical context in which it operates. Education and training for leadership need to include what Mike Nellis has called 'overarching' as well as 'practical' knowledge (see *Chapters 5 and 20*).[14]

The Government recognises the need for the training of civil servants to include leadership in this wider sense, and for it to be extended to ministers. The Centre for Management and Policy Studies was established for this purpose.[15] And yet members of the police service and of the judiciary and other criminal justice services, are still trained separately, within their own professional culture and traditions. Training for leadership, especially in a diverse, modern society, needs a broader base, a wider vision, and a more challenging intellectual environment. And it needs an ethical aspect (see also *Chapter 22*).

AN INSTITUTE OF CRIMINAL JUSTICE

These features could be more easily provided if the Government were to establish an institute or college of criminal justice. The institute would organize and provide joint training for those likely to reach the highest positions in the criminal justice services, the judiciary, relevant parts of the civil service, and indeed perhaps as ministers (and perhaps members of other political parties). The training would be an active rather than a passive experience and it would include opportunities to study and make proposals for dealing with some of the issues of the moment. A supervisory board including representatives of government departments would agree the subjects in advance, and its members should be in a position to see that the proposals were taken seriously in the government's decision-making process. The supervisory board would also include academic members who would ensure a strong academic input to the programme and help to validate it and make proposals for academic research (*Chapter 9* has considered how academic research should be commissioned and funded). There would be close links with universities. The institute would also provide a resource on which former students and others could draw in the course of their own professional lives, and it would publish periodical papers which would help to deepen professional, political and public understanding of current issues and stimulate more informed and rigorous debate. Its functions would in this respect resemble, but go beyond, those of the National Institute of Justice in the United States. It could also complement the Criminal Justice Consultative Council by providing a space in which political and professional leaders could share ideas with each other and their counterparts in other countries in informal surroundings and without arousing suspicion or having to reach definite conclusions.

There is a parallel in the National College for School Leadership, set up by the Department for Education and Employment, which started work in September 2000. Its prospectus states

> The college will set the pace and direction of national debate on school leadership. It will promote a shared awareness of the variety of ways in which the best schools - and other analogous public and private sector enterprises - are led and managed. It will act as a catalyst, bringing fresh perspectives to bear on the challenges facing schools today. It will convene national lecture series and conferences, with high quality contributors including our own best leaders, on its own site, at regional or international venues, and on-line.

> The college will work with government in developing targeted leadership strategies in key national priority areas, for example developing best practice in leadership in the inner cities as part of our Excellence in Cities agenda, and looking at the role of leadership in building racial awareness and inclusion, and celebrating diversity in our schools.

> We shall support government-funded research focused on school leadership issues through the college so that it can act as a powerhouse for high quality research feeding into school-level improvement. The college will commission research into areas of difficulty, challenge and success and then disseminate the results to schools. We expect the college to offer serving teachers and heads opportunities to contribute to research.

A DEPARTMENT OF JUSTICE

Suggestions for reforming the machinery of government by creating a department or ministry of justice have been put forward from time to time for many years. Leon Radzinowicz and Roger Hood describe a protracted debate which took place between 1845 and 1874, with the conclusion that the Lord Chancellor was already the Minister of Justice and no change was needed. The subject was interestingly revived in the context of the reconstruction of government after the First World War, where it was a recommendation of Lord Haldane's committee on the machinery of government, already mentioned in *Chapter 2*. The creation of a department of justice was one of the reforms (along with an independent commission for judicial appointments) to which the Labour Party committed itself in its manifesto for the general election in 1992, and the Institute for Public Policy Research included it among the proposals in *A Written Constitution for the United Kingdom* in 1993.[16]

Arguments for a department of justice are of different kinds and would produce different results. The first is one of efficiency: the present division of functions between the Home Secretary, the Lord Chancellor and the Attorney-General leads to lack of co-ordination and inefficiency, and the three offices should be combined in a single department. Such a department would have a single system for its information technology, and a structure which would allow for a single minister and a single chief executive to direct the whole of the criminal justice system. This argument may look attractive from a managerial perspective, but it does not stand up to close examination. There are already suggestions that the Home Office is too large, and its work too sensitive, complex and unpredictable, for a single minister, or a single permanent secretary, to give it the attention it needs. Adding more ministers or a second permanent secretary would only increase the problems of communication and co-ordination which this argument seeks to resolve. More seriously, it would combine functions and responsibilities which ought in a liberal democracy to be separated as a matter of principle. Maintaining justice and the control of crime and disorder are separate functions, and the first should never be subordinated to, or seen as an instrument for achieving, the second.

A second argument relates to the anomalous position of the Lord Chancellor, and to some extent of the Attorney-General. Since the Lord Chancellor's Department became a major, and in most respects 'normal', department of state with the reform of the higher criminal courts as a result of the Courts Act 1971, and especially since the administration of the civil and criminal courts became the focus of greater political and managerial attention in the early 1980s, the Lord Chancellor's combination of functions - as a government minister, as the head of the judiciary and as the Speaker of the House of Lords - has been hard to justify. The enactment of the Human Rights Act and the recent and prospective reforms of the House of Lords make the situation even more difficult to sustain in a modern democratic country based on the Rule of Law. Diana Woodhouse has drawn attention to some of the arguments, and JUSTICE has done so in its evidence to the Royal Commission on the House of Lords.

Diana Woodhouse[17] writes

> The Lord Chancellor' s Department is no longer detached from the executive and political arm of government. Indeed the research found that the executive, rather than the judicial, responsibilities now dominate. This is

evident from the 'key challenges' set out in its Strategic Plan (1994/5 - 1996/7), none of which makes reference to its judicial responsibilities.

JUSTICE's proposals[18] were that the Lord Chancellor should no longer sit judicially; that serving law lords should no longer sit as members of the House of Lords; and that the judicial functions of the House of Lords and of the Privy Council should be transferred to a newly constituted Supreme Court. They argue that their proposals would enable the Lord Chancellor' s Department to continue to function as a strong and effective Ministry of Justice, but they do not go on to consider the functions of a Ministry of Justice as such or its relationships with the departments of state. JUSTICE have also suggested that the combination of judicial and legislative functions exercised by the Lord Chancellor and the law lords may be open to challenge under the European Convention On Human Rights, as a result of the European Court of Human Rights' decisions in *McGonnell v. United Kingdom* and *Procola v. Luxembourg*.

The anomalies affecting the position of the Attorney-General are less prominent and less frequently discussed. But the combination of minister for public prosecutions, legal adviser to the government, and Head of the Bar is hardly less difficult to justify.

The third argument relates to the quality of decision-making in government as a whole and to the country's conception of justice. Unlike the other two, it demands a redistribution of functions between the Home Office and a new department whose responsibilities would include but go beyond those of the present Lord Chancellor's Department. It starts from the view, expressed in earlier chapters and indicated above, that justice is an aim to be pursued in its own right, across the whole of government and civil society, and is not to be understood as a collective name for the mechanisms by which the state controls crime. On this view there are certain subjects - the principles, content and administration of civil and criminal law; law reform; the organization and management of the courts; the appointment and training of the judiciary; the prosecution of criminal offences; and human rights and constitutional matters. Together they form a coherent and distinct set of responsibilities which needs to have a clear focus and to be separately organized within government. Of course the principles and values to which a government is committed – for the Labour Government those of fairness, opportunity, equal worth, social inclusion, efficiency, effectiveness and modernisation - should inform government departments and public services as a whole. They should be refined and given more explicit content, for example by applying the concept of citizenship in the ways which previous chapters have described. But just as the principles and aims of sustainable growth and of efficiency, effectiveness and value for money have an institutional focus in the Treasury, so should those of democracy, human rights and respect for diversity and freedom under the law have a focus in a Department of Justice, with a minister who can argue for them, if necessary against the Home Secretary.

Those with long memories or a sense of history might claim that they once did so in the Home Office, and a trace of that claim can be found in the letters which the permanent under-secretary of state, Sir Alexander Maxwell, personally sent to newly appointed members of staff in the 1940s.[19] But it is not a claim which other departments would have acknowledged in recent times, and the tradition which Sir Alexander Maxwell described has arguably been compromised (though not destroyed) by policies which successive Home Secretaries have over the years felt obliged to pursue in relation to such subjects as immigration, asylum, official secrets, public order, drugs and terrorism. Sarah Spencer has explored the arguments in more detail, and has suggested a possible distribution of functions between a new department and a reconstructed Home Office, in her paper *Time for a Ministry of Justice?*[20] It is not a subject to be decided on the basis of the personal expectations and ambitions of individual ministers.

The case for a Department of Justice now deserves serious debate.

ENDNOTES for *Chapter 21*

[1]   *The Review of the Crown Prosecution Service, A Report* (Chairman the Right Honourable Sir Iain Glidewell), Cmnd. 3960, London, HMSO, 1998.

[2]   M. McConville, J. Hodgson, L. Bridges and A. Pavlovic, *Standing Accused: The Organization and Practices of Criminal Defence Lawyers in Britain*, Oxford, Clarendon Press, 1994; also A. Cretney and G. Davis, *Punishing Violence*, London, Routledge, 1995.

[3]   Stephen Shute, 'Who Passes Unduly Lenient Sentences? How are They Listed?: A Survey of Attorney-General's Reference Cases 1989-1997', *Criminal Law Review*, 1999, p. 603.

[4]   The debate on the Second Reading of the Bill in the House of Lords took place on 28 September 2000: Lords *Hansard*, Cols. 961-1033. For the argument that the effect of the change would be racially discriminatory, see Lee Bridges, 'Taking Liberties', *Legal Action*, 2000, pp. 6-8. The argument was not that magistrates are themselves racially prejudiced, but that the procedures used in the magistrates' courts had a discriminatory effect and that many members of racial groups believed that they were more likely to obtain a fair trial in the Crown Court. Several of the Bill's opponents in the House of Lords emphasised that their opposition did not imply any criticism of the magistracy as such.

[5]   For a discussion of the magistrates' courts, see Martin Wasik, Thomas Gibbons and Mike Redmayne, *Criminal Justice: Text and Materials*, London, Longman, 1999 pp. 348-64. The literature on the social background of lay magistrates includes John Raine, *Local Justice: Ideals and Realities*, Edinburgh, T & T Clark 1989; Jim Dignan and Arnold Wynne, 'A Microcosm of the Local Community: Reflections on the Composition of Magistracy in a Petty Sessional Division in the North Midlands', *British Journal of Criminology*, 1997, 37/2, pp. 184-97; and Mary Eaton, *Justice for Women?*, Milton Keynes, Open University Press, 1986.

[6]   Rod Morgan and Keith Russell, *The Judiciary in the Magistrates' Courts*, RDS Occasional Paper No. 66, London, Home Office, 2000.

[7]   Andrew Sanders, *Community Justice: Modernising the Magistracy in England and Wales*, London, Institute for Public Policy Research, 2001.

[8]   On local justice, see Christopher Compston, 'Local Justice: A Personal View' in Jonathan Burnside and Nicola Baker (eds.), *Relational Justice: Repairing the Breach*, Winchester, Waterside Press, 1994.

[9]   Charlotte Walsh 'The Trend Towards Specialisation: West Yorkshire Innovations in Drugs and Domestic Violence Courts', *Howard Journal of Criminal Justice*, 40/1, pp. 26-38, 2001.

[10] For a review of the arguments and evidence relating to trial by jury, see Martin Wasik, Thomas Gibbons and Mike Redmayne, *op. cit.*, n. 5, pp. 388-410. Also Warren Young, Neil Cameron and Yvette Tinsley, 'Juries in Criminal Trials', a paper prepared for the Law Commission in New Zealand, Wellington NZ, 1999.

[11] For a discussion of 'perverse verdicts by juries in the Crown Court', see Marcel Berlins and Clare Dyer, 'Perverting the Course of Justice', *Guardian*, 22 January 2001.

[12] Department of Health, *Reforming the Mental Health Act: Part II, High Risk Patients*, Cmnd. 5016 II., London, Stationery Office, 2000.

[13] JUSTICE has for several years argued for the creation of an independent commission to make or advise on judicial appointments, and believes that such a commission has become especially important with the introduction of the Human Rights Act 1998. JUSTICE, *The Judicial Functions of the House of Lords:Evidence to the Royal Commission on the Reform of the House of Lords*, London, JUSTICE, 1999. For the report of the Commission on the Future of Multi-Ethnic Britain, see *Chapter 16*.

[14] Mike Nellis 'The New Probation Training in England and Wales: Realising the Potential', *Social Work Training* (forthcoming).

[15] The Annual Report of the Civil Service Reform Programme for 2000 states that the Centre for Management and Policy Studies has established a strong programme to support ministers and senior civil servants in their leadership role. Two induction programmes have been run to address issues of working with departments and across government. Eight seminars have been held jointly with civil servants and experts from outside government to focus on improving the policy process through cross-cutting working. In addition, 13 seminars and discussion forums have been held specifically for ministers; plus a one-day event for ministers and officials engaged in taking Bills through Parliament. Increased emphasis has been given to leadership in the corporate training the Centre for Management and Policy Studies provides for senior civil servants, and new programmes have been added to tackle new leadership issues, including the strategic leadership in relation to e-government. Cabinet Office, *The Civil Service Reform Programme Annual Report 2000*, London, Cabinet Office, 2001.

[16] Institute for Public Policy Research, *A Written Constitution for the United Kingdom*, London, Mansell Publishing, 1993.

[17] Diana Woodhouse, *The Lord Chancellor : Accountability in a Market Economy*, report to the ESRC, R000222469, Dec. 1999. Also *The Office of Lord Chancellor*, Oxford, Hart Publishing, 2001.

[18] JUSTICE, *op. cit.*, n. 13.

[19] A typical letter which Sir Alexander Maxwell sent to a newly appointed member of staff in April 1947 included the following paragraph:

> One of [the Home Secretary's] chief functions is to see that proper arrangements are made for the maintenance of law and order throughout England and Wales, and as the object of maintaining law and order is to promote the welfare of the community by enabling people to go about their lawful pursuits without molestation, the Home Secretary has a responsibility for preserving the liberty of the subject. This responsibility places on members of his staff a special obligation to carry out their administrative duties in a humane and liberal spirit with a careful regard for the rights and liberties of individuals. Much of our work is concerned with petitions, complaints and applications from all sorts of people, and it is our business to try to understand each applicant's point of view and to take account of the human interests involved.

[20] Sarah Spencer, *Time for a Ministry of Justice? The Future of the Home Office and the Lord Chancellor's Department*, London, Institute for Public Policy Research, 2001 (revised version forthcoming).

PART V Conclusions

CHAPTER 22

Principles and Policies for the Twenty-first Century

> But I do know a regime which provides human beings no deep reasons to care about one another cannot long preserve its legitimacy.
>
> Richard Sennett, *The Corrosion of Character*, p. 148.

Britain is at a stage where it has to ask some difficult and important questions. The answers will both reflect and determine the kind of country it is to be for two or three generations to come. Some of the answers will be within the control of government; others will come from attitudes, beliefs and actions over which governments have little or no control.

A changing landscape
Familiar landmarks in the structure of authority are crumbling or becoming overgrown. New sources of power and influence are emerging. Others are losing their significance. Organizations, processes and individual lives are becoming more complex, more fragmented and often more precarious. Traditional communities are declining; new forms of association are taking their place. The urge to change and modernise in the interests of national progress is matched by a continuing attachment to the past and to traditional values. It is hard to know what to keep, what to discard, and what to create that is new.

Traditions to keep or to restore include: the ethics and values of public service; an individual and collective social conscience; the pursuit and defence of justice and personal freedom; and a sense of trust and confidence in public services and institutions. Public services have to earn and maintain that trust and confidence by their own integrity and legitimacy, and through their relationships with the citizens whom they serve. To be discarded are assumptions of superiority and privilege, and stereotypical views of those who are 'different' for reasons of background, culture or appearance. To be created are: a more inclusive and compassionate society; a stronger recognition and acceptance of the rights and responsibilities of citizenship; a more thoughtful, more accessible and less adversarial approach to politics; and more devolved institutional structures to sustain those values and relationships in citizens' ordinary lives and experience.

Earlier chapters have traced some of the changes which are taking place, in contemporary society (see, especially, *Chapter 2*); in government, governance and public service (*Chapters 2, 3* and *5*); and particularly in criminal justice (*Chapters 6 to 10*). Society has become more unequal, restless and diverse; crime and the fear of crime have come to have an increasing effect on people's lives. Politics has become *more* adversarial, *more* pervasive in its influence over public services and public life, but also more remote from the interest and active involvement of many citizens. This trend has been accompanied by the growth of a 'new public management' or 'new managerialism' in which management becomes a substitute for leadership and competencies for wisdom. Management itself is sometimes presented as if it could be reduced to the 'value-free' promotion of efficiency, effectiveness and 'getting more for less'. Taken together, the changes have brought about a sense of 'democratic deficit' in many areas of national life – acknowledged in effect in the important proposals for innovations in the citizen's participation in government put forward by the House of Commons Select Committee on Public Administration.[1] They have also resulted in declining standards of service, care and maintenance in many public services, and have sometimes led to a loss of consideration, trust and respect in personal and working relationships. Crime and fear of crime are part of a larger pattern of incivility and social instability.

A new sense of direction

A search is beginning for a new sense of political direction and inspiration; for new methods of establishing or restoring confidence in public services, and perhaps especially in criminal justice; sometimes even for a new or restored sense of national identity. In this book I have argued that a sense of direction, confidence and identity could be based on a revival of the spirit of citizenship and public service. That spirit must be generous, open and inclusive rather than closed and exclusionary; it must achieve a proper balance between individual and collective rights and personal and public responsibilities; and citizens must have the opportunity and capacity to exercise those rights and responsibilities. It must be associated with a strong and active civil society. Citizens must always be ready to ask themselves, 'What if it were me? What if it were my child?' (*Chapter 4*, with further references, explanations and specific applications in later chapters).

Restoring authority and respect

Restoring confidence in public services involves more than imposing targets, driving up standards and of measuring performance against them. Those measures have their place, and have brought important benefits, but they can damage trust and even professional integrity (*Chapters 3, 5 and 17*). The primary task is to secure certain vital facets of public services: integrity, accountability and legitimacy, especially if, as in criminal justice, those services have coercive powers. Citizens must feel that they have a sense of 'ownership' of their public services, and some responsibility for and towards them. Public services are not simply the possessions or agents of the government, nor are they (even in criminal justice) simply part of the apparatus of the state. They must work within a framework which is set by government and ultimately by

Parliament, but they must have their own professional identity and sense of purpose. They draw their authority and respect not from government but from the citizens whom they serve.

Questions about 'what works' are a necessary starting point for reviews of policy or practice, but they have to include 'for whom' , 'for what purpose' , 'on what evidence' and 'with what consequences' . Those questions must be answered rigorously and with integrity. The answers need evidence, expertise, vision and sometimes courage (*Chapters 3* and *9*). The academic community must also contribute by making sure that its research, and the interpretation of results, are of the highest quality, and by continually developing research methods. Governments for their part must make sure that the methods by which they fund research are not so rigid or so prescriptive that research produces superficial or misleading results. Nor should they allow a situation in which the country's entire research effort is channelled towards short-term evaluations designed to serve immediate political or operational purposes. Research programmes should reflect a longer term and more strategic vision, and their construction should be a genuinely equal partnership between government and the academic community.

Structural changes should never be introduced for their own sake, to give an appearance of progress or 'modernisation'. But some public services now need a more devolved organization and stronger mechanisms for local accountability, participation and ownership. This is a common theme in the chapters concerned with public service in general, and with the police, prison and probation services in particular (*Chapters 5, 17, 19* and *20*). Changes may also be needed in central government, including the creation of a department for children and a department of justice (and not necessarily with those titles: see *Chapters 14* and *21*).

The civil service
The civil service is a public service of a special kind. Its reputation, and perceptions of its role and responsibilities, have changed and in some ways suffered over the last 30 years. Respect needs to be restored, its role and responsibilities need to be clarified, and it needs the leadership, authority and expertise to discharge them with a proper degree of political independence (*Chapters 2* and *3*). As work on this book was coming to an end, the House of Commons Select Committee on Public Administration published its report *Making Government Work: the Emerging Issues.*[2] The Committee identified a number of issues which it hoped would receive closer attention in the next Parliament, in particular improving the performance of public services at the same time as maintaining or increasing their public accountability, with particular reference to new methods of funding, especially to promote joint working; the change which those methods demand in traditional cultures of ministerial and civil service responsibility; and the need for a cultural change which goes beyond a reorganization of government departments. The Committee expressed concern that new, top down programmes were not matched by adequate capacity, ownership or

accountability at local level. They also discussed public service ethics and professionalism, the implications of new technology and civil servants' relationship with the government of the day. They argued for a system of elected regional government, a Royal Commission on the civil service and a Civil Service Act. More detailed suggestions related to training, recruitment, patterns of civil service careers, methods of risk assessment and arrangements for inspection and audit (including the role of Parliament), where 'in all of this it is important to keep citizens at the front of the picture'.

The issues which the Committee identified are therefore closely in line with those which are the subject of this book. They raise questions not only about organization, policy and practice, but also about the nature and role of the state, and the relationships between the state, the citizen, public services and the government of the day. They include questions which are not just about skills and expertise (or 'competences'), but also about the social and professional wisdom, and the political maturity, which are needed in a modern society and a modern democracy. The Committee's proposals for a Royal Commission on the civil service and a Civil Service Act, together with a system of elected regional government, deserve serious attention. They should not however be approached as a managerial reorganization designed to improve efficiency within existing assumptions and relationships. They should be seen as major constitutional reforms, capable of transforming the whole relationship between the citizen and the state. As such they would be no less signficant than devolution to Scotland and Wales, and perhaps more significant than the Human Rights Act 1998, or any reform of the House of Lords which seems likely to be contemplated.

The nature of justice

The questions identified in the previous paragraph are especially significant in relation to crime and criminal justice. In today's politics, protecting the public - and efficiency and effectiveness in achieving that protection - have come to take precedence over justice and freedom. The word 'justice' is used more often in its secondary sense (as defined in the *Oxford English Dictionary*) as the process of law or the exercise of legal vengeance, than in its primary and substantive or normative sense as the quality or principle of justice or fairness in relation to all the elements in a situation and all the people involved in it. In its secondary sense, justice can be seen as an instrument of the state, even of the government; in its primary sense justice stands *in its own right*. This primary sense needs to be reinforced and where necessary restored.

Changes in the rules of evidence, procedure and substantive law which serve to lessen the effect of longstanding principles concerning the burden of proof, access to trial by jury, the construction of criminal offences and 'double jeopardy' (so that no one can be tried and punished twice for an identical matter), can all be argued individually on their merits. Taken together as weapons of war or as part of a comprehensive programme of 'modernisation', they may appear to put justice itself under threat. The words 'freedom' and 'liberty', once used regularly guide Home Office policy through such expressions as 'freedom under the law' and the 'liberty of the individual' (or sometimes the 'subject'), have all but disappeared from the political vocabulary.

Chapter 6 recalls the ideas, theories and traditions which have historically influenced attitudes to crime and the sentencing and treatment of offenders, the policies and practices which have reflected those attitudes, and the successes and disappointments which have followed. *Chapters 7, 8 and 9* describe the approaches and policies which recent governments have adopted in Great Britain, and more especially in England and Wales. Reflecting on these policies, and on those adopted in the United States, David Garland has written[3]

> Crime strategies and criminological ideas are not adopted because they are known to solve problems. The evidence runs out well before the effects can be known with any certainty. They are adopted and they succeed because they characterise problems and identify solutions in ways that fit with the dominant culture and the power structure upon which it rests.

His analysis gives a dispiriting impression of inevitability and political powerlessness - a sense that governments are trapped by their own politics into promoting policies and programmes which are all to do with appearances, presentation and 'spin', and which have little relevance to the substantive problems which they are supposed to address.

Nature and role of the state
Underlying the more obvious questions of policy and practice are some fundamental questions about the nature and role of the state, and about the relationships between the state, the citizen, public services and the government of the day. They include questions which are not just about skills and expertise, but also about social and professional wisdom, and political maturity, all of which are needed in a modern society and a liberal democracy. They are especially significant in relation to crime and criminal justice.

The state has a clear responsibility to prevent and reduce crime, to protect its citizens from crime, and to support people who become its victims. It has a similar responsibility to defend citizens' freedom and to protect them from unfair discrimination or abuse of power. To enjoy that protection, in all its aspects, is one of the rights of citizenship. But action to prevent crime, to manage its consequences and to deal with those who commit it, is as much a responsibility of citizens individually and of civil society collectively as it is of the state and its agencies. It is also a matter for the commercial sector through both its business customs and its employment practices. It is emphatically not a responsibility which should be left entirely to the state - or the criminal justice system - as a matter either of principle or of practical effectiveness (*Chapters 11, 14, 15*

, especially violent crime, is a symptom of a troubled society. It
symptom - others are unfair discrimination and exploitation,
opportunity, lack of consideration and extremes of social
A liberal democracy will try to treat those symptoms, and to

tackle their underlying causes in human weakness and social injustice, but there is no perfect state in which they will all be resolved. *Chapter 11* has shown that those acts which a society chooses to treat as crimes, and those people whom it chooses to treat as criminals, are to some extent a matter of political choice. But to 'widen the net' so that an ever increasing range of behaviours and more and more people become criminalised, so far from strengthening considerate behaviour or respect for the law, will lead to yet greater social disintegration and alienation. To suppose that human behaviour can be reformed by indefinitely extending or intensifying the mechanisms of control is to ignore its frequent irrationality and unpredictability – and the complex nature of the links between behaviour, the influences to which it may be subjected and human reactions to those influences.

Chapters *6* and *10* have described how attempts to control crime may focus on criminal acts or events, or on criminals as people. The emphasis has been different at different times. Crime has to be prevented and victims deserve to be supported, and those who commit crime have to be dealt with and sometimes (but not always) punished. Action to achieve the first of these objectives is mainly the business of wider social policies and specific programmes of prevention and support (*Chapters 14, 15* and *18*); action towards the second is the business of criminal justice. The distinction is not absolute: preventive measures may also help to catch offenders, and the criminal justice process will certainly have some influence on the general level of crime. But just as a country misdirects itself if it supposes that it can resolve all the problems of crime by programmes of social reform, so it is misguided if it tries to resolve them by concentrating on the criminal justice process and focusing all its attention on individual so-called criminals. Strategies must consider the nature of society as a whole, and of the relationships and responsibilities within it.

The primary purpose of criminal justice is not to prevent crime, nor is it to protect the public unless protection is understood as the defence of freedom - in a sense which includes but which is wider than freedom from crime and fear of crime. Its purpose is to achieve justice.[4]

Making power legitimate

Criminal law and the criminal justice process are a uniquely important part of the apparatus of the state. They set and enforce the framework within which the state controls its citizens and regulates their behaviour. Criminal justice is not only about pursuing, convicting and punishing offenders: it is also about the exercise of the state's powers of interference, intrusion, control and ultimately of coercion, and correspondingly the limits which should be placed upon those powers. In a liberal democracy, the state's possession of those powers, the government's policies for using them, and their actual use in practice, must be proportionate, democratic, accountable and above all legitimate. Criminal justice, or what David Garland calls the criminal justice state, must not become Leviathan.[5]

The notion of legitimacy has been mentioned at several points in the course of the book, especially in *Chapter 5*. Conditions for legitimacy in criminal justice include the following.

- The powers available to the state and its institutions and agencies must be exercised on behalf of its citizens as a whole, and not for the benefit of any particular sector or interest.

- Those powers, and the use which is made of them, must be proportionate to the purpose they are intended to serve. If the state or its agents wish to prevent people from doing what they want to do, it is for the state and not for the citizen to justify its action.

- Proposals for extending those powers, and policies for their use, must be based on a rigorous and honest examination and analysis and well-informed consultation and debate. They must have the consent, the support and the engagement of those who will be affected by them and of those who will have to exercise them.

- Policy and practice must observe the principles of equity, consistency and proportionality, and of equality of consideration and respect for all citizens, including especially members of minority groups.

- Decision-making authorities must be properly constituted and competent for their purpose and the functions they have to perform. They must be accountable to the citizens whom they exist to serve, through mechanisms which are appropriate and effective, which include mechanisms located at the most local practicable level. Citizens have not only the right but also the responsibility to hold those authorities to account.

- Decision-making processes must be open, accessible and similarly accountable. They must be operated scrupulously and with integrity.

- All citizens are entitled to dignity, decency and respect in all their dealings with agents of the state, and to protection from injury, loss or abuse of power or process.

- Any interference with citizens' liberty, lives or privacy must be within a framework of legality, established by domestic and international law, including especially the European Convention On Human Rights, with safeguards and effective opportunities for redress.

Structures and values
These conditions will be set by a combination of statutes, organizational structure and administrative directions. Some changes in structure are now needed, perhaps most urgently within the Prison Service. Within that framework, public servants will have to resolve conflicts and reconcile priorities. Some conflicts will be ethical - for example between

public protection and respect for the individual, or equality and diversity; some will be professional, perhaps between speed or economy and consultation or accountability; some will be managerial, to meet different targets or satisfy different budgetary requirements. Risks must be managed and not simply avoided. How the conflicts are resolved will largely depend on the values of public servants: their ethics, integrity and working culture, their professional wisdom, their sense of confidence and trust, and the extent to which they have discretion to apply their own judgement and common sense. All of these will to some extent reflect, and be affected by, the civic values of society as a whole. Investment in new legislation, management systems and technology will be of small worth unless those wider considerations are taken into account. The demand for safety and the search for efficiency must not exclude the pursuit of freedom and justice, still more a sense of compassion and humanity.

ENDNOTES for *Chapter 22*

[1] House of Commons Select Committee on Public Administration, *Innovations in Citizen Participation in Government*, Sixth Report of Session 2000-01, HC 373-I, London, Stationery Office, 2001.

[2] House of Commons Select Committee on Public Administration, *Making Government Work: the Emerging Issues*, Seventh Report of Session 2000-2001, HC 94, London, Stationery Office, 2001.

[3] David Garland, *The Culture of Control: Crime and Social Order in Contemporary Society*, Oxford, Oxford University Press, 2001.

[4] Andrew Rutherford has written

> ... the purposes of criminal justice reflect choices which are ultimately ideological and matters of political philosophy. If ideology is the permanent hidden agenda of criminal justice ... it is necessary to be explicit about the nature of these choices. Instrumental goals for criminal justice must therefore be considered alongside its underlying and fundamental values. Criminal justice in a liberal democracy is always sold short when it is asserted that its over-riding goal is, for example, the protection of society from crime. Not only should fundamental values temper any instrumental goal of this sort but these may be expected to take precedence as the ends to be served.

Andrew Rutherford, *What is Criminal Justice For?*, London, Institute for Public Policy Research, 2001.

[5] David Garland op. cit. n. 3 and 'Ideas, Institutions and Situational Crime Prevention' in Andrew von Hirsch, David Garland and Alison Wakefield (eds.), *Ethics and Social Perspectives in Situational Crime Prevention*, Oxford, Hart Publishing 2000. Also Thomas Hobbes

> I have set forth the nature of man (whose Pride and other Passions have compelled him to submit himself to government); together with the great power of his Governor, whom I compared to Leviathan, taking that comparison out of the two last verses of the one and fortieth of Job; where God having set forth the great power of Leviathan, calleth him King of the Proud'.

Leviathan Pt. II, ch. xxviii, 1651.

CHAPTER 23

Five Years On

LABOUR'S SECOND AND THIRD TERMS

This book was first published as the Labour Government's first term of office was coming to an end in 2001. A number of themes had already emerged from the political, social and economic context of the time and from the Government's own approach, as discussed in *Chapters 2-6* and *Chapter 9*. A range of new policies was being developed on sentencing, policing, youth justice, the treatment of victims, racism, the prevention of crime and disorder, and the management of the criminal justice services, as described in *Chapters 10–21*.

The last five years have seen the Labour Government's second term of office and the beginning of its third, following its re-election in May 2005. During that period, the Criminal Justice Act 2003 - the outcome of the Halliday and Auld reviews mentioned in *Chapters 12* and *21* - has created a new legislative framework for sentencing, and aims to increase the efficiency and effectiveness of criminal trials (that is, fewer delays and more convictions) by changes in the rules of evidence and procedure. The Government has moved on from its earlier reform of the Probation Service to the formation of a single National Offender Management Service (NOMS), including both the Prison Service and the newly reformed National Probation Service. The Anti-Social Behaviour Act 2003 and the Serious Organized Crime and Police Act 2005, together with the greater use of anti-social behaviour orders (ASBOs) made under the Crime and Disorder Act 1998, has expanded still further the scope and use of the criminal law to cover an even wider range of actions and behaviour. The Sexual Offences Act 2003, and the increased availability and use of technology, have extended the surveillance and control of individuals considered to be dangerous or socially disruptive.

The police have targeted known or suspected offenders in order to 'bring more offenders to justice'. Terrorism has become a major issue as a result of events in the United States in September 2001 and in London in July 2005, which prompted the enactment of the Prevention of Terrorism Act 2005 and the introduction of a new Terrorism Bill in October 2005. Civil renewal, active citizenship and local governance have emerged as new subjects across government as a whole. Not only the Treasury but also the Prime Minister's Office, the Cabinet Office, the Office of the Deputy Prime Minister and the Department for Education and Skills have come to take an increasingly active part in forming criminal justice policy. Crime has fallen overall, quite dramatically in the case of burglary and car crime, but there have been increases in recorded offences of violence and the fall has not yet had much impact on the public's fear of crime or its perceptions of the problem and its possible solutions.

Several of the developments favoured in earlier chapters have now taken place. The formation of NOMS is intended to bring a separation of the 'commissioning' from the 'providing' functions for the combined service and to achieve a better balance between the demands which the courts make upon the Prison Service and National Probation Service and their capacity to meet these demands – see *Chapters 19 and 20*. The Sentencing Guidelines Council created under the Criminal Justice Act 2003 is performing the more dynamic and influential role that was envisaged for the Sentencing Advisory Panel in *Chapter 12*. A new Independent Police Complaints Commission has been established, more separate from the police than the previous Police Complaints Authority. Community policing and local accountability are among the main features of the Government's continuing programme of police reform – see *Chapter 17*[1] - although there is at the same time a continuing movement towards national structures to deal with terrorism and serious and organized crime, and towards the amalgamation of police services into fewer and larger units of management and command.

Responsibility for certain constitutional matters has been transferred from the Home Office to the Lord Chancellor's Department, now re-named the Department for Constitutional Affairs. The Constitutional Reform Act 2005 makes statutory provision for a Judicial Appointments Commission and for a Supreme Court – see *Chapter 21*. The courts, and not the Home Secretary, now set the 'tariff' for the time to be served under a sentence of life imprisonment (*Chapter 13*). The Lord Chancellor is no longer head of the judiciary and no longer sits as a judge. Some of the concerns about the structure and effectiveness of central government have been met by the creation of the National Criminal Justice Board and the Office for Criminal Justice Reform. Local Criminal Justice Boards are becoming increasingly effective at the level of the 42 criminal justice areas. The programme for civil renewal and active citizenship resembles in some ways the framework of principles and values discussed in *Chapter 4*.

Progress has been made in the treatment of victims and witnesses, including the creation of a statutory code of practice and the appointment of a commissioner under the Domestic Violence, Crime and Victims Act 2004 (*Chapter 15*). Reforms are proceeding in the Crown Prosecution Service including its relationship with witnesses and victims, with the possibility that it might become a more powerful representative of the 'public interest' in the prosecution process (*Chapter 21*).[2] Developments in restorative and community justice (*Chapter 10*) include the youth courts' widespread use of referral orders, the establishment of the Community Justice Centre in Liverpool and the Community Justice Initiative in Salford, and a range of other local schemes and initiatives, many of them promoted by the voluntary and community sector.[3] Scepticism remains about the scope for expanding the use of restorative justice in the setting of a criminal court or as diversion from a criminal trial, but its significance should be seen in the wider context of a change in culture and not just as one technique or form of court disposal among others. Work to improve the situation and experience of minority groups has continued (*Chapter 16*), although there are new concerns about religious as well as ethnic groups, especially after the terrorist explosions in London in July 2005.

The reforms of youth justice (*Chapter 14*) have generally proved a success. The Government's programme *Every Child Matters,*[4] together with the Children Act 2004, provide a new structure and new responsibilities for the well-being of children, including the appointment of a Children's Commissioner (as already existed in Wales), new duties for local authorities, and the formation of children's trusts. A Green Paper *Youth Matters*[5] proposes a reform of services for young people to improve the support and opportunities that are available to them.

New technology has brought dramatic changes both in communications and in the supervision of offenders. The changes raise obvious questions about confidentiality, and less obvious questions about their effect on the nature and quality of relationships, of all kinds. Electronic monitoring and satellite tracking are sometimes seen negatively as instruments of coercion and control, but they can be used more positively to promote self-discipline and personal commitment, provided that they are supported by regular human contact as part of a relationship based on humanity and mutual respect.[6]

Most of the wider issues identified in the previous and earlier chapters remain, and the discussion in those chapters is as relevant now as it was in 2001. Tensions between rights of the individual and the protection of the public have become more acute, especially after the terrorist attacks on the United States in September 2001 and the explosions in London in July 2005. What had been thought of as fundamental principles of equality, the rule of law and human rights are now being questioned, in the media and sometimes by the Government itself. A series of disagreements has arisen between Ministers and the judiciary, mostly about the interpretation of the Human Rights Act and its application to new legislation on terrorism, including the Terrorism Bill which was before Parliament at the time of writing.[7]

Unacceptably large numbers of children and young people are still receiving custodial sentences (many of them for breaches of ASBOs), and the accommodation and staffing which the Prison Service can provide are too often unsuitable for them. Many are suffering from mental disorder. There is no sign of any movement towards a situation in which most children who get into trouble can be dealt with outside the criminal justice system altogether, as recommended at the end of *Chapter 14*, and there are even moves to extend a form of ASBO to children under the age of ten.

There is continuing concern over the expansion of criminal justice to deal with social disorder as well as crime, including the use and sometimes abuse of ASBOs;[8] the constant creation of new criminal offences; and the expansion of police powers of arrest and summary justice. There is growing confusion over the nature and purpose of punishment and its relationship to sentencing; anxiety over prison overcrowding and the widening gap between the demands of sentencing and the capacity of the penal system;[9] and uncertainty over what the criminal justice process can realistically and legitimately be expected to achieve, and the reliability and validity of the evidence for 'what works'.

For central government, the suggestions in *Chapter 21* and the arguments in *Chapter 22* are still relevant. There remains a strong case for an independent Institute of Justice responsible for the development of professional leadership in the criminal justice services; and for an independent Criminological Research Council (see *Chapter 9*) responsible for commissioning research. There is an even more compelling case for a Department of Justice, separate from the Home Office, now that the problem of internal terrorism is causing the Home Office to take on even more of the character of a department of home security.

POLITICS, CRIME AND CRIMINAL JUSTICE

The Government has continued to avoid statements of its political vision, except in the most general terms. It has preferred the 'third way', described in *Chapter 4*, dealing with issues as they arise and avoiding criticism by a process of 'triangulation' in which it adopts a pragmatic position, separate from those traditionally associated with the 'right' or 'left', and so not easily attacked from either direction. The Labour Party's Manifesto for the general election in 2005 said simply, 'Our vision is clear; a country more equal in its opportunities, more secure in its communities, more confident in its future'. For criminal justice, the vision is one of 'consistent high standards of service for victims and witnesses; bringing more offenders to justice; ensuring court orders and sentences are carried out; building public confidence; and better services for customers'.[10]

Labour as well as Conservative Ministers have been understandably impatient with the academic arguments of 20 years ago that 'nothing works' to prevent or reduce crime, and with the 'new criminology' (*Chapter 6*) that saw it as the function of the state and the criminal justice system to 'manage' crime rather than find solutions. The Labour Government's frustration has extended to what it sees as the slow pace of change and the obstruction from public servants who refuse or are unable to adopt new methods of working. Even after several years in office, Ministers are still ready to portray the criminal justice system as 'failing' to prevent crime or satisfy the public.[11]

Ministers have continued to demonstrate their belief that a government's function of protecting its citizens from crime extends also to nuisances which may cause inconvenience, annoyance or fear, even if they are not criminal offences as such; and that the criminal justice system needs to be 're-balanced' in favour of the victim. Their language and many of their policies continue to assume the existence of a separate and identifiable criminal class – people who are dangerous or persistently a nuisance, who are different from law-abiding citizens, and from whom law-abiding citizens must be protected. They do not acknowledge that the same people may be victims and offenders at different times. The Government further assumes that by expanding the scope of the criminal law and by increasing the range and depth of its interventions in the lives of actual or potential offenders, it can reduce crime and anti-social behaviour and at the same time increase public confidence in the system and in the Government itself. The new agenda of 'Respect', which the Prime Minister launched in September 2005, is 'about how we change not just the law, but the culture of our country to put the law-abiding majority back in charge of their local communities'.[12] The Prime Minister has argued for a similar 're-balancing' of human rights on the ground that 'the rules of the game' have changed as a result of terrorism.

In a significant speech in August 2005, the then Cabinet Office Minister John Hutton reaffirmed the Government's commitment to the long-standing and constant public service values of 'universality, opportunity, security and equity', and to the mechanisms of the 'market', including choice, diversity and 'contestability'.[13] as the means by which those values had to be realised in modern circumstances. He claimed that 'At the start of the twenty-first century we can be more confident than ever in our ability as a Government to influence the shape of markets, using the tools of regulation, inspection and procurement to secure the social justice the public expects'.[14] He did not however explain the basis for that confidence, or say what he meant by 'social justice'. The expression had not previously been much used in political debate and the Government may see it more in utilitarian terms as the satisfaction of the greatest number than as a matter of upholding principles of equality or human rights.

The Labour Party's vision has brought it success in three elections. The Government deserves credit for the progress described at the beginning of this chapter. But it has come to be criticised for its appeal to self-interest; its commitment to markets, privatisation and contracting-out; and its failure to pay enough attention to issues of equality and social justice.[15] Within criminal justice, it has been criticised for its concentration on the punishment and control of offenders, as distinct from the 'causes of crime' which had equal prominence in its original election campaign (*Chapter 9*), and for its neglect and sometimes rejection of the liberal values described in *Chapter 8*. Critics would claim that there is an underlying ambiguity about the Government's social values and objectives, or even that it has an essentially repressive agenda which is concealed by disingenuous language and the jargon of management, modernisation and effectiveness.

NOMS[16]

The decision to create the National Offender Management Service (NOMS) was the outcome of the Carter Report.[17] The stated aims were to enable resources to be used more effectively and rates of re-offending to be reduced, and at the same time to increase public confidence in the penal system and the criminal justice system as a whole. Its creation was closely linked to the changes in the legislative framework for sentencing brought about by the Criminal Justice Act 2003. The main features were that the Prison Service and the National Probation Service would come together to form a single service; a system of 'offender management' would make a single manager responsible for the oversight of offenders throughout the period of their sentence, whether in custody or in the community; and the 'commissioning' and 'providing' functions would be separated. Services or 'interventions' would be commissioned in accordance with the principle of 'contestability' from a wide range of providers, both from within NOMS itself and also from the private, voluntary and community sectors. Below the Chief Executive, commissioning would be the responsibility of a National Offender Manager, working through Regional Offender Managers appointed for each of the nine regions in England and for Wales. The service would have a new relationship with the courts, within the framework of the Criminal Justice Act 2003, which the Government hoped would lead to sentencing practices which were more 'effective' in reducing re-offending, and at the same time take more account of NOMS' capacity to put sentences into effect.

By the autumn of 2005, the Chief Executive, a National Offender Manager and ten Regional Offender Managers had all been appointed. Many of the common administrative functions of the Prison Service and the Probation Service had been brought together in a single organization, reporting to the Chief Executive or the National Offender Manager; 'end to end' offender management was being piloted in north-west England, and was to be 'rolled out' nationally; a national 'NOMS Sentencing Consultation Group' had been formed to improve communication with the courts; and plans were in hand to establish local liaison committees, reviving the probation liaison committees that had inadvertently been abolished under the Criminal Justice and Court Services Act 2000.

Charles Clarke succeeded David Blunkett as Home Secretary in the spring of 2005, and in September he set out his own ideas for reforming the penal system.[18] He placed particular emphasis on action to reduce re-offending through partnership working and the creation of an individualised 'package of support and interventions ... for each offender and every offender', prepared at the beginning of the sentence. It would have a particular focus on health, education, employment and social and family links. He looked forward to the development of 'community prisons', where prisoners would be kept nearer to their homes and which would be 'far more engaged with their local communities and better at building relationships with a wide variety of other organizations'.[19] He stated his commitment to the creation of a 'vibrant mixed economy within NOMS', referring in particular to the voluntary and community sector, and to 'a strong culture of commissioning and contestability in prisons and probation'.

The Government set out its plans for the Probation Service in more detail in a consultation paper *Restructuring Probation to Reduce Re-*

Offending, published in October 2005.[20] Commissioning of probation services would become a function of the Secretary of State, working through Regional Offender Managers, and not of probation boards as had previously been expected. New bodies to be known as probation trusts would replace probation boards as employers of staff and providers of services, and as bodies with whom the Secretary of State could place or make service level agreements. In accordance with the principle of contestability they would be in competition with other potential providers in the public, private or voluntary and community sectors. Members of the trusts would be appointed by the Secretary of State, with a stronger emphasis on business, financial and management experience. Trusts would need to 'link into local communities' and particularly minority communities, but local links would no longer be a statutory requirement for membership. 'Links with the judiciary will be important' but there would be no requirement for the appointment of a Crown Court judge. A trust which lost its business would cease to exist. The transition 'is likely to impact at local level only gradually' and staff would transfer to the new trusts under their existing contracts or to new providers with their pay, terms and conditions protected. The document invites comments, but only on specified points of detail. Legislation to give effect to the proposals would be introduced later in the Parliamentary session and brought into effect in April 2007.

Some observers originally welcomed the reform as providing a basis for achieving a balance between capacity and demand (or more optimistically a reduction in the use of imprisonment); a more coherent and socially responsible approach to the resettlement of offenders; a necessary division between purchasing and providing, and hence between policy and operations (see *Chapters 8 and 19*); and perhaps the foundation for a service which had a stronger sense of identity, purpose and pride. They were ready to agree with David Blunkett, at that time Home Secretary, that it represented a 'once in a generation' opportunity for a radical reform of the penal system. They were re-assured by Home Secretary Charles Clarke's speech in September 2005.

Most reactions were however critical, or at best sceptical. Critics focused on the absence, as they saw it, of a clear justification or rationale, especially at a time when the Probation Service's performance, as measured by the Government's own indicators, was steadily improving; and on the break-up or, some said, destruction of the Probation Service. More general criticisms were that the reform was in reality a political and ideological attempt to create a 'market' in penal treatment, with as much of the penal system as possible transferred to the private sector; that it was part of a wider policy of expanding the 'net' of punishment and criminal justice in the interests of social cohesion and control; and that a set of impersonal, mechanistic interventions would displace the human and personal relationships with offenders which had been shown to be essential if offenders were to be motivated to change their lives.[21] Previous reforms had already made those relationships harder to sustain.

The consultation paper confirmed many of the critics' fears. It showed that the Government saw the changes as part of its political vision for the reform of public services more generally, without much direct relevance to criminal justice but with close similarities to its plans for the health service and for education. In all three areas, critics argued that contestability and markets would lead to greater confusion and frustration in the services themselves; that despite John Hutton's assurances they were incompatible with traditional social and public service values; and that they would create wider divisions and greater resentment in society as a whole.[22] There no longer seemed to be any serious intention of merging the Prison Service and the Probation Service so that they would share a common sense of values and identity, and it was becoming unclear whether NOMS itself would be a 'service' in any real sense, as distinct from a set of administrative arrangements.

How far those concerns come to be realised in prisons and probation will as usual depend on how the changes are actually put into effect. On the critics' view, the prospect was one of greater central direction, a culture of conformity, standardisation and aversion to risk, founded on coercion and physical and social control. Contestability would be used to punish failure, drive down costs, and fragment the service. Continuing instability would set back the progress which was already being made. They found it hard to see how the changes would by themselves contribute to a reduction in re-offending, or to the vision which the Home Secretary had described in his speech.

An alternative, but critics would say less realistic, view was that the changes would reduce the degree of central control, allow more local imagination and innovation, and encourage greater local accountability and ownership. They could help to generate more constructive relationships with courts and communities, and with other criminal justice services and local authorities, both directly and through local criminal justice boards and crime and disorder reduction partnerships. The culture would be one of challenge, achievement and reward, founded on values of humanity and respect for personal dignity and human rights. Most prisons would remain in the public sector, and offender management and most services in the community could continue to be provided by a recognisable probation service employed by probation trusts. 'Contestability' would be used primarily to introduce more diversity and experiment, not simply to replace the providers of existing services.

The Government had at the time of writing given no indication of which of those views it might hold, but most practitioners and observers would probably agree that it is only by taking and giving effect to the second view that the Government would be able to realise the Home Secretary's vision. It might also be argued that those outcomes could be achieved as effectively by stronger political and professional leadership, without the need for major legislation or another structural re-organization. On any view, the latter is no substitute for the former.

The Government has set a reduction in rates of re-conviction (five per cent by 2008, working towards ten per cent by the end of the decade), and an increase in public confidence, as tests by which the success or otherwise of NOMS will be judged – or in the Treasury's terms, the tests by which increases in expenditure will have to be justified. The first depends however on the co-operation of other agencies and of the public in the re-settlement of offenders, and on the wider social and economic factors which affect levels of crime more generally. The second will be influenced by the public's understanding of the facts and by its degree of confidence in government and public institutions as a whole. Neither is a target at which the service can aim directly or a situation which it can achieve on its own. Failure to achieve them could not be attributed simply to the service's own performance, and would be a matter for which the Government, or society, as a whole should take responsibility.

In reality, the public is more likely to judge NOMS on the extent to which the service 'works' – whether what is supposed to happen does happen, at the right time, in the right place and for the right people, and whether offenders complete programmes and comply with orders and conditions. Courts, other services and voluntary organizations must be able to rely on NOMS to work with them in a spirit of genuine co-operation and understanding, and on equal and mutually agreed terms. Staff, offenders, their families and victims need to know that they will be properly treated, where they stand and what they can expect. Those things do not always happen at present, for various reasons which include pressures on resources and prison overcrowding, but sometimes also the unintended effect of nationally imposed targets and league tables.[23]

Whatever form of organization is eventually adopted, NOMS must have authority and legitimacy - see *Chapter 5*. It must earn the trust and respect of its own staff, of other services and individuals with whom it is in direct contact, and of the general public. Management and staff must be consulted, listened to and taken seriously. They must share a common professional culture. Like all public services, NOMS must be fair, transparent and accountable in all its dealings and contacts. Its accountability must run not only upwards to Ministers and Parliament, but also in other directions through relationships, and the mechanisms to support those relationships, to the organizations, communities and individuals who are affected by its work. That culture and those relationships were not discussed in the consultation paper. They still have to be developed and consolidated.

THE NATURE AND PURPOSE OF PUNISHMENT

Critics have continued to argue that criminal justice has become increasingly politicised and punitive.[24] Those claims may sometimes be overstated.[25] But to-day's 'politics' of punishment could be characterised as demanding greater certainty of punishment (more people convicted and sentenced); greater severity in sentencing (more people going to prison); 'tougher' and 'more demanding' community sentences; and stronger protection from re-offending for the 'law-abiding' public.

Ideally, no offence should ever go unpunished. Many people would say the experience of punishment must be in some way painful if it is to 'count'. At the same time, however, they would probably still agree that for punishment to be legitimate it must be deserved, in the sense that the person must be proved to have committed a criminal offence and the punishment must be related to the seriousness of the offence and the culpability of the offender.

Chapters 10 and *12* have shown how the theory, politics and practice of punishment have become increasingly confused and complicated over the last ten years. Academic debate about theories of punishment has continued, with important contributions from scholars such as Antony Duff, whose idea of punishment as 'moral rehabilitation' deserves more serious attention.[26] The main theories have been conveniently summarised by Lucia Zedner,[27] and there is a set of short and stimulating papers in 'Punishment and Rehabilitation', the Summer 2005 issue of *Criminal Justice Matters*.[28] Theories can often be illustrated by reference to current developments in sentencing, but policy, legislation and practice in sentencing are for the most part developed independently of theories of punishment. Sometimes, theory may be used to explain or criticise, but since the Criminal Justice Act 1991 it has rarely influenced the policy itself. Legislators, judges and penal administrators are all, in their different ways, more interested in the effectiveness, consistency and cost of actual sentences than they are in theories of punishment.

That sounds good sense, but the absence of any serious regard for the theory or principles of punishment has enabled the Government to extend the use of punishment and to introduce new features without much regard to the limits of what should be regarded as legitimate or consistent with the traditional views of British justice as described in *Chapter 12*. The Prime Minister, Tony Blair, has said, 'We are shifting from tackling the offence to targeting the offender.... Just paying the penalty will not be enough'. In a later speech, he said:

> The criminal justice system that we have in this country still asks first and foremost, 'How do we protect the accused from potential transgressions of the state or the police?' That is the attitude the criminal justice system has at its heart... And I think the question should be: 'How do we protect the majority from the dangerous and irresponsible minority?'[29]

On that view, punishment and the rest of the apparatus of criminal justice can be treated as just another form of social intervention which the Government has at its disposal, and as having no particular authority of its own. Principles such as the presumption of innocence, the criminal standard of proof, the right to silence, disclosure of the case against the defendant and 'equality of arms' are no longer of much importance.

In the situation that is emerging, the notion of 'punishment' as applied by the state is becoming increasingly confused. The Government clearly intends that the state, through the criminal justice system, should intervene more actively and intrusively in controlling people's lives in the interests of public safety and comfort, in ways which rely on punishment but which go far beyond punishment as it is ordinarily understood. If the state is to punish people for who they are and not for what they have done, there is a serious danger that punishment will lose its legitimacy, and those who administer it will lose their moral authority.

THE NATURE AND PURPOSE OF SENTENCING

The Criminal Justice Act 2003 sets out, for the first time in statute, five purposes of sentencing - punishment of offenders; reduction of crime; reform of offenders; protection of the public; and reparation (to the victim or the community). NOMS has a set of purposes which are similar but not identical – they do not include reparation.[30] The first is declaratory and retributive – to uphold the law, to condemn, to impose some kind of pain or loss. The test is 'has justice been done?' The next three are utilitarian and instrumental. They can be achieved in various ways – physical control of the offender (typically by imprisonment, but also increasingly by electronic means), rehabilitation, or deterrence. The test is whether the method used 'works' or is 'effective'. The last is reparative – to repair the damage, to achieve some form of reconciliation, to compensate the victim. Here the test is harder to establish. It may be a feeling of satisfaction or relief on the part of those who have been affected by the offence, or a sense that it is now possible to 'move on'. The reparative view has never been as pervasive as the other two and it has not been so clearly articulated, but it is now gaining ground.[31]

It could be argued that only the first of the five statutory purposes necessarily involves inflicting 'pain', and that all the others can be achieved – and perhaps better achieved – by measures which do not harm or hurt, or which may not need to involve the criminal process at all. But then they would not count as 'punishment', and arguably they would not have the confidence of the courts and the public – the problem which has affected community sentences for the last 25 years. Some element of pain therefore has to be added by making sentences 'tough' and 'demanding', in ways which may serve no rehabilitative purpose and which may make any such purpose harder to achieve.

Chapter 12 argued for the traditional view that courts on the one hand, and the Prison Service and the Probation Service on the other, have different and separate functions. The courts dealt with punishment. They decided the amount of punishment that was needed to match the seriousness of the offence and the culpability of the offender. The sentencer's responsibility was to apply the law in accordance with statute, precedent and good sentencing practice, but not to consider longer-term outcomes, wider social consequences, cost, or the services' capacity to give effect to the sentences imposed. The Prison Service and the Probation Service were then responsible for the instrumental purposes including the prevention of re-offending. They had to do the best they could with offenders who were placed in their charge, the resources and powers that were available to them, and more recently the targets and performance indicators that were set for them by the

Government. But it was not their job to punish offenders – that had already been done by the courts. Offenders themselves had no responsibilities except to comply with their sentences and the conditions and demands which those sentences imposed on them.

That division of responsibility preserved the judiciary's independence, and it protected the courts and the penal system from mutual interference. It also, in effect, absolved the offender from any obligation except to comply with the terms of the sentence. But the division will be difficult to sustain under the new legislation.

The courts and NOMS now have a shared statutory responsibility to punish offenders, protect the public, reduce crime or re-offending, and rehabilitate offenders. To do that, they will need a new relationship with one another. That relationship need not compromise the judiciary's independence, but it will require a sense of reciprocal responsibility and mechanisms of accountability which have so far been absent and in some instances resisted. Courts will need to take account of the sentencing guidelines, but they should also consider what NOMS can realistically provide for the purposes of a particular sentence and for a particular offender. NOMS will need to help the court to decide what those purposes might be and what facilities and services are needed to achieve them. The process should be linked with the preparation of the 'package of support and interventions'. Difficulty might arise if under 'contestability' the court were to be advised by an employee of an organization which had a financial interest in the outcome.

A responsible officer, probably the offender manager, will then have to make sure that those facilities and services are actually provided – from the service itself, or by a voluntary organization or private contractor – and should be held accountable for doing so. As part of that new relationship, the offender manager might subsequently be required to give an account to the court of the extent to which sentence plans have actually been carried out, and of what outcomes they have achieved in practice. A similar procedure is already followed for drug treatment and testing orders and for some priority or prolific offenders.

The then Lord Chief Justice Lord Woolf discussed the new situation in his Leon Radzinowicz memorial lecture,[32] although the tentative terms in which he did so show the sensitivity of the subject, and the full implications of the new relationship have still to be considered.

The new situation should also require offenders themselves to take some 'ownership' and responsibility for their sentence plans, and for achieving the plans' objectives. Offenders may not always be willing to accept that responsibility, but the traditional approach to sentencing and penal treatment saw no place for it at all. As Stephen Pryor has argued,[33] it has been a long standing criticism of imprisonment that it removes all responsibility from the offender when the aim should be to motivate and equip offenders to accept and exercise responsibility in the various aspects of their lives. For example, the 'the package of support and interventions' and the pre-sentence report should be prepared in consultation with the offender, and the outcome should if possible have the offender's (and the family's, if there is one) consent and commitment.

Victims should be informed of the process, and given an opportunity to express a view on any aspect which might materially affect them. Communities, including minority communities, should also be consulted in suitable cases, for example to suggest work that might be done to benefit the community under a requirement of a community order, and more generally on the pattern of sentencing in the area. There could well be a role for the prosecutor in assembling and presenting the relevant options and considerations.

There is important work to be done in designing the framework of relationships and accountability in which the courts and NOMS will have to operate. The opportunity presented by the Criminal Justice Act 2003 and the creation of NOMS will be lost if the debate descends into sterile arguments about the need to build more prisons, if too much of the service's energy is turned inwards towards its own internal management, or if it is not allowed the degree of local discretion and authority on which the critical relationships with courts and local communities will depend.

CIVIL RENEWAL, ACTIVE CITIZENSHIP AND LOCAL GOVERNANCE

It is generally acknowledged that the co-operation of local services, authorities and communities, including minority communities, is essential to any success in policing, the prevention of crime or the re-settlement of offenders, and therefore to any prospect of reducing crime, increasing clear-up rates or improving rates of re-offending. Their co-operation depends in turn on mutual understanding, trust and goodwill between services, local communities and individual citizens, and between services themselves, for example in local criminal justice boards and crime and disorder reduction partnerships. All that is now well understood in the police. Within NOMS, the Prison Service has no tradition of engaging either courts or local communities in the management of its own establishments, and the tradition of local involvement which previously existed in the Probation Service had been largely extinguished by earlier reforms. NOMS, like the police, must be able to engage with the relevant organizations, groups and individuals in ways that are both proactive and responsive. Similar considerations apply to the courts and the Crown Prosecution Service, and are being explored in the Community Justice Centre in Liverpool and the Community Justice Initiative in Salford. Local authorities have a significant and so far largely unrecognised contribution to make.[34]

The Government published *Together We Can*, its Action Plan for Civil Renewal, in June 2005.[35] The Action Plan contains important sections headed 'Together we can build safer communities' and 'Together we can reduce re-offending and raise public confidence in the criminal justice system'. One intended outcome is that:

communities are safer and feel safer because the police, crime and disorder reduction partnerships and drug and alcohol action teams, and other local partners work together to involve local people effectively in addressing their concerns about crime, drugs and anti-social behaviour.

Another is that:

communities have more understanding and influence over the activities of the Criminal Justice System (CJS) and are able to work with CJS agencies in reducing re-offending.

Action for the former is to include: the creation of neighbourhood policing teams; holding good practice seminars; supporting Neighbourhood Watch; promoting the Government's messages on anti-social behaviour; and developing targeted neighbourhood prevention programmes involving communities, families, victims and young people. Action for the latter is to include: support for local criminal justice boards in their work to engage and involve local people; developing the pilot Community Justice Centre in Liverpool and the Salford Community Justice Initiative; effective use of community engagement in establishing and implementing offender management policies and practices; and opportunities for work by offenders to meet local concerns, improve the local environment, and be made more visible.

The scope for NOMS to contribute to civil renewal, and the potential significance of its contribution, have been discussed elsewhere.[36] NOMS has published and sought comments on a draft strategy, and the outcome, with a contribution from the Youth Justice Board, was published in November 2005.[37] The approach it described has great potential for reducing crime and for promoting social well-being more generally.

An important report will show how local communities' involvement in community safety could be increased to give it greater scope and vitality,[38] and another has shown how it could be extended to prevent racist violence.[39] The Government has provided encouragement, publicity and some funding, but the driving force has to come from communities themselves, and from voluntary and community organizations, as well as statutory services. The situation has become immensely complicated, and energy, specialist knowledge and sophisticated skills are needed to work within it. Issues to be resolved include the need to build and sustain local capacity, to ensure stability and continuity, and to prevent distraction caused by central government priorities and targets. There are difficult questions about forms of consultation and accountability, including the position of elected members of local authorities. There is a confusing array of Government programmes (Neighbourhood Management Pathfinders, the New Deal for Communities, Police Priority Areas among others), and mechanisms (Local Strategic Partnerships, Local Area Agreements, Crime and

Disorder Reduction Panels and Multi-Agency Public Protection Arrangements) which too often operate in confusing and wasteful isolation from one another (see also *Chapter 18*).

The connection between civil renewal and crime and criminal justice is important. An optimistic view is that civil renewal will re-assert a set of inclusive and compassionate values that is in danger of being overwhelmed by the forces of globalisation and managerialism, and by a politics and a set of public attitudes which appeal to individualism and narrow self-interest. Those values will then shape the professional culture of the criminal justice services, the reasons for which people choose to work for them, and the confidence and trust which they receive from the public. Just as important, they will influence the public's own sense of responsibility for preventing crime and for dealing with its consequences.

There may however be a danger that civil renewal will become a programme that is based not so much on a shared sense of social responsibility as one designed to increase the power and influence of government, by conscripting citizens, communities and voluntary organizations to serve its own political purposes, and subjecting them to its own mechanisms of control – public service agreements, service level agreements, targets, performance measures and the rest. A report prepared for the National Council for Voluntary Organizations suggested that the Government's interest in civil renewal is primarily to further its own agendas, and that voluntary and community organizations and wider civil society are likely to have different perceptions.[40] There may be a further risk that if policies for criminal justice and civil renewal are brought too close together, their combination will work to obstruct progress towards social inclusion and social justice, and come to impose an oppressive form of social control through an expanding process of criminalisation and punishment.

Three further points arise. First, citizens and communities, including minority communities, will need the capacity to respond to the opportunities which civil renewal, active citizenship and local governance provide, and the power and responsibility to do so constructively and in a spirit of public duty and service. Building local capacity - and with it responsibility – may be as necessary as the provision of actual services or interventions. Within NOMS, it should be an important task for Regional Offender Managers.

Second, civil renewal and active citizenship should not be seen as a matter which is only for private citizens. It should also be a matter for public servants themselves. They should be enabled and encouraged to play their own part as members of their own communities, both as informal 'ambassadors' for their service and in interpreting their communities' views and feelings back to the service. Contacts such as those might be one of the most effective means of explaining what each service is and what it does, of enabling views and feelings to be heard and understood, and so of increasing public confidence.

Third, offenders, including prisoners, should themselves have the opportunity to be active citizens and responsible human beings, within the limits of their situation – as argued in *Chapter 19* on page 301. Work for the benefit of local communities is an obvious example, but there are many other possibilities.[41] In particular, as argued in *Chapter 12*, prisoners should not be automatically disqualified from voting in elections – the view taken by the Grand Chamber of the European Court of Human Rights in its judgement in *Hirst v United Kingdom* on 6 October 2005.[42]

RACE, RELIGION, INSIDERS AND OUTSIDERS

Britain still finds it hard to achieve harmonious relationships between people from different ethnic, racial or religious backgrounds. Reactions to the report of the Stephen Lawrence Inquiry, to the report of the Runnymede Trust's Commission on the Future of Multi-Ethnic Britain, and to reforms in the Metropolitan Police Service, and most recently the comments about the Prison Service made in the course of the judicial inquiry into the death of Zahid Mubarek in Feltham Young Offender Institution,[43] have all showed the continued existence of deep resentment towards attempts towards racial conciliation. Religious as well as racial equality has become an increasingly important issue, and religious extremism became a recognised danger as a result of the explosions and attempted explosions in London in July 2005. Various legislative and administrative measures have been taken with the aim of promoting equality, preventing and punishing racist or religious violence, harassment, hatred or discrimination, and providing protection from extremists who promote or commit violence and especially acts of terrorism. Such measures are necessary and important. But programmes to tackle racism or religious extremism must also deal with the social and economic situations in which those problems arise.[44]

Many people, especially young people, feel that they are 'outsiders' in the sense that they can do very little, as they see it, to improve their own circumstances or prospects, and nothing at all to influence the wider situation through the democratic process. Such a feeling of exclusion may derive from lack of faith in the political process and a feeling that it is ineffective against the forces of globalisation, social injustice or, as some of them may see it, moral corruption. The Government for its part focuses many of its policies on the benefits to 'hard working' or 'law abiding' citizens - in effect to 'insiders'. It is understandable that some people, who may come from a wide range of social, ethnic and religious backgrounds, should feel alienated and resentful. Some of them will take part in legitimate protests of various kinds, but the option of idealistic left-wing politics is no longer available and some may be attracted to the politics of the extreme right or become involved in criminal behaviour or public disorder. One or two may become involved in terrorism. Whatever the case for new forms of security, new criminal offences or new grounds for detaining suspects, preventive measures must also confront the social context in which alienation occurs and terrorism has been able to find a place in Britain.

A lot has been said, and quite a lot has been done, to improve the representation of minorities in the country's public institutions. But other questions still have to be considered. Whom will angry or frustrated young people feel they can trust, identify with or rely on for help and support – at school or at work, in their faith or other communities? Or to represent them in their dealings with the state or in national or local politics? What can people in positions of power or authority do to earn that trust, and how can individuals be encouraged to give it? How can trust be spread more widely across divisions of class, ethnicity or faith, or of age or gender? There is a good case for more 'minority' Members of Parliament, police officers and so on – but to represent or work with members of all communities, not just their own. Members of the 'majority' should be enabled and trusted to do the same.

People with different backgrounds, ages and genders may sometimes need help to know and understand each other. They are most likely to do that in settings where they can join together to do something that matters to them, and are not just meeting for the sake of meeting. Schools are one example, both for children and their parents. Community safety is another. So are activities such as sport, drama and music. There are difficulties where schools or housing areas belong predominantly to members of one ethnic or religious group, but there are important questions to be asked about the amount of compulsory 'social engineering' that would be practicable, legitimate and acceptable in areas such as education or housing, and about the position of faith schools. Serious debate is needed.

There are clear attractions to living in Britain – safety, fairness, tolerance, freedom of thought and expression, services which work more or less reliably most of the time. Most people would probably agree about what they are. But they do not make Britain unique or 'special' when compared with a number of other countries in the world, or form the basis for a distinctive 'national identity'. The soldiers who fought on the different sides in the English Civil War knew what they thought was or ought to be special about England, but they had very different ideas about what it was. Those ideas eventually came to be accommodated in a more or less united country under the Bill of Rights in 1689 and the Act of Settlement in 1701 (although the Act still excluded Roman Catholics from succession to the throne). Different visions and values continued to inform social attitudes and politics, but they were for the most part respected and reconciled through the democratic process, and that process was itself progressively reformed during the nineteenth and early twentieth centuries.

It has been one of the special features of England, and later Britain, that it has, usually, eventually and sometimes painfully, found ways to accommodate diverse ideas, ethnic groups, religions and loyalties. But people may legitimately value different British traditions or parts of British history, and they may have different attitudes to the symbols and ceremonies which represent those traditions. Attitudes to ethnic or religious identity which survived for so long in Northern Ireland may have been almost forgotten in Britain, but those who are made to feel 'outsiders' for reasons of race, class or religion may not be enthusiastic about displays of symbols which they associate with privilege or with traditions in which they feel they have no part. Comparisons with the United States are interesting, but the American use of symbols and ceremonies should not be copied without some serious consideration of the values which they may represent, or be thought to represent. There is a strong case for children – all children – to be taught more about their country, its history, its geography and what used to be called civics and might now be called citizenship. But they need to be taught in an open-minded way that respects different views and traditions, and not as a form of political indoctrination or as part of a political attempt to impose a single 'national identity'.

There is still a strong dislike of 'difference' in some parts of British society. It finds regular expression in certain parts of the media, especially on subjects such as immigration, asylum, travellers, policing and of course terrorism; in misrepresentation and attacks on so-called 'liberals'; in contemptuous use of clichés such as 'political correctness'; and in tendentious claims that multiculturalism has 'failed'. To describe Britain as multicultural is no more than a statement of fact. 'Multiculturalism' is not an attractive word, but it describes an approach to the consequences of that fact - essentially one of accepting, accommodating and valuing cultural difference. It argues that awkward issues when they arise should be resolved on a basis of mutual respect and goodwill, and not treated as an insult to one's culture or a threat to one's society, still less as representing a 'clash of civilisations'. It is well within the British or English tradition of accommodating and integrating 'outsiders' of various kinds. 'Multiculturalism' need not and should not extend to encouraging minority groups to live in isolation from the rest of British society, and certainly not to the tolerance of practices which most people find abhorrent. Critics who imply that it does so, or who claim simplistically that it has 'failed', may have various motives but they give encouragement to racism.

The Commission on the Future of Multi-Ethnic Britain showed in its report how the country might come to understand and value its multi-cultural character as a 'community of communities' (see *Chapter 16*).[45] Published in 2000, its analysis and approach remain no less relevant after the events of 11 September 2001 and 7 July 2005, and its arguments have if anything become more powerful and urgent. Examples include the significance of national 'stories' (perhaps more important than 'national identity'); the central concepts of equality, diversity and cohesion; the discussion of religion, politics and representation; and the need to tackle social inequality and injustice. Some of the recommendations may need to be revised to give them a sharper focus and more direct impact, but the report provides a good starting point for a fresh look at the issues in the light of the events in London in July 2005.

RISKS, RELATIONSHIPS AND OPPORTUNITIES

Looking ahead, the prospects have some re-assuring and encouraging features. They include the overall fall in recorded and surveyed crime, and the generally moderate reactions of most people when confronted by crime or asked for their opinions about it. People will express – often justifiably – outrage at particular events or situations, but when the facts are explained they have for the most part a reasonable understanding of what can and should be expected from the criminal justice process. Steady and often unobtrusive progress is being made in several important directions, some of which have been indicated at the beginning of this chapter. The Human Rights Act and the Constitutional Reform Act together provide a more secure framework for the rule of law and the separation of powers, and so for a clearer definition and better understanding of the relationship between the legislature, the judiciary and the executive.

In other respects the prospects are uncertain and precarious. Some of the reasons are of the Government's own making. Central features of the Labour Government's policies have been its emphasis on targets and performance indicators, 'what works', and the assessment, management, and so far as possible the elimination of risk. All have their place in criminal justice as in other areas of public policy. But it has become widely acknowledged outside government that they can have a distorting effect, compromise professional integrity (see *Chapter 17*), and lead to a potentially oppressive culture of caution and blame.

Governments, organizations and individuals have to work with probabilities rather than certainties, in situations which are increasingly variable and complex. Total certainty, safety or security can never be completely achieved: it is always possible to do more, and a judgement has to be made about how much should be sacrificed in searching for them. Outcomes which fall short of expectations are not necessarily indications of failure. Governments should avoid over-stated claims of what can be achieved.[46] In the present context of confrontational politics, the media and opposition parties are keen to seize on any perceived failure or weakness, and to exploit it as a criticism of the Government or the criminal justice system. They are helped by the complexity of the system and widespread lack of understanding of the facts about crime, the working of the criminal justice process or sentencing practice.

The Government regularly consults interest groups and the wider public, but usually on points of detail and within narrowly defined terms of reference. The impression is too often of an attempt to publicise the Government's own actions or to gain legitimacy for a policy or course of action that has already been decided, rarely to allow suggestions for alternative courses of action.[47] Critics are dismissed as 'out of touch', or as 'not caring' about the victims of crime, or even as being disloyal or threatening to the country as a whole. Voluntary and professional organizations, many of them with great experience in their own fields, find it difficult to engage with the Government on constructive terms, and turn instead to public criticism which the Government ignores or contemptuously rejects.[48] They have on several occasions tried to promote serious analysis and debate by setting up their own commissions of inquiry. The outcome has been a number of careful and well-argued reports, but often disappointment that they have had not had more impact.[49]

Ministers try to make sure that they are always in control of the arguments, for example by continually announcing new initiatives (some of them re-cycled several times), so that there is no time or space for other views to be heard or make the news. Critics are made to appear as if they have missed the point or have been left behind because the argument has moved on. Press releases, and sometimes even white papers,[50] are written in the language of political confrontation, and words such as 'tough' and 'effective' are regularly included more for their political effect than for any addition they make to the content. The language of warfare or battle (*Chapters 8* and *9*) is still commonplace: it dramatises social problems such as anti-social behaviour or the misuse of drugs, and trivialises 'real' wars involving nation states.

The 'performance culture' undoubtedly concentrates minds and demands extra effort, but the pressure and sometimes insecurity that go with it discourage innovation, imagination or open debate. Public servants concentrate on what they are told or paid to do; they have little time or appetite for professional reading or activities which provide new challenges or different perspectives (leaving aside any time they may have for their families). If they are required to give comments or advice they will too often think first of what their managers or Ministers would like to hear. Academics, senior officials and Ministers have drawn apart from one another, and the frustrations over the commissioning and funding of research, described in *Chapter 9*, still remain.

By appearing to despise public servants and academic scholarship, by ignoring and dismissing the lessons of history and experience, and by 'talking down' to citizens more generally, the Government risks a loss of the credibility, and ultimately the legitimacy, which are the foundation of any government's authority and vitality. It not only denies itself valuable sources of wisdom and expertise, but devalues the qualities on which the country's future well-being depends.

The result is an administration that seems remote from many public servants and from many of the citizens whose confidence it is keen to gain. It is a situation for which the Government has ultimately to take responsibility, and to which it has contributed by its own actions. But public servants, pressure groups, academics and others must ask themselves how that situation has come to exist, why it is that they have lost authority and respect, and what they should themselves do to regain it. Parliament and the media must also bear some responsibility, both for the situation and for its improvement.

Ministers and public servants would do well to heed the arguments of the economist Paul Ormerod for 'Why Most Things Fail'.[51] To summarise the reasons for failure as they apply to government, they are: refusal to accept the limited capacity of government to change society or human nature, or to achieve complex outcomes; inability to accept the limitations of what can be known or conclusively demonstrated; reluctance to recognise that the purpose of competition should be to promote imagination and innovation, not to just bring in new providers for the same service; and failure to encourage or place their trust in local initiative and responsibility.

CONCLUSIONS

It is hard to judge the social direction which the country will take over the next three or four years. Few people would argue against the Government's vision of a country in which people generally work hard and obey the law: the issues are about how that is to be achieved and sustained, about social justice and equality, and about the limits which the state should place on personal freedom. John Hutton's speech brought social justice back onto the political agenda, but without any clear indication of what it might mean – a censorious, moralistic and controlling society divided between 'good people' who deserve the protection of the state and 'bad people' to whom the normal rights of citizenship need not apply; or one that is open, compassionate, considerate and generous. It is not clear whether 'respect' is to be shown 'downwards' or 'outwards', or only demanded 'upwards' to those in authority or who 'deserve' it. The Government's belief that social justice can be achieved by the mechanisms of the market, suitably regulated from the top by central government, seems at this stage to be more an article of political faith than an argument based on evidence or experience.

In criminal justice, the prospect may be a continuing expansion of the reach and scope of the criminal law and the criminal justice process, increasing criminalisation of the more disadvantaged sections of the population, and an indefinite rise in the prison population. Or the reforms that are now in progress may lead to more accountable, responsible, publicly 'owned' and citizen-focused methods of dealing with crime and disorder, and with people who commit it, on the lines suggested in previous chapters. Whether a system based on such methods would result in less crime, be more compassionate towards offenders and their families, show more consideration towards victims, or be more economical, depends on the country's social values – what kind of a county Britain is to be. But such a system should be more responsive, accountable and responsible, and it should have greater public confidence.

ENDNOTES for *Chapter 23*

[1] Home Office, *Building Communities, Beating Crime: A Better Police Service for the 21st Century*, London, Stationery Office and www.policereform.gov.uk. For a more general and more critical view of policing issues, see Barry Loveday, 'The Challenge of Police Reform in England and Wales' in *Public Money and Management*, 25/4, 275-279, 2005. For a survey of policing as a whole, see Tim Newburn (ed), *Handbook of Policing*, Cullompton, Devon, Willan, 2003.

[2] See www.cps.gov.uk/about/reform.htm

[3] See for example Ben Rogers *New Directions in Community Justice*, London, Institute for Public Policy Research, 2005.

[4] Department for Education and Skills, *Every Child Matters*, Department for Education and Skills, London, 2003.

[5] Department for Education and Skills, *Youth Matters*, CM6299, London, Department for Education and Skills. See also Audit Commission, *Youth Justice 2004: A Review of the Reformed Youth Justice System*, London, Audit Commission, 2004; and Steve Bradford and Rod Morgan, 'Transformed Youth Justice' in *Public Money and Management*, 25/5, 283-290, 2005.

[6] Mike Nellis, 'Out of this World: The Advent of the Satellite Tracking of Offenders in England and Wales', *Howard Journal*, 44/2, 125-150, 2005.

[7] Roger Smith has summarised the issues in 'Changing the Rules: the Judiciary, Human Rights and the Constitution', in the *JUSTICE Annual Report 2005*, London, JUSTICE, 2005.

[8] For a balanced and thoughtful account, see Andrew Millie, Jessica Jacobson, Eraina McDonald and Mike Hough, *Anti-social Behaviour Strategies: Finding a Balance*, published for the Joseph Rowntree Foundation by The Policy Press, London, 2005.

[9] The Coulsfield Inquiry provided an important analysis of the situation and the issues, backed by a valuable survey of the research, and put forward a number of important recommendations. *Crime, Courts and Confidence: the Report of an Independent Inquiry into Alternatives to Prison* (the Coulsfield Report), London, Esmée Fairbairn Foundation, 2004; Anthony Bottoms, Sue Rex and Gwen Robinson, (eds) *Alternatives to Prison: Options for an Insecure Society*, Cullompton, Willan, 2004.

[10] Office for Criminal Justice Reform (2005) 'A Vision for Criminal Justice in 2008', in the *CJS Brief*, issue 4, available at www.homeoffice.gov.uk

[11] See for example the white paper *Justice For All*, announcing the Government's plans for what became the Criminal Justice Act 2003 (Cm 5563, London, Stationery Office, 2002), and the Prime Minister's speech *A New Consensus on Law and Order*, to mark the publication of the Home Office Strategic Plan for criminal justice on 19 July 2004, available at www.number-10.gov.uk/output/Page6129.asp

[12] The Prime Minister speaking at the launch of the 'Respect' agenda on 2 September 2005. The speech is available at www.number-10.gov.uk/output/Page8123.asp

[13] 'Contestability' has entered the Government's vocabulary to denote a form of competition which includes market testing, contracting-out and privatisation, but which extends to voluntary and community organizations as well as the private sector.

[14] John Hutton (2005) *Public Service Reform: the Key to Social Justice*, a paper given to the Social Market Foundation on August 25, available at www. smf.co.uk

[15] Drawing on Philip Bobbitt's *The Shield of Achilles*, the Archbishop of Canterbury has characterised that vision as treating government as a matter of 'insurance' against the hazards of what is seen as an increasingly insecure global and political environment, and representing a shift to a new political mode associated with the 'market state' in which public services such as health, education, justice and safety are treated as commodities to

be traded according to the public's demand for them and the price they are prepared to pay. *The Richard Dimbleby Lecture 2002*, available on the Archbishop of Canterbury's website www.archbishopofcanterbury.org.uk/sermons_speeches/021219.html Ministers, for their part, see the change as a transition to a more democratic, responsive and accountable style of government in which they can take some pride.

16 For a discussion of the National Offender Management Service, see Mike Hough, Rob Allen and Una Padel (eds) *Re-shaping Prisons and Probation: The New Offender Management Framework*, Bristol, Policy Press, 2006.

17 Patrick Carter, *Managing Offenders, Reducing Crime*, London, Prime Minister's Strategy Unit, 2003; Home Office, *Reducing Crime, Changing Lives* London, Home Office, 2004.

18 Charles Clarke, *Where Next for Penal Policy?* Lecture to Prison Reform Trust, 2005. Available at www.prisonreformtrust.org.uk

19 The idea of 'community prisons' has a long history, going back (at least) to the 'neighbourhood borstals' at Hindley and Hewell Grange, and the Young Offender Review in the 1970s (see *Chapter 7*), and to the Woolf Report in 1991 (see *Chapters 7 and 8*). Progress has always in the past been frustrated by the pressures of prison overcrowding, the unsuitable location of many prison establishments, and the lack of collective commitment by the Prison Service itself.

20 Available at www.probation.homeoffice.gov.uk/files/pdf/Restructuring Probation

21 McNeill, Fergus, Batchelor, Susan, Burnett, Ros and Knox, Jo, *21st Century Social Work: Reducing Re-offending: Key Practice Skills*, Edinburgh, Scottish Executive, 2005.

22 John Carvel, 'Feeling the Pressure' in *Society Guardian*, 5 October, 2005; 'Enough Point Scoring', interview with Onora O'Neill, *Education Guardian*, 25 October, 2005, are two of many examples from health and education respectively.

23 See the vivid, if contentious, account in Nick Davies' articles in the *Guardian* on 22 and 23 June, 2005.

24 For example Michael Tonry, *Confronting Crime: Crime Control under New Labour*, Cullompton, Willan, 2003; or less provocatively, John Pratt, David Brown, Mark Brown, Simon Hallsworth and Wayne Morrison (eds), *The New Punitiveness: Trends Theories, Perspectives*, Cullompton, Willan, 2005.

25 Roger Matthews, 'Punitive Myths', in 'Punishment and Rehabilitation' (see note 28), 8-9, 40-41.

26 Antony Duff, *Punishment, Communication and Community*. New York, Oxford University Press, 2001.

27 Lucia Zedner, *Criminal Justice*, Oxford University Press, 2004. See also Sean McConville (ed) (2003) *The Use of Punishment*, Cullompton, Devon. Willan, 2003.

28 'Punishment and Rehabilitation', *Criminal Justice Matters*, no 60, 2005.

29 See notes 11 and 12.

30 Set out in *The NOMS Corporate Plan, 2005-06 – 2007-08*, available at www.homeoffice.gov.uk/docs4/NOMS_Corporate_Plan_2005_2008pdf
The Aims and Objectives in full are :
1: the protection of the public;
2: the reduction of re-offending;
3: the proper punishment of offenders;
4: ensuring offenders' awareness or the effects of crime on victims and the public; and
5: the rehabilitation of offenders.

31 For a discussion of the complexity and potential confusion involved in those statutory purposes, see Andrew Ashworth 'Criminal Justice Reform: Principles, Human Rights and Public Protection', *Criminal Law Review* (2004), 515 – 532.

32 Lord Woolf (2005), *Making Sense of Sentencing,* available at
www.dca.gov.uk/judicial/speeches/lcj120505.htm

33 Stephen Pryor, 'Prison – the Un-responsible Sentence' in *Vista,* 9/2, 121-124, 2004.

34 Local Government Association (2005), *Going Straight: Reducing Re-offending in Local Communities,* available at www.lga.gov.uk

35 Home Office *Together We Can: The Government Action Plan for Civil Renewal,* London, Home Office, 2005. See also www.activecitizen.gov.uk Readers of David Garland's *The Culture of Control* (Oxford University Press, 2001) will recognise the programme as an excellent example of 'responsibilization'

36 David Faulkner and Frances Flaxington, 'NOMS and Civil Renewal', *Vista,* 9/2, 90-99, 2004.

37 NOMS and YJB, *Approach to Communities and Civil Renewal* (2005), available at www.noms.homeoffice.gov.uk/downloads

38 Jean Chinnery, *Improving Community Involvement in Community Safety,* London, Home Office, forthcoming.

39 Sarah Isal, *Preventing Racist Violence,* London, Runnymede Trust, 2005.

40 Veronique Jochum, Belinda Pratten and Karl Wilding, *Civil Renewal and Active Citizenship: A Guide to the Debate,* London, NCVO, 2005.

41 Stephen Pryor, *The Responsible Prisoner: An Exploration of the Extent to which Imprisonment Removes Responsibility Unnecessarily and an Invitation to Change,* London, HM Prison Service, 2001. David Faulkner, 'Prisoners as Citizens', *Prison Service Journal,* 143, 46-47, 2002. Finola Farrant and Joe Levenson, *Barred Citizens,* London, Prison Reform Trust, 2002.

42 Reported in *The Times,* 11 October 2005; the full text is at www.echr.coe.int

43 See the Inquiry's website www.zahidmubarekinquiry.org.uk

44 Sarah Isal, see note 39.

45 Commission on the Future of Multi-Ethnic Britain, *The Future of Multi-Ethnic Britain* (the Parekh Report), London, Polity Press, 2000. Also *Realising the Vision: Progress and Further Challenges,* London, Runnymede Trust, 2004.

46 As regards the evidence from criminological research, see Aidan Wilcox 'Evidence Based Youth Justice: Some Valuable Lessons from an Evaluation for the Youth Justice Board', *Youth Justice,* 3/1, 19-33, 2003. From an economist's perspective, Paul Ormerod, *Why Most Things Fail: Evolution, Extinction and Economics,* Faber and Faber, London, 2005.

47 For example the consultation papers, *Inspection Reform: Establishing an Inspectorate for Justice and Community Safety* (Office for Criminal Justice Reform, 2005) and *Restructuring Probation,* note 20 above.

48 The experience of ASBO Concern is one of several examples. ASBO Concern is a consortium of professional and voluntary organizations, with a large number of corporate and individual supporters, who are concerned about the misuse of ASBOs and its consequences– see www.asboconcern.org.uk

49 Examples include the Prison Reform Trust's Committee on Women's Imprisonment (*Chapter 12*), the Runnymede Trust's Commission on the Future of Multi-Ethnic Britain, and the Esmée Fairbairn Foundation's Commission on Alternatives to Imprisonment.

50 The white paper *Justice for All* (see note 11) was a more politically aggressive document than would be expected for a considered statement of policy. Thomas Mathiesen has written about the mechanisms and devices that are used to stifle dissent and bring about acquiescence in *Silently Silenced: Essays on the Creation of Acquiescence in Modern Society,* Winchester, Waterside Press, 2004.

51 Op. cit., note 46.

Index

New entries for the 2006 Edition

Many more titles at www.watersidepress.co.uk